BRANWELL BRONTË

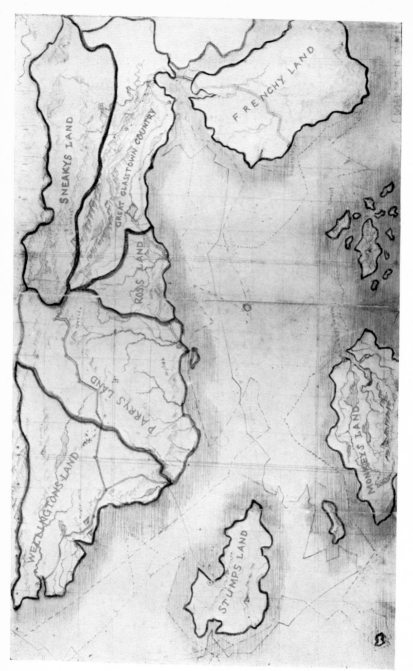

"The Great Glass Town Confederacy", by Branwell Brontë, 1831

BRANWELL BRONTË

by

WINIFRED GERIN

THOMAS NELSON AND SONS LTD

LONDON EDINBURGH PARIS MELBOURNE JOHANNESBURG
TORONTO AND NEW YORK

THOMAS NELSON AND SONS LTD
Parkside Works Edinburgh 9
36 Park Street London W1
312 Flinders Street Melbourne C1

302-304 Barclays Bank Building
Commissioner and Kruis Streets
Johannesburg

THOMAS NELSON AND SONS (CANADA) LTD
91-93 Wellington Street West   Toronto 1

THOMAS NELSON AND SONS
19 East 47th Street New York 17

SOCIÉTÉ FRANÇAISE D'ÉDITIONS NELSON
97 rue Monge Paris 5

———

First published 1961

Printed in Great Britain by
Robert Cunningham and Sons Ltd
Alva

PREFACE

There exists a great body of unpublished writings by Branwell Brontë, both juvenilia and adult compositions, consisting of prose narratives, verse and letters, preserved for the most part in the following places: the Brontë Parsonage Museum, Haworth; the Brotherton Library, University of Leeds; the Ashley Library, British Museum, and various American collections in libraries, colleges and private hands, listed among the "Sources of Information" used in writing this book. All those in the British Isles have been seen and studied by the present author. Wherever quotations have been made from them, their original spelling and punctuation have been preserved.

Because of the close collaboration existing between Branwell and Charlotte Brontë in their juvenilia, all Charlotte's relevant MSS have also been studied in the original, wherever possible, and transcribed directly. In the case of documents preserved in the United States transcripts, photostats and microfilms of the originals have been procured.

The greater part of Branwell's writings has remained unknown and even unsuspected by the general public. Selections from them have appeared from time to time in editions of great scholarship but of very limited number, so that they are virtually to be found only in specialised libraries and private collections. Apart from these not always accessible editions, the public has had no opportunity to assess the work of the brother of the Brontës.

Though this neglect has not been a signal loss to literature, it has been to a better understanding of Branwell. His work must be read—and not in excerpts only but as a whole—for any idea to be formed of the heated imagination, the wholly emotional and irrational outlook the writer brought to bear on life, if that life's cruel disappointments are to be understood. For the very measure of those disappointments can be gauged only by comparison with the extravagance of his dreams.

Because of this, and not because of any great intrinsic merit, lavish quotations from Branwell's writings have been incorporated in the present work. Their importance to the biographer cannot be overestimated. Branwell was, before all things, introspective, and wrote constantly about himself. Without this great body of his imaginative writings, little of the true Branwell could be known today.

Of his vices and misfortunes, all too much has been written by his sisters' biographers. Everybody knows he drank, took opium, and wrote equally fluently with both hands—at times with both hands at once, and in moments of bravado in Greek with his right and in Latin with his left. Of the multiple and contradictory facets that made up his complex personality, however, very little has so far been made known. This book has been written in an attempt to supply that want.

In pursuit of that aim I have followed up every clue left by Branwell in his erratic course; been to every place where he lived or worked; in many cases found the actual houses in which he lodged or which he visited; and met the descendants of the people who were his friends or employers. I have sought out the landscapes that formed his horizons and read the books that roused his enthusiasm and shaped his taste. Particularly fortunate have I been in having access to the private papers of the Robinson family, and this has given me an insight into the background and mentality of the woman whom Branwell loved and who cost him his life.

Living in Haworth has not only made such investigations possible but has enabled me to devote the necessary time to them, and it has also allowed me to see Branwell's world—both the inner and the outer one—with something of the permanence that underlies the seasons' changes.

W.G.

Haworth, 1961

CONTENTS

vii

LIST OF PLATES

ix

TO MY HUSBAND
WHOSE LOVE AND KNOWLEDGE
OF ALL MATTERS RELATING TO THE BRONTËS
IS MY PERMANENT INSPIRATION,
I DEDICATE THIS BOOK

PART ONE

LITTLE BANY

*

Chapter One

THE ONLY BOY

The Rev. Patrick Brontë and his wife Maria, née Branwell, had been married four and a half years when their fourth child and first boy was born on 26th June 1817. He was followed in rapid succession by two more girls (in July 1818 and January 1820), bringing the family up to a total of five girls and one boy, and then the mother died, struck down by a galloping cancer.

The first boy thus became the only son in a family of five daughters, a position which, even in provincial professional classes in the early nineteenth century, carried with it all the prerogative of primogeniture.

He was given the names Patrick Branwell Brontë, as though in his person were embodied (more than in his sisters) the union of his parents. His christening took place at his father's odd-looking old church at Thornton on 23rd July 1817, the officiating clergyman being his mother's uncle, the Rev. John Fennell, minister of Cross Stone in the parish of Halifax. His godparents were Mr and Mrs Firth of Kipping House, the wealthy friends whose benefactions had made the social round at Thornton so pleasant for Mr Brontë and his wife since they first settled there in 1815.

Like many children with a choice of Christian names, the little Brontë boy was called "Patrick" by some, and "Branwell" by others; indeed the Firths' only daughter, Elizabeth, entering his birth in her diary for 26th June, wrote that "Branwell Patrick was born early in the morning." Eventually, the question of his names was resolved by his being called "Branwell" by his family and "Patrick" by other people.

The question of Branwell's name is not so frivolous as might at

1

first sight appear, for it relates to his lifelong need to bolster up his
ego under assumed identities. From earliest childhood, indeed,
neither his Irish nor his Cornish name could satisfy his romantic
exigencies, and, whatever he might be to the world, to himself—
and for many years to his sisters in great secret—he would be known
by a succession of pseudonyms which, he believed, expressed far
better than the names given him at the font the exalted personage
concealed within his breast. These pseudonyms were drawn to begin
with from the Napoleonic saga into which, it must not be forgotten,
he was almost born, and in which he was very certainly nurtured,
and they gained in style and rank as Branwell himself declined, thus
fulfilling not only the mere need for romanticising himself, but of
compensating for his progressive failure.

If Branwell Brontë was born with an extravagant sense of the
high destiny he would achieve, he was not alone in holding it; it was
fostered and fanned by all those who stood nearest to him and who,
from the beginning, made a distinction in his treatment from that
of his sisters. In this, it should hastily be added, his sisters themselves
whole-heartedly shared, neither questioning nor seeking to under-
mine the position accorded their only brother. The little girls might
receive the petting of servants, the confidence and attention of their
father, but it was Branwell who was the main purpose, the fond
hope and pride of that bereaved father's heart.

At the time of their father's appointment to the "perpetual
curacy" of Haworth and of the family's removal there on 20th
April 1820, the children's ages were: Maria 6, Elizabeth 5, Charlotte
just 4, Branwell not quite 3, Emily 1¾ years, Anne exactly 4 months.

There is, surely, something symptomatic in the only memory of
their mother that Charlotte preserved into later life: it dated from
after the family's removal to Haworth and was a recollection of Mrs
Brontë playing with her little boy at twilight in the parlour of their
parsonage home—playing, not with the babies Emily and Anne, not
even with Charlotte herself, but with Branwell, the only boy, in
whom the features of the Branwells and the Irish fire of the father
were so early displayed.

It is doubtful whether Branwell himself retained any distinct
memory of his mother (he was 4 years and 3 months old when she
died) but in one of his fragments written as late as 8th March 1838,
"The Life of Warner Howard Warner", we find a description of a
childhood scene which bears the imprint of authenticity. "Details

of Mr Warner's earlier childhood I find difficult to come at and unimportant in substance. The sickly little child was seldom suffered to run unattended from the house—it was his chief pleasure to sit beside his mother's footstool, a large book spread upon the rug. . . ." The book, he goes on to explain, was either "about Greece or Troy, the Bible, or a Natural History Book". Without forcing the parallel, such reading of precisely those books was Branwell's earliest delight.

Throughout her last illness Mrs Brontë was nursed by her sister, Miss Elizabeth Branwell, her senior by seven years, who had already ventured into the wilds of Yorkshire before Charlotte was born, and had remained with the young clerical household during the first year of its residence at Thornton. Miss Branwell, who had inherited an income of £50 a year from her father, a house in Penzance and the consideration of her fellow townspeople—and fellow Methodists in that Methodist stronghold—had every incentive, besides that of superior climate, to call her back to Penzance once her sister was buried. But Miss Branwell was a woman of rigorous conscience and the plight of her sister's little children, and of her sister's widower, left her in no doubt as to where her duty if not her pleasure lay. Hoping, without doubt, that Mr Brontë would in due course re-marry and liberate her to return to "the palms of Penzance", Miss Branwell established herself in the Parsonage of Haworth, as its virtual mistress and the guardian and instructress of its six little motherless children, in the September of 1821.

She did so without illusions and without great affection for the little girls (whose "wild eyes", the servants later reported, positively frightened her). Only towards her little nephew and the baby, Anne, did she feel her heart go out, because, even thus early, she saw in their features the true Branwell traits of which she was so proud. "Little Bany" as he wrote and evidently spoke of himself at an early age, and Anne, were instantly her favourites and on them she showered all the indulgence of which her unemotional nature was capable.

Though Branwell would write of her when she was dead that she had been "for 20 years as my mother", the fact remains that Miss Branwell never succeeded, even towards the two children who were her favourites, in filling the role left vacant by the death of their mother, or in penetrating the passionate hearts of her little nieces and nephew which thirsted so avidly for affection. The

B

absence of all such tender relationship between parent and child might, indeed, be found to be at the origin of the Brontës' unsatisfied hunger for love which brought such tribulation upon at least three of them in adult life.

Miss Branwell's emotional inadequacy to deal with children of such ardent temperaments need not of itself have injured them permanently; nor, perhaps, need the loss of their mother, occurring as it did when they were all so young, had not another grief followed hard upon it—the death of their eldest sister, Maria, the attendant pathos, injustice and terror of which was indelibly to mark the surviving children. In the case of Branwell it may not be too much to say that the death of Maria was the chief cause of his mental instability and of the consequent disasters that dogged his days.

Chapter Two

MARIA

Of Maria Brontë some imperishable traits remain. She has left behind her an impression not only of "superhuman goodness and cleverness", as Ellen Nussey was later to say, but of wisdom and tenderness almost unaccountable in a little girl.

Her exact age has never been known—only the date of her christening, which took place in her father's then parish of Hartshead, on 23rd April 1814. It can be surmised that she was born in the first months of 1814, since her memorial tablet later recorded that she was "in the 12th year of her age" when she died in May 1825.

Maria was little more than six when her parents removed from Thornton to Haworth, yet it is clearly remembered of her that while yet her father was minister of Thornton she would walk with him the four miles into Bradford and back to visit his publisher, and while the gentlemen discussed business, would herself, set up on a high office stool, correct the proofs of her father's poems.

She was not only a *good* child, but an *educated* child to a degree that many adult women of her day never attained. Since at six she could correct the proofs of her father's manuscripts there is little to surprise us in learning from Mrs Gaskell that at seven and a half she regularly read the Tory dailies and periodicals, gave her brother and sisters an abstract of their contents and then discussed them with her father. Proud as he was of his daughter's attainments, Mr Brontë very certainly did not guess at half Mrs Gaskell's incredulous wonder when he told her that he had been able "to converse with her on any of the leading topics of the day as with any grown-up person".

The servants confirmed his tale, even had Mrs Gaskell seriously doubted it.

Yet, though her intellectual attainments were phenomenal, it was her endowments of heart and soul that made her ever-memorable by those who loved and lost her.

Long before Mrs Brontë died Maria both taught and entertained her little sisters and brother, Miss Branwell being necessarily much taken up with attendance in the sick room and in directing the two

5

young servants brought over from Thornton, Nancy and Sarah Garrs.

In summer, the children's domain was the nursery-cum-study, measuring 9 feet by 5 feet 7½ inches, on the first floor—a slip-room without a fireplace, where the little girls slept at night in camp-beds that could be folded up by day. In winter, it was in the dining-room that, inaudibly to their sick mother and to the astonished servants, they would huddle round the fire, rehearsing their lessons with Maria.

Branwell had a room to himself at the back of the house with a window overlooking the moors, an advantage none of his sisters shared.

All his earliest recollections were bound up with images of Maria, of her care for him, of her tenderness and grave authority. From repeated descriptions, we learn that she was fair-haired and blue-eyed —gris-cendré probably, like Charlotte and Anne in childhood.

"There was a light" Branwell wrote in the poem called "Misery II", written in March 1836:

> There was a light—but it is gone.
> There was a hope—but all is o'er,
> Where, Maria, where art thou!
> O, I do seem to see thee now,
> Thy smiling eyes and shining brow,
> Thy sunny cheek and golden hair,
> All through the noontide of my years
> How thou didst enter all my fears
> And hopes of joy, and smiles and tears!
> How often have thy bright blue eyes
> Driven sorrow shrinking from its shrine
> And banished all my misery
> Before one heavenly look of thine!

Under her benign guidance he learned his letters before his mother died, traced his first pothooks, staged his first games. With her he took his earliest walks over the moors, one of a quaint straggle of little children holding hands all together, that the old villagers remembered long after they were all gone. Sunny days, ending in the crucial evening hour, recalled by him in suffering manhood, when Maria would put him to bed, hearing him say his prayers, singing to him the Wesleyan hymns beloved of their mother, and which by force of repetition and association became like the very expression to him of security and love. Lulled by their strains, there

was nothing to fear in abandoning himself to the darkness of sleep.
Often, his last conscious sensation was of Maria's arms about him.

There were ever-memorable occasions, Christmas nights in
particular, when Branwell was allowed to snuggle into Maria's bed
with her and sleep in anticipation of the thrilling morning which to
most children meant presents, but to the little Brontës brought also
the excitement of pealing church bells by which to spring out of
bed. They had only to run to the window of their nursery and
there, just below the garden wall, stood the old tower of Haworth
Church, as sturdy in that crystal Christmas light as on the far-away
Tudor morning that saw it raised.

For the little Brontës, too, there were presents—books so early
acquired, assimilated, conned, as to be almost coeval with them in
memory: *Aesop's Fables*, *The Arabian Nights*, *Pilgrim's Progress*,
Robinson Crusoe and the precious geography book "Papa lent my
sister Maria", and which set off the spark of the corporate Brontë
genius.

Both Anne and Branwell have celebrated in verse this Christmas
music that was so special a feature of their childhood festivities. To
Branwell the sound of bells would ever after bring back

> ... the hours
> When we, at rest together,
> Used to lie listening to the showers
> Of wild December weather;
> Which, when, as oft, they woke in her
> The chords of inward thought,
> Would fill with pictures that wild air,
> From far-off memories brought;
> So, while I lay, I heard again
> Her silver-sounding tongue,
> Rehearsing some remembered strain
> Of old tunes long agone!
> And, flashed across my spirit's sight,
> What she had often told me—
> When, laid awake on Christmas night,
> Her sheltering arms would fold me—
> About that mid-night—seeming day,
> Whose gloom o'er Calvary thrown,
> Showed trembling Nature's deep dismay
> At what her soul had done. . . .

The portrait of Helen Burns which Charlotte painted of her
admired sister could not be "the exact transcript" she told Mrs

Gaskell it was, had not Maria herself been inspired by the most ardent religious faith. After her death her evangelical father, scrupulously avoiding all appearance of pride in his daughter's intellectual attainments, could yet claim for her that "she had exhibited many symptoms of a heart under Divine guidance". In the language of Methodism this meant a very great deal.

That Maria used every opportunity for awakening in the hearts of the little sisters and brother committed to her love the knowledge and sentiment of religion, the above lines of Branwell's abundantly show. The emphasis on those lovely and comforting aspects of the Christian story that naturally appealed to a little girl was to bear all the more weight thereafter by contrast with the Calvinistic doctrine of Miss Branwell, all too soon to replace the influence of Maria in the younger children's lives.

Maria held sway over their infant hearts for less than three unclouded years, but, by very reason of the contrast with the rest of their childhood, that time would assume in retrospect a state of almost paradisal beatitude to which Branwell in particular would ever after revert.

In the January of 1824, it had been decided to send first Maria and Elizabeth, and then Charlotte and Emily, to boarding school. Only the severe epidemic of measles and whooping-cough ravaging Haworth, from which all the little Brontës emerged seriously weakened, delayed their going until July, when the second "half" of the school year began.

What Maria's going to school meant to Branwell can only be guessed. The successive departure of four of his sisters coincided in all probability with a change in his own routine. Leyland, who knew him, and Clement Shorter, who knew Mr Nicholls, both assert that Branwell for a short time was sent to Haworth Grammar School, though no trace of his passage there can be found in the school registers. If he did, in fact, go there, it must have been in the year his sisters were sent to Cowan Bridge, as he seems to have been at home for good from the time of their return in the following year. An allusion in the fragment already mentioned, "The Life of Warner Howard Warner", contains recognisable biographical data to this effect.

Describing young Warner (the delicate little boy we have seen sitting at his mother's footstool) in the recognisably Branwellian role of hearing the servants read their Bibles aloud, and telling them

about many strange things and strange countries until "their feeling
towards him became far too indulgent", he relates how his father,
"wishing to make a man of him and despite the tears of his wife"
(for wife read "Aunt Branwell") sent him to school at six years of
age to "the celebrated Academy near Hawkcliffe kept by Dr Moray".
Now Hawkcliffe is the name of part of the Manor of Oxenhope—
in which Haworth Grammar School was situated. What kind of
schooling Branwell received there and why he was removed, must
be considered later.

Before Branwell had reached his eighth birthday in June 1825,
the major disaster of his youth occurred, from which, perhaps, it is
not too much to say, all the others stemmed.

The tragedy has often enough been related. Maria and Elizabeth,
taken to the Clergy Daughters' School at Cowan Bridge by their
father on 21st July, their health already undermined by their severe
illnesses of the spring, were there exposed to a regimen of privation
and overwork that in less than a year proved fatal to their fragile
constitutions. Since they were followed to school by Charlotte on
10th August and Emily on 25th November, there can be no doubt
at all that their plight remained unsuspected by either their father or
aunt. Mr Brontë, in taking his little girls to school, would have seen
as much of the institution as its directors chose to show, and nothing
that his own observation registered could in any way prejudice him
against the place. It was a new school claiming to provide a first-
class education for girls and warmly recommended by his clerical
friends. Why should he have suspected it of being a death-trap to his
beloved daughters? Recalling his own eager appetite for learning as
a child, Mr Brontë can but have rejoiced that his little girls would be
given every opportunity for an education that would not only
furnish their minds but fit them for earning their livings thereafter.
This was to have been the great contribution of the Clergy Daughters'
School.

Contrarily to much that has been written about Cowan Bridge,
its natural situation is most beautiful. Set within sight of the high
Westmorland hills and quite surrounded by pasture-lands and sleepy,
wooded villages, it is as wholesome of aspect as any rural scene in
England.

It was not the situation of the school that killed the little Brontës,
but the unkindness of its organisers who chose to disregard the
suffering which their regimen imposed on frail bodies and heart-

sick souls. Maria and Elizabeth Brontë, it must be remembered, were own sisters to Emily, who was twice in later life in jeopardy of dying from homesickness at school.

These things were intimately known to the sisters themselves. Young as Charlotte and Emily were at Cowan Bridge, something of the *heartache* as well as the illness of Maria and Elizabeth reached their childish minds never to quit them again. This it was which added so immeasurably to the children's grief in losing their elder sisters. There was anger mixed with their grief, a sense of revolt that would never leave them so long as they lived.

Notified in February that Maria was critically ill, Mr Brontë sped to Cowan Bridge on the 14th, to find his daughter dying of consumption. Nothing in Elizabeth's *then* appearance can have roused his suspicions respecting her equally threatening state, for he left her behind with Charlotte and Emily, both of whom were in good health.

Many years later only did Charlotte Brontë find words to express, in the burning pages of *Jane Eyre*, what that experience meant to her. Writing to her publisher about her recollections of the Clergy Daughters' School she said, "Early impressions are ineffaceable. My career was a very quiet one. I was plodding and industrious, perhaps I was very grave, for I suffered to see my sisters perishing."

In a "perishing" condition, indeed, Maria reached home, where only Branwell and Anne were present to welcome her.

How much was known of hygiene in that household it is impossible to say. There would seem to have been no attempt at keeping the little ones from her bedside. Branwell bore with him through life the image of that Heaven towards which Maria was hurrying with such speed, and, as she made abundantly clear in all her pronouncements, with such rapture. Follow her, either in body or spirit, he could not do either then or later, to his lasting torment.

Maria died on 6th May 1825, ten weeks after her return home and without ever seeing Elizabeth, Charlotte and Emily again. Her funeral took place on Thursday, 12th May, and was conducted by her "Uncle Morgan", who had held her over the font at Hartshead eleven years before.

Her loss was going to deprive Branwell not only of that maternal love without which his unstable nature could not stand, but of the comfort of that very religion which it had been her chief purpose in life to implant in his heart, and which, in dying, she firmly believed she had bequeathed to him for ever. Through no fault of hers, this was not to be.

When it is remembered that from the very moment when Branwell lost Maria he fell under the religious influence of his aunt— an influence which, as with his sisters Charlotte and Anne, resulted √ in a morbid awakening of the sense of sin—it will be the more readily realised that the sense of severance from Maria was to be yet further heightened by the fear of his own personal unworthiness and damnation. Hence the cruel paradox that was to be created by his saint-like sister's death: her very goodness was going to become an insuperable barrier over which Branwell could never pass. "But we are sundered . . ." he wrote in bitterness of spirit after years had passed.

> I must never look on thee—
> If there's no God, no Heaven, no Hell,
> Thou within thy grave must dwell—
> I, left blackening in the storm—
> Both a banquet for the worm.
> If there is a heaven above,
> Thou in bliss art shining there
> . . . Angel bright and angel fair . . .
> . . . While I stayed where
> Hell's dread night must close my day.

The logical outcome of this sense of severance from his too-perfect sister and the consciousness of his own unworthiness was almost to provoke and certainly to exaggerate every failure in life, until his morbid imagination had made a pariah of him, a true "castaway" in the sense of Cowper's poem, which was so deeply to influence his childhood.

As logical, given his hyper-sensitive temperament, was the virulence of his ultimate reaction to his aunt's teaching.

That with Branwell she achieved but a sorry result is not to say that her admonitions did not cause him exquisite terrors and pains. The evidence shows that it was so. The more his aunt convinced him of the reality of Hell, the more she drove him down the path to it. No wonder that as the distance lengthened from Maria, the boy, the young man, the adult of exceptional morbidity of feeling, should turn cynic and deny his childhood's creed, rather than suffer a Hell of frustration in struggling after it.

In all its aspects the theme of Maria's death would be recurrent in the prose and verse of his adolescent years. Whether he transposed it upon the Angrian scene and lent Maria's lineaments and attitudes to the Duchess of Zamorna, or whether he lent her only a partial disguise of name and appearance, she would be the prototype of all his heroines—fair, frail and touching—so unlike the bold and amoral beauties of Charlotte's childish tales.

The day would come when, after twelve years of repression, the terrible experience of her funeral would rise to the upper layers of his consciousness again and prompt the sequence of his "Caroline" poems in lines of harrowing clarity. From no aspect of that terrifying ordeal was Branwell spared. Maria dying and Maria dead, he saw her through every stage of her slow calvary with every detail branded on his shrinking mind for life.

There have been modern writers to question the relation of the "Caroline" poems to the death of Maria, and to seek to link them with Branwell's experiences at Luddenden Foot in 1841. Let it be said at once not only that they were written in 1837, four years before Branwell could have knowledge of the slightly similar case of a young girl's death at Luddenden, but that Francis Leyland, to whom Branwell gave the poems, stated that they dealt with his sister's death. Even a cursory reading shows their exact relevance to the tragedy that overtook the family at Haworth Parsonage in the summer of 1825. The only transposition made is that the speaker, in the important second poem, is a little girl instead of a little boy; otherwise her experiences are his. The sound of a passing-bell recalls to the writer

> . . . a scene of bygone years—
> Opens a fount of sealed-up tears—
> And wakens memory's pensive thought
> To visions sleeping—not forgot.
> It brings me back a summer's day,
> Shedding like this its parting ray,
> With skies as shining and serene,
> And hills as blue, and groves as green.
>
> Ah, well I recollect that hour . . .
> Was it that bell—that funeral bell,
> Sullenly sounding on the wind?
> Was it that melancholy knell
> Which first to sorrow woke my mind?

I looked upon my mourning dress
Till my heart beat with childish fear,
And—frightened at my loneliness—
I watched, some well-known sound to hear.
But all without lay silent in
The sunny hush of afternoon,
And only muffled steps within
Passed slowly and sedately on.
I well can recollect the awe
With which I hastened to depart;
And, as I ran, the instinctive start
With which my mother's form I saw,
Arrayed in black, with pallid face,
And cheeks and 'kerchief wet with tears,
As down she stooped to kiss my face
And quiet my uncertain fears.

She led me, in her mourning hood,
Through voiceless galleries, to a room,
'Neath whose black hangings crowded stood,
With downcast eyes and brows of gloom,
My known relations; while—with head
Declining o'er my sister's bed—
My father's stern eye dropt a tear
Upon the coffin resting there.
My mother lifted me to see
What might within that coffin be;
And, to this moment, I can feel
The voiceless gasp—the sickening chill—
With which I hid my whitened face
In the dear folds of her embrace;

For hardly dared I turn my head
Lest its wet eyes should view that bed.
"But, Harriet," said my mother mild,
"Look at *your* sister and my child
One moment, ere her form be hid
For ever 'neath its coffin lid!"
I heard the appeal, and answered too;
For down I bent to bid adieu.
But, as I looked, forgot affright
In mild and magical delight.

There lay she then, as now she lies—
For not a limb has moved since then—
In dreamless slumber closed, those eyes
That never more might wake again.

She lay, as I had seen her lie
On many a happy night before,
When I was humbly kneeling by—
Whom she was teaching to adore:
Oh, just as when by her I prayed,
And she to heaven sent up my prayer,
She lay with flowers about her head—
Though formal grave-clothes hid her hair!
Still did her lips the smile retain
Which parted them when hope was high,
Still seemed her brow as smoothed from pain
As when all thought she could not die.
And, though her bed looked cramped and strange,
Her *too* bright cheek all faded now,
My young eyes scarcely saw a change
From hours when moonlight paled her brow.
And yet I felt—and scarce could speak—
A chilly face, a faltering breath,
When my hand touched the marble cheek
Which lay so passively beneath.
In fright I gasped, "Speak, Caroline!"
And bade my sister to arise;
But answered not her voice to mine,
Nor ope'd her sleeping eyes.
I turned towards my mother then
And prayed on her to call;
But, though she strove to hide her pain,
It forced her tears to fall.
She pressed me to her aching breast
As if her heart would break,
And bent in silence o'er the rest
Of one she could not wake:
The rest of one, whose vanished years
Her soul had watched in vain;
The end of mother's hopes and fears,
And happiness and pain.

They came—they pressed the coffin lid
Above my Caroline,
And then, I felt, for ever hid
My sister's face from mine!
There was one moment's wildered start—
One pang remembered well—
When first from my unhardened heart
The tears of anguish fell:
That swell of thought which seemed to fill
The bursting heart, the gushing eye,
While fades all *present* good or ill

Before the shades of things gone by.
All else seems blank—the mourning march,
The proud parade of woe,
The passage 'neath the churchyard arch,
The crowd that met the show.
My place or thoughts amid the train
I strive to recollect, in vain—
I could not think or see:
I cared not whither I was borne:
And only felt that death had torn
My Caroline from me.

Slowly and sadly, o'er her grave,
The organ peals its passing stave,
And, to its last dark dwelling-place,
The corpse attending mourners bear,
While, o'er it bending, many a face
'Mongst young companions shows a tear.
I think I glanced toward the crowd
That stood in musing silence by,
And even now I hear the sound
Of some one's voice amongst them cry—
"I am the Resurrection and the Life—
He who believes in me shall never die!"

Long years have never worn away
The unnatural strangeness of that day,
When I beheld—upon the plate
Of grim death's mockery of state—
That well-known word, that long-loved name,
Now but remembered like the dream
Of half-forgotten hymns divine,
My sister's name—my Caroline!
Down, down, they lowered her, sad and slow,
Into her narrow house below:
And deep, indeed, appeared to be
That one glimpse of eternity,
Where, cut from life, corruption lay,
Where beauty soon should turn to clay!
Though scarcely conscious, hotly fell
The drops that spoke my last farewell;
And wild my sob, when hollow rung
The first cold clod above her flung,
When glitter was to turn to rust,
"Ashes to ashes, dust to dust!"
How bitter seemed that moment when,
Earth's ceremonies o'er,
We from the filled grave turned again

To leave her evermore;
And, when emerging from the cold
Of damp, sepulchral air,
As I turned, listless to behold
The evening fresh and fair,
How sadly seemed to smile the face
Of the descending sun!
How seemed as if his latest race
Were with that evening run!

Such a passage calls for no commentary—unless it is to remind the reader that, following hard upon Maria's death, came the death of Elizabeth, pronounced gravely ill and sent home in charge of the school housekeeper on 31st May. She did not linger so long as her sister and died on 15th June and was buried—doubtless with precisely the same ritual as Maria—three days later.

There may, in this repetition of the nightmare, have been two alleviating factors for Branwell. Elizabeth, for all her stoic qualities of courage, had not been like Maria, his own particular sister, and, when she had been brought home dying, Mr Brontë had rushed to fetch his two other girls away, so that by the same stroke that cut down the main prop of his life, Branwell was given new help and support from another quarter. Certain it is that Charlotte's energetic and passionate nature rapidly responded to the change in her situation. From being the third child in a big family she was left the eldest with the three little ones looking up to her and, unforgiving as her grief for Maria would remain, it was undoubtedly through her death that Charlotte became so devoted to her only brother. On him would now be poured out all the affection of her wounded heart, and though she would never take Maria's place in his life, Branwell would become the chief object of hers for many, many years to come.

Thus began a new phase in the boy's evolution: while the simplicity and tenderness of his relationship with Maria could not be renewed with any living creature, the cleverness and purpose of his sister Charlotte spurred him on to intellectual efforts undreamed of hitherto. What his heart lost, it never regained; but emulating Charlotte made him use his head, spurred his ambition and gave him for a few, illusory years the sentiment of having a great future before him.

Chapter Three

FATHER AND SON

Probably at no other time in Branwell's life was the influence of his father so direct or so strong upon him, as during his sisters' absence at school. His father's tastes, his father's prejudices, the very mannerisms of his father's speech, later so noticeable in Branwell, then held almost undisputed sway over the malleable and emotional nature of the little boy. The frequent interspersings of his talk, even as a child, with the "my dear Sir" and the "verbum sap." and other Latin tags so dear to his father, and so ludicrous in one of his years, raised many a laugh at Branwell's expense, yet the imitation of his only parent may truly, at that stage, have been indicative of nothing but the sincerest flattery. Father and son, thrown so closely together for the first time, enjoyed as never again in their relationship, the delights of conferring favours on and receiving them from one another. If, in the absence of his four older girls, Mr Brontë's whole paternal care was now centred on the budding intellect of his boy, he can have felt nothing but satisfaction with the speed and completeness with which the son became the replica of himself. Yet Mr Brontë cannot be accused of stopping short at impressing his own likeness on his heir.

Whether his very strong nature already recognised the weak nature of his son and feared its unpreparedness for the world, certain it is that he gave Branwell his chance of exposure to other influences than those of his sheltered home. He sent Branwell to school, hoping no doubt, by so doing, to bring him to terms with the world. But, coming to terms with the world—the real world—was always going to be Branwell's stumbling-block in life.

If school constituted the major experience of a year already marked by his sisters' absence, his going there mattered less than the prompt necessity of being withdrawn from it. For, from whatever causes, Branwell can have remained only a very short while at Haworth Grammar School where he met with his first decisive failure—the first of a very long line of failures punctuating the whole course of his career.

Francis Leyland, who, though he had no early acquaintance with

17

Branwell, was later to know two of his boyhood friends, Hartley Merrall and Willie Wood, (Tabby's nephew), stated that Mr Brontë's reasons for sending Branwell to the Grammar School were to please the local authorities, the Haworth Church Lands Trustees— and to give encouragement to a school that had seen better days. This was certainly true respecting the last clause. Founded in 1638 by Dr Christopher Scott, the Grammar School—as its name implied— was required to provide a classical education for boys and girls alike and to fit the former to proceed to university. Provision was made for both a salary and a house for a headmaster, who was required to be a graduate of either Oxford or Cambridge. But in point of fact few of these provisions were being fulfilled by the time Mr Brontë came into the district. The rare families requiring an academic train- ing for their sons, had reduced the call for a "classical" education to the teaching of Latin alone, and after 1818 when the school building was renovated, the headmaster was no longer even a graduate of either Oxford or Cambridge. The number of pupils had fallen, a fact that may have been due to the actual position of the school which was inconvenient for Haworth, being situated some one and a half miles away in Near Oxenhope. It was reached by a field- path only, idyllic in summer but less negotiable in the snows of winter.

The old school house yet stands. A minute edifice, with deep- set windows of tiny leaded lights and a heavy mantle of ivy, it per- fectly evokes the Miltonic Age that saw it built. Even the flagstones of the field-path still remain, hollowed out enough to give credence to the belief that they are the same as those trodden by the little scholars of King Charles's day.

Perhaps the distance proved too much for Branwell, a delicate child at best; perhaps the little Latin he could acquire there was not considered worth the more exceptionable lessons picked up from fellows predominantly rough and rustic in manners and speech (although there, as everywhere in country districts, true refinement of heart and mind was certainly not lacking in his class-mates). Per- haps his eyesight, which early had to be corrected by wearing glasses, was considered to be put to too great a strain from bad lighting and the sharing of lesson-books. One can think of a number of contri- buting causes, but obviously the overruling one was that he broke down under the test, and had to be removed.

It is certain that he was delicate and undersized, even then, for his age, a life-long disadvantage that was galling for so vain a boy, and one which may well have been at the origin of his subsequent passion for pugilism. He had, moreover, inherited the red-gold hair of his father and would not have escaped then, any more than later in life, the inevitable ragging occasioned by "carroty" hair.

All such reasons may have satisfied his anxious aunt and father that he was ill-suited for the rough and tumble of a village school, but there may have been yet another and more conclusive one in deciding them to remove him after only a few months' trial. Whether Branwell manifested symptoms of an acute nervous instability before the death of Maria is not certain, but he was still very young when the incidence of his violent rages was first observed. If he was already subject to them when he went to school, that would be an additional reason for removing him. The child he described himself as being, in the already quoted "Life of Warner Howard Warner", though a "shy-looking little being", would "upon contradiction or scolding" redden violently and bite his lips "which prognosticated something other than a milk and water man"—the man, in short, his friend Grundy described in later years, who in his fits of passion (quite distinct from his fits of drunkenness) would "drive his fist through the panel of a door" and only so find relief.

Charlotte Brontë, wise after the event, saw the taint in retrospect, and described it feelingly in the child Victor Crimsworth in *The Professor*. Though Leyland taxed her with some exaggeration he quoted the passage in full as truly representative of the young Branwell. "Charlotte, who knew well the treasures of her brother's opening faculties, . . ." writes Leyland, "saw also many things that alarmed her in his disposition. She saw the abnormal and unhealthy flashing of his intellect and marked that weakness and want of self-control which left Branwell, when subjected to temptation, a prey to many destructive influences. . . ."

Charlotte, portraying the fictional boy through the eyes of his mother, relates how "she sees a something in his temper—a kind of electrical ardour and power—which emits, now and then, ominous sparks . . .". The mother gives this "something in her son's marked character no name; but when it appears in the grinding of his teeth, in the glittering of his eye, in the fierce revolt of feeling against disappointment, mischance, sudden sorrow, a supposed injustice", folds him to her breast and "reasons with him like any philosopher, and to reason Victor is ever accessible . . . then she looks at him

c

with the eyes of love, and by love Victor can be infallibly sub-jugated . . . ."

The passage finds its echo in the only authentic picture we have of father and son together at this early stage. It is in the story re-lated later to Mrs Gaskell by Mr Brontë himself of the experiment he tried on his children to test their intelligence. In so far as it con-cerns Branwell it corroborates Charlotte's above-quoted description of Victor Crimsworth as being ever "accessible to reason". Mr Brontë asked each of his children a testing question ("What is the best mode of spending time? What is the best book in the world? What is the best mode of education for a woman?" etc.) Of Emily, as he told Mrs Gaskell, he asked, "What I had best to do with her brother Branwell, who was sometimes a naughty boy?" She answered, "Reason with him, and when he won't listen to reason, whip him." The question surely argues a certain perplexity on the part of the father as though he had not himself reached a conclusion on whether to deal more or *less* severely with a son whose ardent temperament gave such ominous signs of instability.

Charlotte, looking back in sorrow over the years to the time when Branwell might still have been saved from himself, wrote of young Victor Crimsworth that the "offending Adam" could have been "if not *whipped* out of him, at least soundly disciplined" and that a little bodily or mental suffering applied then would have been cheap at the price if it had "ground him radically in the art of self-control". Quite obviously she considered that his upbringing had been far too lenient. ". . . Will reason or love," she queries, "be the weapons with which in future the world will meet his violence? Oh, no! for that flash in his black eye—for that cloud on his bonny brow—for that compression of his statuesque lips, the lad will some day get blows instead of blandishments, kicks instead of kisses; then for the fit of mute fury which will sicken his body and madden his soul; then for the ordeal of merited and salutary suffering out of which he will come (I trust) a wiser and a better man."

It is certain that if Branwell ever felt the whip it was no more—and probably far less—than most boys of good homes in the early nineteenth century. The accusation of over-harshness can never be levelled at his upbringing. Far more likely, from Charlotte's evi-dence, that the regimen of his father and aunt was one of "blandish-ments", as corresponding to their overweening love for him and to his many weaknesses, even at that early hour.

An incident, reported to Ellis Chadwick by Haworth residents, which may have occurred as early as Branwell's eighth year, might well also account both for the removal from school and the nervous irritability that followed, and the regimen of indulgence applied to him. He was, apparently, bitten by a mad dog and—for reasons unexplained—never had the wound cauterised. The same accident occurring to Emily as a grown woman, the occasion of her heroic self-inflicted cauterisation of the bite, recalled to the family the neglected accident of Branwell's childhood and wakened their suspicions of its fatal effects on him.

Given his nervous temperament, it is a moot point whether Branwell lost anything by leaving school. Certainly not upon the score of knowledge, for his father was a far better classical coach than the local schoolmaster of the time, with an innate gift for teaching and a genuine passion for learning. The gaps—and many gaps there would be in Branwell's acquirements—would have been different but just as many had he not studied at home. On his classical attainments, his knowledge of Latin in particular, he would constantly be congratulated in after life, and this not only by less educated men than himself, like the engineer Grundy, who was naturally impressed by Branwell's capacity to quote Greek, Latin and French with equal ease, but by men of letters of the standing of Macaulay, Hartley Coleridge and James Montgomery—a result that must be placed entirely to his father's credit.

By the time Branwell was ten, as his first manuscripts show, he had assimilated the Homeric and Virgilian epics; Greek and Latin history; contemporary history, with special reference to the French Revolution, Napoleon's and Wellington's campaigns; the exploits of late eighteenth-century and early nineteenth-century explorers, whose travel books were as much the mode *then*, as their successors', in less arduous fields of discovery, are today. Contemporary politics, Continental as well as English, and the whole field of English literature, from the Elizabethan dramatists to the living "romantic" poets of the day, from all of which Branwell could freely and not incorrectly quote like household words, made up his pasture.

So vast a field of culture could not have been acquired in any village classroom in the time, nor was it solely the effect of his father's teaching, but also of his tastes and influence. Mr Brontë was an overworked minister in a far-flung parish in a mountainous and moorland district, whose duties often took him away from home for whole days at a time. But his great virtues lay in encouraging his children to read for themselves and in never restricting their reading. Branwell's sources of books and periodicals will be examined later; suffice it to say here that he had absolute liberty to browse where he willed and for as long as he willed.

Other liberties were his which his sisters' biographers have again laid to the blame of his father; he was allowed to play with the village boys, a perfectly natural permission on the part of a father who, in his own childhood, had had only the village street for playground. Branwell, as may be imagined, made full use of the permission. What only boy in a predominantly feminine household would not have done the same?

Leyland relates an innocent enough incident which throws light not only on the difference between the kind of life permitted to Branwell and that of his sisters, but upon his highly nervous youthful temperament. The story, reported to him in after years by one of Branwell's surviving friends, Hartley Merrall, described how on the occasion of the "Keighley Feast" (an annual event still today), Branwell and his young friend went down into the town, four miles distant, to enjoy the fun.

"The town," wrote Leyland, "was . . . crowded with booths and shows, and various places of entertainment. Players and riders— men and women—clothed in gay raiments, rendered brilliant with spangles, paced backwards and forwards along their platforms to the sound of drums, organs, and Pandean pipes, cymbals, tambourines, and castanets. There were stalls . . . weighted with nuts and various confectioneries, and there were also rocking-boats and merry-go-rounds, with other amusements.

". . . Branwell's excitement, hilarity, and extravagance knew no bounds: he would see everything and try everything. Into a rocking-boat he and his friend gaily stepped. The rise of the boat, when it reached its full height, gave Branwell a pleasant view of the fair beneath; but, when it descended, he screamed out at the top of his voice, 'Oh! my nerves! my nerves! Oh! my nerves!' On each descent, every nerve thrilled, tingled, and vibrated with overwhelming effect through the overwrought and delicate frame of the boy. Leaving the fair, the two proceeded homeward; and, reaching a country spot, near a cottage standing among a thicket of trees, Branwell, still full of exuberant life, proposed a wrestle with his companion. They engaged in a struggle, when Branwell was overthrown. It was not until reaching the village, and seeing the lights in the windows . . . that he became aware he had lost his spectacles—for Branwell was, like his sister Charlotte, very near-sighted. This was, indeed, no little trouble to him, as he was in great fear lest his father should notice his being without them, and institute unpleasant inquiries as to what had become of them . . . after a sleepless night for both, Branwell's friend was early on the spot in search of the missing spectacles, when the woman living in the cottage close by, seeing a youth look about, came to him . . . brought out the spectacles which she had picked up from the ground just before he came. M—, glad of the discovery, hastened to the parsonage, which he reached to find Branwell astir, who was overjoyed on receiving the missing spectacles, as the danger of his father's displeasure was avoided."

This may be to anticipate, but in such and in less innocuous pastimes, it is necessary to call to mind, many of Branwell's leisure hours were spent. The story does not make it clear whether Mr Brontë's "displeasure" was feared on the score of lost spectacles alone, or upon that of his son disporting himself at the fair. Part of the thrilling experience, one senses from the story, came from Branwell's sense of stolen pleasure. Authority to play in the streets with other boys may not have comprised permission to frequent public places of entertainment! Successful thus early in evading disagreeable consequences, the habit would be confirmed with the passing years, and something like a dual life achieved under the very nose of authority.

For there was very early a dual nature in Branwell, the one as guileless as the other was crooked.

On the subject of boys' education, as distinct from girls', Branwell's sisters, Charlotte and Anne, would both express themselves later in life in terms so heated as to leave little doubt that they had the fiasco of their own brother's upbringing in mind. That he was allowed so much more liberty than they is not their complaint; it is that his freedom was not coupled with necessary warnings against even the commonest pitfalls to which all young creatures must be exposed if not duly protected; it is that he was not fortified against temptation, through the false assumption that being a boy, he was naturally armed to resist it. Both Charlotte and Anne felt the same indignation that their brother, because he was a boy, was not considered to need forewarning against the temptations and vices of the world from which they, as girls, were so sedulously shrouded, as though, wrote Charlotte, "girls . . . were something very frail and silly indeed, while boys are turned loose on the world as if they, of all beings in existence, were the wisest and the least liable to be led astray."

"You think," Anne Brontë makes Helen Huntingdon declare in *The Tenant of Wildfell Hall*, "that a woman cannot be too little exposed to temptation, or too little acquainted with vice . . . whereas in the nobler sex, there is a natural tendency to goodness, guarded by a superior fortitude . . . that the slightest error, the merest shadow of pollution will ruin the one, while the character of the other will be strengthened and embellished—his education properly finished by a little practical acquaintance with forbidden things. . . . You would have us encourage our sons to prove all things by their own experience, while our daughters must not even profit by the experience of others, that they should know beforehand to refuse the evil and choose the good. . . . As for my son, if I thought he would grow up to be what you call a man of the world—one that has 'seen life' and glories in his experience . . . I would rather that he died tomorrow. . . ."

Branwell's sisters blamed the eventual failure of his life on the over-indulgence of his upbringing and the mistaken confidence placed in his moral judgment by his doting elders. But his father's only real mistake in dealing with him lay in not recognising soon enough the need to counterbalance the dangerous hold imagination had upon this dreamer, by firmly rooting his interests in reality. Himself an unworldly man, with a certain streak of naïveté in his character, he gave his son an unpractical education upon romantic lines—lines which, already in the eighteen-twenties had little relevance to the progressive industrial England springing up at his very door, and in which, when the time came, Branwell would find himself a complete misfit. Any failure in such a man was bound to lead to further failure.

The whole emphasis of his education was directed upon heroic example, upon the military ideal, implanted in him in earliest childhood by his father, himself, perhaps, disappointed of a military career that circumstances had put beyond his reach. From Mr Brontë Branwell early imbibed a reverence for the fictitious and real heroes of literature and history that was little short of idolatry. Add to this the very age into which Branwell was born, that post-Napoleonic world only then taking stock of its losses and gains, and who wonders that the flame kindled thus early was fanned into an uncontrollable conflagration? In article after article, in book after book, as it will be the object of the following pages to show, in whatever he read, Branwell's imagination was perpetually excited by the story of the late titanic struggle in Europe, made all the more excitingly real to the boy by the survival of most of the protagonists. With Napoleon's death in 1821 there was released a spate of memorials by his yet-surviving friends and foes which were to rouse opinion for and against the dead lion for a decade to come. When it is recalled that Anne Brontë was born a year before Napoleon died, and that Wellington's entry into politics dated only from 1828, it will be the better realised how it was that the span of the little Brontës' childhood, passed in the afterglow of an already legendary era, should be so deeply influenced by the heroic stature of contemporary politics.

There is a passage in the important autobiographic poem, "Sir Henry Tunstall", (written when Branwell was twenty-one) that feelingly describes the boy's romantic reactions to the heroic examples of the past. With its evocation of the boy's room and treasures, it gives us a rare glimpse into the background of his home.

The protagonist in the poem returns to his home after long absence on the battlefields of India and, seeking the privacy of his own old bedroom, finds among the treasures hoarded there ("guns and rods—wherewith he often trod the breezy hills—") the very picture hanging on the wall that had so stirred his heart in childhood, depicting

> —England's victory, and her Hero's fall
> On cold Canadian hills. With strange delight
> In other days the child would fix his sight,
> Whene'er he wakened, on that time-dimmed view,
> And inly burn to be a hero too;
> Would fill his spirit with the thoughts divine
> Of the loud cannon, and the charging line,
> And Wolfe, departing 'mid commingling cries
> To join immortal spirits in the skies!
> 'Twas that dim print that over Indian seas
> First led his feet and fixed his destinies. . . .

[The reference is, of course, to West's picture, "The Death of Wolfe", first exhibited at the Royal Academy in 1771, of which a famous engraving was made by William Woollett.]

Branwell's feet would never take him farther east than London, and the inescapable reflection is forced on us that much of his suffering and failure would derive from the very extravagance of his hopes kindled in childhood, hopes of fame and fortune based upon a quite illusory identification of himself with the figures of a "world too old" into which it had been his misfortune, he would think, to have been born too late. The predicament, it should be added, was not peculiar to him; it was typical of the post-Napoleonic world. Alfred de Musset would feelingly describe the sense of loss to their generation in his *Enfant du Siècle*, and Chateaubriand, Goethe and Byron all make themselves the elegists of its ruins. Their influence on the youthful Branwell, be it said in passing, cannot be overrated.

The exorbitant expectations such reading fostered informed all his juvenile writings. For the period of his brilliant boyhood, at least, he succeeded in integrating his illusions of grandeur with his every-day existence. In a mass of prose and verse writing of amazing profusion and range, he created a whole world in the very image and to the heroic measure of the Napoleonic Age into which he had so barely missed being born.

Under such influences, it is in no way surprising that the first booklets written by the precocious child should have for title: "My Battell Book" [*sic*] written when he was nine years and nine months old, and "History of the Rebellion in My Army", when he was eleven.

That it was a present from the father that should touch off the creative spark in the son was wholly fitting, and almost in the nature of poetic justice. In June 1824, on the occasion of Branwell's seventh birthday, Mr Brontë gave him a box of toy soldiers. The first of several sets, with them began a new era in Branwell's life—an era of self-expression, of self-dramatisation, of self-transposition—of escape, in short, from a life early shaken to its foundations by the death of Maria.

Chapter Four

THE YOUNG MEN

Maria and Elizabeth were buried. As deep as the grave, the memory of their deaths was buried in Branwell's mind to emerge only after long years of rigorous repression. On the surface, the current of life ran on at an amazing tempo.

The curtain, rung down on the domestic drama in the summer of 1825, was not lifted again in the annals of the family for a whole year. No evidence of any kind has been preserved of the intervening period of mourning. When, suddenly, it is raised again in the June of 1826, it is upon a very different scene. The moment, one senses from the very precision of detail in Branwell's narration, was a moment of immense importance to them, already assuming something of the monumental rigidity of historic fact.

"It was sometime in the summer of the year A.D. 1824 when I, being desirous to possess a box of soldiers, asked papa to buy me one, which shortly afterwards he procured me from Bradford. They were 12 in number, price 1s. 6d., and were the best I ever have had. Soon after this I got from Keighley another set of the same number. These soldiers I kept for about a year until either maimed, lost, burnt, or destroyed by various casualties they

departed and left not a wrack behind!

Now, therefore, not satisfied with what I had formerly got, I purchased at Keighley a band of Turkish musicians which I continued to keep till the summer of A.D. 1825, when Charlotte and Emily returned from school, where they had been during the days of my former sets. I remained for 10 months after they had returned without any soldiers, when on June 5th A.D. 1826 papa procured me from Leeds another set (these were the 12s) which I kept for 2 years, though 2 or 3 of them are in being at the time of my writing this (Dec 15, A.D. 1830). Sometime in 1827 I bought another set of Turkish Musicians at Halifax, and in 1828 I purchased the Last Box, a band of Indians, at Haworth. Both these I still keep. Here now ends the catalogue of soldiers bought by or for me. . . ."

The "catalogue" formed part of the "Introduction" to a work

27

entitled by Branwell "The History of the Young Men" who were, in effect, none other than the toy soldiers brought to life. But to what a life—and what an immortality—their earnest young historian had not even then an inkling.

". . . I must now conclude this Introduction," proceeds Branwell, "already too long with saying, that what is contained in this History is a statement of what Myself, Charlotte, Emily and Anne really pretended did happen among the 'Young Men' (that being the name we gave them) during the period of nearly 6 years, though in some places slightly altered according to the form and taste of the aforesaid Young Men. It is written by Captain John Bud the greatest prose writer they have among them."

"When I first saw them," Branwell further wrote about the incident in a footnote to his "History of the Young Men", "in the morning after they were bought, I carried them to Emily, Charlotte and Anne. They each took up a soldier, gave them names, which I consented to, and I gave Charlotte Twemy (i.e. Wellington), to Emily, Pare (Parry), to Anne, Trott (Ross) to take care of them, though they were to be mine and I to have the disposal of them as I would—shortly after this I gave them to them as their own."

On something more than nodding terms as they might be with the illustrious figures of the day—the obvious giants, Wellington and Napoleon—it gives one pause to hear this nursery party bandying the names of Parry and Ross, even if somewhat mangled, as though they equally were household words.

The fact, of course, is that they were. Reference has but to be made to the pages of *Blackwood's Magazine* for the eighteen-twenties, to find the exploits of both these explorers constantly to the fore in reviews of their "Travels".

That the little Brontës had access to *Blackwood's Magazine* has been known ever since Mrs Gaskell quoted Charlotte's statement to that effect, written in March 1829 when she was barely thirteen. There is, moreover, an important letter of Branwell's written as a young man of eighteen to the editor of *Blackwood's*, which shows that the children were reading and revelling in its monthly issues even at the time of the death of Maria. But what neither statement can give is the direct proof of the influence exercised by *Blackwood's* on their earliest creative writing which a close comparison with the numbers for the eighteen-twenties and early eighteen-thirties alone can do. In article after article, in year after year, one finds the sources of their phenomenally precocious knowledge on matters of history, literature, politics, travel and art; and, more striking still, of the very shape and direction their imaginative writings took.

Both the promise and the pathos of Branwell's early passion for the journal is reflected in the above-mentioned letter written on 7th December 1835. The immediate occasion of his writing was the death of the famous Ettrick Shepherd (James Hogg) who, from the magazine's inception in October 1817, had been, with Wilson and Lockhart, a chief contributor. On hearing of his death Branwell wrote to solicit the reversion of his post. ". . . It is not from affected hypocrisy," he writes, "that I commence my letter with the name of James Hogg; for the writings of that man in your numbers, his speeches in your 'Noctes' [the celebrated symposium of wits which figured almost monthly in the journal from 1822 to 1835] when I was a child, laid a hold on my mind which succeeding years have consecrated into a most sacred feeling. I cannot express . . . the heavenliness of associations connected with such articles as Professor Wilson's, read and re-read while a little child, with all their poetry of language and divine flight into that visionary region of imagination which one very young would believe reality. . . . I speak so, Sir, because while a child 'Blackwood' formed my chief delight, and, I feel certain that no child before enjoyed reading as I did, because none ever had such works as 'The Noctes', 'Christmas Dreams', 'Christopher in his Sporting Jacket', to read."

"Even now," continued Branwell, quoting favourite passages from those old numbers of the magazine, " 'Millions o' reasonable creatures at this hour'—. . . etc. or 'Long, long ago, seems the time when we danced hand in hand with our golden-haired sister, . . . Long, long ago, the day on which she died. That hour, so far more dreadful than any hour that now can darken us on this earth, when she, her coffin and that velvet pall descended—and descended—slowly—slowly—into the horrid clay, and we were borne death-like, and wishing to die, out of the churchyard. . . .' Passages like these, Sir, (and when the last was written my sister died)—passages like these, read then and remembered now, afford feelings which, I repeat, I cannot describe."

The familiarity such reading bred with figures in all walks of public life can be measured only when viewed in the light of the children's unselfconscious statements, meant for no eyes but their own.

Wishing to record how their principal "plays"—as they called their games—arose, Charlotte wrote on 31st June [*sic*] 1829,

The Play of the Islanders was formed in December 1827, in the following manner.

One night about the time when the cold sleet and dreary fogs of November are succeeded by the snow storms, and high peircing night winds of confirmed winter, we where all sitting round the warm blazing kitchen fire having just concluded a quarel with Taby concerning the propriety of lighting a candle from which she came of victorious, no candle having been produced. a long pause suceeded, which was at last broken by Bany saying, in a lazy maner, I don't know what to do. This was re-echoed by E & A.

T.: Wha ya may go t'bed.

B.: I'd rather do anything than that.

C.: Why are you so glum to-night? supose we had each an island.

B.: If we had I would choose the Island of Man.

C.: And I would choose the Isle of Wight.

E.: The Isle of Aran for me.

A.: And mine should be Guernsey.

We then chose who should be chief men in our islands: Branwell chose John Bull, Astley Cooper, and Leigh Hunt; Emily, Walter Scott, Mr Lockhart, Johnny Lockhart; Anne, Michael Sadler, Lord Bentinck, Sir Henry Halford. I chose the Duke of Wellington and sons, Christopher North and Co Mr Abernathy. Here our conversation was interrupted by the, to us, dismal sound of the clock striking seven, and we where sumoned of to bed.

The names of Sir Walter Scott, "Mr" Lockhart and "Johnny" Lockhart, chosen by Emily for her chief islanders, though of general interest no doubt in that day and age, refer in particular to closer contacts the little Brontës had with them. On 1st January 1828, Miss Branwell made a very welcome New Year's present to the children, in the shape of Scott's *Tales of a Grandfather* in three volumes, and wrote in the fly-leaf:

A New Year's Gift by Miss E. B. to her dear
little nephew and nieces, Patrick, Charlotte,
Emily and Anne Brontë. 1828.

Less obvious were the personalities chosen by Branwell and Anne, "Astley Cooper" and "Sir Henry Halford", the court physicians. Reference to *Blackwood's Magazine* for May 1827, however, shows that in an article on "The Last Illness and Death of H.R.H. The Duke of York", particular mention is made of "H.R.H.'s gratitude to his physicians"—the Duke of York was shortly to play a major role in the children's secret games.

Though not his earliest literary composition, Branwell's "History

of the Young Men" was the most ambitious to date (1830) and is the
keystone to the whole future edifice of his and Charlotte's "Glasstown" creation, the absorbing occupation of their childhood and
adolescence.

Sprung originally out of the acquisition of the twelve soldiers
(the "Twelves" as they became), the plot was equally based upon
the children's early readings of *The Arabian Nights* and *Aesop's
Fables*, with its insistence on Giants Ten Miles High and Genii dis-
pensing the powers of life and death and the restoration of life, and
upon the practical lessons of geography received from studies with
their father and the stirring reports—constantly echoed in the pages
of *Blackwood's*, of the explorations of John Ross and William Edward
Parry and Mungo Park.

The directions taken by genius are impossible to track, but there
would appear to have occurred a strange converging of forces at a
given moment in the Brontës' childhood, upon a given point: in
their case the point was the west coast of Africa and the Gulf of
Guinea.

The travels of Mungo Park, lost in 1806 while exploring the
upper reaches of the Niger, had brought the interior of the African
west coast into the news. His own account of his first voyages of
discovery had been published in 1799 and it is significant that a copy
of the book, in its edition of 1800, existed in the library of Ponden
House—a source of reading open to the children of Haworth
Parsonage possibly even before *Blackwood's Magazine* came their
way.

Frequent references to Mungo Park occur in Branwell's juvenilia.
More contemporary still were the explorations in northern and
central Africa of Major Denham in 1822, 1823 and 1824, of which a
detailed report appeared in the June issue of *Blackwood's* in 1826,
accompanied by a map of the district—so far as it had yet been
charted—which may indeed be said to be the deciding factor in
locating the "Young Men's Play" for, as examination of the original
manuscript of Branwell's "History of the Young Men" shows, he
very closely *copied* the map from *Blackwood's*.

It has hitherto been supposed that the choice of the west coast of
Africa for the setting of the "Kingdom of the Twelves" and later
of the "Great Glass Town Confederacy" as it became, arose from the
children's study of the map of Africa in the old geography book—
still to be seen at the Brontë Parsonage—Goldsmith's *Grammar of*

General Geography, which was the great delight of their childhood. A comparison of Branwell's map with that appearing in *Blackwood's* and with the map of Africa in Goldsmith, reveals two things: firstly, that Goldsmith's map, which is on a very small scale, represents the whole continent of Africa, while the Blackwood map, which is on a large scale, represents only the west coast from the Gulf of Guinea northwards. It is this map that Branwell copied. Names in the Blackwood map, i.e. the province of Ardrah and the rivers Calabar and Etrei, became household words in the history of the Young Men and later throughout the chronicles of "Angria", into which the Young Men's kingdom evolved, but these names do not appear in Goldsmith's map of Africa. Nevertheless Goldsmith played a very large part in the children's creation of their African make-believe kingdom.

In Goldsmith's map of Africa, as in the Blackwood map, the Kingdom of the Ashantee figured. This tribe became in the children's play of the "Young Men" the inveterate enemy who, from the very outset, opposed their disembarkation on African territory and years later in the last phase of Branwell's sanguinary campaigns, supported the traitor in the Angrian Wars—the Earl of North-angerland—against the elected monarch, Arthur Augustus Adrien Wellesley, Duke of Zamorna and King of Angria. The long tale, branching out over the nine years of its creation into countless ramifications and complexities, retained constant factors which were the country, as first mapped by Branwell, and the "Twelves" who, starting as teen-agers in the "History of the Young Men", grew up with their creators and assumed the main roles in the evolving tale.

The names bestowed on the four chief soldiers of the children's choice—Wellington, Parry, Ross and Bonaparte—also supplied the names for the principal geographical divisions of the African Kingdom of the Twelves, shortly to be conquered by the intrepid warriors. On Branwell's Map of the West Coast of Africa, in place of the divisions shown on the Blackwood map, we find the divisions "Wellington's Land, Parry's Land, Ross's Land"—and, Bonaparte being voted a sneak by the time the "play" was thus far evolved, "Sneaky's Land" figures instead.

Islands charted in neither Blackwood's nor any geographer's map, figure large in Branwell's Gulf of Guinea—"Stumps Land", "Monkey's Land" (later "Donkey's Isle") and "Frenchy Land"— derived from names gradually bestowed on the rank and file of the twelve soldiers. Listing them at the beginning of his "History of the Young Men", Branwell gives their names and ages as follows:

In the beginning of the year A.D. 1770 there set sail from England a ship named the "Invincible". It was bound for Ashantee. Its crew consisted of 13 men all strong healthy and in the highest spirits imaginable. Their names were

Butter CRASHY	Captain	aged 140 years
Alexander CHEEKY	Surgeon	„ 20 „
Arthur WELLESLEY	Trumpeter	„ 12 „
William Edward PARRY	„	„ 15 „
Alexander Sneaky	Sailor	„ 17 „
John Ross	Lieutenant	„ 16 „
William BRAVEY	Sailor	„ 27 „
Edward GRAVEY	„	„ 17 „
Frederick GUELPH	„	„ 27 „
STUMPS	12 Middy	
MONKEY	11 „	
TRACKY	10 „	
CRACKY	5 „	

(Of Branwell's thirteen adventurers, only twelve in fact survived to become what he termed "Founders of our City and Fathers of our Nation".)

The interesting feature both of Branwell's imaginary characters and of the actual wooden soldiers, was the marked differences in their appearance; they were not, like modern toy soldiers, all of a piece. As the children described them, Charlotte's "Wellington" was "the prettiest of the whole" and "the tallest", while Emily's was "a grave-looking fellow" and Anne's "a queer little thing much like herself". The names given the remaining Twelves—"Cheeky", "Cracky", "Bravey"—were obviously derived from characteristic features or physical disasters, like poor "Stumps". The venerable age given "Crashy" corresponded doubtless to his appearance, which Branwell described as "a patriarch full of years and wisdom".

For all the dissimilarity in their physique, the Twelves were yet clad in a uniform which Branwell described in detail. "Their dress for occasions of state was curious, if we may judge from the statues, bas-reliefs, and illuminations remaining to this day. It consisted of a high black cap with several hieroglyphical figures on it, the meaning of which is unknown, their coat or rather jacket was shaped after the manner of a sailors and was in colour a light scarlet. They also wore light pantaloons of the same colour, but their shoes were the most curious part of their apparel. This shoe, for each man only had one! was like a round flat cake with two holes in the middle into which his feet were inserted as in a stocks. Many have been the attempts made to find out how this shoe could possibly be used, and many the volumes written on the subject, all of which are improbable and many impossible. The only guess which I conceive to be near the truth is that suggested, by my learned friend Professor Gifford, R.A.S." Having, he hopes, sufficiently mystified his readers by now, Branwell, like the competent editor he was fast becoming, inserted a note here to the effect that "The state dress here spoken of was what my first soldiers (i.e. the 12s) were really carved and painted in; the curious shoe was the little stand which each soldier had to keep him from falling."

The likeness of the "12s", moreover, has been preserved in colour in Branwell's earliest booklet, mentioned earlier, "My Battell Book", written and illustrated when he was only nine years old.

Two water-colour sketches (now sadly faded) measuring $2\frac{1}{2}$ inches by $2\frac{1}{4}$ inches (the size of the booklet) represent Branwell's soldiers in action. Particularly noticeable are the "round flat cakes" of their stands in the drawing entitled "Battel of Washington".

In the second scene of action, more distinctly decorative in style than the first, with the flags of the combatants supplying the main pattern, Branwell's soldiers—still clearly recognisable—are headed by an officer with a hat such as Wellington wore.

Some doubt has been expressed as to the title "Washington" in the first of these pictures, as the writing is almost obliterated. Some scholars have read it as the "Battell of Wch-not-on"—hesitating to recognise the word "Washington" in the title. However, the identification can plainly be established by reference to the other end of the booklet, where Branwell has written in pencil and in longhand: "the Battle of Washington was fought the 12th Sep between the British and their Allies 2,2000 and the United States and their Allies 3,0400."

Confirmation of Branwell's preoccupation with the Battle of Washington at the very time of his compiling his "Battell Book", in March 1827, can be found by referring to the numbers of *Blackwood's Magazine* for the March and April of that year. In them can be found a serialised "Narrative of the Campaign of the British Army at Washington and New Orleans" in a "relation of the late war in the Southern States of North America". A detailed account

Queen Esther handwritten inscription on image: "Queen Esther — Painted by Martin and copied by P. B. Brontë Decr. 1830"

"Queen Esther", from the water-colour by Branwell Brontë, after Martin, 1830

"Painters of this class (when they *do* shew us Nature)
shew us Nature in hysterics. . . ."
—*Fraser's Magazine*

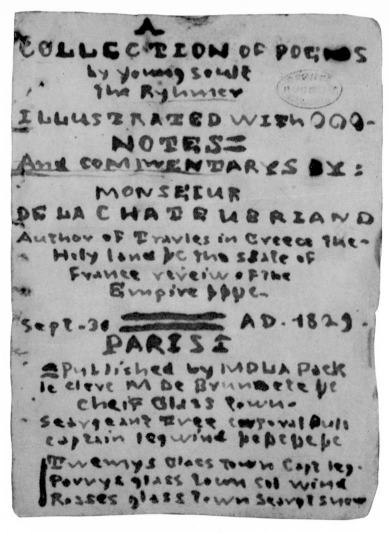

Facsimile of "A Collection of Poems by Young Soult the Rhymer",
dated 1829

"This truly great poet . . . appears constantly labouring
under a state of strong excitement. . . ."—*Charlotte Brontë*

of the Battle of Washington (Virginia) and its destruction by the British is given, the action being dated in the late August and early September of 1814.

The articles formed part of a serialised narrative called "A Subaltern in America", a companion series to one published in *Blackwood's* in 1825 which ran through seven numbers and was called "The Subaltern—A journal of the Peninsular Campaign", from which Branwell and Charlotte quite obviously "lifted" not only many of their *dramatis personae*, but numbers of place-names and titles as well, later incorporated by them in the "Young Men's Play" as it evolved towards the complex creation of Angria. "The Subaltern", with its close-up narrative of the struggle between Wellington and Soult, was undoubtedly the reason why, of all ✓ periods of the Napoleonic War, the Peninsular Campaign should most particularly have inspired the little Brontës in the creation of their imaginary world. In identifying themselves with the characters of the "Marquis of Douro" and "Marshal Soult", Charlotte and Branwell were doing more than assuming pseudonyms—they were projecting themselves into an heroic existence far more in keeping with their temperaments than their own modest identities. Add to this that Southey, their favourite author, had brought out a *History of the Peninsular War* in 1823, which *Blackwood's* reviewed with much encomium in its May number for that year.

From such specific sources were the adventures of the "Young Men" drawn.

The babyishness of his second booklet, "History of the Rebellion in My Army", dated 1828, makes one suspect it was considerably post-dated. One of the main characters is called "Boaster" and a boastful effort it is, containing such challenges as the following letter from a bad character called "Goodman". With a force of 10,000 foot and 11,000 horse, "Goodman having marched into Lorraine, wrote me this letter in his hand-writing.

Sept. 1827. I will go to war with you, little Branwell.
September 1827. To Little Branwell.
Signed Good-
Man."

Branwell's "History of the Young Men", written between 15th December 1830 and 7th May 1831, was the first lengthy work he wrote without the collaboration of Charlotte. It covers eighteen pages measuring 7¾ inches by 6½ inches, runs to six chapters and

D

numbers 15,000 words. It has no literary merit. Its interest lies in revealing how the children built up their games and transposed them, from a basis of reality, to a structure of high fantasy.

The plot can be condensed as follows: The Twelves, having set sail as already described, at last sighted land, the "long wished-for termination of their pilgrimage—the coasts of Ashantee, and soon the far-off and indistinct mountains of the interior and the low sunny coast of Guinea burst full in their view, and after 2 days' farther sailing they landed at what is now called the Glasstown Harbour, now the most splendid one in the world, then a deserted, stormy and reed-choked bay. It was," dramatically concludes Branwell, "6 o'clock in the morning of the 5 of June A.D. 1770", a date, indeed, to be remembered by the little Brontës.

The Ashantees did not delay in attacking the new arrivals. "They were tall, strong, well-made and of a black or copper colour. Their garments were skins and their arms spears, bows and shields." In a note from the editor, P.B.B., we read that "The Ashantees" "were small nine pins which were bought from Leeds at the same time with the twelves: one of them remains at this time, i.e. January A.D. 1831."

War with the Ashantees looked like being a condition of their existence in Africa, but shortly after their first bloody encounters, the Twelves received evidence of support from superior powers under whose aegis they were encouraged to proceed with their work of colonisation.

"They soon arrived at the town," the narrative proceeds, ". . . and then deliberated in the great hall what further means should be taken to rescue Crashey" (taken prisoner by the Ashantees). While sitting together in the common hall and, as the unknown author of the romantic tale (Charlotte) graphically says, "the wine cups standing upon the round table filled to the brim", the air suddenly darkened, the hall shook and streams of fire continually flashed through the room, followed by long and loud peals of thunder. While all were standing pale and affrighted at the unusual phenomenon, "a dreadful Monster . . . entered the room with Crashey in his hand. He placed him down and said in a loud voice, 'I am the Chief Genius Brannii, with me there are 3 others; she, Wellesley, who protects you is named Tallii, she who protects Parry is named Emmii; she who protects Ross is called Annii. . . . We are the guardians of this land. . . . I prophecy unto you that we shall one day become a great and mighty nation, and rule all the world. . . .' " After which providential intervention, the Twelves, relates their historian, "enjoyed 8 years uninterrupted prosperity". This should be the less surprising since, even in war, the Twelves resorted to a practical method of dealing with casualties: the simple device of "making alive again". Even in extreme cases, where the Ashantees, who were sometimes cannibals, had half-eaten the heroic fallen, a prayer to the Chief Genii restored the slain.

They could not establish themselves in their new kingdom without electing a king, and their choice fell on "Frederick Guelph, Duke of York, and second son to his majesty George III . . ." who mounted the throne with the title of Frederick I.

In renewed hostilities against the Ashantees, mention is made for the first time of the Ashantee Prince—Quashia Quamina—the black devil who, through various evolutions, would go right through Branwell's juvenilia and on into his adult writing, appearing in his last attempt at fiction, "And the Weary are at Rest", as late as 1845.

The very name "Quashia" was probably taken from *Blackwood's Magazine*, appearing under the variant "Quashee" in the September serialisation of the novel *The Man-of-War's-Man*. He is described by his messmates as a "little silly blackamoor boy", a "little black majesty", who has, in fact, just died and must be conveyed overboard for burial. Dead, he is the source of terror to his messmates as the agent of evil overtaking their ship.

The figure of an orphaned, abandoned black boy occurs and recurs not only in the Brontë juvenilia but in their mature works. Charlotte introduces him both in her "Green Dwarf", 1829, and in the "African Queen's Lament" of 1833, as found by the Duke of Wellington lying under a tree by the dead body of his mother. The Duke takes the boy home and adopts him, thus causing bad blood with his own sons—a theme which Emily was to develop to its ultimate limits when in *Wuthering Heights* Mr Earnshaw brought home the black changeling from Liverpool. Throughout Branwell and Charlotte's "Glasstown" fiction, Quashia, Prince of the Ashantees, plays the villain's part in ceaseless warfare against the British, finally leaguing himself with the traitor "Earl of Northangerland" against Arthur Wellesley, "Marquis of Douro, The Duke of Zamorna and King of Angria".

Thus early in the children's corporate games were the seeds sown of their ultimate achievements.

In pitched battle against Quashia and the Ashantees, King Frederick was killed in the region of Coomasie (Kumasi, the capital of the Ashantees) at the battle of Rossendale Hill, a mountain described by Branwell as "shaped like Pendle Hill".

A local landmark to the Brontë children, and visible to them every time their walks took them from home across the Lancashire border, Pendle Hill has a very characteristic flat top and sides reminiscent of Table Mountain. Like Quashia, it would appear constantly in Angrian literature and figure in Branwell's last novel, "And the Weary are at Rest", where the setting is recognisably that of the district round Haworth.

"The reason why we let Guelph be killed," Branwell explained in one of his editorial notes to the "History of the Young Men", "so as he could not be got alive at this battle is that at the time in which we let this battle take place [i.e. in the beginning of A.D. 1827] the real Duke of York died of a mortification and therefore we determined that he should die so that he could not be got alive, the which however was unusual among us."

The reason for the Brontës' infatuation with the Duke of York need not perhaps be sought further than that he was Commander-in-Chief of the British Army—and was violently anti-Catholic.

Frederick I, Duke of York, was succeeded as King by "Stumps" for a reason explained by Branwell in an editorial note: "The reason why we really let Stumps be King was he was the same wooden soldier which the Duke of York had been."

In successive campaigns where always, in spite of enormous enemy superiority of numbers, the Twelves were victorious, several feats of prowess are recorded by Branwell as reminiscent of, but superior to, similar exploits performed by Homeric heroes. Passages are frequent showing the young author's acquaintance with Greek history and literature, confined so far to the translation of Pope. "Now indeed there ensued a scene utterly unparalleled in the annals of the world," writes the historian of the Young Men; ". . . the battle of Marathon and the conflict at the pass of Thermopylae are not to be compared to this. . . ." The battle to regain the dead body of Frederick I killed at Rossendale Hill is compared to "the conflict for the dead body of Patroclus on the shores of Troy . . . which must sink to nothing before the actions of this memorable day. . . ." The bravery of the Twelves was in all circumstances, their historian claimed, "superior to that of Leonidas the Spartan".

Charlotte, in the meantime, had been writing on matters closely allied to the central subject of the Young Men—she had written her own account of their voyage in the *Invincible* and their landing in the Country of the Genii, in a tale written in April 1829 called "The Twelve Adventurers". Her stories, unlike Branwell's, were little concerned with the military aspect of these events, but with the fabulous, the human and the romantic. By introducing the Duke of Wellington and his two sons, the Marquis of Douro (Arthur Augustus Adrien Wellesley) and Lord Charles Wellesley into every story, always as heroes and sometimes as narrators (a habit of projecting herself into a male protagonist, which she carried over into her adult novel *The Professor*), Charlotte rapidly and radically altered the essentially *epic* character of Branwell's Young Men sequel, and converted it into a commentary on the social and political world of their day. The chief pastime of the Wellesleys, "père et fils", in her pages was no longer war but courtship, and their fabulous Glass Town was hardly erected before she had peopled it with a society of wits and beautiful women.

The scene set, the chief and subsidiary actors in place, chroniclers were not wanting to record their doings. Charlotte was soon director of policy of the organ of "Glass Town" society, the monthly journal which, it is hardly surprising to learn, had for title: "Blackwood's Young Men's Magazine".

Running almost concurrently with the "History of the Young Men", from January 1829 to December 1830, these amazing replicas of the children's favourite reading permitted them to deal in a variety of matter and style that was invaluable to them as a literary apprenticeship.

PART TWO

YOUNG SOULT THE RHYMER

*

Chapter Five

THE EDITOR

The idea of bringing out a magazine on the model of *Blackwood's* came, like so many of the children's joint efforts, from Branwell. The first three numbers, indeed, of the series bore his name: "Branwell's Blackwood's Magazine". But again, as in so many of their enterprises, it was soon Charlotte who took over control. In the July issue of 1829 Branwell thus announces the transfer of responsibility in a "Concluding Address" to his readers.

> To my Readers P.B.B——te.
>
> We have hitherto conducted this magazine, we hope, to the satisfaction of most (No one can please all) but as we are conducting a newspaper which requires all the time and attention which we can spare from other employments, we have found it expedient to relinquish the editorship of this magazine. But we recommend our readers to be [   ] to the new editor as they were to me. The new one is Cheif Genius Charlotte. She will conduct it in future, though I shall write now and then for it.
>
> Signed P. B. Brontë

(The addition of a Greek symbol to the signature showed that Greek was now added to Branwell's other studies.)

Charlotte's own comment on the take-over betrayed another cause than that advanced by the editor, none other than rebellion on the part of his readers. In "Lines by ONE who was Tired of Dulness" she celebrates the cessation of the "Rule of Dulness" in the magazine.

Fifteen numbers of the joint production of brother and sister have survived, and the overall impression created by them is astonishment at the sheer manual competence of the young compilers. The booklets are of varying minuteness, some measuring $1\frac{7}{8}$ inches by $1\frac{3}{8}$ inches and none of them more than $2\frac{1}{2}$ inches by 2 inches. The number of script pages varies from nine to twenty-two, the majority remaining at a figure of twenty. They are neatly stitched into paper covers, mostly a rough grey or brown paper of the sort used by grocers for bags of sugar, with elaborate title pages on which are minutely set out the names of authors, publishers, bookseller and stationer—all, it need hardly be added, of Glass Town provenance. The writing, minute throughout, is already an astonishingly adept imitation of print.

A glance at some of the tables of contents, especially of the earliest numbers, shows the persistent interest in all things French. A serial runs through several numbers called "Journal of a Frenchman", each instalment totalling some 1,150 words. (Most monthly parts consisted of four or five contributions.)

In a tale called "The Swiss Artist" a boy prodigy painter, called Alexandre, has his work seen and admired by a benighted traveller, who offers to take him to Paris. Paris, to the Brontës, evokes "the splendour of the Tuileries, the grand collection of painting and statues which adorned the Louvre Gallery, taken by Napoleon from the Eternal City . . . since restored by the mighty Wellington. . . ." (In the "boy prodigy" it is not difficult to recognise Branwell, so soon to impress his family with his artistic gifts.)

The majority of articles in "Blackwood's Young Men's Magazine" deal with themes connected with the Great Glass Town and its inhabitants, such as: "Review of the Causes of the late War", "Scene on the Great Bridge", "A Scene at my Inn", "On seeing the garden of a Genius", "The Bay of Glasstown", etc., a review of "The Cheif Genii in Council" (a painting). Many of the verse contributions are signed "U.T." (Us Two) or "W.T." (We Two).

Editing "The Young Men's Magazine" was far from occupying all Branwell's play-time, curtailed as it very likely was in his thirteenth year by the addition of Greek to his other studies. Between the ages of ten and seventeen he became the author of some thirty named and distinct volumes of tales, poems, dramas, journals, histories, literary commentary, etc. and of almost as many fragments. It has, also, to be taken into consideration that a quantity of others may have been lost. Apart from any literary merit this body of juvenilia may possess, the question of sheer quantity must not be forgotten in considering a life "so misspent" as Charlotte was later to say, and which, indeed, in the aggregate, achieved so little.

Branwell would appear, as a child, to have worked at fever heat, speed and intensity being the condition of his writing. Small wonder

that on more than one occasion the editor, interrupting the work of
the chronicler or poet, will interject some such comment as the
following with which he ended a "commentary on Ossian 29 vols
folio". "This is one of the most long-winded books that have ever
been printed. We must now conclude for we are dreafully tired."
The date was July 1829 and Branwell was twelve. "Dreafully tired"
the over-eager brain must often have been, and the thought will
occur: how much of its final collapse can be attributed to too much
early pressure?

The "History of the Young Men" purported to be written by
John Bud, Esq. ("the greatest prose writer they have among them").

Bud's genius was confined to prose, but the Great Glass Town or,
as shortly it was to be called, "Verdopolis", would not long lack a
poet to sing its praises. In two diminutive booklets, size $2\frac{3}{4}$ inches
by $2\frac{1}{8}$ inches, had already appeared in September 1829 "Young
Soult's Poems", a very unequal performance, but shortly to be
followed by a veritable spate of verse in magazine and story. As
Branwell grew up and his personal predicament invaded more and
more of his creative writing, poetry would seem to express his state
of mind more naturally than prose.

The source of the pseudonym "Young Soult" is interesting to
trace.

In the children's games, in which, as Mr Brontë told Mrs Gaskell,
Charlotte's hero Wellington was always "sure to come off con-
queror", Branwell had to seek a foil of equal stature. His first choice
very naturally fell on "Bonaparte", but the universal and, particularly, the parsonage opprobrium having disqualified him as a
"sneak", Branwell had to look elsewhere for a figure of sufficient,
if not equal importance.

It has already emerged that the children's knowledge of Wellington's exploits concerned the Peninsular Campaign rather than that
of Waterloo, and throughout the Peninsular war it was Marshal
Soult who commanded the French forces against Wellington.

Of Marshal Soult the children had read in Southey's *History of
the Peninsular War* which appeared in successive volumes over the
years 1823-32 and received considerable publicity in *Blackwood's*.
But it was in the thrilling pages of the serial, "A Subaltern", running
through seven numbers of *Blackwood's* during 1825, that the children's almost personal feeling for Wellington—already here given
the style of his freshly-won title, "Marquis of Douro"—and for his

opponent Marshal Soult, was undoubtedly aroused, for both constantly figure in the story which closely follows the evolution of the Peninsular Campaign.

Marshal Soult had won the esteem of the British public by his chivalrous conduct on the occasion of the burial at Corunna of Sir John Moore, Wellington's predecessor as Commander-in-Chief. Soult had ordered the French forces to fire a salute of guns during the hurried and midnight burial of the British Commander. The incident, described by Southey in the *Annual Register* and referred to by the Irish poet Charles Wolfe in his lines on "The Burial of Sir John Moore", was widely publicised and never forgotten. When, many years later, under the Orleanist King Louis Philippe, Old Soult was sent to London on the occasion of the coronation of Queen Victoria—and entertained by Wellington at Apsley House—he received a rapturous reception from the British public.

As Charlotte adopted Wellington's sons—Arthur Adrien and Charles Wellesley—for her special playmates, identifying herself so completely with them as to write under their names in all her youthful stories, so Branwell invented a son for Soult who, in his turn, assumed the chief onus of his authorship.

Branwell's sympathies and interests appear to have been predominantly French at the period of his writing "Young Soult's Poems" (September 1829).

In notes relegated to the bottom of the tiny pages, and in script so microscopic as to need a magnifying glass to decipher it, the author explains to the ignorant reader his more obscure terminology, thus: "Guillotine . . . A instrument used in France instead of the Gallows." "Paris a city and Capital of French-land situate on the River Siene 50 m. from the open sea. It is a Glass Town and very large. . . ."

The name of Chateaubriand appearing on the title page and figuring in most of the editorial notes, where further references to his *Travels in Greece and the Holy Land* appear, reminds us of another source than *Blackwood's* for much of the Brontë children's early reading: the library of Ponden House, the moorland home of the Heaton family.

A copy of Chateaubriand's *Travels* in its translated edition of 1812 figured in that library, as the catalogue shows, and Branwell very obviously saw it, for he copied the title page even to the error in giving Chateaubriand's *particule* a capital "D".

Ponden House, which served Emily Brontë for the model of Thrushcross Grange in *Wuthering Heights*, was well known to the Brontë children and the object of many of their walks. Closely associated since 1684 with Haworth Church, the Heatons of Ponden were something of a power in the district, and at the time of Mr Brontë's appointment to the living, the current owner was lately married and rapidly fathering a family of five sons. Younger than the Brontë children, they became eventual playmates of theirs. The famous library, numbering 1,393 titles, which included a First Folio edition of Shakespeare, had been collected by generations of Heatons, and was kindly put at the disposal of Mr Brontë and his family. The first-floor room in which the library was housed was described by Emily as Edgar Linton's and later as that in which Lockwood, the tenant of Thrushcross Grange, had to lie up from the ill-effects of his chill. The panelled bookshelves, with their fine Adam moulding, still line one complete wall.

The *Travels of Mungo Park*, as already mentioned, figured in that library, with other works on African explorations such as *The Proceedings of the Association for Discovering the Interior Parts of Africa* in two volumes, published in 1810, and a large section given up to the classical French authors, including Voltaire's *Henriade*, which Charlotte translated at the age of thirteen. A very large section composed of Elizabethan dramatists accounts for the surprising knowledge shown by Charlotte and Branwell of long-forgotten plays and characters, including Beaumont and Fletcher's *Hermaphrodite*, which seems to have given rise to a long-continued and uncomplimentary exchange of epithets between the young authors.

"Warner Howard Warner", whom there has been occasion to mention before, would, moreover, be called a "Hermaphrodite" by his political enemies, and for his slightly effeminate appearance and high voice.

Branwell's astounding knowledge of the topography of London, which later surprised his acquaintances, and which was reputedly due to a long study of maps, may have been acquired from a volume in Mr Heaton's library called *The Pocket Companion Through London*.

Suffice it to say that "Young Soult" for a period was permeated with matter relating to French history and literature, which he very certainly derived from his browsings among the bookshelves of Ponden House.

As "Young Soult", Branwell's literary personality was established by the time he was twelve and his "character" described by Charlotte in one of her earliest contributions to the Glass Town literature, "The Characters of Celebrated Men", written in December 1829. "This truly great poet," she wrote, "is in his 23 year. . . . His apparel is generally torn and he wears it hanging about him in a very careless and untidy manner. His shoes are often slipshod and his stockings full of holes. . . . He appears constantly labouring under a state of strong excitement, occasioned by excessive drinking and gambling to which he is unfortunately much addicted. . . ."

The reader is almost tempted to ask: was this written of Branwell at twelve or Branwell at thirty? So apposite is the portrait to the man.

Glimpses of the true likeness of Branwell can yet be perceived in many of his own and Charlotte's references to "Young Soult". In "Visits in Verdopolis" written by Charlotte a year later than the preceding passage (i.e. in December 1830) after quoting some of Branwell's verse, Charlotte proceeds:

"When Young Soult had concluded this extempore effusion, which was uttered in a strange variety of tones—first speaking which gradually changed to recitative, then chanting, and last to regular singing, he sat down and said: 'Pray, Lord Charles, forgive my enthusiasms, but really my feelings do sometimes carry me utterly beyond the control of reason and politeness.' "

"Young Soult" would further evolve under Charlotte's pen and appear before us in all his changeable aspects, as poet, enthusiast, musician, painter, the portrait keeping step with the mutations in the boy. He was, already in 1829, when she was thirteen and he was twelve, the focal point of her existence, the pride and delight of her young days.

Laugh at him as she might in their games, a very different tone creeps into her references to him in the very first letter of hers to be preserved by Mr Brontë and which dated from September 1829. With their aunt, the children had gone on a week's visit to "Uncle Fennell", recently bereaved of his wife and incumbent of the church at Cross Stone, Todmorden, some twelve miles from Haworth.

Dated from the Parsonage House, Cross Stone, 23rd September 1829, the letter runs:

My Dear Papa,
   At Aunt's request I write these lines to inform you that "if all be well" we shall be at home on Friday by dinner-time, when we hope to find you in good health. On account of the bad weather we have not been out much, but not

withstanding we have spent our time very pleasantly, between reading, working [sewing] and learning our lessons, while Uncle Fennell has been so kind as to teach us every day. Branwell has taken 2 sketches from nature, and Emily, Anne, and myself have likewise each of us drawn a piece from some views of the lakes which Mr Fennell brought with him from Westmoreland. The whole of these he intends keeping, Mr Fennell is sorry he cannot accompany us to Haworth on Friday, for want of room, but hopes to have the pleasure of seeing you soon, All unite in sending their kind love with your affectionate daughter,

Charlotte Brontë

Already then, while his sisters were copying prints, Branwell was "taking sketches from nature", and the fact accepted and recognised that he had a pronounced artistic talent.

For the time being, however, "Young Soult" concentrated his activities on literature. He followed up the first volumes of his poems with two plays in the November and December of 1829, "Laussane, A Tragedy" and "The Revenge, A Tragedy", in which the decidedly French flavour of the "Poems" is maintained.

But the main attraction, both for Branwell and Charlotte, lay in their "Glass Town" creation upon which most of the voluminous output of their early teens was spent.

By using such literary conventions as the portrait "Character", especially dear to seventeenth-century French and English writers, the "Dialogue", the "Visit" and the perennial "Letters", in the manner of Montesquieu's *Lettres Persanes* and Goldsmith's *Citizen of the World*, Branwell and Charlotte built up a whole body of literature on and around the original theme of their Glass Town Adventures. They further instituted, on the model of the famous "Noctes Ambrosianae" of *Blackwood's* (the symposium of wits supposed to hold its sittings at Ambrose's Hotel), a series of dialogues at "Bravey's Inn", the premier hostelry of the great Glass Town, containing criticism and comments on the chief events of their imaginary capital. "Bravey", it will be remembered, was one of the original "Twelves".

What the children visualised by their Glass City they made quite clear, but the actual origin of the name—if any specific origin there were—escapes detection.

Branwell stated in the "History of the Young Men" that the city rose by enchantment, the work of those benevolent Genii Brannii, Tallii, Emmii and Annii, who protected the Young Men on their landing on the coast of Guinea.

In the "Bay of Glass Town", a poem by "U.T." that appeared in

"Blackwood's Young Men's Magazine" for December 1829, we
are told that

> . . . like fair piles of burnished gold
> those marble pillars stand,
> palaces of immortal mould
> and castles towering grand
> While murmuring sounds of pomp and mirth
> Rise from the mighty walls. . . .

The chief features of the city were the Tower of all the Nations,
the Palace, the Hall of Justice, Bravey's Inn.

The harbour, we learn from "The Pirate", presents "a gorgeous
and vast view, with its endless shipping, crowded quays and mighty
expanse of blue water stretching away till one might fancy they beheld over its horizon the hills of Stumps Land and the towering
heights of Monkey's Isle".

The setting of their imaginary world could not very well present
a more perfect contrast to the reality of the little Brontës' daily life.

But the fabulous element would end with the creation of the
Great Glass Town. Its inhabitants and their way of life would increasingly reflect current events in the political and social world of
Europe of the early eighteen-thirties—a period of political upheaval
almost as telling in its consequences as the revolution of 1789.

The summer of 1830 was marked by two major occurrences, the
"Revolution of July" in Paris, which drove the Bourbons permanently from the throne of France, and the revolt of the Belgian
people against the Dutch king imposed on them by the Congress of
Vienna (21st July). The repercussion of these predominantly liberal
rather than revolutionary movements in neighbouring countries,
profoundly influenced the English elections that followed. The
Whigs did so well that Palmerston could write from Cambridge
on 1st August with reference to the deposition of Charles X,
". . . We shall drink to the cause of Liberation all over the world. . . .
This event is decisive of the ascendancy of Liberal Principles throughout Europe. . . ."

The immediate effect on English politics was the introduction by
Lord Grey of the Reform Bill in November 1830 and the beginning
of the long agitation that preceded its passing two years later.

All these events were followed passionately by the young
Brontës and reflected in their Glass Town literature.

What politics meant to them, Charlotte eloquently described

with regard to Catholic emancipation in her Introduction to Volume II of her "Tales of the Islanders" written in 1829 when she was thirteen.

... Parliament was opened and the Great Catholic question was brought forward and the Dukes measures were disclosed and all was slander violence party spirit and confusion. O those 3 months from the time of the Kings speech to the end! Nobody could think speak or write on anything but the catholic question and the Duke of Wellington or Mr Peel. I remember the [Sun] day when the Intelligence Extraordinary came with Mr Peels speech in it containing the terms on which the Catholics were to be let in. With what eagerness papa tore off the cover and how we all gathered round him, and with what breathless anxiety we listened as one by one they were disclosed and explained and argued upon so ably and so well and then when it was all out how aunt said she thought it was excellent and that the catholics [could] do no harm with such good security. I remember also the doubts as to whether it would pass the house of Lords and the propheceys that it would not and when the paper came which was to decide the question the anxiety was almost dreadful with which we listened to the whole afair: the opening of the doors the hush the Royal Dukes in their robes, and the Great Duke in green sash and waist-coat the rising of all the peeresses when he rose the reading of his speech papa saying that his words were like precious gold and lastly, the majority one to four in favour of the Bill. ...

In a character shortly to be created by Branwell the political agitator of the times was represented forcefully, as using every device of sedition and revolt to overthrow the established government of the Wellesleys in Africa. This was the figure of Alexander Rogue, M.P. (possibly an evolution of the original Alexander Cheeky), better known as Alexander Percy, Viscount Elrington through marriage with the beautiful Zenobia Elrington, and finally created Earl of Northangerland.

Glass Town in Charlotte's hands would too soon have settled down into a sophisticated society of nobles and wits, dependent for interest upon domestic intrigues and love passages, with the Duke of Wellington and his sons changing wives and mistresses with capricious frequency and as fast as their gorgeous uniforms. The social background of their lives—the banquets, the receptions, the balls, the theatres, the concerts, the art exhibitions—these fully occupied her pen. Not so Branwell. His contribution, predominantly military and political as might be expected, increasingly introduced the elements of violence, of treachery and disaster into the tale. In the six volumes of his "Letters of an Englishman" written between 1830 and 1832 the Civil War provoked by Rogue is sometimes tediously—and always sanguinarily—related at large.

How persistent was the influence of his old passion for France, revived by the recent Revolution of July, can be seen in descriptions like the following, taken from the sixth Letter. The narrator, James Bellingham, the unwilling witness of the civil broils, writes ...:

I am now while writing to you confined in a large, dark, damp dungeon, in which are 600 of my fellow prisoners, and the door of the room is continually opening and shutting either to take out to execution, or to bring in to the horrid apprehension of execution some unhappy victim. But oh! what shall I do? I am undone. A messenger has sent for me to take my trial. There is no hope for me— I must die—Farewell.

March 20. I now resume my story. I was conducted from the prison to a large, open area which was covered with blood and dead carcases which several persons were engaged in carrying away. This area was crowded with people and at one end of it, at a large table which was covered with papers, sat Alexander Rogue and several members of the provisional government. Before them was placed on a blood-covered scaffold a block and 2 executioners. I was conducted up to this horrid tribunal where Rogue questioned me as follows:

ROGUE: "You are, I suppose, James Bellingham, the English banker?"

MYSELF: "I am."

R. "It is reported that you favour the 12s. Answer me, do you, or not?"

M. "I do favour the 12s and likewise I abhor and detest you as the most wicked, cool-blooded and inhuman tyrant that ever existed."

R. "This is enough, is it not, gentlemen?"

COUNSEL'S: "It is, it is."

R. "Executioners, do you duty."

The executioner immediately dragged me on to the scaffold, placed my head on the block, and was about to lift up the axe when a tremendous shout of "The 12s are coming, hurry, the 12s are coming", was heard through the city, and instantly the executioners jumped from the scaffold, Rogue and his company jumped out of the yard, and in a short time all were under arms, and jumping from the scaffold in an ecstasy of delight, I ran to the gate of the area. . . .

Rogue, at the end of the fourteenth letter finds himself in his turn placed before a firing-squad. The narrator, having suffered many ups and downs of fortune since the above-quoted incident, looks out of his prison window on to ". . . a yard vast surrounded by high gloomy houses, partly unroofed and shattered with balls . . . in the middle was an empty space floored with black cloth and the paling round it covered with the same. Dead silence and utter motionlessness pervaded the vast assemblage below me till a swaying to and fro among them announced the approach of some one. It was the King's, Sneaky, Wellington, Parry and Stumps, who with their attendants ranged themselves on one side of the open space. Next followed 10 soldiers with muskets guarding a tall man dressed in black, with a countenance as pale as death . . . it was Alexander Rogue." Giving the order himself to the firing-party, Rogue is shot. "He fell dead," writes Branwell. "Rogue is no more."

But so strong was the old compulsion born of the game of "making alive again" that Branwell could not leave Rogue dead. Without explanation, he was brought back. In a narrative called "The Pirate" and written more than a year later (January 1833) Branwell relates how "Alexander Rogue has just returned from no one knows where. He has bought a fine house in George's Street, where he lives in the utmost style of magnificence. But what are his means, or from whence he draws his evidently princely income, no one can guess."

w H ?

Heathcliff, it will be remembered, also returned after a similar period of disappearance, with an equally unexplained source of income, a detail that reminds us that Emily and Anne were still, at this period of the young people's literary evolution, playing the Glass Town game with Charlotte and Branwell, though already evolving a different one of their own.

Emily and Anne did not like the tedious military paraphernalia of Branwell's most characteristic contributions, the repetitive mustering of forces, the fabulous numbers engaged, the indiscriminate slaughter, and so withdrew more and more from their elders' game to create their own Gondal Saga. Both Branwell's control of the plot and the younger girls' withdrawal from it was mainly brought about by Charlotte's being sent away to school from January 1831 until May 1832. This was precisely the period when Branwell evolved and established the character of Rogue, a character which was apparently so acceptable to Charlotte that when she returned from school she herself wrote an account of Rogue's early life in a story called "The Green Dwarf", in which he abducted a Lady Emily Charlesworth, falsely accused a rival of high treason, and got himself exiled for fourteen years.

The time of the brother and sister's closest collaboration had come, for the separation from Charlotte that left Branwell in undisputed control of their cherished creation served rather to emphasise his dependence on her than to develop any real capacity to strike out on his own. On her part, the severance served only to confirm and further heighten her absorbing love for him. Never apart since the disastrous year of Cowan Bridge, Charlotte and Branwell seemed in this first serious separation of their lives to take stock of

Cross Stone Parsonage

"We have spent our time very pleasantly, between reading, working and learning our lessons."—*Charlotte Brontë*

Bolton Abbey, from a sketch by Charlotte Brontë

their mutual position and to realise how necessary they were to each other. A need which they may not yet have realised proceeded from the initial weakness of the one and the strength of the other. For the time being Charlotte yet looked up to Branwell and he basked in the sunshine of her favour.

Chapter Six

"CHEIF GENIUS CHARLOTTE"

Charlotte's departure for school on 25th January 1831 marked the emergence from childhood for her brother too. It required of both that they step outside their imaginary existence as mere puppet-manipulators and to accept, in their own persons, the first contacts with an alien outside world.

After the first agony of separation, Charlotte assumed her new responsibilities with undivided purpose. She was resolved to benefit fully, not only for her own sake but for her sisters', from all the advantages to be derived by three terms at Roe Head. For the time being she would heroically eschew all composition not devoted to the set subjects of the Miss Woolers' excellent and comprehensive curriculum.

The event roused Branwell also to a new sense of realities. We see him, like any other loving brother, going to call at his sister's school for a blissful "half-day" in Charlotte's company—with the difference that Branwell, certainly very short of pocket-money, walked the fourteen miles to Roe Head and back again.

The glow of delight his unexpected visit caused Charlotte is reflected in the letter she wrote after his return. Dated 17th May 1831, it reads:

Dear Branwell

As usual I address my weekly letter to you, because to you I find the most to say. I feel exceedingly anxious to know how and in what state you arrived home after your long and (I should think very fatiguing) journey. I could perceive when you arrived at Roe Head that you were very much tired, though you refused to acknowledge it. After you were gone, many questions and subjects of conversation recurred to me which I had intended to mention to you, but quite forgot them in the agitation which I felt at the totally unexpected pleasure of seeing you. Lately I had begun to think that I had lost all the interest which I used formerly to take in politics, but the extreme pleasure I felt at the news of the Reform Bill's being thrown out by the House of Lords, and of the expulsion or resignation of Earl Grey, etc. etc., convinced me that I have not as yet lost all my penchant for politics. I am extremely glad that aunt has consented to take in *Fraser's Magazine*, for though I know from your description of its general contents it will be rather uninteresting when compared to *Blackwood*, still it will be better than remaining the whole year without being able to obtain a sight of any periodical publication whatever; and such would assuredly be our case, as in the little wild, moorland village where we reside, there would be no possibility of borrowing or obtaining a work of that description from a circulating library. I hope with you that the present delightful weather may contribute to the perfect restoration of our dear papa's health, and that it may give aunt pleasant reminiscences of the salubrious climate of her native place.

With love to all,—Believe me, dear Branwell, to remain your affectionate sister, Charlotte.

Even to the last dig at Aunt, the depth of their understanding and devotion is expressed in every passage. That their absorbing confidences should include politics and literature was a matter of course. To keep Charlotte in the picture Branwell described the new periodical launched that year, *Fraser's Magazine*, and which, thanks to Aunt, they were now taking to compensate for the loss of *Blackwood's*, which Dr Driver was obviously no longer lending to them.

Branwell may or may not have had time to expatiate on one article in particular in the April number of *Fraser's Magazine*, which was dedicated to the great favourite of their childhood, "Christopher North", in his real person of John Wilson, editor of *Blackwood's Magazine*. The accompanying portrait, showing him as a handsome man in his forties, surrounded by all the insignia of his chief interests—sparring pugilists, fighting cocks, etc., must have finally dispelled the belief, if they still entertained it, of "Christopher North's" being "an old man, 70 years of age". The spurious crutches, made famous in many a scene of "Noctes Ambrosianae" figure in the picture with all the other less congruous attributes of Wilson's talents and tastes. Perhaps Branwell was made to realise for the first time that his hero was a reputed pugilist, "a sixteen stoner who has tried it, without the gloves, with the Game Chicken, and got none the worse . . . a cocker, a racer, a six bottler, a twenty-four tumbler—an out-and-outer . . . .".

Be that as it may, in all these declared tastes and prowesses of his idol, Branwell would seek to emulate him, remembering, no doubt, that another of his idols, Lord Byron, subscribed to them also. Being Branwell, he would not rest content until he had surpassed them both.

The passion for boxing, soon to become almost an obsession with him, finds its first echo in a passage of one of his "Letters of an Englishman" written in the very next month after his visit to Charlotte at Roe Head: on 8th June 1831.

There we read that "Brandy . . . rallied and laid on Naughty in good style, giving him a slinger on the throat apple, and one or two black and red patches on the eye closing up one peeper . . . until Naughty delivered his antagonist a closer on the collar-bone which smashed through the skin and caused the blood to stream."

The use of "fancy" terms already shows Branwell as a devotee of the sport. The language of the ring was chiefly known to him through the perusal of *Bell's Life in London*, the sporting weekly which was taken by the landlord of the *Black Bull* hotel, and eagerly devoured by the members of the Haworth boxing-club of which, according to Leyland, Branwell became a member about this time. The village lads had "sundry gloves, and, at intervals," Leyland tells us, "amused themselves with sparring in an upper room of a building in Haworth".

To a lonely boy with no brothers, the discipline and sheer pluck involved would appear of obvious benefit, if it had not brought him contacts sometimes with older and less disingenuous professors of the art.

In any village a boy from a better home has to accept compromises if he is to mix with the majority. The fact that Branwell was always so accepted, welcomed by all circles, admitted to every clique, is evidence of the truth of his reputed charm and also of his easy-going virtue. ". . . In early youth," wrote Mrs Gaskell, "his power of attracting and attaching people was so great, that few came in contact with him who were not so much dazzled by him as to be desirous of gratifying whatever wishes he expressed."

To gratify even such a simple wish as seeing his sister at school, Branwell had not the pocket-money, it must be remembered, to pay for a lift. The origin of a number of his earliest peccadilloes, if the truth were known, would be found to lie in his total lack of funds. None of the young Brontës at any time had any pocket-money, not even the price of a stamp, as Charlotte had the humiliation to confess to her friend Ellen; but whereas this total poverty led the girls into no temptations, with Branwell it very certainly did the reverse. Even to borrow sparring gloves must sometimes cost an odd shilling and it is not always possible to cadge the odd meal out, even when freely offered by generous Mrs Sugden of the *Black Bull*. Certain it is that all too early in his ill-fated life, Branwell got into debt. Doubtless the sums were insignificant, but the habit was formed of accepting at first, and then of cadging for, small favours which he very soon found he could not do without. "While the rest [of the family] were almost ascetic in their habits," wrote Mrs Gaskell, "Branwell was allowed to grow up self-indulgent." Increasingly, while Charlotte was away at school, Branwell sought his pleasures outside.

It was not unnatural that he should gravitate towards the two kindliest and most welcoming circles within his ken; that of the *Black Bull* under the flourishing and respected proprietorship of Thomas Sugden and his wife, and that of the family of his father's sexton, John Brown, general factotum in the parish and living in his own house, the first one in Church Lane, only a stone's throw from the parsonage.

Apart from his parochial functions John Brown's profession was that of stonemason, which he exercised with consummate artistry and taste as visitors to Haworth Church can yet judge today. His stone-cutter's yard lay only a few paces from the parsonage garden gate and Ellen Nussey, recalling in after years her earliest impressions of Haworth, spoke of the perpetual "chip, chip" of his mallet on marble as the most characteristic sound of the Brontës' home.

Much blame has always been laid at John Brown's door for the early perversion of Branwell, but the charges are seldom precise in definition and do not bear inspection.

Leyland accuses Brown of entertaining Branwell by cracking "coarse jokes while . . . employed in digging . . . graves", as though grave-diggers since Hamlet's day had not made a practice of keeping up their spirits with ribaldry; a reaction moreover wholly in keeping with north-country humour and not, by itself, a stigma on the character of a man reputedly witty and intelligent beyond his sphere.

For if one thing emerges more clearly than another from investigations into John Brown's life and character, it is that he was neither the drunken sot nor village ignoramus successive Brontë biographers would make him appear.

Of the "two or three individuals" in the village deserving "particular note" according to Ellen Nussey, "men of remarkable self-culture and intelligence", vying with "Mr Brontë himself in his knowledge of the dead languages", John Brown was one. He was never known at home, so a surviving granddaughter of his still avers today, without a book in his hand.

Branwell's portrait of him shows a gentlemanly-looking man of gigantic strength and height, with a fine forehead and an alert expression in his eyes.

With John Brown, a man in his mid-thirties when Branwell was fifteen, the boy could spar not only with his fists but with his tongue, while the sexton held his own with Latin tag for Latin tag.

How the Brontë children saw the "factotum" and his wife, who was twenty-six at the time, is reflected in one of Charlotte's "Tales of the Islanders" written over the years 1829 and 1830. There she describes how "Little King" (as Branwell's then title was), Emily, Anne and herself, in the guise of three old fairies, were invited inside that functionary's typical Haworth cottage.

It was a small apartment neatly white-washed, an oaken dresser furnished with the brightest pewter . . . above it was suspended a highly-polished musket and sword, several ancient books were carefully piled on a black oak kist, two substantial armchairs stood at each end of a blazing fire and opposite the window seat a number of stout 3-legged stools were ranged in a row, the floor and hearth were as clean and white as scouring could make them. Mrs Seringapatan [Charlotte's name for the Duke of Wellington's "factotum"] sat mending her husband's stockings by a round deal table. She was clad in a dark green stuff gown with snow-white cap and apron and looked as sedate as if she had been 60 instead of 26. When "Little King" and the "old women" entered, she rose and begged them to be seated. They complied. After chatting a while she got up again and went out but in a short time returned with a plate of rich currant cake and a bottle of perry [?] these dainties she invited her guests to partake of which they did of course and then prepared to depart. . . .

In the Brown household Branwell thus felt himself completely at home. Mrs Brown and her six little girls—Anne, Martha, Eliza, Tabitha, Mary and Hannah—were almost as much inmates of the parsonage as the incumbent's family itself. In turn they would almost all of them work there in one capacity or another, Tabitha, Hannah and Eliza figuring in the family letters, and Martha attaining almost legendary fame for her twenty-three years' devoted service and friendship with the parson's family.

Mr Brontë held the Browns in the highest esteem and if one thing is certain it is that, had John Brown really exercised such a disastrous influence on Branwell, he could easily have been dismissed from his post and the daily close intercourse between the two households interdicted. But this was never the case. On the contrary, as time went on, and Mr Brontë's blindness increased, John Brown became in more senses than one the parson's right-hand man, and his confidant in caring for Branwell when the disaster came.

This is not to say that John Brown was not a heavy drinker—as who was not in those days?—and did not introduce his parson's son into some rough company. John Brown himself was a man of forceful character and he may not have early enough gauged Branwell's fundamental lack of moral and physical stamina. What John Brown thought suitable for a young lad who could have been his own son (and there was certainly something paternal in Brown's love of Branwell) might have been wholesome diet for an altogether tougher fibre than Branwell's; on him it acted like poison.

The sad time was not yet when Branwell realised his fatal incapacity to cope with life. As yet every pleasure was a delirious excitement, every expectation miraged in a rosy light.

During her year and a half at school, Charlotte formed two lifelong friendships, those with Ellen Nussey and Mary Taylor, both girls from the vicinity of Roe Head. To Ellen's home at the Rydings, Birstall, Charlotte was invited for a fortnight in October 1832, shortly after her return from school. To the Rydings, Ellen Nussey related in after years, Charlotte was escorted on this first visit by Branwell.

Ellen's home, far more luxurious than any house the young Brontës had yet entered—including Ponden House—had such romantic adjuncts as a park of chestnut trees, a battlemented roof and a rookery, evoking, as it still does today for all its altered circumstances, the perfect setting for such romances as "Nightmare Abbey" or any poem by Byron or Scott, the prime favourites of Haworth Parsonage. How Charlotte saw it she later described in the "Thornfield" of her Jane Eyre.

The Nusseys were considerable landowners in the district and had connections in Parliament and the county. Ellen, who was the youngest of a family of twelve children, had an elder brother established in London, who was Court Physician and with whom she frequently stayed in Cleveland Row. Though Mrs Nussey lived in comparative retirement with her younger sons and daughters after the death of her husband in 1826, Ellen could never wholly avoid, in her attitude to Charlotte Brontë, a sense of her own social superiority, however much she was prepared to concede to her friend's over-riding intelligence. The feeling permeates even her account of that first visit to the Rydings in 1832, so valuable for its observation of Branwell at that time.

"Charlotte's first visit from Haworth," writes Ellen, "was made about three months after she left school. She travelled in a two-wheeled gig, the only conveyance to be had in Haworth, except the covered cart which brought her to school. Mr Brontë sent Branwell as an escort; he was *then* a very dear brother, as dear to Charlotte as her own soul; they were in perfect accord of taste and feeling, and it was mutual delight to be together.

"Branwell probably had never been far from home before and was in wild ecstasy with everything. He walked about in unrestrained boyish enjoyment, taking views in every direction of the old turret-roofed house, the fine chestnut trees on the lawn (one tree especially interested him because it was 'iron-garthed', having been split by storms, but still flourishing in great majesty), and a large rookery, which gave to the house a good background—all these he noted and commented upon with perfect enthusiasm. He told his sister he 'was leaving her in Paradise, and if she were not intensely happy she never would be!' Happy, indeed, she then was, *in himself*," comments Ellen across the intervening years of heart-break, "for she, with her own enthusiasms, looked forward to what her brother's great promise and talent might effect. He would be at this time between fifteen and sixteen years of age." (He had turned fifteen in the preceding June.)

In the following summer Ellen paid a return visit to Haworth, her first and for that reason an ever-memorable one, in spite of the many others that followed during her twenty-two years' intimacy with Haworth Parsonage.

Of Branwell, then turned sixteen, Ellen left no physical description as she did of his sisters—Emily's "kind, kindling eyes" and "dear, gentle Anne's very pretty light-brown hair". What she recalled was that he "studied regularly with his father, and used to paint in oils, which was regarded as study for what might be eventually his profession. All the household entertained the idea of his becoming an artist, and hoped he would be a distinguished one."

This is the first direct reference to painting being seriously considered by the family as a career for Branwell.

The ever-increasing reference to art and artists in Charlotte's and Branwell's writings of the time, show in what direction their tastes were developing, although it would be difficult, without this pointer from Ellen Nussey, to know by which of Branwell's many predilections and enthusiasms—poetry, painting, music—he actually contemplated making a living. He would, before his course was run, have attempted them all.

That painting had the full support of the family is again confirmed by Ellen in her description of "the interior of the now far-famed parsonage", in which she adds that "on the right, at the back, as you mount the staircase, was a small room allotted to Branwell as a studio . . .", the one room in the house with an open view to the moors above Stanbury and the Sladen Valley. Up that valley, "in fine and suitable weather", as Ellen remembered, "delightful excursions were made over the moors, and down into the glens and ravines that here and there broke the monotony of the moorland. . . . Emily, Anne, and Branwell used to ford the streams, and sometimes placed stepping-stones for the other two. Emily especially had a gleesome delight in these nooks of beauty—her reserve for the time vanished. . . . No serious care or sorrow had so far cast its gloom on nature's youth and buoyancy, and nature's simplest offerings were fountains of pleasure and enjoyment."

As Ellen saw the young Brontës on that first encounter, so independent, free and united, there appeared no limits to their endowments or to their enviable self-reliance.

That Emily was normally reserved, Ellen had been forewarned by Charlotte, unnecessarily warned, as she judged on finding Emily all consideration and kindness on a solitary ramble they took together. But that the whole family, and Branwell in particular, could be blighted by shyness, she would not have credited were she not shortly to see the effect very different surroundings could have on them.

A few weeks after this first visit to Haworth, an excursion was planned on which Ellen was to meet her new friends at a renowned beauty-spot; the appointed tryst was the *Devonshire Arms Hotel* at Bolton Bridge, the objective of the outing being a visit to the famous ruins of the Priory.

Given a day of lovely weather, as the early September morning proved itself to be, the prospect held nothing but pleasure in store for the unspoilt young people from the parsonage. Ellen, relating the circumstances of that day many years later to T. Wemyss Reid for his *Memoir* of Charlotte Brontë, described the spirits in which they drove along to meet her. Once again the humble Haworth gig was hired, with Branwell in charge of the horse—Branwell in full spate of eloquence and in high glee with himself, the day and the passing lovely scene. So rare were outings undertaken in "such style" by these hard-walking, weather-beaten children of the moors, and the present treat such an obvious present from Papa and Aunt, that the excitement was general and the tongues of his sisters almost as unloosed as his own.

Bolton is at some fourteen miles from Haworth on the farther side of the romantic village of Addingham, and it would have taken the one-horse gig some two-and-a-half hours to get there. Ellen, whose home at Birstall was at almost double that distance, may have been staying in the district. Ellen's mistake, as she was to learn that day, was not to have come alone or accompanied by a brother or sister only. What she did was to come surrounded by a whole party of brothers and sisters and friends, grown-up young men and women from another world to that inhabited by the desperately shy quartette from Haworth, and unable by one simple word to bridge the gap between their sophistication and the Brontës' inexperience.

Ellen never forgot the impression of that day, nor the insight it gave her into her friends'—and particularly Branwell's—uneasy pride. In the presence of patently successful persons, Branwell found himself totally at a loss. If incomparably better read and more gifted than any of Ellen's brothers would ever prove themselves to be, he was defenceless before their prosperity and assurance. The unpleasant feeling may have lasted only for the day, but it was to recur every time in his life that the situation was repeated and that an effort was required of him to prove his worth. Only among intimates or in *inferior company* could he expand and the quality of his mind declare itself uninhibited.

No man ever bore the signs more clearly on him of what the psychologists would later term the "inferiority complex".

In Wemyss Reid's narration of that unhappy day is to be found, still further heightened, Ellen's own objectionable awareness of the difference between the Brontës' social background and her own.

One bright morning in June 1833 [the month was in fact September], a handsome carriage and pair is standing opposite the Devonshire Arms at Bolton Bridge. In the carriage with some companions is a young girl . . . Miss N—— waiting for her quondam schoolfellow and present bosom friend Charlotte Brontë, who is coming with her brother and sisters to join in an excursion to . . . Bolton Abbey. Presently, . . . the sound of wheels is heard, mingled with the merry speech and merrier laughter of fresh young voices. . . . Their conveyance is no handsome carriage, but a rickety dog-cart, unmistakably betraying its neighbourhood to the carts and ploughs of some rural farmyard. The horse, freshly taken from the fields, is driven by a youth who, in spite of his countrified air, is no mere bumpkin. His shock of red hair hangs down in somewhat ragged locks behind his ears, for Branwell Brontë esteems himself a genius and a poet, and, following the fashion of the times, has that abhorrence of the barber's shears which genius is supposed to affect. But the lad's face is handsome and a striking one, full of Celtic fire and humour, untouched by the slightest shade of care, giving one the impression of somebody altogether hopeful, promising, even brilliant. How gaily he jokes with his three sisters; with what inexhaustible volubility he pours out quotations . . . applying them to the lovely scene around him. . . . Beside him, in a dress of marvellous plainness and ugliness, stamped with the brand "home-made" . . . is the eldest of the sisters. Charlotte is talking too; there are bright smiles upon her face; she is enjoying everything around her . . . most of all, perhaps, the charm of her brother's society. . . .

Suddenly the dog-cart rattles noisily into the open space in front of the Devonshire Arms, and the Brontës see the carriage and its occupants. In an instant there is silence; Branwell contrasts his humble equipage with that which . . . stands at the inn door, and a flush of mortified pride colours his face; the sisters scarcely note this contrast, but to their dismay they see that their friend is not alone. . . . The laughter is stilled; even Branwell's volubility is at an end; the glad light dies from their eyes, and when they alight and submit to the process of being introduced to Miss N's companions, their faces are as dull and commonplace as their dresses. . . . Miss N—— still recalls that painful moment when the merry talk and laughter of her friends were quenched at sight of the company awaiting them, and when throughout a day to which all had looked forward with anticipations of delight, the three Brontës clung to each other or to their friend, scarcely venturing to speak above a whisper, and betraying in every look and word the positive agony which filled their hearts when a stranger approached them. . . .

The following letter of Charlotte's, dated 11th September 1833, gives some further details of the event. The ordeal of lunching at the *Devonshire Arms*, whose imposing Georgian dining-room can still be admired today, had evidently to be further endured, before the relative relaxation of the walk to the ruins could be earned.

Dear Ellen,

. . . I was at first rather at a loss to understand what you meant by saying that "George had made a mistake in his arrangements with Branwell respecting the Gig", but at length I conjectured that the expression must have been in allusion to the agreement of paying the price of the conveyance in equal shares. If this conjecture is correct, allow me to assure you dear Ellen, that there is no mistake, for if you recollect your Brother Richard most kindly disbursed all the expenses incurred at the Inn which amounted to more than your share of the stipulated sum; consequently *we* are in reality the debtors, and *you* the creditors. . . .

Ellen's brothers referred to in Charlotte's letter, Richard and George Nussey, were respectively twenty-seven and nineteen at the time—already "men of the world" from the viewpoint of the

Brontës; Henry Nussey, who six years later proposed to Charlotte, was then at Magdalene College, Cambridge.

All who know the beauty of the scene will hope that the day's pleasure was not totally spoilt for the young Brontës and that they were able to appreciate the genius of the founders of the Abbey who built it in spreading parklands at a double bend in the Wharfe, thus adding by a position of natural grandeur to its own nobility—that, looking above and all about them, at the wooded cliffs that overhang the wide sweep of the river, their gaze was led to the farther hills so reminiscent of home, rolling northwards in unfolding range on range. It would have been a sight to uplift their spirits.

Nor, on any normal occasion, would a single detail of the great historic interest of the place have been lost on them: the fact that the stepping-stones fording the Wharfe, so like their stepping-stones in Sladen beck and so tempting to the fleet-footed Emily and Anne, were coeval with the Priory's foundations; that the "town field", stretching from the Priory walls to Bolton Bridge and reputed since medieval days of "an inexhaustible fertility", had been "foiled" by Prince Rupert on his way to Marston Moor; that, anciently, a Chapel for the "benefit of travellers" (certainly less alarming to in-experienced travellers than the *Devonshire Arms*) had formed a part of the bridge; that Wordsworth had visited and commemorated the spot in more than one poem; that it had been painted innumerable times by countless artists of the eighteenth and their own nineteenth centuries—all these were so many passports to their favour, and may, in recollection, have converted the day into one of rare delight.

For them, even a day's holiday was a great event, affording spiritual nourishment for months to come.

Her schooldays ended and home for good, Charlotte's main task now consisted in teaching her sisters everything she had learned during her three "halves" at Roe Head. That she was scrupulously conscientious in benefiting them with all her fresh acquirements is not to be doubted and can be seen from the following account of her days sent to Ellen.

You ask me to give you a description of the manner in which I have passed every day since I left School: this is soon done, as an account of one day is an account of all. In the morning from nine o'clock till half past twelve, I instruct my sisters and draw, then we walk till dinner, (2 o'clock) after dinner I sew till tea-time, and after tea I either read, write, do a little fancy work or draw, as I please. Thus in one delightful, though somewhat monotonous course, my life is passed . . . .

Of the true occupation of her time she said nothing. The voluntary "abstinence" of her schooldays ended, her liberty regained, she returned with immeasurably heightened powers and rekindled zest to the chief passion of her life, her dream creation. In this she collaborated with Branwell more closely than ever before as to subject-matter, while at the same time launching out into a new idiom of her own.

To the years 1834 and 1835 belongs the creation of "Angria", the culmination not only of their long African adventure, but of their partnership. Never again would brother and sister so mutually inspire each other, so shape each other's visions and ecstasies, come so close in mind and heart and purpose.

While Charlotte was at school Branwell's chief literary output had been his "Letters of an Englishman" (September 1830—August 1832). Consisting of six tiny manuscript booklets and cast in a literary form copied from Goldsmith's *Citizen of the World*, they relate the events of Alexander Rogue's rebellion against the four kings of Twelves Land, i.e., Wellington, Sneachie (or Sneaky), Ross and Parry, ending, as has already been noted, in the execution of Rogue.

Something more than the political and dramatic utility of such a character—a sympathy so deep that gradually Branwell would identify himself with him—connived at the survival of Rogue and brought him back to the Great Glass Town more formidable than ever before. Marriage with the lovely and influential Zenobia Elrington further assured his position in Verdopolitan society, where he emerged anew with the style and title of Alexander Percy, Viscount Elrington.

Fresh from his first visit to the Rydings, Branwell thus describes the luxurious residence of his hero.

Ordering my carriage I drove off for George's street and alighted at the door of his splendid mansion. Upon delivering my card I was ushered by a foreign servant through many noble passages, and up a grand staircase to his study. I entered, with the usual compliments. He was seated alone on his sofa. . . . The apartment was spacious, as most drawing-rooms, the ceiling painted in Arabesque, and the walls lined with books; fine bay-windows, curtained with velvet lighted the apartment, and opened on a gorgeous view of the vast Glass Town harbour. . . . Over the rich Persian carpet were scattered a vast number of naval maps plans and charts; the table groaned beneath a profusion of atlases and treatises on navigation; while round the room in rosewood stands and cases were placed the rarest and most valuable curiosities from every shore and ocean. In the midst of this princely profusion sat Rogue upon his sofa . . . sipping incessantly from a bottle of the most fiery liqueurs. . . .

In an equally Ouida-like description of Rogue's country seat, Elrington Hall, contained in the first issue of "The Monthly Intelligencer" dated April 1833, Branwell assures his readers that Rogue's dining-room was "the summum bonum of magnificence".

With Rogue firmly re-established in Verdopolitan society, Branwell was obviously seeking a new dramatic twist in the old plot to keep his hero before the public eye. Through the remainder of 1833 he can be seen feeling his way to set a new scene for Rogue's activities.

"The Monthly Intelligencer", a perfect replica of the journal of those days, set out in four columns of microscopic script, which he inaugurated on 27th March 1833, served only for a short time to absorb the editor's colossal energy. One issue alone survives. It contained no contribution from Charlotte—a cause perhaps for its ill success and for Branwell's dissatisfaction. She was obviously not to be caught up at the moment in political journalism, but was far too busy celebrating the rapture of regained freedom by writing love romances around the figure of the Marquis of Douro ("The Bridal", "The Foundling", "Arthuriana"). With a dig at her provoking self-absorption, her abandoned colleague prefaced his new journal with the following note:

A Few Words to the Cheif Genii

When a parent leaves his children, young and inexperienced, and without a cause absconds, never more troubling himself about them, those children, according to received notions among men, if they by good fortune, should happen to survive this neglect and become of repute in society, are by no means bound to believe that he has done his duty to them as a parent merely because they have risen, nor are they indeed required to own or treat him as a parent. This is all very plain and we believe that four of our readers will understand our aim in thus speaking.

A Child of the G. . . ii.

Charlotte would come racing back to her colleague's side when in February 1834 Branwell hit on the new theme that was the ideal solution to exercise both their talents: his for political intrigue and military "reportage", and Charlotte's for romance.

It was no less than the foundation of a new kingdom, the Kingdom of Angria, territory wrested by conquest from the Ashantees by the ubiquitous Marquis of Douro, Duke of Zamorna, and claimed by him before the Verdopolitan Parliament as his right by conquest—a right supported by no lesser peer than the quondam Viscount Elrington, now elevated to the title of Earl of Northangerland and newly allied to the Duke of Zamorna through the latter's marriage with his daughter Mary.

Mary Henrietta Percy, Duchess of Zamorna and Queen of Angria, Rogue's daughter by a first marriage, was originally a creation of Branwell's. He first mentioned her in a manuscript of November 1833, "Politics in Verdopolis", as a débutante in Verdopolitan society freshly engaged to be married. The marriage, however, never took place, because her very first encounter with Zamorna plunged them both fatally in love. Already married as he was, Zamorna cruelly abandoned his wife, Marian Hume (an early and fond creation of Charlotte's) and proposed to Mary Percy. As a heroine she was eagerly seized upon by Charlotte, who was not content with merely writing about her, but painted her portrait on several occasions. Indeed, of all the figures jointly created by Charlotte and Branwell, Mary Percy may be said to be the one nearest to both their hearts, and to occupy the front rank in countless stories, dramas and poems for years to come.

The idea of founding a new state outside Verdopolis, with all the attendant architectural, political, social and military activity that such a removal must cause, was pregnant indeed, and plunged Branwell and Charlotte into a fever of composition for the next fifteen months, when a fresh change in their situations caused a break in invention, only to be resumed at every return of leisure with redoubled zest.

Descriptions of the new kingdom flow from Branwell's pen. How real the geography of "Angria" was to Branwell can be judged by the minute details into which he entered relating to distances and even to the new "Coach Services" plying between Verdopolis and Angria—the Morning Mail being called the "Royal Angrian, towering in the broad lacquered pride of glossy green and scarlet . . .".

Irrespective of any literary or dramatic merit the Angrian legend may contain, its sheer scale is astonishing. Reared upon Homer, Virgil and Milton, Branwell took epic creation in his stride. That the result could bear no comparison with his models is less surprising than the magnitude of his conception, a circumstance to which it owed both its vitality and its death.

With the erection of the new kingdom's capital, Adrienopolis, on the banks of the Calabar, an exodus of society in the wake of the new monarch almost emptied Verdopolis and caused a reshuffling of official appointments which, together with Zamorna's coronation and the opening of the new Angrian Parliament, were so many themes requiring celebration, and exploited to the full by Charlotte and Branwell over the following months.

Six main documents by Branwell written between February and December 1834 relate to these recent developments: "The Conferring of the Kingdom of Angria on Zamorna by the Verdopolitan Parliament" (18th February 1834), "The Coronation of Zamorna" (June 1834), "The Wool is Rising or The Angrian Adventurer, A Narrative of the proceedings of the foundation of the Kingdom of Angria", eight chapters (26th June 1834), "Northangerland's Letter to the Men of Angria" (12th September 1834), "The Opening of the First Angrian Parliament" (September-October 1834), "The Massacre of Dongola"—ten pages, a recapitulation of Zamorna's campaign in conquering his kingdom from the Ashantees (December 1834).

Quite naturally, Charlotte's contribution to the new creation was the establishment of the fresh *dramatis personae* called for by the foundation of the young court at Adrienopolis. Zamorna's wife—and before very long, Zamorna's mistresses—the generals, functionaries, painters, poets, musicians, architects who thronged the court, the precincts, the elegant streets and squares of the new capital.

At the same time she did not abandon her old favourite, and mouthpiece, Lord Charles Albert Florian Wellesley, the new king's brother, who by remaining at the former capital, Verdopolis, permitted a constant exchange of news and visits between the two.

Charlotte's chief contributions to the Angrian creation are contained in eight manuscripts written between May and December 1834, the most important to her brother's biographer being "My Angria and the Angrians" (October 1834).

Although her characterisations, wildly romantic as they are, probe deeper than Branwell's, range further and sometimes even ring true to life, there is no marked inequality, at this stage, between their contributions to their story, and, without the proof of their handwriting and of their signatures, it would not be obvious at all times which of the two, brother or sister, had written a passage. Both are declamatory, emphatic, arrogant; both can completely

"The Bay of Glass Town", water-colour by Charlotte Brontë

"Like fair piles of burnished gold
those marble pillars stand,
palaces of immortal mould
and castles towering grand. . . ."
—"*Blackwood's Young Men's Magazine*"

"Percy at the Death-bed of his Daughter", from the water-colour by Charlotte Brontë

submerge their personality in that of the dramatic character by whose mouth they speak.

Inevitably their individual sympathies attached them more particularly to one or the other of the rival protagonists, and Charlotte increasingly spoke for the Duke of Zamorna, while Branwell gradually identified himself with Northangerland.

The term is not too strong. As time passed and the disappointments of his actual circumstances threw him more completely back on his dream world to satisfy his growing demands on life, Branwell became his hero (endowing him even with his own physical characteristics) and allowed that hero so to possess his mind and emotions as finally to suggest and direct his actions. The importance of the creation of Northangerland cannot be over-emphasised if one would understand the evolution—and wreck—of his creator's life. Thus, tedious as a study of much of Branwell's early writings must be to modern readers, they are essential to any understanding of his destiny.

While Charlotte at twenty-three would squarely face her responsibilities and have the courage to say "farewell" to Angria and all the bliss it brought, Branwell would never quit the imaginary kingdom of his dreams. It would gradually invade his whole world, while with Rogue he pursued his *doppelgänger* kind of life to perdition.

F

Chapter Seven

PATRICK BENJAMIN WIGGINS

The temporary separation of schooldays had brought Charlotte back with fresh eyes and sharpened perceptions with which to study her brother. Once again she was thrown into close contact and collaboration with him during the three years following her return from Roe Head and she had now both the opportunity and the critical faculty to see him anew.

For years past Branwell had fascinated her, as her two sisters had never done. Emily and Anne were an indissoluble entity, strong in their alliance—their isolation almost—and sufficient unto themselves. (Ellen Nussey, seeing them for the first time, said they were like twins.) Charlotte accepted them without question. Their secrets she might not often share, but their motives she could divine; they were made of the same material as herself.

Branwell was different. He was not only a boy, a being enjoying immunity from the laws that bound his sisters, but a mystery. She was not always quite certain, when they were all children together, whether he was of the same race as themselves. It was not merely for the purposes of fiction that Charlotte in her "Tales of the Islanders" written when she was twelve and thirteen, represented Branwell as a "brownie" as opposed to the "fairies" she imagined herself and her sisters to be. "Brownies", as she would have learned from a series of articles by the Ettrick Shepherd in *Blackwood's*, were malignant beings, small, shrivelled and spiteful in most of their activities, while "fairies" were good. Occasionally, "little king", as Branwell was called in these stories, played a benevolent part in conjunction with the three "little queens" but mostly his conduct is unpredictable and occasionally savage. "I forgot to mention," writes Charlotte about the school upon their imaginary island, "that Branwell has a large black club with which he thumps the children upon ocasion and that most unmercifully."

When not actively malicious, "little king" is imperious and indolent. It is the three "little queens" who run all the errands. The Duke of Wellington came upon them one day in his park at Strathfieldsay and found them in characteristic guise, as "the figures of 3

68

old women seated on a green bank under a holly knitting with the utmost rapidity and keeping their tongues in constant motion all the while. Stretched in a lounging posture beside them lay little king languidly gathering the violets and cuckoo plant which grew around. At the Duke's approach he started up, as likewise did the old women. they curtseyed and he bowed. . . ."

Fairies, benevolent and malicious, were a part of the world of childhood, and doomed like it to disappear in the light of common day. When next Charlotte reviewed the personalities of her brother and sisters, after the lapse of years, there was very little glamour left, but the beginning of a lifelike and recognisable portrait.

In "My Angria and the Angrians", finished 14th October 1834, she introduces into the Angrian story the figure of "Patrick Benjamin Wiggins", the caricature of Branwell which, like most good caricatures, is instinct with far more than a superficial truth. Unfalteringly, even in this comic skit of her brother at seventeen, Charlotte put her finger on the cause of his ultimate failure: his inability to act with an undivided purpose. While she sees the extravagance of his pretensions, not only literary, artistic, and musical, but social, sporting, and gastronomic, she sees just as clearly also his timidity, his modesty, and his subservience even, where his heart is most engaged. She sees how his emotions are too strong and too easily aroused; how the very range of his tastes and talents is too extended ever to allow of concentration upon one object; how his ambitions are too inordinate ever to be satisfied with moderate achievement—the very walk, language, demeanour, of such a man are here portrayed with an uncanny insight into the future. The passage where Wiggins is first introduced into the narrative must be quoted at length to convey the "odd mixture of folly and enterprise, absurd toadyism and bold ambition" which, as Charlotte herself summed it up, composed the portrait of what her brother was then. The narrator is Lord Charles Wellesley.

Being in no hurry I threw myself under the hedge and sat to watch for a fellow traveller. . . . Only about eighty yards off and, striding fast and firm, there advanced a low slightly built man attired in a black coat and raven grey trousers, his hat placed nearly at the back of his head, revealing a bush of carroty hair so arranged that at the sides it projected almost like two spread hands, a pair of spectacles placed across a prominent Roman nose, black neckerchief adjusted with no great attention to precision, and, to complete the picture, a little black rattan flourished in the hand. His bearing as he walked was tolerably upright and marked with that indescribable swing always assumed by those who pride themselves on being good pedestrians. I rose at his approach and proceeded to accost him. "Well Wiggins" said I (for it was no other), "How d'ye do, it's a fine morning."

"An uncommonly fine morning Lord Charles. I'm excessively glad to see you. Hope you're going a good way along the Road. Shall be proud of your company, that is if you can keep up with me."

"O never fear Wiggins I'll do my best, but pray are you going to the end of the world? Should think so from the spirit with which you progress."

"Not *quite* to the end of the world, that is not altogether. Just at present. I don't think of walking much farther than Zamorna. I came to Edwardston last night, and slept there. Mr Greenwood sent for me from VERDOPOLIS. The distance you know Lord Charles is forty miles and I did it all in twelve hours,— indeed it's more than forty, nearer fifty. O yes, and above sixty I daresay, or sixty-five. Now sir, what do you say to a man's walking sixty-five miles in one day?" As I knew Wiggins' style of exaggeration I made no answer. . . .

"Spare us Wiggins," interrupted I. ". . . answer a few questions I shall ask you respecting your own particular self. In the first place, where did you first see the light and what part of Africa had the honour of giving you birth?"

"Why Lord Charles I was born partly at Thorncliffe, that is after a fashion, but then I always account myself a native of Howard, a great City among the Warner Hills, under the domination of that wonderful and superhuman Gentleman WARNER HOWARD WARNER, Esq., (here he took off his hat and bowed low). It has four churches and above twenty Grand Hotels, and a street called the TAAN Gate, far wider than Bridgenorth in FREE TOWN."

"None of your humbug, Wiggins," said I, "I know well enough Howard is only a miserable little village, buried in dreary moors and moss-hags and marshes. I question whether it has one church or anything nearer an Hotel than that wayside Ale-house you are now eyeing so longingly. . . ."

"I'm rather thirsty," replied he, "and I think I'll call for a pot of porter or a tumbler of brandy and water, at the Public yonder."

He bolted across the road. A fat landlady met him at the door.

"Well, sir, what's your will," said she, for he stood a moment without speaking.

"If you please ma'am will you be kind enough to give me a ha'-penny'orth of milk, or a gill of whey, or even a draught of ditchwater, if it would be too much trouble to procure the other liquids for such a mere Tom-cat as I am."

The Hostess, who seemed to be a good-natured soul, was no doubt accustomed to Wiggins' manner, as he is a frequent traveller on this road. She laughed and said: "You'd better step into the House, Sir, and get a cup of warm tea into you. I've set the Breakfast things on the table."

Wiggins scraped his feet very carefully and followed her in. I could see him through the open door, take a seat by the fireside, swallow two or three cups of tea, with a due quantum of bread and butter very rapidly dismissed. Then, rising from his seat, he took from his pocket about twenty shillings in silver, (how he came by it I don't know), and offering it with an air to the Landlady said, "Pay yourself out of that, Ma'am, just take what you will, I never call a reckoning."

She helped herself, laughing at the same time, and with a gallant "Good Morning," he quitted the house and rejoined me.

"Well!" was his first exclamation, "I feel like a Lion now at any rate. Two bottles of Sneachie's Glasstown ale, and a double quart of Porter, with cheese, bread, and cold-beef have I devoured since I left you Lord Charles. That's what I call doing the thing in a handsome way. . . . But, however, let us resume the talk. What were you asking me, Sir?"

"I asked you where you were born, Sir, and now I ask you what relations you have?"

"Why in a way I may be said to have no relations. I can't tell who my father and mother were no more than that stone. I've some people who call themselves akin to me in the shape of three girls, not that they are honored by possessing me as a brother, but I deny that they're my sisters. . . .'"

"What are your sisters' names?"

"CHARLOTTE Wiggins, JANE Wiggins, and ANNE Wiggins."

"Are they as queer as you?"

"Oh, they are miserable silly creatures not worth talking about. CHARLOTTE's eighteen years old, a broad dumpy thing, whose head does not come higher than my elbow. Emily's sixteen, lean and scant, with a face about the size of a penny, and Anne is nothing, absolutely nothing."

"What! Is she an idiot?"

"Next door to it."

"Humph, you're a pretty set, but pray Master Wiggins, what first induced you to leave Howard, and come to Verdopolis?"

"Why you see Lord Charles, my mind was always looking above my station. I was not satisfied with being a sign-painter at Howard, as Charlotte and them things were with being sempstresses. I set before myself the Grand Plain of Africa, and I traced a path for my own feet through it, which terminated at the door of a splendid Palace situated on Cock-hill, whose portal bore inscribed 'Residence of the Duke of Thorncliffe', and beyond that a tomb under the oaks of my own Park, showing to the passenger such words as these 'Erected to the memory of PATRICK BENJAMIN Wiggins, Duke of Thorncliffe and Viscount Howard. As a Musician he was greater than Bach, as a Poet he surpassed Byron, as a Painter, Claude Loraine yielded to him, as a Rebel he snatched the Palm from Alexander Rogue, as a Merchant Edward Percy was his inferior, as a mill-owner, Granville came not near him, as a Traveller De Humbolt, Ledyard, Mungo Park, etc. etc., never braved half his dangers or overcame half his difficulties. . . .'

"With ideas so sublime as these in my mind you may imagine Lord Charles how I longed for an extended field to put them into practice. At length the wished for opportunity arrived. In the month of May last [1834] a fine full new Horgan was hoppened in Howard Church. At that period John Greenwood Esqur., the musician and composer, chanced to return. . . . That great man was compelled, shortly after landing, to seek a temporary refuge in the house of a humble acquaintance of his, one Mr. Sudbury Figgs who resided within four miles of Howard, and who, being a Pianist by profession, was accustomed to give music-lessons to the various families in the neighbourhood. When I heard of his arrival I stood upon my head for fifteen minutes running. It was news almost too glorious to be believed, but afterwards, when Mr Abey Figgs told me as he was drinking tea at our house, that through his influence Mr Greenwood had been prevailed on to preside at the Horgan's Hoppening and Re-Hoppening (for the business was twice performed) I positively fell into a fit of joy. He came—I saw him—yes I remember the moment when he entered the church, walked up to the Organ-Gallery where I was, kicked Sudbury Figgs, who happened to be performing Handel's 'And the Glory of the Lord' from the stool, and assuming it himself, placed his fingers on the keys, his feet on the Pedals, and proceeded to electrify us with 'I Know that My Redeemer Liveth.' 'Then' said I, 'this is a God and not a Man.' As long as the music sounded in my ears, I dared neither speak, breathe, nor even look up. When it ceased I glanced furtively at the performer, my heart had previously been ravished by the mere knowledge of his fame and skill: but now resistlessly was it captivated, when I saw in Mr Greenwood a tall man dressed in black, with a pair of shoulders, light complexion and hair inclining to red—my very beau ideal of personal beauty, carrying even some slight and dim resemblance to the notion I had formed of ROGUE. Instantly I assumed that inverted position which with me is always a mark of the highest astonishment, delight, and admiration. In other words I clapt my pate to the ground and let my heels fly up with a spring. They happened to hit Mr Sudbury Figgs' chin, as he stood in his usual way, picking his teeth and projecting his underjaw a yard beyond the rest of his countenance. He exclaimed so loud as to attract Mr Greenwood's attention. He turned round and saw me. 'What's that fellow playing his mountebank tricks here for?' I heard them say. Before anybody could answer I was at his feet licking the dust under them and crying aloud, 'O Greenwood! the greatest, the mightiest, the most famous of men, doubtless you are ignorant of a nit the foal of a louse like me, but I have learnt to know you through the medium of your wonderful works. Suffer the basest of creatures to devote himself utterly to your service, as a shoe-black, a rosiner of fiddlesticks, a great-coat carrier—a Port-music, in short a thorough going toadie.' Greenwood laughed. He gave me permission to stand by his side. That night I handed him his hat when he left the church, tumbling over William Rad, Henry Lock, and John Mildmay (the organ builder's son) in my hurry to get it. Afterwards I had the Supreme felicity of running down to the Inn with his Indian Neckerchief which he had left behind him. During the remainder of his stay at Howard I had various other little opportunities of currying favour with him. At last one evening when he was sitting in the BLACK-BULL PUBLIC HOUSE . . . he told me that I might accompany him to Verdopolis when he went there and welcome. Before my extasy of thanksgiving and gratitude was over he rose and told me to pack up my alls for he was going to set off that minute for the cross-roads, where a coach passed west-ward at ten o'clock p.m. I just ran home to tell the children, get my best clothes on, my clean shirt and collar, and in an hour's time was rattling as fast as four Coach-Horses could carry me towards Free Town.

The passion of the day was obviously music, greatly heightened at the moment by the inauguration in the May of that year, of the "new full organ" in Haworth Church, with all the attendant stir and bustle that such an event provokes in village life.

Since the previous year Mr Brontë had been active in trying to meet his parishioners' desire for a new organ. To open a fund for this purpose, a committee had been formed on which Branwell served with other local personalities like the Haworth surgeon, Mr Thomas Andrew. Miss Branwell had early sponsored the scheme with the offer of a contribution of £5.

The inaugural ceremony, as we learn from Charlotte's account in "My Angria", was marked by performances from the "Sacred Oratorios" and graced by the presence of the famous Leeds organist.

That Branwell had already had occasion to attend orchestral performances of the great oratorios then frequently given in Leeds, Bradford and Keighley, can be seen by his description, as far back as 1831 in one of his "Letters of an Englishman" (11th June) of the Celebration of the Olympic or "Great African Games" when an "assembly of 5 or 6 million persons" came to hear an "orchestra of 10,000 performers on the organ, trumpet, flute and clarinet, these being the only instruments allowed to be used" in an "Ode to the praise of the Twelves in a solemn strain of the sublimest music that ever I heard. Handel, Mozart, and all those who till now I considered the best musicians in the universe sunk to nothing before it. It began by a single flute which was scarcely heard through the building, but which seemed to float on the air, like the music of a fairy. This was in time joined by a trumpet, then 2 or 300 instruments, and at last the whole orchestra of 10,000 joined in the chorus. To give you an idea of its sublimity, I will tell you that through the mysterious influence of music on the soul, not a dry eye was seen. . . .'

Leyland, who was much struck in later years by Branwell's ecstatic response to music, reported that: "Mr Brontë had obtained musical tuiton for his son and daughters, and Branwell was enthusiastically fond of sacred music, and could play the organ. He was acquainted with the works of the great composers of recent and former times; and, although he could not perform their elaborate compositions well, he was always so excited when they were played for him by his friends that he would walk about the room with measured footsteps, his eyes raised to the ceiling, accompanying the music with his voice in an impassioned manner, and beating time with his hand on the chairs as he passed to and fro. . . . He was an enthusiastic admirer of the oratorio of *Samson*, which Handel deemed equal to the *Messiah*, and of the Mass music of Haydn, Mozart and others. . . ."

Besides playing the organ, Branwell, for a time at least, studied the flute. A manuscript notebook of his contains the transcription of twenty-one airs for the flute.

All the Brontë children were lovers of music; though Emily alone would appear to have achieved anything like a professional standard of performance after a year's intensive study in Brussels under a first-class professor, they were all given an early opportunity to study the piano and singing.

When Ellen Nussey first visited Haworth in July 1833 she noted the absence of a piano in the house but recalled that "A little later on, there was the addition of a piano." Signed and dated albums and pieces of music still preserved in the Brontës' old home show that the three girls were having lessons as from 1832.

The children's teacher was Mr Abraham Stansfield Sunderland, organist of Keighley Church and referred to by Charlotte above as "Mr Sudbury Figgs" who "being a pianist by profession, was accustomed to give music-lessons to the various families in the neighbourhood". Did we need confirmation that Mr Sunderland taught the young ladies of Haworth Parsonage, we have but to look at Emily's and Anne's diary paper of 24th November 1834, where, after blithely confessing that ". . . Anne and I have not done our music exercise which consists of b major . . ." the entry occurs: "Mr Sunderland expected. . . ." By then there was a piano at the parsonage.

It was doubtless also with Mr Sunderland that Branwell first studied the organ. Though never regularly organist at his father's church, Branwell was reported as playing there on several occasions, and as late as Christmas 1839.

In 1834 his interest in music seems to have been at its height. Writing on 20th February to Ellen Nussey, then on a visit to London, Charlotte added the postscript: "Will you be kind enough to inform me of the number of performers in the King's Military Band? Branwell wishes for this information."

But, of course, there was never any question of his taking up music as a profession. The proposal to be shortly approved by Mr Brontë, to have Branwell trained as a professional painter, must already have been under debate within the walls of Haworth Parsonage, thus relegating music and literary composition to second and third place in Branwell's interests. The deciding factor, always a matter of great emotional stress where he was concerned, would appear to have been an exhibition at Leeds in this same summer of

1834. The work of two Yorkshire artists, the Halifax sculptor Joseph Bentley Leyland and the portrait painter William Robinson, was on show there and to it, according to F. A. Leyland (the sculptor's brother), Mr Brontë took his children. To understand the impact of such a visit, not only on Branwell and Charlotte but on their father, who was led by it to so momentous a decision, one has to recall the whole course of their childish obsession with painting, and of his encouragement of their budding talents.

There is not a margin, not a fly-leaf of a book belonging to the Brontë children that they did not scribble over with attempts at portraiture. The very walls of their nursery, presenting what must have appeared to their childish minds as an unlimited area of whitewashed surfaces, are covered with faces—pretty, ugly, serious, gay— from every angle. Drawing was an accomplishment with Branwell and Charlotte at a time when to wield a pen legibly was still an uncertain hazard demanding great concentration and firmness of touch. From the age of nine Branwell was drawing little pictures inscribed "for Anne", which he proudly signed as gifts for his youngest sister. They represented Gothic ruined castles and thatched cottages and date from a time even earlier than his first "Battel Book".

All their childhood the little Brontës would run to the village carpenter, Mr Wood, begging for tiny frames for their latest artistic efforts; in exchange for which they, having no pocket-money and being too proud to accept benefits, would solemnly offer other drawings and paintings of their own; making up by the quantity of those for the one frame coveted for the favourite picture of the moment. Mr Wood, to humour them, would stuff his drawers full of their offerings, judging them on their exact face value—as so many childish daubs. The day came when his descendants realised their worth, but, as so often happened in connection with the Brontës, it was too late; the mass of little pictures had disappeared—no one knew precisely when, how, or why.

According to the recollections of an old Haworth resident, the son of Mr Brontë's tailor, interviewed in *The Bradford Observer* of 17th February 1894, the Brontë children's earliest art teacher was Thomas Plummer of Keighley. By 1829 certainly, when Branwell was twelve, they had begun regular drawing lessons. Charlotte's letter from their Uncle Fennell's parsonage at Cross Stone, is evidence of this. The views of the lakes they sedulously copied there were undoubtedly taken from William Gilpin's enormously successful sketches published in 1786. His style left a very deep imprint on the mass of landscapes they produced.

To the same year belongs "the list of painters whose works I wish to see", drawn up by Charlotte, and though it includes such obvious names as Titian, Raphael, Michelangelo, da Vinci, Van Dyck and Rubens, it contains also a number of others that can only have come to Charlotte's knowledge by very specialised reading, doubtless in *Blackwood's*. That the children read everything they could about painters and painting, would shortly appear in their own writings, where such references abound.

That the young Brontës had some opportunity to study the works of the great contemporary illustrators is known: Bewick's *British Birds* they possessed as early as 1829, as verses by Charlotte, and Emily's drawing of the whinchat testify. Very possibly, too, they knew Fuseli's illustrations to the *Iliad*, the *Odyssey*, and *Paradise Lost*, all of which figure in the list of books at the Keighley Mechanics' Institute Library.

An obsession with dungeons, spiral staircases, and massed pillars, evident in such early writings as Charlotte's "Tales of the Islanders", raises the question whether they had occasion to see reproductions of Piranesi's fantastic etchings of "The Prisons of Rome", then much in vogue, thanks to Flaxman's admiration.

The overruling influence on their early drawings, however, was undoubtedly that of John Martin, engravings of whose apocalyptic scenes hung in the parsonage, and in whose perspectives of massed colonnades and battlements in the antique style can be seen the direct genesis of Charlotte's surviving panorama of the Great Glasstown.

Four of Branwell's earliest water-colour drawings, dating from 1830, are preserved in the Parsonage Museum, and though three are endorsed as "original" they all share something of the characteristic of the fourth, which is a copy of Martin's "Esther and Ahasuerus". This characteristic is a quality of melodramatic sensationalism for which Martin's paintings were often censured. "Mad" Martin's historical paintings, then much in vogue, were obviously to Branwell's taste and struck a responsive chord in his nature. The three examples of his early work to be seen at the parsonage are a reflection of Martin's choice of the dramatic moment of any given theme. In the picture called "Terror", Branwell has indeed succeeded in giving his giant-like central figure in primitive combat a look of terror. In the "Hermit", all the paraphernalia of a studious recluse is dramatically displayed. The picture was drawn on 30th April 1830, and possibly lent its subject to its companion, "Study", drawn only six days later and depicting a seated figure holding a parchment scroll. All three sketches are overdone—too dramatic in gesture and too emphatic in facial expression to give pleasure. They strangely exemplify the faults for which Martin would be rated by the art-critic of *Fraser's Magazine* in the June issue for 1831. Writing of his "Esther and Ahasuerus" then being exhibited in the Suffolk Street Galleries, the critic deplores his "ultra-magnificence", adding: "painters of this class (when they *do* shew us nature) shew us Nature in hysterics. . . ."

Branwell's copy of Martin's "Esther and Ahasuerus", painted while the original was being exhibited in London, raises the whole question of how the young Brontës saw reproductions of contemporary paintings. That they saw exact replicas of the outstanding paintings of the day is instanced by a water-colour of Charlotte's still to be seen at the Brontë Parsonage Museum, which she entitled "Lycidas", but which a succession of coincidences has revealed to be a copy of Fuseli's "Dawn" exhibited in the Royal Academy Exhibition (Somerset House) in 1823.

Fuseli's painting, discussed in the *Blackwood's* for July 1823 and described there in detail, was, so the critic explained, suggested by the lines from "Lycidas":

> Under the opening eyelids of the morn
> What time the gray fly winds her sultry horn

which gives the clue to Charlotte's choice of title. It also goes to show that she had read the description of the picture in *Blackwood's*. Fuseli's picture, still privately owned, was shown again in London at the Arts Council Exhibition of "Romantic Art" at the Tate Gallery in the summer of 1959, when its exact resemblance—as regards the figure in Charlotte's little water-colour copy—made it instantly recognised by the present writer.

The picture was thus described in *Blackwood's*: "A Youth is asleep in the foreground, the air is filled with rolling mists—the grass is deep and dewy—a long pyramidal flash of pale purple shoots up from the verge of the horizon—the general expression of the picture is touching and true."

Description alone could not have made so exact a copy possible; an engraved reproduction must have been procured by Charlotte—from an art periodical of the time.

That art albums held a place in their lives is instanced by a passage in Branwell's "Monthly Intelligencer" (March-April 1833) describing a banquet given in honour of the marriage of Rogue and Zenobia Elrington at which "divers groups of visitors admired the various and costly works of art. Before one party lay spread the magnificent, nay, glorious work, De Lisle's 'Verdopolita delineata' representing the most splendid Architecture which ever existed. Others were examining the five quartos of Dundee's scenery of the Glass Town. . . ."

With them admiration was synonymous with emulation, to look at pictures was to wish to copy them. Leyland relates that Charlotte copied the engravings of Fittler, David Brown (the landscape painter in the manner of Morland) and William Woollett, the line-engraver, one of whose best-known works was the engraving of West's "Death of General Wolfe", a copy of which hung in Branwell's bedroom when he was a boy. Charlotte used her eyesight in such minute reproductions, spending as much, sometimes, as six months copying one engraving. It was not till years later that the cruel truth was brought home that to "produce curiously finished fac-similes of steel or mezzotinte plates", as she wrote in *Villette*, was "about as valuable as so many achievements in worsted work . . .".

Copy as they all might, Branwell early showed more originality than his sisters and had an unmistakable bent for portraiture.

It is tempting to see, in an article by Charlotte in "Blackwood's Young Men's Magazine" for December 1829, an account of an early portrait-group of the four children by Branwell. Purporting to be a review of the picture of the "Cheif Genii in Council by Edward De Lisle" (the leading Verdopolitan painter mentioned in many of Branwell's and Charlotte's juvenilia), it describes the four genii seated on their thrones in their immense hall, by which euphemism they constantly referred to their own tiny nursery-study. Branwell's now world-famed portrait of his sisters, preserved in the National Portrait Gallery, is known to have been only one of several similar groups painted over the years, and the 1829 picture of the "Cheif Genii in Council", though unlikely to have been in oils, was yet probably an early attempt at a group-portrait. "It is many years," comments Charlotte in the role of editor, "since any painting of great merit has appeared if we accept the Spirit of Cawdor by George Dundee [another Verdopolitan character] which we reviewed in our number for September. The one which is the subject of our present article almost atones however by its excellence for the mediocrity of those which have preceeded it. . . . The Cheif Genii in Council . . . is of large almost gigantic dimensions, and none the worse for that. . . . The Genii are seated on thrones of pure gold . . . in the midst of an immense hall surrounded by pillars of fire and brilliant diamonds. . . ." The background is composed, not unsuitably when the view outside the Brontë nursery window is remembered, of "gentle hills rising in the distance".

Leyland assumes that it was following a visit by Mr Brontë and his children to the "Annual Exhibition of the Northern Society for the Encouragement of the Fine Arts" at Leeds in the summer of 1834, where both the sculptor Leyland and the portrait-painter William Robinson had works on show, that Mr Brontë decided to engage Robinson to give his children—and particularly Branwell—lessons in painting. An echo of Branwell's fresh absorption in the art which was now being considered as his future profession can be found in a fragment of Charlotte's written on the following 5th December, by which time Robinson was giving regular lessons to the young people at the parsonage.

Purporting to be "Extracted from the last number of the Northern Review", Charlotte's article plunges without preamble *in medias res*.

"Well, Etty," said I, as I entered the artist's studio at Adrienopolis, one fine afternoon last week, "What's the last news with you? anything fresh on the canvass?" I knew that this mode of adress was likely to be the most unpleasing possible to so sensitive a person as William Etty Esqr R.A. and therefore I was not at all surprised when instead of answering me he turned his back on me and continued the assiduous prosecution of some works he was then engaged on. Undaunted by so cold a reception I calmly walked in and began to amuse myself by examining the pictures framed and unframed that hung around. Portraits, landscapes, half-finished Historical scenes . . . single figures, comical sketches formed the splendidly varigated canvass pannelling of this apartment.

Mr Brontë paid Robinson two guineas a visit to teach his children painting. The sum, for a clergyman of his restricted means, was considerable and argues the father's absolute belief in the son's ability.

Robinson was a successful young artist whose rapid rise in fortune can only have inspired old and young at the parsonage with the fondest hopes of a similar result for Branwell. Leyland clearly says that "a knowledge of the master's career did not a little to fire the mind of the enthusiastic Branwell . . . to aim in the same direction . . .".

William Robinson was born at Leeds in 1799 and had studied painting there under the water-colourist John Rhodes the Elder. In 1820 he had gone to London taking with him a precious letter of introduction to Sir Thomas Lawrence, who was not long in recognising the quality in him. He agreed to teach him and insisted on doing so gratis. Robinson was admitted to the Academy Schools, where he came to know the fashionable painters of the day—among others, Fuseli.

Within four years he was a portrait painter in great request, with such sitters as Wellington, the Duke of York and the Princess Sophia for his subjects. He was commissioned to paint a series of portraits for the United Service Club (still to be seen there today), and returned to Leeds at the height of his celebrity and achievement.

Such a success story was very certainly not lost on Branwell Brontë and his family. Without considering whether he had Robinson's talent, they were unhesitatingly confident of his achieving Robinson's success. The enthusiasm for art in the home-circle far exceeded any practical knowledge of the fundamental requisites for an art-career. Branwell was swept forward in such a surge of optimism that nobody—least of all himself—was aware, until it was too late, that he had lost his footing.

What Robinson's views of his pupil were has not been disclosed. A sensitive and kind-hearted man, already assailed by the tuberculosis that was to end his career so prematurely in 1839, he may have over-encouraged the sanguine expectations of the boy, remembering the lack of encouragement he had himself met with at home.

To this year 1834 has been assigned Branwell's group-portrait of his sisters preserved in the National Portrait Gallery. Recent X-ray examination shows that it once included a fourth—male—figure, presumably of Branwell himself, painted out by the pillar that divides the picture all too exactly in halves.

The picture is not signed or dated, a proof of its unfinished condition. Mrs Gaskell saw it on her visit to Haworth in 1853 and gave a very exact description of it in her *Life of Charlotte Brontë* (Chapter VII). She clearly states there that "the picture was done I know not when, but probably about this time." She is referring to 1835 and Branwell's projected departure for London, but goes on to add that it must then (1853) have been "ten years or more since the portraits were taken".

In a letter to a friend written during her actual stay in Haworth in September 1853, Mrs Gaskell mentioned the picture again but without going into details; she said it represented Charlotte as "a little rather prim-looking girl of eighteen, and the two other sisters, girls of sixteen and fourteen, with cropped hair, and sad, dreamy-looking eyes . . .". If the ages given here are correct, the picture would indeed have been painted in 1834.

But the only evidence for attributing it to that year is Mrs Gaskell's, and that she herself has rendered inconclusive and conflicting. Her two accounts of the picture do not tally. In the one she owns that it was painted "I know not when", possibly more than ten years before 1853, in the other she gives the girls' ages as though she *did* exactly know. She had obviously no certain knowledge of the date and was basing her assumption on the fact that Branwell was studying portrait-painting with Robinson from 1834. That the picture could with far greater likelihood have been painted as late as 1838, when Branwell was again intensively working at portraits and setting up a studio of his own at Bradford, she had not considered.

Mrs Gaskell did not think much of the picture; she described it as a "rough, common-looking oil-painting . . . little better than sign-painting as to manipulation . . ." yet she conceded its excellence as a likeness. "I could only judge of the fidelity with which the other two were depicted, from the striking resemblance which Charlotte, upholding the great frame of canvas, and consequently standing right behind it, bore to her own representation. . . ."

As biographical evidence about the sisters, the picture must remain beyond price; as an example of their brother's work, of great importance. In either connection, the exact date of its composition must affect the judgment of posterity not a little.

On 17th June 1834, Charlotte drew a water-colour sketch of Anne, aged exactly fourteen and a half at the time, which is yet to be seen at the Brontë Parsonage Museum. If Branwell's group-portrait dated from about the same time, a profitable comparison of the two portraits can be made.

They recognisably represent the same subject. Anne's arched brows, pouting lips and delicate curving nose are strikingly similar, and yet Charlotte's picture obviously shows a far younger girl than does Branwell's.

Her hair is worn in almost childish close clusters of curls that fall about a very thin throat and bony shoulders, which the cut-away frock emphasises only the more. Mrs Gaskell, in speaking of the frocks worn by the three girls in the group-picture, said Charlotte was "in the *womanly* dress of that day of gigot sleeves and large collars", adding that the others wore "a more girlish dress". (In fact there is no difference in the style of the girls' dresses in Branwell's picture.) What Mrs Gaskell was wishing to emphasise was that young women wore high-necked dresses whereas young girls still wore them off their shoulders, as reference to the fashion-plates of the day clearly shows. This, Charlotte's portrait of Anne exemplifies.

The Anne of Branwell's portrait no longer wears her hair in clustered curls, but cut fairly short (though not "cropped" as Mrs Gaskell described it) and parted down the middle in a far older style. She has filled out considerably since Charlotte's portrait—the frail throat and angular shoulders are gone—the eyes have not only what Mrs Gaskell described as a "dreamy look", but the visionary abstracted gaze of someone who has already thought much and felt deeply. Precocious as the Brontës were, such a face hardly fits a girl of fourteen, whereas Charlotte's portrait of her does perfectly.

According to "Patrick Benjamin Wiggins's" estimate of his sisters in that very winter of 1834, as related by Charlotte, Emily was "lean and scant, with a face about the size of a penny". Even allowing for brotherly malice, there was doubtless a measure of truth in this remark as relating to Emily in 1834—but the Emily of the group-portrait, seen only with the artist's earnest regard for truth, is fresh-cheeked and almost plump, bearing no relation at all to such a description. Nor, for that matter, does Anne to the brotherly flattering judgment of being "nothing, absolutely nothing . . . next door to an idiot".

The likeness of Charlotte alone corresponds to "Wiggins's" view of her in 1834 as "a broad dumpy thing", but Charlotte could describe herself as "very fat" as late as 1839 when writing to Ellen Nussey. If the group-portrait belonged to 1838 when Charlotte was at home for a long period of rest, she might well have looked so.

Finally, the blocked-out male figure in the group-portrait wears the high black stock then fashionable for gentlemen. Was it not

William Robinson of Leeds, from a self-portrait

"I thank you for your great kindness towards my son."—*The Rev. Patrick Brontë*

Charlotte Brontë,
from the portrait by J. H. Thompson, *c*.1838

more likely to be worn by Branwell at twenty or twenty-one than at seventeen, when his dress was reported so ill-fitting and slovenly?

Only the experts can judge of the quality of the actual painting of the group-portrait. It shows many of the faults noted by Leyland as typical of all Branwell's oil-painting. "It is quite clear," he says, "that he never had been instructed in the right mode of mixing his pigments, or how to use them when properly prepared. . . . He was, therefore, unable to obtain the necessary flesh tints, which require so much delicacy in handling, or the gradations of light and shade, so requisite in . . . a good portrait . . . the colours he used have all but vanished and scarcely any tint, beyond that of boiled oil . . . remains."

Leyland conceded that Branwell was a fine draughtsman, knew how to place his subjects, and, very important in the particular art-form he had adopted, could capture a likeness admirably. A view endorsed by Mrs Gaskell, as we have seen. The power and spiritual character of at least two out of the three heads in the group are amazingly conveyed. Would such a result come more likely from a tiro of seventeen, only just beginning to study painting seriously, or from a man of twenty or twenty-one after a few years' experience? In default of absolute proof of the date of the painting, every consideration points to its being at least later than 1834.

There remain evidences of two other family group-portraits by Branwell to which no exact date can be given either. One is the now lost "gun-group", known only by a copy published in J. Horsfall Turner's *Haworth Past and Present* (1879), and the profile fragment of Emily—Branwell's greatest claim to immortality—now preserved in the National Portrait Gallery.

It was cut away from a group of the three sisters by Charlotte's widower, Arthur Bell Nicholls, and sold at his death by his second wife. Its resemblance to Emily was vouched for by Nicholls, who excused the destruction of the rest on the score of its total lack of resemblance to Charlotte and Anne.

Before this group-portrait of the sisters was removed to Ireland by Nicholls, it was seen by the Haworth stationer John Greenwood, who took exact tracings of the three figures, carefully naming each. These tracings still exist today in the possession of descendants of John Greenwood. The tracing named "Emily" was compared with the original now in the National Portrait Gallery a few years ago by Mrs Edgerley, then Honorary Secretary of the Brontë

G

Society, and found to fit over it exactly. Hence, no doubt can sub-
sist that the famous profile fragment is indeed a portrait of Emily.
From the tracings bearing their names a good idea can be gathered
of the portraits of Charlotte and Anne.

As in the "gun-group", the girls are painted half-length and
seated about a table. John Greenwood wrote the name of each under
the individual figures—in Anne's case he added "in the 14th year
of her age"—which would date the picture 1834. Anne, like Emily
in the profile fragment, is wearing a low-necked frock with gigot
sleeves and wears her hair half-long, falling to her shoulders. The
general effect of the outline is youthful.

The figure of Charlotte bears a close resemblance to that in the
"gun-group"; she would appear to be wearing the same frock with
high neck and frilled collarette. Her hair is worn parted in the
middle with a high chignon; she is shown three-quarter face from
the same angle as in the gun-group. It seems a pleasing likeness of
her (though Nicholls denied its resemblance); there is no trace here
of the "broad dumpy thing" of the pillar portrait; yet, from Greenwood's dating, it would seem to show her at a younger age.

The fact remains that if Greenwood's ascription of a date is
correct, the profile portrait of Emily, the only fragment of the
picture to survive, shows her at the age of sixteen. It would, further,
show that even at that early stage Branwell was capable of inspired
painting. Nothing he did subsequently—and several finished portraits of friends and customers remain—would ever again achieve
the enchantment of that pose. But then, he would never have
another subject comparable to his sister Emily.

The comparative lack of literary compositions dating from the
autumn and winter of 1834 would seem to indicate that "William
Etty Esqr R.A." as Charlotte was now calling Branwell, was indeed
spending more and more time in his studio, painting feverishly.

A ten-page manuscript describing Zamorna's victorious campaign over the Ashantees called "The Massacre of Dongola" belongs
to this time (December 1834—January 1835). Its chief interest lies
in the identity of its reputed author, "Henry Hastings, the poet of
Angria" (who had succeeded and superseded "Young Soult" in that
role). As Young Soult had been the emanation of Branwell's
innocent boyhood, so Henry Hastings would shortly assume the
uglier role of his evolving personality.

Perhaps the last document to evoke the care-free home-life of the Brontës' adolescence is Emily's and Anne's diary paper for 24th November 1834. Among the themes that had absorbed their eager childhood—love of animals, politics, secret writings, baiting Aunt and Tabby, the freedom to do or not to do their "bed work" or their "music exercise"—there emerges also, as yet unchallenged, the old ingrained acceptance of Branwell's superior position. How he stood first in importance with his family cannot be better exemplified than by that unselfconscious document.

I fed Rainbow, Diamond Snowflake Jasper phaesent (alias) this morning Branwell went down to Mr Drivers and brought news that Sir Robert Peel was going to be invited to stand for Leeds Anne and I have been peeling Apples for Charlotte to make an apple pudding and for Aunt nuts and apples Charlotte said she made puddings perfectly and she was of a quick but limited intellect Taby said just now Come Anne pilloputate (i.e. pill a potato) Aunt has come into the kitchen just now and said where are your feet Anne Anne answered On the floor Aunt Papa opened the parlour door and gave Branwell a letter saying here Branwell read this and show it to your Aunt and Charlotte—The Gondals are discovering the interior of Gaaldine Sally Mosley is washing in the back-kitchin It is past Twelve o'clock Anne and I have not tidied ourselves, done our bed work or done our lessons and we want to go out to play we are going to have for Dinner Boiled Beef Turnips, potatoes and apple-pudding The kitchin is in a very untidy state Anne and I have not done our music exercise which consists of b major Taby said on my putting a pen in her face Ya pitter pottering there instead of pilling a potate I answered O dear, O dear, O dear I will directly with that I get up, take a knife and begin pilling (finished pilling the potatoes) papa going to walk Mr. Sunderland expected

Branwell was seventeen and a half. The first major decision regarding his future had been taken; he was already actively engaged in preparing himself for the career which he had freely chosen, and yet neither then nor when it was within his grasp did he feel any real joy. Nothing but the bewilderment of a departure into the unknown is apparent in the verses he wrote almost at the same time as Emily and Anne wrote their diary paper—on 10th November—and which he attributed to his *alter ego* "Northangerland", describing his voyage into exile.

Byronic in substance and style and transposed upon the Angrian plane, the lines yet bear a haunting personal application to the radical alteration in his life he was even then having to envisage in the immediate future.

> Waves of the ocean, how nobly ye roll!
> Endless and aimless, nor pathway nor goal;

Proudly ye thunder, your white crests on high
Shaking their foam to the spray-beaten sky.
Winds of the ocean, your voices arise,
Shriek on my canvas and storm to the skies;
Ye tell me that life is an ocean of woe
Where the fierce blasts of fashion eternally blow.
. . . I ride upon the raging sea,
And long long leagues of Ocean roar
Between me and my native shore.
Oh, all the scenes of a lifetime past
Far, far behind me lie;
There tossing o'er a stormy waste
Oh, who so lone as I!

PART THREE

THE GREAT VERDOPOLIS

*

Chapter Eight

ANGRIAN POLITICS

A preoccupation with the political scene marked the opening months of a year that was to bring far-reaching domestic changes in the lives of all four young Brontës. Never so completely before as during the first half of 1835 had the personalities of the hour and the great political issues then being debated between them formed the very substance of Branwell's and Charlotte's literary outpourings. It was as though, on the threshold of a new life demanding a closer contact with the outer world, they awoke from the long dream of their childhood to the sensation of living in the stirring England of the thirties, of actively participating in the history of their own times. Certainly Branwell was using the latest projection of himself—Captain Henry Hastings, the "Poet of Angria", author of the recently composed Angrian panegyric "History Stood by her Pillar of Fame"—to chronicle events in Angria which were directly inspired by the actual politics of the day.

When Emily and Anne noted in their diary paper for 24th November 1834 that Branwell had brought news from Mr Driver's that "Sir Robert Peel was going to be invited to stand for Leeds", they were commenting on the government crisis caused by the dismissal on 14th November of Lord Melbourne's (first) ministry—the last "dismissal", incidentally, of any government by the sovereign. Summarily ending the triumphal Whig regime of the last four years, it quickened Tory hopes throughout the country and, not least, those of the inhabitants of Haworth Parsonage.

The collapse of Melbourne's government (due largely to the death of its main prop, Lord Spencer) after only four months in office, had followed close upon the previous break-up of the Whig

ministry, when Lord Grey had resigned—and finally retired from
office, on 9th July 1834. Both crises had been brought about by
dissensions within the Cabinet itself, the bone of contention in each
case being the Government's Irish policy.

Having disposed of the Whigs—as he hoped—in November
1834 William IV called on Wellington to form a government.
Wellington's advice was to call in Peel, who had been Home
Secretary and Leader of the House in his former government
(1828-30), because he believed that Peel alone could now unite the
Tory party. Brought back from Rome with all the haste that
existing communications allowed, Peel in December 1834 formed
his first ministry which soon achieved the sorry distinction of being
defeated six times in six weeks. Lord John Russell, allying himself
with the Irish Members in the House, created an Opposition strong
enough to put through his Irish Bill—and to bring down the
government again in April 1835. Only an appeal to the country
could now resolve the stalemate and elections were called for the
May and June of that year. (The polls remained open at that time
from anything up to three weeks.) The results returned Melbourne
to power once again, where he remained for the next six years.

These events are widely commented on in Charlotte's letters of
the time. Writing to Ellen Nussey on 13th March 1835 after a visit
to The Rydings, during which she had obviously worked up some
spark of interest in her unpolitically minded friend, she breaks out:
"What do you think of the course Politics are taking? I make this
inquiry because I now think you have a wholesome interest in the
matter; formerly you did not care greatly about it. Brougham you
see is triumphant. Wretch! I am a hearty hater, and if there is anyone I thoroughly abhor, it is that man. But the Opposition is
divided, red hots, and luke warms; and the Duke (par excellence *the*
Duke) and Sir Robert Peel show no sign of insecurity, though they
have already been twice beat; so 'courage, mon amie'. Heaven
defend the right! as the old chevaliers used to say before they joined
battle. . . ."

On 8th May, as Election Day approached, Charlotte wrote again
to Ellen. ". . . The Election! The Election!

"That cry has rung even amongst our lonely hills like the blast
of a trumpet, how has it roused the populous neighbourhood of
Birstall? Ellen, under what banner have your brothers ranged themselves? The Blue or the Yellow? Use your influence with them,

entreat them if it be necessary on your knees to stand by their Country and Religion in this day of danger. . . ."

The election fever of 1835, as felt even in "little Haworth" was adroitly transposed by Branwell to the Angrian scene. From the wording of the posters stuck up all over Verdopolis, echoes of the election issues bandied by Lord Morpeth the Whig and by the Hon. Stuart Wortley the Tory candidate reach us today—

Men of Angria
Be present in Elrington Square
At 6 o'clock in the evening
of Friday June 19th 1835
To — Hear
The Rt. Hon. The Earl of Northangerland
Explain to you
The Character and Measures of
The Present Government
And bring before the only free Parliament
A bill for the reform of the Verdopolitan NAVY

proclaimed one poster, while its refutation by the rival candidate could be read across the way.

Reformers of Africa,
I pledge Myself
That the instant that
Renegade Northangerland
Has concluded vociferating
I will Rise —
And in your Presence
Confute every word he says.
Show up his Blackened Treachery
And adorn the Tree of Reformation
With fresh flowers of truth and
Liberty.
Signed. H.M.M. Montmorency.
June 17th
1835

Branwell had missed nothing of the excitement of the occasion as appears from the new Angrian chronicle then absorbing his thoughts.

I passed that evening through Elrington Square and beheld workmen erecting a Hustings in front of the splendid Elrington Hall, while directly opposite another was in progress for the Yellows (Whigs) and their speaker Montmorency. . . . Night came on. Then Morn, and with it the fated 19th day of June. What were the feelings of the Men in power—the Reformers the "Maritimes" at breakfast that day . . . the hour of dinner arrived . . . hastily I swallowed a few mouth-fuls for past the windows of my Hotel I saw the crowds of people already filing past the streets . . . and what I particularly noticed above everything else was the number of Rare Lads and men from the country whose strong rough forms mingled so thickly with the more dashing citizens. I sallied forth at ½ past 5 and repaired to the Square where the crowds were thickening every instant. Having secured a good place on a sort of hustings not far from the great one. I resolved to stand and view the sight—Twice before had I seen a Verdopolitan crowd and twice I have said none other is like it . . . I need not particularly describe it there were thousands here—orange crimson scarves and blood-red favours mingled in the multitude. At 7 o'clock the Yellow Hustings began to fill with the Ministerial Grandees. . . . Shortly after 6 or 7 foreign looking persons sallied forth from the portal of the Great Hall and mounted the blood red Hustings. Then law givers and ministers . . . then mounted a gentleman supported by a page and wrapt in a black military cloak and cavalry Helmet. What a horrid and universal groan was that which greeted his appearance, how haughtily he bore himself advancing to the very front of the Hustings. Was there none to applaud him? Where were the Angrians to shout long live Zamorna? The Balconies and windows of Elrington Hall were adorned as by exotic flowers with a Brilliant Display of Aristocratic Beauty. . . . Ere I was aware Another Person stood in the full front of the Bloody Hustings. But the roars of Hate and Triumph rose in such deepening volleys that I could hardly steady my eyes to see him. But tall and solemnly, with his head uncovered and the high bald forehead pale features and sunken eye—My sight almost grew dim while I felt in my mind that I saw before me the immortal Alexander Percy—immortal for his greatness and crimes. . . . His lordship was attired in black frock coat, light trousers and the red ribbon round his neck while his profuse dyed whiskers and scarlet lips contrasted strongly with his fork beard and eyes. . . .

That the Haworth campaign was rowdy and that Mr Brontë and his son were in the thick of things can be seen from an eye-witness account given many years later to *The Bradford Observer* of 17th February 1894 by an old Haworth man, the son of Mr Brontë's tailor in the village. The glimpse it affords of Branwell is curiously in character, and reminiscent of Patrick Benjamin Wiggins.

As was to be expected in a predominantly Whig community like Haworth, the Tory minority, consisting of local gentry, the parson, the doctor and a few farmers, was exposed to constant heckling during the campaign. On the occasion when Mr Brontë rose to speak on the "Blue" hustings erected outside the *Bull*, he suffered such repeated interruptions that Branwell leapt up, beside himself with rage, and screamed: "If you won't let my father speak, *you* shan't speak!"—a gesture which earned him the distinction of being burned in effigy, holding a potato in one hand and a herring in the other—a Haworth way of reminding him of his Irish origin.

In midsummer 1835 Branwell began the longest sustained literary composition of his life—the document called for convenience by Brontë bibliographers, the "History of Angria", which was to run into ten parts and extend over two and a half years of writing.

Such an absorption at precisely that moment might seem surprising if something more than an objective interest in public events were not discernible in his motives. Branwell knew himself to be on the eve of taking his first practical steps towards starting out on a career. According to the plan cherished by the whole family since the previous year, he was shortly to go up to London to qualify for admittance to the Academy Schools and—in the fond opinion of them all—to do as well as William Robinson had done and come back to his native Yorkshire a successful portrait-painter.

London—or the Great Verdopolis with which for years past it had been inextricably identified in Branwell's imagination—now loomed a present reality on the horizon. Since childhood he had pored over maps of the great city (one of them he borrowed from Ponden House library) until every side-alley had become known to him; so certain had he always felt of being called there one day. That day was fast approaching. The very thought of seeing with his own eyes the gorgeous buildings he had pictured from earliest childhood, of mixing with the crowd of illustrious and uniformed figures so familiar to that inner eye by which he and his sisters had always lived, imposed on him now an obligation, almost, of *feeling* himself into the part of denizen of the greatest metropolis of the world. To follow public events was not the mere indulgence of a passion, but a necessity to anyone intending—as in moments of exaltation he intended—"to push out into the open world".

Perceptible now as a characteristic later to develop into a monomania is the sense of self-importance which informed all his anticipations of what to expect and of what was expected of him. No humble role, but one in the forefront of events. How much of disappointment and misery would have been spared him could he then have seen his prospects with the sober eye of the author of *Villette*! But Charlotte herself, who was to learn so quickly and so indelibly the disillusioning lesson of life, might never have reached such true humility but for the early overthrow of Branwell's hopes. She too, in that summer of 1835, shared in his naïve anticipations.

Whether hers were unmixed with certain qualms—not respecting Branwell's talents but his character—appears unlikely in one so closely bound to him as she had been, particularly during the last two years. No one becomes suddenly vile. In Branwell there must already have become apparent to her shrewd eyes the shadows and traces of that deterioration already perceptible in his writing of the time.

London, to the members of the Brontë family except perhaps Emily, awakened feelings of the highest awe, deriving as much from their great sensibility to artistic beauty as from their veneration of human greatness. They imagined London only in terms of the magnificence and nobility of its buildings, its court and its government; the squalor and misery of an overpopulated city, housing every degree of misfortune and ruin, was inconceivable to them. (It is doubtful whether, at that time, Branwell had yet read De Quincey's indictment of the "stony-hearted" city—since the effect of the *Confessions*, when it came, would be so overmastering.) The exaggerated sense of what awaited them in London was typically voiced by Charlotte in a letter to Ellen the previous year during one of her friend's visits to the capital.

"I was greatly amused," she wrote on 20th February 1834, "at the tone of nonchalance which you assumed while treating of London, and its wonders, which seem to have excited anything rather than surprise in your mind: did you not feel awed while gazing at St Paul's and Westminster Abbey? had you no feeling of intense, and ardent interest, when in St James's you saw the Palace, where so many of England's Kings had held their courts, and beheld the representations of their persons on the walls. You should not be too much afraid of appearing *country-bred*, the magnificence of London has drawn exclamations of astonishment from travelled men, experienced in the world, its wonders, and beauties. Have you yet seen any of the Great Personages whom the sitting of Parliament now detains in London? The Duke of Wellington, Sir Robert Peel, Earl Grey, Mr Stanley, Mr O'Connell etc? If I were you Ellen, I would not be too anxious to spend my time in reading whilst in Town, make use of your own eyes for the purposes of observation now. . . ."

With the awe and the anticipatory delight in the prospective encounter, there mingled the credulity of the "country-bred" girl and youth in both Charlotte and Branwell; they believed that the paths of even the most casual visitor to the capital, crossed those of the illustrious great even then making history.

For Branwell the public scene and the great figures of the hour held a fascination that was both frightening and irresistible. They drew him like a magnet. The sensation of being himself a part of such unattainable spheres was, at the same time, torture and delight. He needed to brace his nerves to the idea—to experience in anticipation that encounter, so that like an actor, he might have his part by rote when the moment of his entry on the stage arrived. He was thinking about the London he must shortly enter and the great folk he had inevitably (so he imagined) to face, when he plunged into his "History of Angria".

The short preface, written on 15th June 1835, betrays both the excitement and the apprehension with which he viewed the prospect. "Reader, however devoid of general interest may be the publications I have hitherto presented to you, I can answer for this one that its contents shall come home to the hearts and feelings of you all—and I am sorry to say that I take my pen in haste because I see some clouds fast gathering . . . whose effects I must describe."

In the person of Captain Henry Hastings, fast making a name for himself in Verdopolitan society as the chronicler of the Duke's victorious "campaign on the Calabar", Branwell imagines his entrance into London life. But already in the character of his new protagonist he was pushing out into troubled waters, sounding depths he had hitherto shuddered to approach and frantically trying to give himself the semblance at least of that self-confidence whose lack he knew to be his Achilles' heel.

Plunged straight away into the thick of things by a dinner in government circles, Hastings has to own to his correspondent: "I must confess that I felt slightly embarrassed amid persons who call up so many thoughts and ideas to my mind, and you must excuse my diffidence among founders of an Empire, Heads of Parties, men intwined with History, Rulers of Northangerland [the Province], Ministers of Zamorna. . . ."

As the great day of departure approached and his goal stood within measurable attainment, what Branwell saw in his mind's eye, like the original Glass Town of his childhood, was pure enchantment.

Now I have entered the Newborn Capital of Zamorna, doomed perhaps as the seat of Arts and Sciences and riches and arms. What I saw seemed like the beginning of a city destined to rule the world. . . . We . . . soon entered under a vast gateway of three Noble Arches into the great inhabited streets of the Calabar, whose finished buildings, all resembling rather palaces than houses, and the noble shops, blazing on each hand of us, with the thickly-peopled state of the promenade and the air of life and bustle which seemed to reign through this thoroughfare . . . all conspired to fill us with sensations of unmixed astonishment and wonder. As we neared the top of this very long and fully finished street which swept and curved most grandly before us, the majestic colonnades and royal entrances of the Palace of Adrian the First rose up and unfolded its splendour before and beyond the Ministerial Square. This square of vast size, and surrounded by . . . houses of Regal Magnificence, is to be devoted entirely to the residences of the Ministry of the Angrian Parliament. Above it stretches the entrance of the Palace. On one side, the street sweeps on to the vast roofs of Northangerland House, and on the other side it makes an opening down toward the wide, bright, oceanlike Calabar. It was a lovely sight as we passed this magical scene to view the quays stretching along below us, the long forest line of vessels laden with materials . . . the gay morning waves all dancing in the light, and miles off, over the blue bounding water, the yellow burning sands of the desert region of Africa. . . .

No element, indeed, was lacking in Branwell's far-off vision of London to invest it with all the paraphernalia of mirage. How much of the unsubstantial pageant he actually found at the end of the two hundred and ten miles that separated it from Haworth, he himself could never precisely tell; all was obliterated in the mighty storm—not of desert sands—but of his bitter disappointment.

One of the few glimpses we get of him before setting out, is of a visit to Liverpool at the end of May, during which he bought— with what an application to his own case may be guessed—a copy of *Childe Harold's Pilgrimage*.

Chapter Nine

LONDON

For reasons that will later become apparent the actual date of Branwell's visit to London, and of its attendant circumstances, cannot be traced in the Brontë family records. That he went there, his friends Leyland, Grundy and Searle Phillips and many others later heard directly from himself.

His own account of his experiences, written as part of the fifth section of his "History of Angria", dates from May 1836. Some biographers have suggested that his journey took place early that same year, but that is to ignore the evidence of his writings dated from home intermittently during December 1835 and continuously from 1st January 1836. He was admitted to the Masonic Lodge of Haworth on 1st February 1836, and the minutes show that he was in attendance at every meeting throughout that year. The internal evidence of his writings, which reflect a deep moral upheaval as from December 1835, indicate strongly that his London journey took place in the autumn of 1835. Moreover, his original application to the Academy Schools was for the autumn term and Leyland, the best informed about his movements because of his brother's intimacy with him, places Branwell's London visit in the autumn of 1835.

For the causes of his failure to be admitted to the Academy Schools, which later so puzzled Mrs Gaskell, Ellen Nussey guardedly offered the solution: "conduct and lack of finances". But, in the event, what brought Branwell back to Haworth a permanently disillusioned man had little to do with outward circumstances. Neither want of cash nor indulgence in the first heady orgy of his youth could have wrought on him so devastating a change, without the realisation of that fatal flaw of character which left him helpless before the challenge of real life. Poverty and drunkenness have never yet turned a true artist from his goal, but the horrible lesson of London was precisely to show Branwell that he *had* no goal: that so far from being a painter, he was not even man enough to stand on his own feet. Painfully typical of just such a man was the growing impatience also and disregard for those very props—the family—whose absence he would shortly hail as "a pleasant and delightful reflection". He was tired of being beholden to them, but also incapable of steering a course without them.

At the beginning of July (1835) a family dispersal was decided upon. Charlotte was to return to her old school, Roe Head, in the capacity of teacher, and Emily to accompany her there as pupil, her fees being in part defrayed by Charlotte's services. Writing to Ellen Nussey about the plan on 2nd July, she clearly gave her reasons for it; it was not merely to give Emily a chance of getting as good an education as herself, but to help her father with Branwell's expenses in London. "I had hoped to have the extreme pleasure of seeing you at Haworth this summer," she wrote, "but human affairs are mutable, and human resolutions must bend to the course of events. We are all about to divide, break up, separate, Emily is going to school, Branwell is going to London, and I am going to be a governess. This last determination I formed myself, knowing that I should have to take the step sometime, and 'better sune as syne' to use the Scotch proverb, and knowing also that Papa would have enough to do with his limited income should Branwell be placed at the Royal Academy and Emily at Roe Head. . . ."

The bulk of Branwell's expenses must fall on the family. If he qualified for admission to the Academy Schools the normal period of training was three years. Though entrance to the Schools was purely on merit and entailed no fees, the whole cost of his keep would have to be met. He might contribute something towards this by making himself useful to his teachers, as Robinson had done to Lawrence; he might, even, as all young Royal Academy students dream of doing, get an early commission from a patron on the lookout for budding talent—but the cost of his three years' residence in London must in the main fall on the family.

That Branwell was sent to London by the united efforts and generosity of family and friends alike is apparent from the letter Mr Brontë wrote to the former Elizabeth Firth of Kipping, now Mrs Franks, on 6th July. It plainly shows that Branwell's godmother, Mrs Firth (Elizabeth's step-mother and long since widowed), was contributing towards the venture. Reference in the same letter to other "sponsors" of the children—Miss Outhwaite and Mrs Franks herself, both of whom were Anne's godmothers—shows the practical help he could rely on in getting his children educated. "It is my design," Mr Brontë wrote, "to send my son, for whom, as you may remember, my kind and true friends Mr Firth and Mrs

Firth, were sponsors, to the Royal Academy for Artists in London; and my dear little Anne I intend to keep at home for another year under her aunt's tuition and my own. For these dispositions I feel I am indebted, under God, to you, and Miss Outhwaite and Mrs Firth and other kind friends; and for every act of kindness I feel truly grateful."

Charlotte and Emily set off for Roe Head on 29th July "sad, very sad at the thoughts of leaving home". They would not be there to see Branwell off on his great adventure. The earliest prospect of reunion for the four inseparables was Christmas—after, who could tell what changes and losses to them all?

In her note to Ellen, there was perceptible for the first time something like a shifting of the centre of Charlotte's gravity towards Emily and away from Branwell. Caused as yet by outward conditions mainly, it is a pointer of the direction her inner life would increasingly take, as Branwell's erratic course removed him beyond her orbit. "Emily and I," she wrote, "leave home on the 29th of this month, the idea of being together consoles us both somewhat. . . ."

In the event, Emily stayed barely three months at school. She fell gravely ill from homesickness—an illness of the spirit Charlotte well understood—and had to be hurried home in mid-October, her place at Roe Head being immediately taken by Anne.

Before that date Branwell had, in all probability, started for London, the autumn term at the Academy Schools beginning early in October.

A draft letter of his, unsigned and undated, to the Secretary of the Royal Academy, shows that he planned to take up his drawings for inspection some time in August or September. The letter, if he ever sent it, was not preserved in the Academy files because he was never admitted there. It reads:

Sir

Having an earnest desire to enter as probationary student in the Royal Academy, but not being possessed of information as to the means of obtaining my desire, I presume to request from you, the Secretary to the Institution, an answer to the questions—

Where am I to present my drawings?
At what time?
and especially,
Can I do it in August or September?

That Branwell was working with William Robinson almost up

to the time of his departure emerges from a letter that Mr Brontë wrote to Robinson on 7th September. The letter is notable for its revelation of Mr Brontë's own personal response to art, of his faith in his son, and of the kindliness and generosity of which he was capable when his heart was touched. The text, with Mr Brontë's punctuation, reads:

Dear Sir,

I am greatly obliged to you, for your very acceptable present; both on account of the good principles, and great talents of the man whom it represents, and the fidelity and skill of its execution. I thank you also for your great kindness, towards my son. Your picture which he has brought home, has so much in it of truth and life, and that something which cannot be expressed and which genius alone can give, that when it is not in use I frequently have it in my own room— for the pleasure of looking at it—for, though I have, comparatively, but little skill in the fine arts—I greatly admire them—and in their excellence, they afford me particular pleasure. The Child has a fine, expressive countenance—I trust that under providence, as she grows up, her mind will harmonize with her features. I wonder how you could get her to sit—If I were in Leeds I would buy her a pretty little Book or something else that would amuse, and profit her.—But as I am not likely, soon to be there, I have taken the liberty of enclosing under a seal in this letter—half a sovereign, which I beg you to present her with, in my name, and to lay out for her, as my proxy; in the manner, in which you may think, will corres-pond best with her infantile fancy; telling her, at the same time, that I am greatly obliged to her for the trouble she has had on my account—

If all be well, Branwell hopes to be with you on Friday next, in order to finish his course of lessons. . . .

In 1835 the journey to London was still made by coach. For Branwell it meant either a very early start from Haworth, by gig or carrier's cart, to catch the Keighley coach at 6 a.m. thus getting to Bradford (the *Bowling Green Hotel* in Bridge Street) by 8.30, or a late night departure. The London coach, the daily *Courier*, left Bradford from the *White Swan Hotel* in Market Street, only a street's length away.

The journey took two days, the coach getting into London on the afternoon of the second. What Branwell thought as every stage brought him nearer his goal, he recorded in great detail in a fragment of his "History of Angria" written in the following May. Whether the disillusionment of that document was really coincident with the event, or added in retrospect, it makes sad reading now. If he told the truth about himself, he was beaten before ever he started out. Like many another enthusiast he felt no joy in the actual moment of attaining his desire.

View of Somerset House, home of the Royal Academy until 1837.
After the painting by Thomas Malton, 1796

Interior of the *Castle Tavern*, Holborn

"The Temple of the Fancy"

Relating his adventures in the person of Charles Wentworth he explains how "he set forth on his journey of 300 miles . . . with plenty of letters of introduction in his pocket." On examining his feelings on this day of days, he realised almost at once that his departure for "the mightiest city in the world, where he was to begin real life, and in a while, maybe, take a lead in it", did not give him half so much pleasure as he had always fancied it would. "Now this, thought he, was always looked to by me as one of my grand fountains of happiness." While he was "nearing the great spring where all my thirst would be gratified", he made the blighting discovery that "Happiness consists in Anticipation."

He was nearly twenty-one, he reflected [actually eighteen], and, realising he was on his own for the first time in his life, turned over in his mind the parting injunctions of his elders which go far to show that they had already seen the red light where Branwell was concerned. "Next he recollected his advisers had told him when they saw him in expectation of an ample fortune . . . give himself up to idleness and go about doing nothing and caring nothing, but building air-castles for the adornment of his future life. . . . Now, they said, you can never have real happiness without working for it," to which typically Brontëan philosophy, subscribed to and practised by his father and all his sisters, he replied: "Why should I labour?"

The confusion of mind in which he set out on even so clear a course as his present venture is all too evident in his indecision "what road to take in life". He thinks that the truly great men like Zamorna and Northangerland could advise him and the idea possesses him to seek their council. "It was his disposition when he thought a man truly great, to adore him as a god . . . but if any of these great men went against his feelings, they became instantly dust and ashes. For Wentworth was most obstinate in his generalised feelings—but as to fixed detail of character, he had none."

On the second day of his journey he arrived in "the mighty City of Africa and took up his abode at Johnson's Hotel, first walking through his room in a pleasant sort of excitement, then, as that ebbed off, longing for supper . . .".

By "Johnson's Hotel" Branwell was indicating the *Chapter Coffee House* in Paternoster Row, noted in the eighteenth century as a meeting-place for publishers and men of letters, and boasting proudly of its connection with Goldsmith and Johnson in particular.

H

By the turn of the century it had a clientele predominantly provincial and clerical in character, and there Mr Brontë had stayed on his first visit to London, and on his way to and from Cambridge and his first curacies. At the Brontë Parsonage Museum there is preserved a rough plan of the position of the *Chapter Coffee House* drawn by Mr Brontë, no doubt on this occasion of Branwell's journey to London. Later, Mr Brontë took Charlotte and Emily there on their way to Brussels (1842) and again in 1848 Charlotte and Anne stayed there when visiting their publishers. Mrs Gaskell could therefore in all truth say that every member of the Brontë family had stayed there at one time or another.

There was a coffee room downstairs and there Branwell preferred to have his first and one of his few meals in London, rather than to go out and face the city in its evening mood. He had not the tranquillity of mind to undress and go to bed: "His thoughts kept him up all night though tired enough with his hasty and lengthened journey."

Next morning he reflected that he had not a relation in the city, which to him was a pleasant and delightful reflection. Then he examined his letters and put them up again, thought of his wealth and independence, took breakfast and sallied out into the streets with an outward appearance of remarkable dejection, and something very like broken circumstances, but which really arose from constant thinking. . . . He threaded the dense and bustling crowds and walked for hours, never staying to eat or drink, never calling a coach or attending to personal appearance, but with a wildish dejected look of poverty-stricken abstraction. His mind was too restless to stop and fully examine anything. He was not searching for information or gratifying his tastes or curiosity. Here is what he was doing. He was going about striking sparks from his mind by a contact with scenes connected with glorious events, associations, persons. He felt the want, that restless uneasy feeling with which rest is torment and ease begets stupor. The flashes of feeling, which were constantly scintillating thrilled into his soul and he cared and thought of nothing more. . . .

Branwell has often, wrongly, been pitied for his irregular education and chronic poverty, as though they could wholly be attributed to his family; but where so supersensitive and vain a young man must greatly have suffered, and through no fault of his own, was, in addition to his gallingly low stature, in the out-moded and provincial cut of his clothes. The glimpse he caught of himself in shop windows as he hurried through the prosperous crowds, was destined only to add to his "wildish and dejected look of poverty-stricken abstraction", and may well indeed have acted as yet another deterrent from seeking those contacts which he had expressly come to make.

His friend Grundy has something to say in his *Pictures of the Past* (published in 1879) on Branwell's physique and personal appearance which, in spite of Grundy's genuine liking for him, speaks for his unprepossessing exterior. Unlike his father, Branwell had not "an air" about him. Grundy speaks of "his downcast smallness", of his small deep-sunk eyes, nearly always cast down and only very occasionally glancing furtively upwards, and he had to admit that at first sight Branwell was the "reverse of attractive" (an opinion, it should be added, not shared by another of Branwell's friends, Leyland).

Young and supersensitive, there was nothing in the buffeting crowds his frail person had to breast to bring him reassurance. The great city stupefied Branwell Brontë, and so pressed upon him as to drive him into the farthest recesses of his being; but surely no more lucid account was ever confided to paper of a mind imprisoned in itself. It could no more emerge than the last defenders of a keep, unless by jumping to its death.

He had, as he had already twice mentioned, "plenty of letters of introduction in his pocket". Some were certainly from his teacher Robinson, who had, not so long before, come to London on the self-same errand. Prospective Academy students had two particular courses of study to follow before they could hope for actual admittance to the Schools: they had to "study from the antique", which meant weeks, sometimes months spent in copying the Elgin Marbles, and they had to make a prolonged study of anatomy. As his biographer, F. A. Leyland, was later to write, Branwell had not even a rudimentary acquaintance with either subject.

The Elgin Marbles, housed for a long time after their arrival in England in "a damp dirty pent-house" in the back yard of Lord Elgin's house in Park Lane, had, by the time Branwell arrived in London, reached their permanent home in the British Museum, by way of Burlington House. Access to them, however, for all purposes of study, was only by permission of their Keeper, who, at that time, was William Young Ottley, the art-critic and author. To him, Branwell very certainly carried a letter of recommendation from Robinson.

Another letter he also certainly carried was for Robinson's— and his own eventual—friend, the Yorkshire sculptor Joseph Bentley

Leyland. Robinson and Leyland, it will be remembered, had both exhibited at the Leeds Annual Exhibition of 1834, visited by the Brontës, where Leyland had shown his colossal bust of Milton's "Satan". He had, only the year before, gone to London to study from the Elgin Marbles, and had achieved so rapid a success that he was now permanently established there. He was on friendly terms with Chantrey, Westmacott and Benjamin Robert Haydon, with whom he had studied anatomy. He had lodgings with yet another Yorkshire artist, the mezzotintist Geller, with whom Branwell was also to make friends eventually. From his studio in Queen Street, Oxford Street, Leyland, a devoted son and witty correspondent, headed his letters home: "City of Crime!"

With such contacts, the doors of artistic London stood open for Branwell Brontë had he but chosen to raise his hand and knock.

Instead, he wandered down to the Embankment and, leaning on the parapet of the river, stood for hours staring down at the sight below.

The Academy Schools were still housed in Somerset House at the time of his visit (they moved to the National Gallery only in 1837), and the scene at the riverside which caught his eye with so compelling a fascination and riveted him there for hours was probably as near as he ever got to presenting his letter of introduction to the Academy's Secretary, Henry Howard, R.A.

Howard, who combined the purely administrative office of secretary with that of professor of painting at the schools, would, had Branwell so willed it, have become his teacher. But, "before him stretched docks and shipping and merchandise, and the blue boundless main", and he preferred to turn his back on Somerset House.

Charles Wentworth leant over a parapet with the sun shining upon him, and on one side a great merchantman just come in from Stumps's Land—and before, the wide waving main. Then, on a sudden, the tears came, starting into his eyes, and a feeling like a wind seemed to pass across his spirits, because now he felt that not even the flashes of glory which these streets and buildings had struck from his soul, not even these feelings which he had reckoned on as something to supply years of dullness, could preserve his thoughts from aimless depression. We cannot tell often what impulse it is which changes our mind from one state to another; nor could he tell why the sudden sight of the sea made him learn at once "what shadows we are, and what shadows we pursue". . . . The contrast between the spring waters at home in their far-off summer loneliness and the stir and bustle of Verdopolis too violently broke his current of thoughts and from his mind being overstrained, the relapse was as strong as the spring; yet it was long ere he quitted the spot, and then he turned, passing through many noble streets without hardly turning his eyes to look at them. He entered his hotel, stretched himself on a sofa, and listlessly dreamed away his time till dark.

The emphasis Branwell lays repeatedly in his account upon the fact of his having "plenty of money in his pocket" may have deluded him into thinking he also had plenty of time, but as the event showed the longer he delayed the greater his disinclination grew to make any effort at all. He was living shut up with himself and perhaps for the first time realising what lack of purpose there was inside. The futility of his attempt was all that was made clearly apparent to him.

No greater contrast could perhaps exist between his response to the stimulus of the great city and that of another young art student who left on record his comparable yet, at the same time, totally different experiences there.

Exactly thirty years before Branwell Brontë, Benjamin Robert Haydon had travelled up to London from his provincial home to make a name for himself as a painter. He, too, was just eighteen; he was an only son, with a mother and sister looking to him for their eventual support; he, too, had a kind father prepared to finance his training, though he would have far preferred his son to enter his own bookselling business. The journal he kept of his student days in London, later expanded into his classic autobiography, is as eloquent a commentary as could well exist on Branwell Brontë's lost opportunities.

The coach from Plymouth had barely deposited Haydon in the city than he started hunting for lodgings. To be near the Academy Schools he took a "second-floor" at No. 342 in the Strand. Without unpacking, he went straight to Somerset House to see the Exhibition of that year's paintings; then hurried to Drury Lane to buy a plaster cast of the Laocoon's head which, together with some hands, feet and arms, he bore back to his lodgings; unpacked his anatomy books "and before nine the next morning was hard at work, drawing from the round, studying Albinus his anatomy primer and breathing aspiration for 'High Art' and defiance to all opposition."

For three months he saw nothing but his books, his casts and his drawings. "My enthusiasm was immense, my devotion to study that of a martyr," he remembered. Only at the end of three months' intensive study of anatomy and the antique, did he deliver his first letter of introduction and show his drawings to Northcote, the illustrator and portraitist. They were so good that Haydon was at once sent to present himself to the Keeper of the Academy Schools, the great Fuseli, who ordered him in his broken English to attend the schools on "de first nights". The very next evening he went. Then began for Haydon three years of unremitting toil, but also of the greatest happiness. "Happy period!" he wrote of it in after years, "painting and living in one room—as independent as the wind —no servants—no responsibilities—reputation in the bud—hopes endless—ambition beginning—friends untried. . . ."

All day long the art students were either copying the Elgin Marbles, working from plaster-casts in their lodgings or, if in funds and the luck of the day sent a coal-heaver with "a fine muscular arm" to deliver coals in the house, engaging a model to make drawings "from the life", and every evening from 6 to 8 attending the Academy Schools. There the two porters, ex-guardsmen with splendid physiques, served as permanent models for the "Life" classes; and Fuseli savagely criticised their work in his guttural English, and keen students clubbed together, at a cost of two guineas each, to pay for an extra course of lectures in anatomy.

The daily round was not all grinding work. There were joyous meals at their ordinary in the Strand and occasional—very occasional —oyster-suppers at a student's lodgings to which all the others flocked and the talk was all of art, the opera and Drury Lane. They were all secretly working at a "masterpiece" in their lodgings and living in hopes that Sir George Beaumont, or some other wealthy connoisseur, might come to see their work and give them the longed-for commission for their first painting—an eventuality not at all so remote in those days of keen patronage. Portraits were commissioned at a fee of fifteen pounds; historical compositions or landscapes at anything from fifty guineas to a hundred and fifty pounds. It happened to Haydon—it had happened to William Robinson and to Leyland—as Branwell very well knew.

He took not one step towards entering that world which, now it was within his grasp, only repelled and frightened him. He neither delivered his letters of introduction nor went to show his specimen drawings at the Schools. The effort required was quite beyond him. He did not even write home to tell his family he had arrived.

On his third morning, he found himself "wending his way toward the central square, shrinking from introductions, and letting his letters slumber in his desk, and his friends remain in ignorance of his arrival". He went out with some definite objective of seeing some of the great buildings he had dreamed about, and written about, all his childhood and youth: "the Tower of All Nations" (the Tower of London), the two "Houses of the Twelves" (the Houses of Parliament, burned down in the previous October) and "St Michael's Cathedral" (St Paul's) "swelling its enormous dome into the cloudless sky". His reaction to St Paul's sums up the whole of his approach to London—he dared not enter it for fear of disappointment.

But after he had asked himself the reason of his hesitation and found it proceeded from instinctive fear of ending his pleasure by approaching reality . . . he dashed through the dread, walked up the grand flight of steps and soon found himself, hat in hand, pacing the marble pavement in the still shadow of coolness beneath the vast expanding roof and glorious dome. Standing upon the pavement immediately beneath this enormous concave, and gazing upward through a wide uninterrupted void of 450 ft, the effect to him was overpowering for the air . . . itself seemed to dissipate all harshness, left him nothing but the sublime to gaze on. He looked till to his dimmed eyes it seemed to rise and soar beyond his sight. He lay on the pavement and still looked till he thought it would thunder down in ruins on his head. . . . All was utterly still. The lonely mountain tops of Sneachie's Land could not be more sublimely solitary. Men might be in the Church but no one noticed another, and hundreds would not have dissolved the spell; and when the stunning crash of the great bell struck one at noon it did not so much break as yet more express the silence.

Wentworth lost the calculation of time while he was here gliding about as successively attracted to the Cupola, the nave, and the aisles. Then he stepped beneath the organ screen and entered the Choir, turning back upon the imposing front of gilded pipes above him and thence to the high, dark, aged mass near the altar whose gloomy and mysterious form attracted a nearer gaze . . .

This was the tomb of the Duke of York, his boyhood's hero, the "Frederick I, King of the Twelves" killed at the battle of Rossendale Hill, of their far-away "secret plays". No wonder the real world receded before the inner phantom world that he carried with him everywhere like his shadow. At the same time he was observing the dual nature of his experience with a perfectly detached sense.

Next day found him still unknown and unvisited, without participating in the splendours of wealth, no more than if he had not a pound in his pocket. Nor was he bent studiously on ransacking the great libraries or studying in the picture galleries. He was restlessly, aimlessly, and with the same anxious face feeding his feeling with "little squibs of rum", as he called them to himself, since he was perfectly aware that they would only the more depress him afterwards. But that evening, while walking from the eastern dock he struck into a new line of streets in the fashionable quarter of the city, and ere long found himself in a great square fronted by an enormous palace surrounded by columns which reached from base to pediment. He asked one passing, Whose residence was that? "It's Elrington Hall, to be sure then" . . . [Apsley House]. And forthwith he knelt down upon the lowest step of the portico and kissed the stones. Turning from Elrington Hall after looking and stopping to take in its soul, he hurried to Johnson's. . . . At midnight there came upon his mind the word ANTICIPATION and he remembered all his present feelings were those of anticipation. How anxious and impatient and incomplete was his greatest pleasure, and was it all there was to be? For those who possessed what he *thought about*, in reality, were they happy? Was Percy happy? And Zamorna? or Zenobia? If they were not, was there a hope of his being so?

At morning, he arose cast down and melancholy with these and such like reflections. Again the world looked futile and he spent that day without an aim till late in the afternoon, when at the east-end coffee house he noticed much bustle. . . .

The evening papers had arrived with their contradictory reports, foreshadowing further political upheavals. For Wentworth, his aimless visit to the metropolis was over. Using the prospect of impending elections for his excuse to return home the next day, "he hurried through the crowded and troubled streets, repaired to his hotel, dressed himself, took a coach, and drove to Lofty Square" [Trafalgar Square], the point of departure for the mail coach home.

According to Charles Wentworth's narration, he was no more than five days in London. Some further evidences of Branwell's actual visit would suggest that he stayed longer than that.

In his account of Charles Wentworth's use—or misuse—of his time, he left it to be supposed that all his evenings were spent miserably shut up in his room at the *Chapter Coffee House*, whereas in reality he spent some at least at the *Castle Tavern* in High Holborn. This he later confided to Leyland, whom he was to know intimately at Bradford in 1838, and to other friends. By a strange coincidence, also, Branwell's presence at the *Castle* was remarked by a fellow traveller, a Mr Woolven, an engineer from the north, soon to be in a key position on the new railways, who was so impressed with Branwell's eloquence as to recognise him after four years when chance threw them in each other's way again.

It was not chance that took Branwell to the *Castle* in High Holborn among so many hundreds of other taverns in London. It had for him an attraction, if not as sublime as St Paul's, as compelling at least, for it had been licensed since 1828 to no less a hero in Branwell's esteem than Tom Spring, the champion pugilist. Had the urge to meet and shake hands with so eminent a member of "the fancy" not impelled Branwell on his own account, it is certain that his Haworth cronies, with John Brown at their head, had impressed on him with their last farewells not to miss such an opportunity on any account.

As far back as he could remember Branwell had heard about Tom Spring (whose real though equally seasonal name was Winter). His encounter on Hinckley Down with the Bristol favourite, Neat, followed by two other victories in the same year, bringing him in prizes worth £1,000, had been commemorated in mock-heroic verse by William Maginn, in the July number of *Blackwood's* for 1823. Branwell's enthusiasm for Tom Spring, had it needed any justification as a gentlemanly hobby at a time when Lord Byron had brought pugilism into the fashion, had received further impetus from the admiration of John Wilson, the editor of *Blackwood's* himself, and its most genial contributor under the pseudonym of Christopher North.

Of Tom Spring since his retirement and establishment as Mine Host of that "Temple of the Fancy", the *Castle Tavern*, Branwell had read in the numbers of the sporting journal, *Bell's Life in London*, taken by Thomas Sugden, landlord of the *Black Bull*, and available to the members of the Haworth boxing club. Strangely enough, for Branwell Tom Spring's premises possessed a second attraction: they were much frequented by painters in search of models among retired, or merely disengaged, pugilists.

The old *Castle Tavern*, now disappeared, was situated on the north side of High Holborn, at No. 25, three doors down from the archway into Gray's Inn, and nearly opposite the opening of Chancery Lane. It had no frontage on the street but gave on to an inner courtyard, access to which was reached through a coach entrance. The pillared porticoes of London's West End that Branwell had always visualised as typical of Verdopolis gave place here to the narrow high premises dating back to the early or mid eighteenth century, occupied by small shops and warehouses.

The tavern had assumed a predominantly sporting flavour since the turn of the century, when a predecessor of Tom Spring's, the Lancashire pugilist Ben Gregson, had run it as a chop house.

He was such a fine figure of a man that he had been in great request as a model for both the Academicians and the students at the Academy Schools, sitting to Lawrence and being recommended

by the then teacher in anatomy, Mr Carlisle, as "a most excellent
subject".

Tom Spring himself was, according to the many accounts left
by his patrons and supporters, an equally striking-looking man,
standing 5 feet 11 inches, with a fine figure and remarkable face and
head. He had, long before his years of fame, been employed, like
Ben Gregson, by the Royal Academy, and bore a high character
for honesty and humanity.

Situated as the tavern was at a half-way position between the
east and west ends of the town, it attracted a very big clientele of
strangers to the capital with both sporting and artistic interests. To
meet Tom Spring himself, a former champion of England, to be
served by him and to shake his hand, was accounted a rare and
pleasurable experience. To be invited into the "Snug" behind his
bar, was a signal honour indeed, and one to be boasted of for ever
back in the provinces. Pierce Egan, writing in 1832 about Tom
Spring's establishment, had nothing but praise for it. It was, he
could vouch, "most respectably conducted. The appearance of
Mine Host is very much in his favour; there is a manly dignity about
his person that is prepossessing; his language is mild and perfectly
correct—he is truly civil and attentive to his customers." Altogether
it was Egan's opinion that "a night spent at Tom Spring's need not
be regretted by the most fastidious visitor."

Here Branwell came, and here, of all the places he saw and visited
in London, he alone felt at home. The evidence of his fellow visitor
there on at least one night, states that Branwell's "unusual flow of
language and strength of memory had so attracted the attention of
the spectators that they had made him umpire in some dispute
arising about the dates of certain celebrated battles . . .". Though
the gentleman had never met him before, both the subject and the
manner are recognisably Branwell, and go far to confirm Pierce
Egan's claims for the standard of conversation and clientele to be
found at the *Castle Tavern*.

The *Castle's* patrons were by no means all drawn from sporting
or even artistic circles. A great variety of original and interesting
characters assembled in the coffee room which, to quote Pierce Egan
again, "together with every part, was very attractive to the eye",
the walls being hung with sporting prints and etchings by Robert
Cruikshank. Here, "visitors from the country who had never
visited such houses and felt anxious to take a peep at the 'resort of

the Fancy' merely to see what it was like . . ." would find themselves "seated next an M.P. without being aware of that honour, or
rubbing against some noble lord"; they could hope to meet "poets
on the look out for a hero, boxers for customers and artists and
surgeons on the look out for 'subjects' ".

"Every Friday evening there is a most excellent Free-and-Easy
where some first-rate singing can be heard," continued Pierce Egan.
"Tom contributes himself to the harmony of the evening." Tom,
moreover, was a very charitable individual and encouraged acts of
charity in his customers. On many a Friday evening a collection
would be taken to help some particular case of distress, while the
habitués urged on the passing strangers to join in the chorus of one
of their favourite ditties:

> Then let us be merry,
> While drinking our sherry,
> For friendship and harmony can't last too long:
> Be still our endeavour
> That nothing shall sever
> The Lads of the Fancy, at the Castle so strong.

In this setting Branwell could be himself, revived by something
more than "little squibs of rum"; his tongue was at its most be-
guiling, his memory sharp and clear. In such society he shone. The
overpowering impact of London's size and noise was softened down
in Tom Spring's red-curtained parlour. His sense of inferiority to
everything and everyone his projected career would bring him into
contact with was forgotten in the warmth and cordiality of this
mixed company, where nothing but flattering attention was paid
to the eloquent and informed young man who could arbitrate on
matters of history. With plenty of money in his pockets for the
first time in his life, it is not surprising that, being the man he was,
he should spend it in Tom Spring's parlour, so reminiscent of the
Black Bull at Haworth, rather than in calling on his contacts and
testing his chances of acceptance at the Academy Schools.

Leyland, writing many years after Branwell's failure estimated
those chances as very poor, but it is impossible not to think that, had
his heart been in his work, he could have learned, as Haydon did
before him, the mechanics of his art, and overcome those deficiencies
that were due only to want of training.

Face to face with the masterpieces of Reynolds, Gainsborough
and Lawrence, he realised the hopelessness of trying to compete

with them. To emulate them even from afar, meant drudgery—and madly as he admired, indiscriminately as he praised the wonders of painting, he knew quite well that he lacked the one requisite for achieving anything by it himself—the force of character to pursue any objective to its end.

Late in his visit to the Great Verdopolis, he roamed through the exhibitions and galleries; he went to the British Museum; he saw the Elgin Marbles. There was nothing there for him. The proximity of such unattainable perfection only acted like an irritant on his nerves —those poor nerves that could not stand the "rocking-boat" of his boyhood without screaming. Without delivering a single one of his letters of introduction, without attempting to seek the advice of men truly competent by their position and experience to help him, he turned his back on it all and fled home.

Being Branwell, his loss in retrospect would take on a truly tragic tone. What he had rejected, having the occasion to possess, he would deplore later as an unattainable dream. Writing to Leyland in 1847, after the last of his desires had been frustrated, he recalled those wasted opportunities. "I shall never be able to realise the too sanguine hopes of my friends, . . ." he wrote. "I used to think that if I could have for a week the free range of the British Museum—the library included—I could feel as though I were placed for seven days in Paradise, but now, really, dear Sir, my eyes would roam over the Elgin Marbles, the Egyptian saloon and the most treasured volumes like the eyes of a dead cod fish."

The seven days had been his—and the truth was they had been Hell.

The grand adventure was over—the one real opportunity of his life to get away from the predominantly feminine regime of home, from the "uncouth society" of his village, from the authority of his father, from all those things for which Branwell Brontë has been pitied by successive biographers—and without which, he now found he could not live. He had had his chance—London, the world of art, the stimulating society of intellectual equals, he could have had it all, but he preferred otherwise.

Chapter Ten

"MISERY"

The worst problem facing him as the coach bore him northwards was how to explain what had happened, how to present his tale with any prospect of being believed. There was not only his father to face, but his teacher William Robinson, who would be better placed even than anyone at home to put his finger on discrepancies in Branwell's story. Robinson knew the London to which Branwell had gone and the characters of the men to whom he should have presented himself. To reward Robinson's kindness by owning that he had neglected all his advice, and wasted all his efforts to get him known in the right quarters, was a worse ordeal in some ways than to placate the elders at home. *They* might easily be put off with a cock-and-bull story. For, if one thing becomes apparent from this time on, it is that Branwell's sense of guilt makes a liar of him.

He came back without any money. What he told his astonished father and aunt, and what shortly ran like wildfire through the village, was that "before he had really reached the City he had fallen a prey to 'sharpers' and been robbed of most of his money". In this form the tale reached Ellis Chadwick many years later, through Haworth folk who still remembered that deplorable return. Pity for Branwell's inexperience, rather than disapproval of his wasted opportunities, was the first reaction to his tale. That his family gradually guessed something of the truth, that his London journey eventually appeared to them in its true aspect of moral failure, is apparent from the absolute silence in which they passed it over. No direct reference to it can be found in the Brontë correspondence of the time, nor in any later statement of theirs. Branwell might, for all the evidence supplied by his family, never have gone to London at all. By their reticence alone the magnitude of their disappointment can be measured, the first major disappointment suffered on his behalf. Yet it was rather a disappointment *for* Branwell than a disappointment *in* Branwell as yet.

He found the family much depleted on his return. Only Emily of his sisters was there: Charlotte and Anne were away at school until Christmas.

It may have been as well for Branwell that it happened to be Emily who was at home, for Emily could understand his predicament if anybody in the family could. She had just, herself, suffered a mortifying failure at Roe Head and fled home on an impulse of self-preservation, different in degree but not in nature, from his. It was not work that daunted Emily, but the removal from surroundings essential to her nature.

It may well be that in that first association of brother and sister, there was formed that closeness of understanding and tolerance which united Emily to Branwell in his direst need at the end of his life.

It did not save him from suffering intensely as the realisation of his failure was borne in on him. The poem written those autumn days and called by him "Misery I" strikes a genuinely desperate note, quite new in his writing.

Before it was finished he received yet another blow, which, though it struck him under different circumstances from his London experience, hurt him perhaps even more, in that he really cared more about writing than about painting.

On 21st November 1835 there died James Hogg, "the Ettrick Shepherd", an event which, while reviving all his childhood's passion for *Blackwood's*, stirred Branwell to a sudden burst of hope and energy. He imagined himself capable of assuming the succession of Hogg on the staff of *Blackwood's*, and sat down to write the editor an offer of his services. The letter remained unanswered. He wrote a second to which, like the first, no reply came. On 7th December he wrote yet again, a letter which has been preserved and whose whole tenor is evidence of the mental commotion into which his successive frustrations had thrown him. More than any acknowledgment of failure, its extravagant claims to literary merit are a declaration of failure. It is the crescendo of the shriek of an ignored child frantically striving to draw attention to himself.

"Sir," it abruptly begins, "read what I write."

And would to Heaven you could believe it true, for then you would attend to and act upon it.

I have addressed you twice before, and now I do it again. But it is not from affected hypocrisy that I commence my letter with the name of James Hogg; for the writings of that man in your numbers, his speeches in your "Noctes", when I was a child, laid a hold on my mind which succeeding years have consecrated into a most sacred feeling. I cannot express, though you can understand, the heavenliness of associations connected with such articles as Professor Wilson's, read and re-read while a little child, with all their poetry of language and divine flights into that visionary region of imagination which one very young would believe reality, and which one entering into manhood would look back on as a glorious dream. I speak so, sir, because while a child, "Blackwood's" formed my chief delight, and I feel certain that no child before enjoyed reading as I did, because none ever had such works as "The Noctes", "Christmas Dreams", "Christopher in his Sporting Jacket", to read. . . . Passages like these, sir, passages like these, read then and remembered now, afford feelings which, I repeat, I cannot describe. But—one of those who roused those feelings is dead, and neither from himself nor yourself shall I hear him speak again. I grieve for his death, because to me he was a portion of feelings which I suppose nothing can arouse hereafter: because to you he was a contributor of sterling originality, and in the "Noctes" a subject for your unequalled writing. He and others like him gave your Magazine the peculiar character which made it famous; as these men die it will decay unless their places be supplied by others like them. Now, sir, to you I appear writing with conceited assurance: but *I am not*; for I know myself so far as to believe in my own originality, and on that ground I desire of you admittance into your ranks. And do not wonder that I apply so determinedly: for the remembrances I spoke of have fixed you and your Magazine in such a manner upon my mind that the idea of striving to aid another periodical is *horribly repulsive*. My resolution is to devote my ability to you, and for God's sake, till you see whether or not I can serve you, do not so coldly refuse my aid. All, sir, that I desire of you is—that you would in answer to this letter request a specimen or specimens of my writing, and I even wish that you would name the subject on which you would wish me to write. In letters previous to this I have perhaps spoken too openly respecting the extent of my powers. But I did so because I determined to say what I believed. I *know* that I am not one of the wretched writers of the day. I know that I possess strength to assist you beyond some of your own contributors; but I wish to make you the judge in this case and give you the benefit of its decision.

Now, sir, do not act like a commonplace person, but like a man willing to examine for himself. Do not turn from the naked truth of my letters, but *prove me*—and if I do not stand the proof, I will not farther press myself on you. If I do stand it—why—You have lost an able writer in James Hogg, and God grant you you may gain one in

Patrick Branwell Bronte.
Haworth, near Bradford,
Yorks, December (7th) 1835

The Editor of "Blackwood's Magazine".

Mrs Oliphant, employed in the publishing firm of *Blackwood's* shortly after the period of Branwell's correspondence with it, regretted the callous silence with which all his communications were met, but she was told they were considered the letters of a madman and only kept in the files as a curiosity.

The emotional range of the poem "Misery I" (finished 18th

December 1835) and of its immediate sequels, "Misery II" (2nd March 1836), "Memory" (July 1836), "Still and bright, in twilight shining" (August 1836), "Sleep, mourner, sleep!" (January 1837), "Well, I will lift my eyes once more" (February 1837), and "Alone she paced her Ancient Hall" (March 1837), which led up to the "Harriet" poems and "Caroline" sequence of 1837-8, is far in advance of anything attempted yet by Branwell. He had suffered, and, in flashes of truth piercing the fustian rhetoric, the sincerity of his suffering comes through.

The poems represent his first serious attempt at philosophic speculation. He is aware that he has reached a point in his existence from which a review is possible of the path by which he has come, and a first sight afforded of the one he may have to take. His strongest sense of the moment is one of complete loss of direction; over and above all the frustration and shame, it is that feeling which is the predominant source of his anguish in returning from London. Where, he cries, looking down the vistas radiating before him, where is he to go?

That at this precise moment of acute mental depression he should associate the memory of his first great loss—the death of his sister Maria—with his present pain, is hardly surprising. After the total suppression of that initial grief—the unbroken silence of almost a dozen years—that the ghost of Maria should rise from the depths of his consciousness was only natural and to be expected. As though she personified the total weight of his sorrows, her gentle image ranges through passage after passage of his prose and verse of the next few years, sometimes directly evoked by name, at other times disguised, as in the "Harriet" and "Caroline" sequences, sometimes transposed upon the Angrian scene as in the numerous accounts of the death of Mary Percy, but always she is shown as standing at the heart of his desolation, as the prime cause of all his suffering.

The Maria-theme of these poems, interwoven as it is with the subject of defeat, loss of direction and simple loss of all wish to live, leads quite naturally to the subject of death, and through death to judgment and damnation. In this sequence of poems which reached their culmination in "Sir Henry Tunstall" (which for many reasons may be considered his finest achievement) Branwell examines his religious position and receives scant comfort from it. Yearning as his heart would ever do after Maria, the sense of the gulf between

John Brown, from the portrait by Branwell Brontë

"—Old Knave of Trumps—"

The Lodge of the Three Graces, Haworth

them makes him wish for obliteration rather than for eternity, since to survive death can only mean relegation to outer darkness for him, excluded as he must ever be from the presence of her perfection. This is unadulterated Calvinism.

Though Branwell would cast off the teachings of his aunt more absolutely than any of his sisters, and for reasons far less edifying than theirs, the hold of Calvinism on him would not be broken lightly or without enormous cost. Possessed as none of his sisters could ever be with an acute sense of personal sin, for Branwell there was a kind of voluptuous delight in ensuring his damnation that was not merely Byronic plagiarism but the effect of genuine perversion. In lines of a newly-acquired power and pungency, he reviews what is lost in "Misery I".

> I thought just now that Life or Death
>   Could never trouble me,
> That I should draw my future breath
>   In silent apathy,
> That o'er the pathway of my fate
> Though steady beat the storm,
> As I walked alone and desolate
> I'd to that path conform.
> Affection should not cherish me,
> Or sorrow hold me down,
> But Despair itself sustain me,
> Whom itself had overthrown.
> I know that fame and glory
> Were names for shame and woe,
> That life's deceitful story
> I had finished long ago,
> That all its novelty was gone,
> And that thus to read again
> The same dull page in the same sad tone
> Was not even change of pain . . . .

The resurgence of Maria in the poems of this period was gradual. In "Misery I", where the physical details of her death-bed are enumerated as if for a rehearsal of the complete performance given in the "Caroline" sequence, the theme is subject to the over-riding one of defeat.

The protagonist of the poem is a Lord Albert, sole survivor from a bloody battle, who rides by night back to his castle where his beloved one waits. Branwell, for the first time, is writing with artistry and power, with a painter's eye for the telling detail.

I

How fast that courser fleeted by,
His arched neck backward tossed on high,
His snorting nostrils opened wide,
His foam-flecked chest and gory side. . . .

Intermittently the light from the tower in which the beloved one
lies breaks through the darkness of the forest trees; it is the recollection of her that alone supports him.

Defeat has crushed me in the dust,
But only laid my head
Where head and heart and spirit must
Be soon for ever laid.
My fearless followers all were slain,
My power and glory gone,
. . . I am now alone!
Not so! I thought it till that light
Glanced glittering down the glen,
And on my spirit's dreary night
Flashed brighter back again.
Yes! I had thought I stood alone,
That I need sigh or weep for none,
Had quenched my love in apathy,
Since none could sigh or weep for me.
Yes! But the single silver beam
Which flashes in my eye
Hath waked me from my dreary dream
And bade my darkness fly;
But pardon that the storms of woe
Have whelmed me in a drifting sea,
With death and dangers struggling so
That I, a while, forgot even THEE.
The moment that I gained the shore,
And clouds began to disappear,
Even steadier, brighter than before,
Thou shinest, my own—my Guardian Star!
Oh could I speak the long lost feeling,
The inward joy its Power revealing,
The glimpse of something yet to come
Which yet shall give a happy Home,
Oh should I speak my thoughts of thee
Whom soon again my eyes shall see,
The dove that bore the olive leaf
Could never bring such glad relief
To wanderers o'er the hopeless main
As in my weariness and pain
That single light hath given to me. . . .

Here appears for the first time the "leitmotiv" of the evening, or "Guardian Star", and of the dove with the olive branch, which would constantly recur in the following years whenever his dead sister Maria was the subject of a poem. For Branwell these symbols represented her both in the beauty and the peace they evoked, as in a kind of eloquence with which he imbued them as *speaking* directly from her.

In "Misery II" he takes up the simile:

> Can I forget how toward my eye
> Still ever gazed, for guidance, thine,
> As if I were thy star on high,
> Though well I knew 'twas thou wert mine.
> That azure eye, that softened smile,
> That heavenly voice whose tones to me
> The weariest wintriest hours could wile
> And make me think that still might be
> Some years of happiness with thee;
> That thou, amid my life to come,
> Shouldst be my hope, my heaven, my home. . . .

And again from "Misery II":

> . . . When general darkness clouds the day,
> That single star amid the sky
> Will shed a brighter light on high,
> And in the horizon only one
> Is yet the ALL that can be shewn.
> Well o'er me shining let it be
> That thus one glimmering I may see
> Fixed far above to show my gloom
> And light my spirit to its Tomb!

The terrified child, understanding nothing of the funeral rites performed over his "sunny-haired sister", knowing only that the grave was dark and deep under the cold flags, survives in the baffled man who questions in vain the message of the heavens.

In "Misery II" and in "Harriet II", the important poems of the following year, Branwell referred constantly to the terrors of judgment and damnation from which, for all his cynicism, he had neither his sister Anne's force of character nor her light of faith to shake himself free.

> Oh, how my eyes have stretched to see that land!
> . . . Have strained its mysteries to understand.
> . . . Though those vast waves which bear such thousands thither

Have never brought again one spirit hither . . .
Oh might I send across yon sea that Dove
Which bore the Olive Branch! Oh might it bear
From thence some token, reward my hovering here,
Even though it were the fruit of bitterness,
So I might cease this doubt and fearfulness
While I embark to sail—I know not where.

And again, in lines strangely reminiscent of Anne's, he cried:

Where is the rest beyond the tomb?
Where are the joys of his heavenly home? . . .
God, if there be a God, look down,
Compassionate my call!
Oh! clear away thine awful frown,
Oh! hearken to my call!—

("Misery II")

It is the same cry, directly addressed to Maria in "Misery II":

But we are sundered . . .
I must never look on thee—
If there's no God, no Heaven, no Hell,
Thou within thy grave must dwell
I, left blackening in the storm—
Both a banquet for the worm—
If there is a Heaven above,
Thou in bliss art shining there . . .
   Angel bright and angel fair . . .
                    While I stayed where
. . . Hell's dread night must close my day.

And again, in the same poem:

Nay, all is lost. I cannot bear
In mouldering dust to disappear,
And Heaven will not the gloom dispel—
Since were there one, my home were Hell—
No Hope, no Hope, and oh, farewell
The form so long kept treasured here. . . .

The sense of guilt apparent here and, shortly, to be personified in the figure of Henry Hastings, is one of the strongest and most frequently recurring themes of the prose and poetry of the two years following his London failure.

Harriet (another transposition of the Maria figure), in the poem called "Harriet II", voices the age-old terror and the new despair now obsessing him.

'Tis not the agony of death
That chills my breast and chokes my breath—
. . . Oh no!—'Tis something far more dread
Which haunts me on my dying bed!—
I have lost—long lost—my trust in Thee!
I cannot hope that Thou wilt hear
The unrepentant sinner's prayer!
So, whither must my spirit flee
For succour through Eternity? . . .

The agony of doubt from which Branwell suffered now, and by which both Charlotte and Anne would in their turn be tortured, could be known only to children brought up as the Brontës had been. Not lightly did Branwell throw over the tenets in which he had been reared and whose acceptance was as the corner-stone of family life at the parsonage. Not the least of his predicaments at this time was to feel himself so utterly adrift from the sheet-anchor to which the family bark was bound.

"Eternity!"—he cries, "Oh, were there none!
Could I believe what some believe,
Soon might my spirit cease to grieve
At the cold grave and churchyard stone!
But—God!—To appear before Thy face
In all a sinner's nakedness,
Without one little hour to spare
To make that sinner's grief more fair,
Without the slightest power to shun
Thine Eye whose lightning looks upon
All things I've thought and deeds I've done. . . ."

Whereas the great strength of his sisters would lie in their very power to transcend all limitation of faith and form when the moment of doubt assailed them, and to stretch out fearlessly like eagles to the light—towards a greater truth by which to live and die —Branwell had neither the range of intellect nor the heart of fire to raise him out of the dust into the light of day. His imagination could offer in place of the fires of Hell, nothing but the darkness of obliteration.

Transposed upon the Angrian scene, the terrors of Harriet, who has sacrificed her God for the "guilty love" of Percy, are patently those felt by Branwell, come, in that year of failure, to a parting of the ways.

The sense of being cut adrift, inspiring such a poem as "My ancient ship upon my Ancient sea" (written in July 1836, and describing Zamorna, defeated and exiled, leaving the known regions of his Angrian kingdom), was one of the deep-rooted causes of his revolt against religion and the accepted order of things. Increasingly Branwell would take sides with the outlaw figure of his own Northangerland, now in the political ascendant and piling crime upon crime in defiance of all law. To defiance would be added cynicism, and to cynicism boastfulness of the very deeds for which his conscience tormented him—a truly Byronic state, and one for which Branwell had no natural affinities at all. The tenor of all his writings, during these two years of rapid mental growth, is one of vacillation and weakness, immeasurably removed from the diamond-hard purpose of the Byronic prototype.

The defiant note, ushering in his new favourite hero, Henry Hastings, is struck in the resumed "History of Angria" with which he opened the year 1836.

This is the first of January 1836, and it is New Year's Day. Truly, Readers, to you and to me and to All Africa it is a New Year. Must I alter the word and say a New Era. The future alone can determine that. But the present seems strongly to indicate it most certainly our Native Land was never in so tremendous a darkness before with so many Elements of Discord so thoroughly stirred up— And Wrongs inflicted and Tyranny exercised and . . . courage roused upon so mighty a scale—

But I am writing not a History of my nation but describing my own prospects of and experiences in it therefore I may well ask—and what is this new year to me?

Branwell's own prospects did not keep pace with his writing and indeed appeared to have come to a complete standstill. For the whole of 1836 and for most of 1837 he remained at home. That no concrete plan was in preparation for anything different, is shown by his admission to the local Freemasons' Lodge whose minutes for these two years give evidence of his assiduous attendance at their meetings.

He was proposed as a Brother on 1st February 1836 and accepted; initiated on 29th February, passed on 28th March and installed full member on 25th April. The fact that he was so accepted when still considerably under the requisite age (he had just turned eighteen the previous June) was a concession due, doubtless, to the fact that his father's sexton, and his own particular crony, John Brown, was Worshipful Master of the Lodge; and his father's parish clerk, Joseph Redman, its secretary.

Branwell attended eleven meetings of the Lodge in 1836; on one occasion (13th September) he acted as secretary and entered the minutes and on another (20th December), performed the duties of "Junior Warden". During 1837 he entered the minutes of seven meetings and acted as organist for the Masons' Christmas Day Service.

That the Haworth Masons were flattered at counting their parson's son among their members is obvious; his education and musical abilities could stand them in good stead; but the gesture was also one of solidarity and kindness extended to Branwell at a moment of signal distress. It was both intended, and understood, to raise him in local estimation. Whatever his subsequent follies and disasters, his popularity with his fellow-villagers never waned. In estimating his final failure, it must never be forgotten that Haworth took him to its heart as it never took any of his sisters, except possibly Charlotte at the very end.

It has often been asserted that Branwell's "village gossips" were men of the lowest order and directly responsible for debauching him. Among the members of Haworth Lodge, "The Three Graces", who represented a good cross-section of professional classes and upper tradesmen, Branwell was, as a matter of fact, among as decent a group as he was likely to find in the district. As Leyland reminds us, "Masons were pledged to high moral principles". The old accusations when examined are found to have very little basis in fact. As an example: Branwell's early addiction to drink has been imputed to the fact that meetings of the Lodge took place at the *Black Bull*, whereas ever since 4th February 1833, and all through Branwell's membership, the Lodge meetings were held in premises of its own in a private house, and only the annual dinner on St John's Day (26th December) continued to be held at the *Bull*.

The Masonic meetings were held in a new house in a little street, known yet today as Lodge Street, just off Main Street, where a room was rented at £4 per annum from a family of the name of Eccles (still resident in Haworth today), and "furnished with a carpet, chairs and the usual fittings and regalia of a private Masonic Lodge". Considering the period and the region—the West Riding of Yorkshire in the thirties—it is unthinkable that the evenings passed off without potations, and, indeed, the acquisition of a piano, very certainly played upon by Branwell, was recorded as allowing of "songs and toasts" becoming a regular feature of the meetings. But, in the main, it seems only fair to say that Branwell's connection with the Lodge helped rather to keep him out of mischief than to plunge him further in it. His peculiar tragedy was that the seeds of his destruction were laid in himself and need not be sought outside.

In the last analysis, had the Haworth Lodge had a bad reputation or an obvious ill effect on Branwell, Mr Brontë would not have countenanced its activities as he did. The records remain of his being feed to preach a sermon (10s) on the occasion of the opening of the Lodge's premises in February 1833. A procession formed of brethren from all the neighbouring Lodges, one hundred and twenty strong, paraded to St Michael's, dressed in the insignia of their order —white gloves, aprons and regalia—and were headed by the famous Keighley Band engaged at a fee of 30s. The bells of Haworth Church were rung and singers specially engaged for a comprehensive fee of 4s.

Among its more overt activities the Lodge founded a "Sick and Death Benefit Society" with a yearly premium of 10s for its members for which a sick benefit of 5s a week up to £20 could be received.

Dating from before his London visit, but continuing after it as well, was Branwell's appointment as secretary to the local Temperance Society of which his father was President. The appointment, arising from his double suitability as his father's son and one of the more literate villagers, however surprising it may be, is but another indication of his interest in local matters—an interest which would only have been heightened by his recent realisation that London was not for him. The fact remains that, in whatever light his London failure was seen at home, an effort was obviously made by family and friends alike, to help Branwell rise above that failure, by giving him a sense of widening responsibilities.

It is, perhaps, surprising to learn that, like Charlotte, he taught in the Sunday School. He was chiefly remembered afterwards for his violent temper and impatience. The slow droning reading of his scholars put him into a passion and many a time he could hardly keep his hands off the boys. They were not impressed by his tantrums and on one occasion that he screamed at a pupil to "Get on! Get on! or I'll turn you out of the class!" the unruffled pupil stared at him and slowly articulated: "Tha willn't, tha old Irish ——" and slowly picking himself out of his desk, took his own departure from the school.

The same witness, an old pupil of Branwell's, recalls that immediately after Sunday School the boys were marched to church, where they occupied one of the big box-pews under the north gallery. Branwell sat with them but retired to a corner of the pew close to the window "where he read with avidity during the service some book which was not the Prayer-Book. If any of us disturbed him," continued the witness, "he was very cross. He would come to the interrupter, and, turning a lock of the lad's hair round his finger, he would lift the offender from the floor and finish by giving him a sharp rap with his knuckles. . . ."

If village life provided his only background for the time, Haworth was—and is—an unpredictable village with unexpected facets to the smooth front it presents to the world, and, wherever the surface stirred, Branwell was sure to be at the centre of agitation.

From 1835 to 1836 Mr Brontë had a curate to help him—a Mr Hodgson—who lodged in the village, and whose son-in-law had later the following story to tell to Clement Shorter. Mr Hodgson was troubled by ghostly visitations in his lodgings which were in a house at the beginning of West Lane. The ghost had, among other propensities, "an unpleasant habit of disturbing him at night. He slept in one of the old four-posters which had an understructure of sacking. . . . When he got comfortably settled the bed would begin to heave as though someone underneath were uplifting it, but nothing could be seen. This fact he communicated to Branwell Brontë who was very sceptical on the subject. . . ." Mr Hodgson asked him to test the truth of his tale by coming and spending a night at his lodgings. Branwell might make a show of scepticism to a partial stranger but there was nothing in reality which had a stronger hold on his romantic mind than just such a manifestation as this, and he accepted Mr Hodgson's challenge with alacrity.

"He came," the narrator continues, "and took every precaution for excluding anyone from entering the room after they were in it. He closely examined the room in every way, and satisfied himself that no one was there but themselves. He locked and bolted the door and securely fastened the windows. But they had not been long in bed before the upheaving began. One night's experience was quite enough for Branwell, and he would not renew it. . . ."

This was a period of prolonged separation from Charlotte, who remained as teacher at Miss Wooler's school from July 1835 to May 1838, Anne remaining with her until the Christmas of 1837. While brother and sister moved inevitably apart in a widening moral rift of which Branwell was naturally more aware than Charlotte, their old literary collaboration remained strangely unimpaired.

The theme of the death of Mary Percy, wife of Zamorna, treated by Branwell in verse and prose with varying detail, aroused in Charlotte a frenzy of excitement which she could only calm by confiding in the sporadic journal she kept at Roe Head. "About a week since I got a letter from Branwell," she wrote in October 1836, "containing a most exquisitely characteristic epistle from Northangerland for his daughter [Mary Percy]. It is astonishing what a soothing and delightful tone that letter seemed to speak. I lived on its contents for days—in every pause of employment—it came chiming in like some sweet bar of music bringing with it agreeable thoughts such as I had for many weeks been a stranger to. . . ." And again, a little later: "I wonder if Branwell has really killed the Duchess [of Zamorna]. Is she dead, is she buried, is she alone in the cold earth on this dreary night with the ponderous gold coffin plate on her breast under the black pavement of a Church in a vault closed up with lime and mortar . . .? I hope she's alive still, partly because I can't abide to think how hopelessly and cheerlessly she must have died, and partly because her removal if it has taken place, must have been to Northangerland the quenching of the last spark that averted utter darkness. . . ."

In Part VIII of his "History of Angria", dated 19th September 1836, and written a few days before Charlotte's journal entry, Branwell had, in fact, anticipated her queries, by killing the Duchess of Zamorna.

Her father, Alexander Percy, Earl of Northangerland, is brought to her death-bed at the moment of his greatest triumph against Zamorna, now driven from his capital Adrienopolis and exiled overseas.

This chamber of death was opened now in all its dreary magnificence, lofty and airy, but hung and fashioned with velvet so dark as to seem shadowy in despite of the softly shining silver lamps that glistened from their white marble pedestals and centred their radiance on the bed where lay the shadow rather than the substance of the forsaken wife and crownless Queen. Over her the vast festoons of drapery hung from the coronetted tester as if even they were mourning. . . . Above them and right opposite Mary's eyes, a wide and lofty arch opened sublimely to the sky, its curtains were drawn aside to display the full extent of waste midnight heaven and sad struggling moon. . . . Here was the principal figure, cold white and wasted, supported by a pile of pillows. . . . All the once rich auburn curls were fallen back, and parted in long locks from her brow which, with her cheeks and lips, was stricken with the glistening light of death. . . .

The scene, directly inspired by his memories of Maria was so dramatically described by Branwell, and with such accompanying detail of stage properties, that Charlotte was able to illustrate it in a water-colour sketch still preserved at the Brontë Parsonage Museum. Its relevance to the prose passage above and to such passages in the poems as the following, becomes apparent when the texts and the drawing can be compared. In "Misery I" we read:

> Lo, on that stately couch alone
> Reclines thy Lady fair.
> But—cold and pale is her marble brow
> Dishevelled her sunny hair. . . .

In "Well! I will lift my eyes once more" the scene has become theatrically more contrived. Here she dies soliloquising upon the westering sun.

> What pleasant airs upon her face
> With freshening coolness play,
> As they would kiss each transient grace
> Before it fades away;
> And backward rolled each deep red fold
> Begirt with tasselled cords of gold
>   The Open Arch displays.
> O'er towers and trees that orb divine
> His own unclouded light decline
> Before her glist'ning gaze.
>
> On pillows raised, her drooping head
> Confronts his glorious beam,
> And all her tresses backward strayed
>   Look golden in the gleam,
> But her wan lips and sunken cheek
> And full eyes eloquently speak
> Of sorrows gathering near,
> Till those dark orbs o'erflowing fast
> Are shadowed by her hand at last.
> To hide the streaming tear. . . .

In "Harriet II" the description is taken further:

> The curtain drawn obscured her lying,
> But all distinct each window pane
> Was starting into form again . . .
> So back I drew the curtain shade,
> And started at the noise I made.
> There, then, her gentle cheek declined;
> All white her neck and shoulders gleamed,
> White as the bed where they reclined. . . .

In his prose description of the death of Mary Percy, Branwell introduces a sentiment of revolt quite unknown and even alien to the remote figure of his sister Maria, but which looks forward startlingly to the sentiment expressed on another death-bed and written by a very different hand. Like Catherine Earnshaw, Mary Percy's heaven is *not* elsewhere and is bounded by a purely earthly love.

"This is the end of a child of earth," wrote Branwell of her, "all whose soul and spirit were rooted in earth and perishing on being torn away from it." Her thoughts were expressed plainly by her a day or two before this time, "It does not matter where I am going, I know I am going and I know from whom I am going." It is surely not fanciful to see in this text the influence of his sister Emily, even then, during their relative isolation together at this period, unconsciously infusing into his weakness something of her strength.

That literature was still the strongest lure of his life, stronger than art, is seen by the quantity of his output during this period: eight parts of his "History of Angria" and a large body of verse; by his renewed attack on the fortress of *Blackwood's* in April 1836 and again in January 1837; and by his direct approach to Wordsworth immediately afterwards (19th January 1837). To both he sent examples of his recent work (to *Blackwood's* he sent "Misery", to Wordsworth the pointedly philosophic poem "Still and bright, in twilight shining"), appealing to them, in the role of arbiters "from whose sentence there is no appeal", to pronounce once and for all whether he should "write on, or write no more". The violent and ill-mannered tone of both communications brought their own inevitable and cruel reward—the silence of contempt.

The letter to *Blackwood's*, written 8th April 1836, reads:

Sir, Read now at least . . .

The affair which accompanies my letter is certainly sent for insertion in "Blackwood's" as a *Specimen* which, whether bad or good, I earnestly desire you to look over; it may be disagreeable, but you will then KNOW whether, in putting it into the fire, you would gain or lose. It would now be impudent in me to speak of my powers, since in five minutes you can tell whether or not they are fudge and nonsense. But this I know, that if they are such, I have no intention of stooping under them. New powers I will get if I can, and provided I keep them, you, sir, shall see them.

But don't think, sir, that I write nothing but Miseries. My day is far too much in the morning for such continual shadow. Nor think either (and this I entreat) that I wish to deluge you with poetry. I send it because it is soonest read and comes from the heart. If it goes *to* yours, print it, and write to me on the subject of *contribution*. Then I will send prose. But if what I now send is worthless, what I have said has only been conceit and folly, yet CONDEMN NOT UNHEARD.

> P. B. Bronte,
> Haworth, nr. Bradford, Yorkshire.

The second letter, written nine months later and begging for a personal interview—*Blackwood's* offices were, of course, in Edinburgh—shows the longing for a decision, even a negative decision, to be reached.

Dated 9th January 1837 it reads:

In a former letter I hinted that I was in possession of something, the design of which, whatever might be its execution, would be superior to that of any series of articles which has yet appeared in "Blackwood's Magazine". But being prose, of course, and of great length, as well as peculiar in character, a description of it by letter would be quite impossible. So surely a journey of three hundred miles shall not deter me from a knowledge of myself and a hope of utterance into the open world.

Now, sir, all I ask of you is to permit this interview, and in answer to this letter to say that you will see me, were it only for one half-hour. The fault be mine if you have reason to repent your permission.

Now, is the trouble of writing a single line to outweigh the certainty of doing good to a fellow-creature and the possibility of doing good to yourself? Will you still so wearisomely refuse me a word when you can neither know what you refuse nor whom you are refusing? Do you think your Magazine so perfect that no addition to its power would be either possible or desirable? Is it pride which actuates you—or custom—or prejudice? Be a man, Sir! and think no more of these things. *Write* to me: tell me that you will receive a visit; and rejoicingly will I take upon myself the labour, which if it succeed, will be an advantage both to you and me, and if it fail, will still be an advantage, because I shall then be assured of the impossibility of succeeding.

After ten days of anxious waiting for the answer that never came, he wrote to Wordsworth on 19th January 1837—

Sir,
I most earnestly entreat you to read and pass your judgment upon what I have sent you, because from the day of my birth to this the nineteenth year of my life I have lived among secluded hills, where I could neither know what I was or what I could do. I read for the same reason that I ate or drank, because it was a real craving of nature. I wrote on the same principle as I spoke—out of the impulse and feelings of the mind; nor could I help it, for what came, came out, and there was the end of it. For as to self-conceit, that could not receive food from flattery, since to this hour not half-a-dozen people in the world know that I have ever penned a line.

But a change has taken place now, sir; and I am arrived at an age wherein I must do something for myself; the powers I possess must be exercised to a definite end, and as I don't know them myself I must ask others what they are worth. Yet there is not one here to tell me; and still, if they are worthless, time will henceforth be too precious to be wasted on them.

Do pardon me, sir, that I have ventured to come before one whose works I have most loved in our literature, and who most has been with me a divinity of the mind, laying before him one of my writings, and asking of him a judgment of its contents. I must come before some one from whose sentence there is no appeal; and such a one is he who has developed the theory of poetry as well as its practice, and both in such a way as to claim a place in the memory of a thousand years to come.

My aim, sir, is to push out into the open world, and for this I trust not poetry alone; that might launch the vessel, but could not bear her on. Sensible and scientific prose, bold and vigorous efforts in my walk of life, would give a further title to the notice of the world; and then again poetry ought to brighten and crown that name with glory. But nothing of all this can be ever begun without means, and as I don't possess these I must in every shape strive to gain them. Surely, in this day, when there is not a *writing* poet worth a sixpence, the field must be open, if a better man can step forward.

What I send you is the Prefatory Scene of a much longer subject, in which I have striven to develop strong passions and weak principles struggling with a high imagination and acute feelings, till, as youth hardens towards age, evil deeds and short enjoyments end in mental misery and bodily ruin. Now, to send you the whole of this would be a mock upon your patience; what you see does not even pretend to be more than the description of an imaginative child. But read it, sir; and, as you would hold a light to one in utter darkness—as you value your own kind-heartedness—*return* me an *answer*, if but one word, telling me whether I should write on, or write no more. Forgive undue warmth, because my feelings in this matter cannot be cool; and believe me, sir, with deep respect, your really humble servant.

P. B. Bronte.

It was hardly the letter to invite sympathy from the receiver, but one cannot help wondering what Branwell's destiny might have been if someone of the standing and authority of Wordsworth had held out a helping hand. The scorn with which all his advances were met only heightened his vanity and self-centredness, and hardened his vacillating heart. So much of what was naturally lovable in his nature, his enthusiasm, his impulsiveness, his very naïveté, was petrified by the cold stare of the world. From now on he would evolve in the image of his own Northangerland, at war with society, but neither strong enough nor purposeful enough to achieve anything but irremediable harm to himself and to his family.

He was already taking on the definitive characteristics by which he would ultimately be known: increasingly shiftless as the winds of

chance buffeted him in contrary directions; hiding his deep unhappiness below a surface of scepticism and his unworldliness under
a show of depravity; drowning his want of direction in whatever
opiate offered—drink, and before very long, drugs. By the age of
twenty the distinctly Branwellian qualities would be developed from
which he would never again shake himself free.

PART FOUR

THE WANDERER

*

Chapter Eleven

THE PORTRAIT PAINTER

The hurt received to his pride as a writer threw him back again on the old alternative—art. But before changing course once more, it was as though he needed to take stock of his situation; to see himself —if such a thing were possible—as others saw him.

A new self-consciousness pervades this period. In the person of his latest hero, Henry Hastings, he is constantly portraying himself during the year 1837, notably in two fragments dated January and July, where the truth breaking through the fiction affords a clear indication of his own view of his case, and of his changing relations with his family.

There is no doubt that these were rapidly worsening. Criticisms of his conduct which he mocked at as dramatisation of mere peccadilloes were fast hardening his opposition. He could not bear criticism of any sort. He was already reaching the stage where the blame for his situation must be laid on others—on his father and sisters in particular. His own detachment from them, already perceptible in the account of his London journey, was developing consciously or unconsciously into something very near indifference. What they thought of him at home, he hints, has no particular significance.

Branwell at twenty is altogether impatient of the old standards by which life at the parsonage was ruled. In the prolonged absence of Charlotte and Anne, and under the unrelieved regime of his father and aunt, life could be not only bleak, but intolerable at times. Branwell had the vision to see that he was not "up" to the level of his family. Their standards crushed him; their absolute integrity, irritating his sense of failure, only heightened his guilt complex. He had the critical acumen to realise that he would be far better living away from them.

He had yet to realise, after many and repeated failures to do so successfully, that his tragedy lay in *not* being able to live outside their orbit.

The year 1836 had brought him no satisfaction of any kind. The letters, written early in January 1837 to *Blackwood's* and to Wordsworth, appealing for their encouragement of his literary efforts, had, as we have seen, remained unanswered. Both at home and in his work he was "misunderstood". In the revealing fragment of his Angrian history written on 23rd January 1837 all these causes of discontent are stated, together with a new one which would appear to concern his sisters, his "forsaken comrades", no longer the compliant and complacent partners in his childish games. The "Reader" he was addressing, it must be remembered, could not be other than his sisters.

"Reader—" he opens the narrative on 23rd January,

Reader—I think I owe an Apology for the long time for which in spite of your former favourable reception of me I have absented myself from your company and neglected my task of amusement and information. But inasmuch as a young man when he rises above the station he before moved in is looked on by his forsaken comrades as one removed from their sympathy and affections and by the new society that he neighbours on as a plebeian intruder into their aristocratic circles, so I since I published my first volume of the Campaign of the Calabar experienced from my lofty associates and patrons repulses and jealousies and mean efforts to keep down the aspiring plebeian, while, when I looked for friendship and fellowship from my former companions I found only the shyness of that pride which scorns to hang for promotion on another's sleeve and the coldness entertained toward a man who has forsaken their company for higher fortune. For my own part I have never forgotten Auld Lang Syne any more than I have remembered the petty flatteries and compliments of my new-fashioned Janus-faced friends. I would have kept hearty and whole with everyone I respected either high or low but this was not decreed to be. My patron thought proper first to appropriate to himself all the little praise I could earn from a benignant public . . . and when I looked for consolation under these slights to you with whom my public character was entrusted, I found that you were engaged in readily devouring long stories of the dissipation and drunkenness of the mushroom Henry Hastings! . . .

The word is out. For the first time, even if writing in bravado and banter for the eyes of his sisters only, Branwell is acknowledging the fact that, in the judgment of those whose standards used to be his, he was drinking too much. That the accusation hit home, the

K

self-justifications with which he follows it up make it only too
apparent.

Now, with respect to the reports about my conduct, I must say one word
further. It has been stated that within the last year past I have done nothing but
drink and gamble and do everything that is Bad, but had I gone on in the course
————represented, I could not by this time write one page of consecutive reason
or decency. . . .

In his representation of the case that follows, laying the blame
not on *his* indulgence but on his family's austerity and narrowness,
he touches the heart of the matter standing between him and them:
by his lax standards he was doing relatively no harm—but already
he was learning that in his family's code there was no place for
laxity at all.

I like my glass of a night, the same as another. Well, "I am in a continual and
beastly state of intoxication." I bet a nominal guinea on the issue of our topics of
daily curiosity, I am "an abandoned gambler", and if successful, "an arrant
swindler". . . . No matter; Henry Hastings is pronounced to be a debauched and
reckless desperado. But I'll give over this talk or else people will say that he who
is always complaining is generally found particularly worthy of suffering!

By the summer, the situation had clearly become envenomed.
Allowing for the swaggering tone consistent with the character of
his hero, in Henry Hastings' next confession Branwell was speaking
all too obviously from the heart, and with rare perception, was
putting his finger on the cause of his misconduct: his sense of guilt.
Dated 12th July 1837, the fragment opens in mid-action.

"This will never do", thought I, as I came reeling home through the streets of
Rosses town, after a night of debauch and drunkenness. "I am a gone man, and by
th' heart I'll go and drown myself. Steady, heigh ho!—" In fact, I was going as
fast as a man can go . . . and I, not being personally concerned in negotiations,
had nothing to do but revel away as fast as my means would permit me. Besides,
conscience with withering sting was constantly striking into my heart—king,
country and cause forsaken, old associations severed, friendships torn away—and
had I not received a letter from my father coldly saying he and all at home had
cut me for ever and ever. All which matters, like hot sweetmeats, the more and
more incited me to drink; and good credit with the tradesmen for a while supplied
me with the means for such rioting. . . .

The readers to whom Mary Duclaux's transcription of Branwell's
now famous letter to John Brown, in the *Life of Emily Brontë*, came
as a shock, had had no opportunity of reading Branwell "in the
raw", as he habitually appeared in his later Angrian manuscripts,

here and elsewhere. Long before he wrote that unfortunate letter to John Brown, Branwell had assumed both its swagger and its desperate tone. The Hastings text continues:

In staggering along the pavement of Dock Street it was my luck to tumble down just before the leader of a coach, that barely found time to back ere death had made a speedier end of me than even the one I was seeking, but I got up prettily bemired and called lustily,

"For Tartarus bound, eh? E'gad, I'll take my passage with ye!"

"The Sneachie Mail, Sir," cried the driver.

"The coach to H——" cried I, "lend me a hand. Who-hoop! And now, off as if Daddy were at th' back of us!"

Setting myself on the seat I did not care where we were going to. . . . I first burst into a roaring song, then swore an oath at each of the outsiders, then strove to pull the reins from the coachman, and then dropping back . . . I fell quietly asleep . . . [till Banbarra]. There was a halt here . . . and in that time I managed to get again so righteously drunk that the set off and the route to the City was swallowed in the Lethe of another dose which only woke into consciousness at the Inn table before a rattling company and a half-dozen of wine. . . . I was hardly a man till I was half seas over, and when fairly landed on t'other side I was not a man again. . . .

The tedium of such descriptions cannot remove the authentic tone of their evidence. Drinking might be a new addiction and its effects still interesting to the neophyte, but it was becoming an addiction all the same.

That this was so is confirmed by certain entries made by Mr Brontë in his copy of Graham's *Domestic Medicine* relating to the treatment of drunkenness, applied at this time, 1837, with varying results on a case obviously at hand.

The intense wretchedness of the poem "Sleep, mourner, sleep!—" written on 13th January 1837, seems a fitting commentary on the disappointments of that year. The speaker, as in the two versions of "Misery", mourns the death of a long-lost "angel Mary" and spurns all comfort or "lying sympathy" from reputed friends. It is a cry for withdrawal, both from life and friendship.

> Sleep, mourner, sleep!—I cannot sleep,
> My weary mind still wanders on;
> Then silent weep—I cannot weep
> For eyes and tears seemed turned to stone.

The only comfort to be accepted is in the memory of a past irremediably over—in the realisation of his present loneliness.

> For I've been consecrate to grief . . .
> And all my prospect of relief
> On earth would be to grieve alone!

Forgetfulness is both a necessity and an agony.

> To live in sunshine would be now
> To live in Lethe every thought;
> What I have seen and been below
> *Must* first be utterly forgot . . .

The sense of guilt for what he has become, all too cruelly blots out the radiant memories of the time when he was innocent and happy.

> So there's no choice. However bright
> May beam the blaze of July's sun,
> 'Twill only yield another sight
> Of scenes and times forever gone. . . .
> All—all is over, friend or lover
> Cannot awaken gladness here. . . .
> I cannot weep as once I wept
> Over my Western Beauty's grave, . . .
> I feel and say that I am cast
> From hope and peace, and power, and pride—
> A withered leaf on Autumn's blast;
> A shattered wreck on ocean's tide. . . .

The reckless, defiant mood associated with his hero, Henry Hastings, and increasingly characteristic of this period of desultory activity, finds further expression in an important prose fragment of some length (twenty-six pages of microscopic script) classified as "Percy" by bibliographers in default of any title of its own, and written during October, November and December 1837.

The scene—for the narrative never progresses beyond one scene —is set in ". . . a Beershop situated far up one of the gloomiest glens that open up from the main valley in . . . that northern wilderness of moors . . ." in what are recognisably Branwell's home surroundings. The "noisy and riotous-looking company stretched round the peat fire" and occupying "the old oaken settle and the three-legged stools beside the Bed-end" are accompanied by dogs and armed with fowling-pieces. They have come in from a day's shoot on the moors and the landlord (who "didn't look over-pleased with his company") when ordered to supply clay-pipes and the wherewithal to concoct "fiery Punch", answers in Haworth dialect. Here, in marked contrast to the majority of his prose writings up till then, which had artificial settings and "intellectualised" action lifted from the political, military, and social events of the day, Branwell is launched on a piece of purely realistic writing. If for nothing else but this, the "Percy" fragment would be of importance; but it furthermore looks forward, both in theme and setting, to the only known novel Branwell attempted, "And the Weary are at Rest", written in 1845, with which he closed his ill-fated literary career. Because of the extravagant claims put forward posthumously on his behalf by some of his friends, that Branwell was, in fact, the author of *Wuthering Heights*, it is necessary to give both the fragments "Percy" and "The Weary are at Rest" more attention than they aesthetically deserve. As it is, their intrinsic interest goes no further than to make us pose the question: how far Branwell's writing might have evolved had he, like his sisters, come to maturity of mind, capable of drawing inspiration from actual experience. Vulgar and violent as both these attempts at fiction are, they are little further removed from good writing than, to be just, his sister Charlotte's "Caroline Vernon" is, at that time, from *Jane Eyre*. It is a matter of quality of mind rather than of literary capacity; the latter all the Brontë children abundantly possessed, but it is a moot point whether, even under favourable circumstances, Branwell would have achieved the former in any degree, irrespective of all comparison with his sisters. Had fortune been kind to Branwell, he might very well have become a novelist of the calibre of Bulwer Lytton, but very certainly not of the Brontë sisters.

Between "Percy" and "And the Weary are at Rest" there are many startling resemblances that separate them in substance from Branwell's "Angrian" prose writings, with which he was still engaged right up to the end of 1839 (his twenty-second year). The setting, a lonely, moorland district, with an inn in one story and a country house in the other, and the characters, a group of dubious or disreputable people, are drawn in great part by name from his Angrian cycle. Percy himself (Northangerland), increasingly anglicised and physically resembling Branwell (whereas he originally was given black whiskers and hair, he appears with flaming red hair and whiskers in "And the Weary are at Rest"), Henry Hastings, Hector Montmorency, Grafton, Ellan, and the black, ubiquitous Quashia (finally evolved as merely "deeply tanned by tropical suns") are transplanted to Yorkshire soil and, particularly in the later novel, deeply conditioned by the atmosphere of village Methodism and country-house life of which, by then, Branwell would have had some searing experience.

How strong is the link binding the two tales is revealed by a clue that only a comparison of the two manuscripts makes apparent.

The setting for "And the Weary are at Rest", as already mentioned, is a moorland district recognisably Haworth, where the Thurstons have a country house called "Darkwell Farm" at which they receive their friends during the shooting season.

In "Percy" Branwell is at some pains to explain the local belief in the "Gytrash", the ghost-dog described by Charlotte in *Jane Eyre*, and familiar to all moorland folk round and about Haworth. "The 'Gytrash'," he writes, "is a spectre neither at all similar to the Ghosts of those who once were alive, nor to fairys nor to demons." It mostly appears in the form of some animal—"a black dog dragging a chain, a dusky calf, nay, even a rolling stone". The point of interest here in the "Percy" manuscript is that Branwell goes on to explain: "The Darkwell Gytrash was known by its form of an old dwarfish and hideous man, as often seen without a head as with one and moving at dark along the naked fields which spread round the aged house." Branwell knew his local lore and here he is evoking the apparition peculiar to Ponden House, known as the "Headless Man" (which generation after generation of Heatons saw whenever disaster threatened their family), unless it appeared in the alternate form of a flaming barrel bowling across the fields. The background of "Percy", even to the name "Darkwell", is thus the background to the novel "And the Weary are at Rest", written years later to distract his grief.

In 1837 when "Percy" was written, his mood was one of defiant cynicism. The narrative is confined to a drunken orgy broken into by a party of revellers and ending in a "free for all". The dialogue, liberally spiced with Haworth dialect (where to get drunk is to get "fresh") is peppered with blasphemies and jests in doubtful taste.

The company, which among the old Angrian puppets includes a local doctor and clergyman, is distinctly raffish, and, were it to be taken as literally portraying Branwell's usual cronies, would indeed reflect little credit upon the Freemasons of Haworth. One "red-cheeked young squire", evidently in the hardware trade, "was just proceeding to ask a thickset companion 'Whats nails a pack?' when, the door opening, he espied a young damsel pass in and out again in a moment. The stout youth sat silent and then with a "By Jove!" he started up, walked to the door and disappeared into the midnight winds.

The President demanded of the sturdy villain: "Southwell, what's Grafton up to?" "Gone, for a bit of trash," said the shooter. "Egad, man, and I think he could have got fresh enough here if he had waited. Hastings! Fill up, Man! . . . May our hearts be warm while we live! We are to turn to ashes when we die. Bumpers, Gentlemen!" "Egad"! cries a stout old gentleman still indignant at the youth who has gone after the damsel, "my old body would fry rarely in its own grease. Hang such brimstone trash!"

Among the company is a clergyman who "protests at the most distant allusion to his cloth", but is obliged to submit throughout the evening to tasteless witticisms at the expense of religion. Indeed, the company's preoccupation with blasphemy is symptomatic of the general immaturity of its wit; it supplies half the evening's pleasures. After the incursion of the second band of revellers, a mighty clash ensues in which both the doctor and the clergyman are knocked out. Neat whisky is poured down their throats by their respective supporters, the parson's swearing that "the parson must pardon him for administering Infant Baptism but he thought they had better all be confirmed and begged he should stand excused if he likewise practised upon himself baptism for such a one of ripe years!"

Projecting his own thoughts and his own dilemma into the character of Henry Hastings, Branwell gives us a clear insight into his then state of disillusionment. Only Hastings of all those present, he writes, sat "thinking of something beyond present things. He was here drinking with a set of atrocious devils . . . he who a few years ago had entered life ambitious of distinction and to run a bright race. . . . But there was an end of Hope now to him, broken from one military service and a fugitive in another, with a heart and a constitution that was yielding to his unchecked intemperance. . . ." Hastings, unlike his companions, has had his ambitions, his dreams of a better life. While the "long loud wind and the bitter beating of the rain without" recall his years of service in Africa, and "carry his heart away to nights of encampment . . . and the wet winter of the Angrian War . . .", he is made to feel ashamed of his present life. The effect is momentary only and "when the blast had howled over the Heath into silence", he grasped his glass and swilled it to "the speedy entombment in our stomachs and its resurrection with us in another world!" So Branwell, at many a convivial meeting of his Haworth cronies, must have sat and moralised, and wished things were different, and himself a better man.

According to Leyland he made an effort to end the miserable

situation at home, by taking a post as usher in a school near Halifax
that autumn. No evidence of this exists apart from Leyland's, and
Leyland himself knew only the bare fact, without either the name
of Branwell's employers, the situation of the school, or the date
at which he went there. It was certainly not before midsummer,
because no mention is made of it in the family record kept by Emily
and Anne in one of their diary papers, written on Branwell's
birthday, 26th June 1837. It was the summer holidays, and Charlotte
and Anne were home from school. Outwardly, the old union
binding the four inseparables appears as strong as ever.

Branwell is reading aloud *Eugene Aram* to Charlotte in Aunt's
room; Emily and Anne are writing Gondal poetry in the parlour.
All is "tight and right", as the authors hope they will all be "on this
day 4 years . . ." and seem to see no reason why it should not be so.

Eugene Aram, published in 1832, was one of the books possessed
by the Keighley Mechanics' Institute Library. The copy Branwell
was reading aloud to Charlotte may have been borrowed from there,
but one likes to think it may have been a present from his sisters on his
birthday. The macabre story, much publicised by various theatrical
versions then in vogue, together with its Yorkshire setting, would
have appealed to him.

At the time of writing that diary paper the girls could not fore-
see that Emily would shortly be leaving home to take up a post in a
school at Southowram called Law Hill, and the probabilities are
that it was this move of hers that decided Branwell to imitate her
and take a post in her district.

Emily at Law Hill was subjected to a regimen of "slavery"
according to Charlotte, in a school with forty boarders (a large
establishment for the period) and suffered torments of frustration
and home-sickness, as her poems written in the brief intervals from
the day's duties bear witness. Intolerable as the effort required of her
was to her freedom-loving spirit, she stuck to her post for a full
eighteen months. Branwell, fair game to pupils and teachers alike,
with his carroty hair and diminutive stature, deserted his after one
term only.

Neither literature nor pedagogy had brought him any returns.
As 1838 opened and his twenty-first birthday drew in sight, the
need to make some definite choice of profession became imperative
as never before. The choice was not very wide for a young man of
his classical education.

He had not been trained with an eye on the evolving economy of industrial England, and living in the very heart of the woollen trade, no thought seemed further from his family's or his own mind than that of making a living in its flourishing centres, as the brothers of Charlotte's friends were even then doing. He had been brought up to believe his literary and artistic abilities considerable enough to carry him to affluence, if not to fame.

In default of literature, he must fall back on art. By the month of May 1838—the year in which he attained his majority—and in full accord with his family, he set up as a portrait painter with a studio of his own in Bradford.

The transition from the ill-prepared art-student of his London venture to the quasi-professional status he assumed at Bradford had not, of course, been made without some further training. From the beginning of that year, if not before, he had resumed lessons with his old teacher William Robinson. But not under the same conditions. Robinson, who had taught the parsonage children in their home at a fee of two guineas the lesson, charged far less in his studio at Leeds. According to Leyland, a new arrangement was made by which, thanks to the generosity of his aunt, Branwell went over to Leeds and worked directly in his master's studio. Even so it meant putting up for the night at an inn in Briggate, an additional expense which also, apparently, was borne by Miss Branwell. The implication is that this was a last bid to launch Branwell on a reputable career and that without the continuing good offices of his aunt, it could not have been made. As Branwell's letters would shortly show, from his father and aunt he systematically hid the shady side of his life. They might be increasingly dissatisfied with much that they saw, but he was careful to let them see by no means all. He was already cultivating that hypocritical exterior of which he would come to boast to his confidant John Brown.

Having worked at his master's studio, and carried his pictures home to study and copy; having painted his sisters and any other patient sitters whom he could cajole into the task for several months, Branwell was impatient—and for more reasons than one—to set up on his own.

Bradford was chosen, rather than Leeds, for his centre of activity, for in Bradford the family still had numerous connections and friends. In Fountain Street lived the Rev. William Morgan, his father's oldest friend, Maria's godfather, the minister who had baptised most of the Brontë children, and the giver of many kindly and generous gifts from their early childhood; a bustling, busy man with a wide circle of clerical acquaintances; under his wing Branwell, the anxious elders believed, could come to no harm. William Morgan was vicar of Bradford's second most important church, Christ Church, situated at the top of Darley Street, almost within sight of whose spire Branwell lodged in Fountain Street.

Within five minutes' walk, at No. 11 Eldon Place, lived Mr John Outhwaite, surgeon, and his daughter Fanny, Anne's godmother and a close friend of Mr Brontë's and Miss Branwell's Thornton days. Their circle, comprising a good cross-section of the professional classes of Bradford—doctors, chemists, lawyers, preachers and teachers—would be invaluable in finding clients for the newly-established portrait-painter.

In Bradford, too, lived the Brontë children's old nurse, Nancy Garrs, long since married and gone from the parsonage, but a lifelong friend with whom they never lost touch. Nancy lived to be photographed, and recalled with amusement Branwell's insistence that she should sit to him for her portrait in oils; but she laughed him off with the excuse that she was not good-looking enough. Nancy, who outlived all her charges, and her old master as well, recalled how Charlotte, hearing of her severe illness on one occasion, hurried over to Bradford to see her and disregarding fear of infection threw herself on the bed beside her, covering her with kisses and imploring her to get well.

The good sense and affection of an old friend like Nancy were worth their weight in gold to the fundamentally diffident Branwell.

On no count would his progress be easy in Bradford. What his unworldly clerical connection did not appreciate was that Bradford, a highly prosperous town of 40,000 inhabitants at the hub of the woollen industry, was practically devoid of cultural interests, and one where grudging recognition only was afforded to local artists. Artists, writers, and musicians of quality, as Branwell was to find, abounded there, but, for the most part, only those who broke away and went to London made a living and a name.

It was not the fault of his friends, however, nor—in this instance —of Branwell himself, that portrait-painting had, all-unsuspected by them, already passed its apogee and entered into its final phase in the provinces. The dramatic introduction of the daguerrotype, so soon to supplant it as a means of preserving a likeness, would kill the profession stone dead except at its highest levels. To these at no time could Branwell have aspired, but with a good connection among the smaller *bourgeoisie* he might have made a living as a portraitist.

His beginnings at Bradford were propitious. Uncle Morgan, doubtless appealed to by Mr Brontë to find respectable lodgings for his son where he could at the same time receive sitters and exercise his art, found him a room and a studio in the very street where he himself lived, at No. 3 Fountain Street with a family named Kirby. He did more. To start Branwell off on his career, he sat to him for his own portrait and brought him another influential client, his patron the Rev. Henry Heap, Vicar of Bradford. Neither portrait can now be traced.

Mr Isaac Kirby, as reference to the Bradford trade directory of the time reveals, was a "Porter and Ale Merchant" (a not unsuitable host for Branwell some might say), with business premises at 33 Market Street, the very centre of the busy town's activity. At home at 3 Fountain Street, Mr Kirby lived with his wife and two children in all the aura of respectability. Fountain Street, a steep side-turning off Manningham Lane, is still a very respectable street, where the residential character of the Georgian house-fronts belies the adaption of some to commercial purposes. The discreet brass plates announcing the trading activities of their owners might yet be the brass-plates of the doctors and solicitors who, together with such clerical gentlemen as Branwell's Uncle Morgan, abounded in the district in the late eighteen-thirties.

Throughout the period of Branwell's residence with the Kirbys, they had living with them a young niece, a Margaret Hartley, who never forgot him and who, many years later, married and living at Dewsbury, came to the defence of his memory. Margaret Hartley's evidence, agreeing as it does with that of so many other outsiders, places Branwell in a favourable light, such as he could never achieve by comparison with the great superiority of his family. *Away* from them, he exercised many of their virtues; modesty, politeness and, where no sacrifice was asked of him, consideration and honesty. He had, beneath all the Byronic swagger, a natural fund of gentleness and kindness remarked upon by all who ever met him.

Mrs Kirby had, Leyland relates, "a beautiful little girl" who was Branwell's special favourite. "At his frequent request, she dined with him in his private sitting-room, her pleasant smiles and cheerful prattling always charming him."

The picture conjured up by Margaret Hartley, though possibly over-simplified through the eyes of a young girl, gives some valuable evidence of his way of life at the time.

From my girlhood for several years I resided with my uncle and aunt, Mr and Mrs Kirby, of Fountain Street, Manningham Lane, Bradford. At a time when Patrick Branwell Brontë was about 22 or 23 years of age [actually 21-22] he came to lodge with us and had one room as his studio, and there painted many portraits. He was low in stature, about 5 ft 3 inches high, and slight in build, though well proportioned. Very few people, except sitters, came to visit him; but I remember one, a Mr Thompson, a painter also. I recollect his sister Charlotte coming and I remember her sisterly ways. She stayed a day, and I believe that was her only visit. They left the house together, and he saw her off by the Keighley coach. I am not aware that his other sisters or that his father, the Rev. Patrick Brontë ever came to Mr Kirby's. It was young Mr Brontë's practice to go home at each week-end, and I remember that while sometimes he took the coach for Keighley, he on other occasions walked to Haworth across the moors. He was a very steady young gentleman, his conduct was exemplary, and we liked him very much. He stayed with us about two years and left, he said, to go to a situation, as a book-keeper [in fact as tutor to the Postlethwaite family at Broughton]. Whilst lodging with us he painted my portrait and those of my uncle and aunt, and all three were accounted good likenesses.

The portraits still exist and can be seen today at the Brontë Parsonage Museum at Haworth. They are the most finished of any of Branwell's to be preserved, and were it not for his subsequent correspondence with the "Mr Thompson" of this account, neither their authenticity nor Branwell's unclouded relationship with the Kirbys would be called into question. As it is, the evidence suggests that Thompson had a hand in finishing the portraits and that Branwell's feelings for the Kirby family were not quite so cordial before the end as young Margaret Hartley supposed.

He had made friends with John Hunter Thompson in Robinson's Leeds studio, where they were fellow-pupils. They had much in common, though Thompson was nine years the elder. His father, like Branwell's, was a poor Ulsterman, a mechanic who made his way in the world. Finally settling in Bradford, he had apprenticed his son to a house-painter and decorator, and it was while young Thompson was employed in decorating the reception-rooms at "St Ives", the home of Major and Mrs Ferrand of Bingley, that his talents were remarked and that they had persuaded the father to let the boy be trained as an artist. He had learned his profession the hard way, studying anatomy under a Bradford doctor, but by the time he reached Robinson's studio, he was much further advanced on the road to achievement than Branwell. A fine draughtsman (due to his study of anatomy), Thompson made a reputation for himself and lived to the age of eighty-two.

His genial temperament, in strong contrast to Branwell's fundamentally morbid one, at once attracted his fellow-student. Thompson was an inimitable raconteur and they struck up a friendship that was wholly beneficial to Branwell.

Through Thompson, Branwell had the entrée to the artistic, literary and musical circles of Bradford, which, in a sort, stood to him in place of the university he never knew. It threw him into the society of all that was keenest and best among the young intelligentsia of the place, and brought him friendships which lasted into later life. His sojourn there was probably the happiest period of his adult life.

United in their open war upon the Philistines (in the persons of the wealthy mill-owners), the Bohemian circles of Bradford had their separate and distinct centres where they met to discuss the burning topics of the day. The "men of letters" met at the *George Hotel* in Market Street, a noted hostelry where Dickens in his time was to stay; at the *Bull's Head* at the bottom of Westgate, the predominantly musical element foregathered; at the *Queen's Hotel* in Bridge Street kept by William Oddy, it was the artists, painters, engravers, sculptors, while the newly-formed Bradford Philosophical Society met at the *New Inn* in Tyrrel Street.

At all of these Branwell soon made friends and became an assiduous customer. At the *Talbot*, too, though its clientele was markedly snobby and "select", he was at home, as it was the Tory headquarters for Bradford and as such had even been frequented by his father.

Of special delight to him would be the rehearsals of the Bradford Choral Society held at the *Bull's Head* on Tuesdays of each month "on or before the full moon" to accommodate those musicians having a long return journey into the outlying and unlighted country districts. Among them Branwell was in paradise, because they made a rule of performing nothing but oratorio. Here he met a type of landlady—characterful, generous and motherly—who was to constitute for many years in his increasingly *déclassé* existence his chief experience of women. Mrs Illingworth of the *Bull's Head* was noted for her liberality to musicians, catering generously on rehearsal nights and seeing that "there was a tit-bit for all".

Mrs Reaney (spelt alternatively Reenie) of the *George Hotel*, maintained an equally high character for decency, generosity and intelligence. She presided over the meetings, vociferous always but seldom riotous, of the predominantly literary coteries in the town. Here, Branwell first met Hartley Coleridge, a "regular" of the place, and one who, while engaged on writing his "Northern Worthies" for the Leeds publishing firm called Bingley (not to be confounded with the township of the name), was constantly over at Bradford. Another member of the literary circles to become a friend of Branwell's through the same contacts, was John James, the future historian of Bradford, a worthy man of great learning, with a passion for architecture and archaeology. John James was a close friend of Thompson's and of two other noted Bradford artists, the brothers Charles and John Cousen.

A friend—a patron almost—of whom Branwell was always to speak with bated breath, was the poet James Montgomery, who launched the Bradford Philosophical Society early in 1839, by contributing six lectures on "The Poets of England" to its opening meetings. Branwell was no sooner introduced to Montgomery than he confided to him his literary ambitions and ever after quoted him as giving him the strongest encouragement to proceed.

Comforting to Branwell in his luckless life as the friendship of such men as Hartley Coleridge and James Montgomery would be, his chief contacts at Bradford must necessarily be among fellow artists. Introduced by Thompson, he made the friendship of such men of established reputation as Joseph Bentley Leyland, the Halifax sculptor, Wilson Anderson, the landscape painter, William Overend Geller, the mezzotintist and exquisite engraver, the two Cousens, Richard Waller, the portrait painter, and many others. Of these, J. B. Leyland would become a life-long friend, and the close confidant of his ultimate disasters.

Early success had crowned the first exhibition of Leyland's work at Leeds, where he showed, among others, his gigantic bust of Milton's Satan. Hailed instantly by George Hogarth (Dickens' father-in-law and editor of the *Halifax Guardian* at the time) as an artist of exceptional merit, Leyland received every help and encouragement to go to London and show his work there. The welcome of Chantrey and Westmacott, and of Benjamin Robert Haydon (under whom he was soon studying anatomy) assured him of a position in the capital. He established himself there, though frequently returning to Halifax to work in peace on the commissions received in London.

When Branwell first knew him he was working on a group called "African Bloodhounds", which won the enthusiastic encomiums of Landseer. There was in Leyland's work a lyrical quality and a propensity to seek his inspiration in literary subjects, that immediately attached him to Branwell. One of his most reputed works is in York Minster. It is the monument to Dr Beckwith, one of the Minster's benefactors and a generous supporter of orphanages and schools—a recumbent figure of great serenity and charm with hands of a startling eloquence.

In London Leyland lodged with his fellow-Yorkshireman Geller mentioned above, the mezzotintist, whose engraving of Leyland's group "Bertram" (from the tragedy of that name by Mathurin) enormously enlarged Leyland's following and at the same time made Geller's reputation as an engraver. Geller, who frequently returned to Bradford and there met Branwell, had studied in London under John Martin, the painter whose extravagant style had so appealed to Branwell as a boy, and whose pictures he had attempted to copy when only eleven or twelve years old. This was a contact of peculiar interest to Branwell.

While in Bradford, Geller painted several portraits of Bradford worthies, among them one of Branwell's own "subject", the Rev. Henry Heap, Vicar of the Parish Church.

There were two other Bradford circles frequented by Branwell: the Freemasons of the town, the "Oddfellows", whose Lodge met in a fine hall in the Thornton Road, and to whose members he may have had introductions from Haworth; and the local theatre— Skerret's Theatre, so named after its manager—whose performances were given in the "Oddfellows' Hall". During Branwell's residence in Bradford, the scenery for Skerret's Theatre was painted by another artist friend of his, J. Wilson Anderson, the exquisite landscape painter, whose work achieved considerable repute in the region.

Bradford did a very great deal for Branwell, but it did not furnish him with a living. The fact was, it was too small a centre to contain so many talents and provide a livelihood for all. Branwell was neither experienced enough nor gifted enough to compete with portrait painters like Waller, Geller and Thompson. Those artists who made their way sought their livelihood outside, and had the resolution to uproot themselves and pursue a career in London.

The idea never seems to have presented itself to Branwell or his family that he might, like the brothers Charles and John Cousen, or John Clayton Bentley, study engraving so as to work for the fashionable art journals of Messrs Virtue, or Fisher and Son, who regularly employed young artists to reproduce the pictures then most in demand. Branwell's one venture into the vortex of London seems to have discouraged him for life. Neither he nor his family seemed to have seen further for him than Bradford. When the commissions given him by connections or friends had been exhausted, not all the efforts of his well-wishers could bring him further custom. Bradford, as a source of income, very quickly played itself out.

As clients fell off and the effort to build up a connection began, unpleasantly, to resemble drudgery, Branwell yielded more and more to the charms of trusting to luck, living from day to day, improving his friendships with the many and gifted men whose acquaintance he had made, and whose society was certain to be found at the bars of *The George*, *The Bull's Head*, *The New Inn* or *The Talbot*. He greatly preferred it to any regular occupation, for, in proportion as it stimulated and inspired him as a speaker, it made him forget his failures in all other domains. Like his friend Hartley Coleridge and that friend's greater father, he found his truest release in desultory talk.

It was from this period, undoubtedly, that he became a brilliant talker. Innately so from childhood, but for the crushing Brontë timidity, he needed something more than his sisters' admiration or the Haworth villagers' facile wit, to "strike sparks", as he himself put it, from a mind all too often clouded by muddled thinking. Like many another unfulfilled artist before and after him, Branwell needed an exact temperature in which to flower. This temperature he found in the sympathetic and vital society of his Bradford contemporaries—and in drink. Increasingly, voluptuously, he submitted to its potent aid. Like an actor fearing to break down without a prompter, from then on he came to rely increasingly on its support.

Mr and Mrs Kirby of Bradford, from the portraits by Branwell Brontë, painted 1839

View of Bradford in 1840, drawn by Charles Cousen and engraved by John Cousen, friends of Branwell Brontë

Chapter Twelve

"MY HOME IS NOT MY HOME..."

By mid-May 1839 he had given up his studio and returned home. Two letters of his written to Thompson that summer show under what unsatisfactory conditions and in what a humour he had left Fountain Street. No sentiment of regret is evident, except regret for the premature death that summer, at the age of thirty-nine, of their master William Robinson—a circumstance which may have contributed to his decision to cut his losses with the Leeds and Bradford connection.

Though Branwell's biographer, Francis Leyland, hotly denied Mary Duclaux's allegation that he left Bradford in debt (see her *Emily Brontë* published in 1883), it is obvious that he was at least in debt to Thompson, and that his landlady was also claiming he had not finished her portraits or varnished them as agreed.

That she could do so as *by right* looks uncommonly as though he had left the portraits as part payment for his rent.

Branwell's first letter, addressed to "J. H. Thompson, Artist, Care of Mr Ogden, Carver & Gilder, Bradford", reads:

Haworth May 17
1839

Dear Sir,
Your last has made me resolve on a visit to you at Bradford for certainly this train of misconceptions and delays must at last be put a stop to.

I shall (Deo Volente) be at the Bulls Head at 2 o'clock this afternoon (Friday) and DO be there or in Bradford to give me your aid when I arrive!

I am astonished at Mrs Kirby—I have no pictures of hers to finish. But I said that if I returned there I would varnish 3 for her and I do not understand people who look on a kindness as a duty.

Once more my heartfelt thanks to you for your consideration for one who has none for himself.

Yours faithfully
P. B. Bronte

The text of the second letter, written three months later but still bearing on the same questions, reads:

Mr J. H. Thompson Artist
    At the George Hotel
    Bradford

                                    Haworth Bradford
                                    Augt 24th 1939
Dear Thompson,
    It had been my intention to see you at Bingley on the Tide Monday or Tues-day and there settle accounts with you but, last night I saw young Mr Craven who told me that you desired an answer to your last letter as soon as possible—so understanding what you meant I have forwarded the needful enclosed under the seal of this letter.
    I am rejoiced to hear that Bradford continues to like you, and you it well enough to incline you to settle there—Do you mean to raise your prices?—or could it be done in the same place where you have painted in the old ones?—
    I hope nothing has occurred been [sic—for "between"] yourself and Ogden. Has the little man shown any meaness to you who have benefited him more than any one I know of? Because if I understood you you must have left him and taken up your quarters at the George.
    You say that you mean to invite Mrs Robinson [widow of his former teacher] to see you on your settlement in Bradford—and this shows your goodness in an admirable light—I heartily wish I could have gone, with you to Leeds but I was then at Liverpool and there I staid so much longer than I had intended that it along with the payment of several depts of which my Father or Aunt had no knowledge has positively left me too poor to send as I had hoped—along with this letter, a sovereign or two as an acknowledgement of the kindness with which I was treated by her and our poor Master. But I am going to Leeds I believe shortly and then I hope to be able in some degree to help one whom too many—I am afraid—have injured—indeed It astonished me when I read the hints contained in your letter though I need not have wondered for this world is all rotteness—as for Robinson's brother I never had any good will to his wooden head.
    Mrs Kirby's name is an eyesore to me—What does the woman mean?—How can I come paddling to Bradford with my wallet on my Back in order to varnish her portraits—for I know of no other finishing she stipulated for? I dare not trespass farther on your extreme kindness toward me but I would give the amount contained in this letter or twice it to silence her chattering. The sentence comes ill off my pen point for it is neither pleasant or profitable to finish another man's daubs but I would gladly stand by what I have said.
    I am afraid I must deny myself the pleasure of seeing you at Bingley but my heart is with you.
    With prosperity to you and happiness to Mrs Thompson
                Believe me to remain Yours
                                    P. B. Bronte

Though the world was "all rotteness" and he had debts of which he dared not let his father and aunt know anything, outwardly his relations with his family had suffered no further deterioration by his failure at Bradford. It only created a fresh problem—or rather, perhaps a fresh aspect of the old problem—what profession should he adopt next? Yet once again it was met with stoicism, if not with optimism, by his father. There exists at the Brontë Parsonage Museum touching evidence that in the June following Branwell's return from Bradford, Mr Brontë set himself once again to coach his son in Latin—with a view, doubtless, to preparing him to take up teaching as a profession.

In the fly-leaf of a little shabby *Concordance to the Holy Scriptures* Mr Brontë noted that "In June 1839—I agreed with Branwell, that, under Providence, we should thoroughly read together the following Classics . . ." the first six Books of the Aeneid, the four Gospels in Greek, the first six books of the Iliad, some of the Odes of Horace and the Art of Poetry, "besides translating some English into Latin." Mr Brontë, with all the method he had brought to his own studies, duly noted that their progress should "be regularly set down in this and the following pages". In the event, the blank pages of the little Concordance were not much needed: progress stopped at "line 320 of the third Book of the Aeneid" and the "4th Chapter of St Matthew's Gospel". There is nothing to surprise us in this. What is surprising when Branwell's emotional condition at the time is considered, is the use to which he turned his classical studies in the eventual translation of Horace's Odes, begun then and emerging finally as his most abiding claim to literary merit. The achievement, if judged merely as an exercise in application, would be remarkable in him—quite irrespective of its poetic excellence.

The summer of 1839 was an unsettled time for all the family. Emily had returned home at Christmas after three exhausting halves at Law Hill, unequal to going away again. Charlotte, after only three months with the Sidgwick family at Stonegappe, came home in July. While there she had written her complaints to Emily with the strict injunction ". . . Don't show this letter to papa or aunt, *only to Branwell*. They will think I am never satisfied." Only Anne was earning her living with any resolution, and after the summer holidays returned to her post at Mirfield with the Ingham family of Blake Hall.

Branwell, it would seem, was not alone in lacking direction. That neither Charlotte nor Emily made a better job at earning her living than he did, must have been a source of secret comfort to him.

How little Charlotte judged him at that time, though acutely observant of his increasing failure and frustration and debt becomes apparent on examining the important and revealing Angrian narrative on which she was engaged in the spring of 1839 and whose finishing date—May 1939—coincided with Branwell's return from Bradford.

Branwell's debts were fast becoming a condition of life to which his sisters had to become inured as the growing size and frequency of his duns would necessitate urgent intervention. At the very time that Branwell was writing to Thompson that he had pressing debts of which his father and aunt knew nothing, the only certain friends to whom he could look to extricate him were his sisters. Charlotte's manuscript, given by Brontë bibliographers for convenience the title "Henry Hastings", but left without a title by Charlotte herself, is concerned with a brother and sister relationship, only thinly disguised from that existing at the moment between herself and Branwell. It deals with Branwell's own recent creation Henry Hastings and takes him on some considerable steps further than his originator perhaps intended. The Henry Hastings of Branwell's fragments of January and July 1837, already in trouble with his family for "doing nothing but drink and gamble" and "cut off for ever and ever" by all at home "for doing everything that is Bad", has in Charlotte's narrative further added desertion to his other list of offences, and is a fugitive from authority. In this predicament, with military and police forces converging upon the region where he is suspected of hiding, he finds an unexpected asylum in the house where his sister, Elizabeth, is employed as governess and lady companion to the haughty Angrian beauty, Jane Moore. The hunted youth (whose age is given as twenty-one—Branwell's precise age at the time) breaks into the house by the french windows of the drawing-room, where he finds his sister sitting over the fire in twilight solitude. The interview is full of perception on Elizabeth's part and of self-knowledge on his. Among Charlotte's very last Angrian stories, it is also the subtlest in characterisation, the least exaggerated, the most realistic, and the nearest to the great novels to come.

Watching her exhausted brother slump in the chair opposite her, Elizabeth notices how he looks at her "with that kind of mistrust born of conscious degradation. 'Come,' he said, 'with regard to you I'm just the same Harry Hastings that I always was. I daresay by this time you've learnt to think of me as a kind of ogre.' Her glance, more than her words, said: 'Your faults and yourself are separate existences in my mind.'"

In her description of brother and sister, Charlotte emphasises their resemblance—a resemblance as strong as that constantly remarked on as existing between Branwell and herself. "Neither was handsome—the man had wasted his vigour and his youth in vice—there was more to repel than charm in the dark fiery eye—in an aspect marked with the various lines of suffering, passion and profligacy ... his sister was almost as fair as he was dark, but she'd little colour—had she dressed herself stylishly and curled her hair, no one would have called her plain. She tried to speak cheerfully, desirous to conceal from his vigilant jealousy those pangs of anguish which his changed appearance ... must have forced into her heart. ...

"I am not as bad as you think me," said Henry Hastings, in words that Charlotte must repeatedly have heard in the last few months. "I am a man who has been atrociously wronged." His relation of his misfortunes and the injustices of which he has been a victim, evoke from her the cry that "she had always believed in him". Elizabeth Hastings, going one further perhaps than Charlotte Brontë had dared do, tells her brother how she had defied their father in his defence, and on the occasion when he had crossed his son's name off his will had cried, "You have done wrong and unnaturally." "My father was then scarcely himself," Elizabeth continues, "and he is always quite as passionate as his son—he knocked me down. ... I got up and said the words over again—I cared nothing, ..." and, true to character, she left home and earned her bread by her own efforts.

Contemplating their two characters objectively, Charlotte accepts unquestioningly their great imperfections and concedes that "neither of them was the brightest, mildest or gentlest of human beings ...". Her analysis of the man's mind is most perceptive, and strangely unrelieved by any optimism. This is no longer the glamour portrait of a Zamorna, amoral and seductive, but the analysis of a real person observed at first hand. Hastings' mind, she writes, "was of that peculiarly agreeable conformation that if anyone conferred a bounty upon him he instantly jumped to the conclusion that they expected some minor act of submission in return and the consequence was he always bit the hand that caressed him. ... His passions were naturally strong, his imagination warm to fever . . . the two together made wild work especially when Drunken Delirium lashed them up to a gallop. . . .''

In spite of Elizabeth's efforts, Hastings is arrested and given the choice of life with ignominy—on condition that he betrays the names of his confederates—or execution. He chooses life. Charlotte, summing up his conduct and his sister's acceptance of it, has this to say, which, in view of her own position vis-a-vis Branwell, is of the utmost importance in any attempt to understand their relationship.

It was very odd that his sister did not think a pin the worse of him for all his dishonour: it is private moments not public infamy that degrade a man in the opinion of his relations. Miss Hastings had heard him cursed by every mouth, saw him denounced in every newspaper, still he was the same brother to her he had always been—still she beheld his actions through, she saw him go away with a triumphant Hope—that his future actions would nobly blot out the calumny of his enemies. Yet after all she knew he was an unredeemed villain—human nature is full of inconsistencies—natural affection is a thing never rooted out where it has once existed.

Elizabeth and Henry Hastings may be characters in a novel— and Charlotte was before all else a novelist—but the sentiment in that passage is of the stuff of life. It is not to diminish the creativeness of the Brontës' writings to say that the more the details of their lives and backgrounds are examined, the more apparent become the sources of their inspiration. Without the experience of a brother like Branwell, Charlotte could not at that time have written "Henry Hastings", any more than she could have created Paul Emmanuel without M. Heger. And from this it follows that what she wrote regarding Henry Hastings was true of her sentiments *at the time*: nothing that Branwell had yet done made her "think a pin the worse of him". That the time would come when she would eat her words, is indicative rather of the great change that would take place in her, than of any further marked deterioration in him who was only pursuing the course predictable even then to any wide-awake eyes.

A recollection of Ellen Nussey's, relating to the autumn of 1839, shows us perhaps the last image of the old impregnable alliance existing between brother and sister. It can be found in the touching account, written many years later, of Charlotte's first visit to the sea—a visit to Easton near Bridlington, made in her friend's company that autumn—in which Branwell is made to appear in the role of Knight Errant supporting his sister against all the head-shaking of the elders, dubious of the propriety of two young ladies going away by themselves.

Mr Brontë and Miss Branwell, had all manners of doubts and fears and cautions to express and Charlotte was sinking into despair—there seemed only one chance of securing her the pleasure, her friend must fetch her; this she did . . . in a carriage that would bring both Charlotte and her luggage—this step proved to be the very best thing possible, the surprise was so good in its effects . . . everybody rose into high good humour, Branwell was grandiloquent, he declared "it was a brave defeat, that the doubters were fairly taken aback", "You have only to *will* a thing to *get* it", so Charlotte's luggage was speedily prepared and almost before the horse was rested there was a quiet but triumphant starting; the brother and sisters at home were not less happy than Charlotte herself in her now secured pleasure.

Except for the short visit to Liverpool that autumn (mentioned in his letter to Thompson) and made, if not in the company at least at the expense of his father and aunt, Branwell's prospects were unrelieved now by any immediate hope of escape from home.

That home was no longer to him what it still was to his sisters— the centre of being to regain which after an absence was very bliss— Branwell had become acutely aware during the last year. How he saw his changed relationship can be seen in the important poem written during 1838-9, to which he first gave the name "The Wanderer". Both for its exceptional literary merit and for the illumination it casts on his state of mind and emotional development, it must be ranked among his most valuable achievements. For the maturity of thought and, on the whole, the sobriety of its expression, it is indeed singular among his poetry.

The subject is absence—absence and return, and the sad inevitability of change.

Ever since the London fiasco, these themes had haunted Branwell and found expression in many passages of his Angrian history. Here, in "The Wanderer", without the bitterness and cynicism that characterised many of those other passages, he considers, as applied directly to his own case, what his home has yet to offer him, and with genuine sorrow recognises that the old familiar circle has "lost him beyond recall".

The poem, while it explores new ground in his subjective attitude to the old subjects, is at the same time his last and most complete evocation of his sister Maria. Written after the two main "Caroline" poems of 1837, it sums up his philosophy of loss, with a courageous acceptance of the mutability of things and faith in the consoling power of memory. Moreover, the advance in this poem on the previous Maria poems in the subjection of the purely physical and morbid aspects of her death to its spiritual and eternal implications, is notable. It shows Branwell at last having emerged from the heart of the furnace and able to stand outside it as a chastened observer.

The poem describes the return after sixteen years' active service in India of "Sir Henry Tunstall" (whose name became the title of the poem in its final version), whose parents, sister and children, form "the parlour group", so strongly reminiscent of that other parlour group in Haworth, eagerly waiting him. The true images of home are here tenderly and simply recalled and recognisably belong to Haworth Parsonage: the

> Clock slow ticking in the Hall—
>
> The parlour group . . . seated all together,
> With long looks turned towards the threatening weather
> The agèd Father, on his customed seat,
> With cushioned stool to prop his crippled feet,
> Averting from the rest his forehead high
> To hide the drop that quivers in the eye . . . .

—The sister "fast by the window . . ." turning pale "with every leaf that falls, a breeze that blows"; the children—such children as Branwell and his sisters once were,

> O'er the table bent,
> And on the map with childish eyes intent
> Are guiding fancied ships through ocean's foam
> And wondering—"What he's like" and "When he'll come"—

In retrospect he evokes the things that made home most dear—

> The shaggy pony he was wont to ride—
> The dog so faithful to its Master's side—
> The rooks and doves that hover round the door . . .
> The flowers he planted many seasons past. . . .

He knows, in advance, how they will all be gone.

He arrives. All is joy for a moment, in spite of the outward change in him now, a "war-worn warrior" whose "golden locks" have "waved dark and dim"—

> for India's clime
> Had touched him with the iron hoar of time.

They are confident of finding behind the altered mask, the old face, but he, after a few moments' effort to hide his dismay in all the alteration he feels in himself, asks to go to his old room to hide his distress.

> The twilight hour appears,
> The hour ordained by God for man's repose,
> Yet often made by man an hour of woes,
> A summing-up of daylight's toils and grief
> Of moody musings, not of wild relief.

He goes up to his old room, the room Branwell knew so well, with its faded print of "The Death of Wolfe" on the wall, and suffers at the realisation that it means nothing any more to him.

> 'Twas that dim print that over Indian seas
> First led his feet and fixed his destinies.
> So why on what was childhood's chief delight
> Will manhood hardly deign to bend his sight?
> The old print remains—but does the *old mind* remain?
> Ah World!—why wilt thou break enchantment's chain?

There, too, he finds the very bed on which

> Long years ago had lain his infant head
> In sleep unstained by sorrow.

In the darkened room he sits reflecting on what this return in fact means.

> Yes—now at last I've reached my native home,
> And all who love me joy to see me come . . .
> I have seen my Father full of honoured days,
> Whom last I saw adorned with manhood's grace, . . .
>   . . . I have seen her too
> The first I loved on earth—the first I knew—
> She who was wont above that very bed
> To bend with blessings o'er my helpless head,
> I have seen my Sister—I have seen them all—
> All but myself. They have lost me past recall,
> As I have them. And vainly have I come
> These thousand leagues—my Home is not my Home.

He tries to analyse the cause for this and finds it has nothing to do with physical change. The family, he reflects, is unaware of the change in his heart.

> They did not think my head and heart were older,
> My strength more broken, and my feeling colder—

and he faces the fact that the very name of "Home Affections" has no abiding sense; mutability is the law of life.

> . . . Where have we a home
> For ever doomed in thought or deed to roam,
> To lay our parents in their narrow rest
> Or leave their hearth stones when we love them best.

He is aware, as never before, of the effect of a changed heart.

Tintern Abbey.

> Well! I have talked of change—but oh, how changed
> Am I from him who o'er those dim hills ranged
> With trusty dog—poor Rover!—where art thou?
> I seem to see thee looking upward now
> To thy young Master's face, with honest eye
> Shining all over with no selfish joy. . . .

To deflect his thoughts he picks up an old book left lying in his room and finds, inscribed on its fly-leaf a prayer, written and signed many years ago by "Caroline", and recalls his parting from her, and her prophetic words foretelling the very change he is now aware of in himself.

> "You'll perhaps survive," said Caroline,
>   "through many a field of blood,
> You'll perhaps gain fame's rewards—but never more
> Those far-off climes *my* Henry shall restore
> To England's hills again. Another mind—
> Another heart than that he left behind—
> And other hopes he'll bring—if hope at all
> Can outlive fancy's flight and feeling's fall
> To flourish on an iron-hardened brow—
> The soldier may return—but never Thou!"

Then, in a flight where truth and feeling meet in a fine fusion rare indeed in his writing, Branwell faces the fact that he can no more recover Caroline than she can him.

> Alas, Lost Shade! Why should I look upon
> The mouldering letters of thy burial stone!
> Why should I strive thine image to recall,
> And love thy beauty's flower, and weep its fall?
> It cannot be—for far too well I know
> The narrow house where thou art laid below. . . .
> I know that if from weeds I cleared thy name . . .
> 'Twould be of no avail—*Thou* couldst not come. . . .
> No, Caroline—the hours are long gone by
> When I could call a shade reality,
> Or make a world of dreams, or think that one
> Was present with me who, I knew, was gone.
> No—if the sapling *bends* to every breeze,
> Their force shall rather *break* the full-grown trees.

> If Infancy can catch at every toy,
> Pursuits more solid must the Man employ.
> He feels what *is*, and nought can charm away
> The rough realities of present day.
> Thou art dead—I am living—my world is not thine,
> So keep thy sleep—and, Farewell Caroline!

At the age of twenty-one, when the first draft of this poem was written, Branwell was taking a last farewell not merely of his childhood and all its fond memories, but of the imaginary world which had for all too long been his life—not gradually and painlessly, but brutally had the chrysalis been broken that cast him now with maimed wings upon an uncomprehending world. How alien it was to the incurable romantic he had been born and bred to be, the poem goes on to tell:

> Yet—while I think so, while I speak farewell,
> 'Tis not in words the dreariness to tell
> Which sweeps across my spirit—for my soul
> Feels such a midnight o'er its musings roll
> At losing—though it be a vapour vain—
> What once was rest to toil and ease to pain.
> I knew not while afar, how utterly
> These memories of Youth were past from me. . . .
> . . . I did not think I *could* be seated here,
> After the lapse of many a toilsome year
> Once more returning to accustomed places
> Amid the smiles of "old familiar faces"
> Yet shrinking from them—hiding in the gloom
> Of this dull evening and secluded room,
> Not to recall the spirit of the boy,
> But all my world-worn energies to employ
> In pondering o'er some artifice to gain
> A seat in council or command in Spain. . . .

Sir Henry, remote indeed as he is from Branwell's destiny, can sit and contemplate the fulfilment of all his ambitions. He has risen to the highest military command, he has been knighted for gallantry in the field and has but to ask for "gain and glory—place and power" to have all and even more accorded him—but even in the heart of his success he sees the hollow centre—

> Thou gavest them all—I have them all this hour
> But I forgot to ask for youthful blood,
> The thrill divine of feelings unsubdued,
> The nerves that quivered to the sound of fame,
> The tongue that trembled o'er a lover's name,

> The eye that glistened with delightful tears,
> The Hope that gladdened past and gilded future years. . . .

It is as though, acutely sensible as he was of the succession of failures behind him, Branwell was tasting the dust and ashes even of that success which he would never know, and which, if achieved, could never compensate now for the loss of the kingdom and crown which once had been his in the realm of fairyland.

> So, Caroline—I'll bid farewell once more
> Nor mourn, lost shade, for though thou'rt gone before,
> Gone is thy Henry too—

Here, in this last encounter face to face with his dead sister, he reaches to a truth which, while it bereaves him of all hope, stills once and for ever the heartache of the intervening years. Returned a changed man to an unrecognisable home, he realises now that even had Caroline, his perfect sister, lived, she too would have been changed (as even then he was sensing the change in Charlotte, Emily and Anne) and become "cold, perhaps" to him. For

> . . . hadst thou lived, thine angel heart, like mine
> Would soon have hardened with thy youth's decline—
> Cold, perhaps, to me, if beating, as when laid
> Beneath its grave-stone 'neath the churchyard shade. . . .

With this acceptance he exorcises once and for all the ghost of Caroline. Comfortless he lies on the old bed as twilight gathers outside. And then, from the dome of darkness framed by the window, he sees the evening-star, the old, old symbol to him of his sister Maria. It has one more message to bring him with which to face the future. In all this remarkable poem nothing is more symptomatic of the change in Branwell than the sanity and courage of its end. Here, for the first time, we are made to feel he has become a man—here, in his acceptance of loss as a law of life, in his abiding faith in love, he has reached a philosophy of compromise astounding indeed in so intemperate a romantic. Could Branwell have walked by the light of this revelation to the end, he would not have made such a pitiable fiasco of his life.

> So, while he lay there, twilight deepened fast . . .
> Till chairs and pictures lost themselves in gloom
> And but a window glimmered through the room,
> With one pale star above the sombre trees. . . .
> And though his eye scarce saw it, yet his mind,

As, half to wake and half to dreams resigned,
Could scarce help feeling in its holy shine
The solemn look of sainted Caroline,
With mute reproachfulness reminding him
That faith and fondness were not all a dream;
That form, not feeling, should be changed by clime;
That looks, not love, should suffer hurt by time;
That o'er life's waters, guiding us from far,
And brightening with life's night, should glisten
                                    Memory's star.

This poem, of which two manuscripts exist, was first copied by
Emily Brontë for her brother with the inscription "Bradford July
31st 1838". The later completed version with the altered title, "Sir
Henry Tunstall", was sent by Branwell both to *Blackwood's* and to
De Quincey on 15th April 1840, and published in Mrs Oliphant's
Annals of a Publishing House (1897) and in the *De Quincey Memorials*
in 1891. Representing the labour of more than a year, it marks the
climax of Branwell's poetic achievement.

· · · · ·

According to Grundy, who became his intimate in 1841, it was
during the depression following on his Bradford failure that Branwell took to opium. The habit, started, so he confessed to Grundy,
in imitation of De Quincey, whose *Confessions* he then read for the
first time, "seized on his nervous system" till he "underwent the
torture of the damned".

Like De Quincey, he had capital motives—so he could convince
himself—for taking to it. The current belief, propagated by De
Quincey, that opium arrested the development of tuberculosis,
would find ready credence with Branwell, all too conscious as many
of his writings of the time attest, of his physical decay, and living
ever in the recollection of his sisters' deaths from the scourge.

Not least among De Quincey's revelations was that respecting
the absolute ease with which opium could at that time be procured.
Every druggist sold it in its liquid form (laudanum) or made up in
pills—the known panacea unaffectedly resorted to for all pain, and
very cheap and effective. "So much so," relates De Quincey, "that
on a Saturday afternoon the counters of the druggists were strewed
with pills of one, two or three grains in preparation for the known
demand of the evening. The immediate occasion of this practice

was the lowness of the wages which, at that time, would not allow them to indulge in ale or spirits."

With opium undercutting the price of spirits, a plausible secondary reason might be found for Branwell's new-found preference. He was finding drink an increasing drain on his resources, yet without some stimulant he could not get through his day. The extent of his excesses at the time can be gauged by the confession contained in the letter he would shortly write to John Brown—from Broughton in March 1840—that since taking up his post in the New Year and eschewing whisky, his hand no longer shook.

Branwell learned from the pages of De Quincey "that no quantity of opium ever did, or ever could, intoxicate"—a piece of advice not lost upon the parson's son, whose growing problem must have been how to hide from his father and aunt the state in which he all too frequently now returned home. If the same degree of comfort and consolation could be achieved by the cheaper anodyne, he would account himself a fool not to try it. For De Quincey was at the moment one of his gods, whose judgment he would shortly be consulting and whose example he would slavishly follow with all the old infatuation for great men displayed by Patrick Benjamin Wiggins. De Quincey clearly indicated the way to pleasures more lasting than and superior to any he yet knew—and exempt, so he deceived himself, from the known hazards of drink. "The pleasure given by wine," wrote De Quincey, "is always rapidly mounting, and tending to a crisis, after which it rapidly declines; that from opium, when once generated, is stationary for eight or ten hours: the first, to borrow a technical distinction from medicine, is a case of acute, the second of chronic, pleasure; the one is a flickering flame, the other a steady and equable glow. But the main distinction lies in this—that, whereas wine disorders the mental faculties, opium, on the contrary . . . introduces amongst them the most exquisite order, legislation and harmony. Wine robs a man of his self-possession; opium sustains and reinforces it. . . ."

The arrival in August 1839 of a new curate to help Mr Brontë— the Rev. William Weightman, M.A.—may have determined Branwell to make another effort to earn his living. Ultimately he would count "Willie" Weightman among the small number of his "best friends". Weightman had a sanguine temperament, high spirits, and a kind heart, which eventually procured him, in varying degrees, the love and friendship of the entire Brontë family, including Papa and Aunt. He may have helped Branwell, both practically and morally, to find a way out of the morass in which he was foundering. Willie Weightman came down from Durham with a glowing record of classical attainments and must have aroused, like all Branwell's friends, a fierce, if transitory emulatory spark—enough, at least, to influence him to seek that post of tutor for which his father had been coaching him since June.

Weightman's home town was Appleby, in Westmorland, and in considering Branwell's present destination—Ulverston in the Furness peninsula, so removed from all the Brontës' previous haunts —it is tempting to wonder whether Weightman had no hand in recommending him there.

Be that as it may, by the end of December 1839, Branwell's departure was imminent. Charlotte, writing on the 28th to Ellen, thus announced the fact, not without some illuminating remarks about her brother and about her own attitude to him.

> ... One thing will make the daily routine more unvaried than ever. Branwell, who used to enliven us, is to leave us in a few days to enter the situation of a private tutor in the neighbourhood of Ulverston. How he will like or settle remains yet to be seen; at present he is full of hope and resolution.
>
> I, who know his variable nature, and his strong turn for active life, dare not be too sanguine. We are as busy as possible preparing for his departure, and shirt-making and collar-stitching fully occupy our time. ...

Even so soberly would Elizabeth Hastings have written of her brother's chances of rehabilitation. Still, "he was the same brother to her he had always been", and his departure, far from relieving the home-circle of a burden, would deprive it of an enlivening influence.

The post to which Branwell was going on the last day of 1839 was as tutor in the family of Mr Postlethwaite of Broughton House, Broughton-in-Furness, ten miles north-west of Ulverston.

Chapter Thirteen

MR POSTLETHWAITE'S TUTOR

He was indeed breaking new ground, and, whether intentionally so or by mere accident, going to a part of the country peculiarly cherished by De Quincey. As a Lancastrian, De Quincey had always felt, so he explained in the *Confessions*, a "kind of mystic privilege" in the fact that some of the English Lakes were situated in Lancastrian territory—Esthwaite and Coniston Waters and the west shores of Windermere—and rejoiced in possessing "some fraction of denizenship in the fairy little domain of the English Lakes".

Their beauty had been known to Branwell all his life by the writings of the very group of poets who were his favourites—Wordsworth, Southey, Coleridge—and even their semblance partially known to him by the sketches of William Gilpin, whose studies in the "Picturesque", published the previous century, and particularly his *Tour of the Lakes* (1786) had supplied so many models for Branwell's and his sisters' earliest attempts at drawing. That Ulverston was only eighteen miles from the shores of Windermere, Grasmere and Rydal, where the Wordsworths, Hartley Coleridge and De Quincey himself yet lived, can have had no small share in making Branwell decide to accept the post.

The journey would have to be broken at Kendal, and probably at Ulverston as well. The early fall of darkness and the almost equally certain fall of snow before the day's end in that district, made this a necessary as well as a welcome prospect.

He was starting out, as Charlotte had written three days before, "full of hope and resolution". The resolution lasted all the fifty odd miles to Kendal, when the hazards of the road threw him into the kind of company best calculated to reduce all such resolutions to nonsense.

Branwell's famous letter about his night at Kendal has been quoted and re-quoted in evidence against him, since its first publication by Mary Duclaux in her *Emily Brontë* and there is nothing to add to the chorus of obloquy—except the reflection that on his way to Kendal the coach would pass, shortly after leaving Ingleton, a place that even then, after all those years, would so stab the heart

Broughton House

"My employer is a retired county magistrate,
a large landowner. . . ."

Broughton Church, from the drawing by Branwell Brontë, March 1840

within him that any extravagance of behaviour might be expected to follow.

Whether Branwell anticipated it or not, the buildings of the Clergy Daughters' School—the school itself long since transferred to Casterton—stood, and still stand, at the bend in the lane below the little bridge that gives its name to the village of Cowan Bridge. There, for the first time he saw, from the coach windows that bore him northwards, the place whose name was anathema in his family, and about which he had fretted his heart for almost as long as he could remember. There were the low buildings, the meagre gardens, the whole confined area that had been the last sorrowful setting of his beloved Maria's life. In summer, the pleasant pasturelands, the wooded streams, the great hills rolling in gathering crests away to Westmorland, impart a nobility to the place which relieves much of its sadness. But to Branwell on that dying winter day, there can have been little to alleviate the pain of memories too poignant to be borne.

Kendal lay little more than ten miles ahead and, once snugly ensconced in the hospitable bar of the *Royal Hotel*, it was easier to obliterate the image. How the evening was spent he wrote in great detail several weeks later from Broughton to his crony John Brown. The text, extensively bowdlerised by successive editors, reads as follows:

OLD KNAVE OF TRUMPS—Don't think I have forgotten you, though I have delayed so long in writing to you. It was my purpose to send you a yarn as soon as I could find materials to spin one with, and it is only just now that I have had time to turn myself round and know where I am. If you saw me now you would not know me, and you would laugh to hear the character the people give me. Oh, the falsehood and hypocrisy of this world! I am fixed in a little retired town by the sea-shore, among wild woody hills that rise round me—huge, rocky, and capped with clouds. My employer is a retired county magistrate, a large landowner, of a right hearty and generous disposition. His wife is a quiet, silent, and amiable woman; his sons are two fine, spirited lads. My landlord is a respectable surgeon, and six days out of seven as drunk as a lord! His wife is a bustling, chattering, kind-hearted soul; and his daughter!—oh! death and damnation! Well, what am I? That is, what do they think I am? A most calm, sedate, sober, abstemious, patient, mild-hearted, virtuous, gentlemanly philosopher—the picture of good works, and the treasure-house of righteous thoughts. Cards are shuffled under the table-cloth, glasses are thrust into the cupboard, if I enter the room. I take neither spirits, wine, nor malt liquors. I dress in black, and smile like a saint or martyr. Every lady says, "What a good young gentleman is the Postle-thwaites' tutor!" This is fact, as I am a living soul, and right comfortably do I laugh at them; but in this humour do I mean them to continue. I took a half-year's farewell of old friend whisky at Kendal on the night after I left. There was a party of gentlemen at the Royal Hotel; I joined them. and we ordered in supper and "toddy as 'hot as hell!'" They thought I was a physician, and put me in the chair. I gave them some toasts, of the stiffest sort . . . washing them down at the same time, till the room spun round and the candles danced in their eyes. One was a respectable old gentleman with powdered head, rosy cheeks, fat paunch, and ringed fingers . . . he led off with a speech, and in two minutes, in the very middle of a grand sentence, he stopped, wagged his head, looked wildly round, stammered, coughed, stopped again, and called for his slippers and so the waiter helped him to bed. Next a tall Irish squire and a native of the land of Israel began to quarrel about their countries; and, in the warmth of argument, discharged their glasses, each at his neighbour's throat instead of his own. I recommended bleeding, purging, and blistering; but they administered each other a real "Jem Warder", so I flung my tumbler to the floor too, and swore I'd join "Old Ireland"! A regular rumpus ensued, but we were tamed at last, and I found myself in bed next morning, with a bottle of porter, a glass, and a corkscrew beside me. Since then I have not tasted anything stronger than milk-and-water, nor, I hope, shall, till I return at Midsummer; when we will see about it. I am getting as fat as Prince William at Springhead, and as godly as his friend, Parson Winterbotham. My hand shakes no longer. I ride to the banker's at Ulverston with Mr. Postlethwaite, and sit drinking tea and talking slander with old ladies. As to the young ones! I have one sitting by me just now—fair-faced, blue-eyed, dark-haired, sweet eighteen—she little thinks the devil is so near her!

I was delighted to see thy note, old squire, but I do not understand one sentence—you will perhaps know what I mean. . . . How are all about you? I long to hear and see them again. How is the "Devil's Thumb", whom men call —— ——, and the "Devil in Mourning", whom they call —— ——, and —— —— and the Doctor; and him who will be used as the tongs of hell—he whose eyes Satan looks out of, as from windows—I mean —— ——, esquire? How are little —— ——, —— "Longshanks", —— ——, and the rest of them? Are they married, buried, devilled, and damned? When I come I'll give them a good squeeze of the hand; till then I am too godly for them to think of. That bow-legged devil used to ask me impertinent questions which I answered him in kind. Beelzebub will make of him a walking-stick! Keep to thy teetotalism, old squire, till I return; I will mend thy old body. . . . Does "Little Nosey" think I have forgotten him? No, by Jupiter! nor his clock either. I'll send him a remembrancer some of these days! But I must talk to some one prettier than thee; so good night, old boy, and Believe me thine, THE PHILOSOPHER. Write directly. Of course you won't show this letter; and, for Heaven's sake, blot out all the lines scored with red ink.

What time he reached Ulverston after waking the next day, "with a bottle of porter, a glass and a corkscrew" beside him, does not appear.

The distance to Broughton was thirty-six miles, and the road, lying westwards and seawards, was markedly different from the straight line of the preceding day. It brought him constantly round abrupt turns and precipitous rises and falls, now veering northwards, and again violently sweeping over to the west, bringing him his first breath-taking sight of the mountains round Windermere and Coniston from the plateau of High Newton.

From there on the mountains of three counties were about him all the way, towering away to the farthest north and west in tier upon tier of heaving crests, soaring peaks and stark ridges. A more romantic prospect it would be difficult, at any time, to imagine, till the sheer drop down to the Greenodd estuary confronts the traveller with the first sight of the sea, and he realises only then that his cup is full.

In those days Ulverston was at the end of the coach run. Branwell would have many occasions to get to know it thereafter, as it was the administrative centre for the Furness district, and before the railways deflected much of the commerce from its port—with a wealth of shipping lying in its docks—a prosperous little town with a weekly market dating back to the reign of Stephen. Enough remains of its old-world character today, its coaching-inns and cobbled streets and narrow alleys, its many bow-fronted shops and overall Georgian character, to realise the charm it exercised in its hey-day.

From Ulverston, his journey had to be completed by gig, unless Mr Postlethwaite sent over a carriage or a servant and horses to meet him.

There were ten miles yet to go and it being mid-winter and darkness long since fallen, the probabilities are he stayed overnight at Ulverston. Whenever it was he had his first sight of the country round Broughton, he would not have regretted the decision that brought him there.

Rising and falling at gradients of 1 in 6, the road traverses nothing but the wildest and most mountainous country, culminating in the sudden vision of the Duddon estuary and, beyond it, the massive head and deep brow of Black Combe (1,969 feet) detaching itself from the surrounding heights and seeming to rise like a great isolated bulwark straight from the sea.

To any Brontë surroundings of natural beauty were an essential, and here was everything to stir the poet in Branwell to excitement and rapture. When at Grisebeck the road suddenly twisted and dropped down to sea-level and all the reality of Broughton lay before him, he might indeed have exclaimed, as all those years ago at the Rydings, at finding himself in paradise. Unfortunately, at Broughton, there were his employers to be reckoned with, and they had now to be faced with whatever courage he could summon.

The greater part of the little town had to be traversed first—a small market town pleasantly enclosed within itself and conveying even now an impression of timeless and changeless repose. The houses, like those of the West Riding, were built of stone, but a light grey stone, and roofed with bluish slate. At the bend in the road leading to the central square where the Postlethwaites lived, stood the *Old King's Head*, which has every appearance yet today of being coeval with Charles I, whose head graces its sign. The small square, hemmed in with private houses and bordered with chestnut trees, had more the air of a cathedral close than that of a market place, yet here the markets were held and here, on the corner opposite the *King's Head* stood Broughton House, the home of Branwell's employers and the end of his present journey.

It stood flush on the street, a solid two-storied house, stone-built throughout, with pedimented doorway and a fine array of Georgian windows. It had been built by the father of Branwell's employer in the previous century.

The family into which Branwell now entered as tutor had been established in the district since the thirteenth century, and had held high posts in the magistrature and civil administration. When Branwell knew them, the family consisted of father, mother and two boys, John and William, aged respectively 12 and 10½. The parents had been unfortunate in losing four other children before this date, two little girls (one of whom was John's twin and christened Margaret) and two other sons, Robert and Thomas, who had died in infancy.

Mr Postlethwaite had been born in 1784 and was thus a man in his early fifties when Branwell arrived at Broughton. He was a vigorous, active man, filling the functions of Justice of the Peace and Deputy Lieutenant for the county, and a noted fox-hunter to boot. His prowess in the field is yet remembered in the family and commemorated by a chased silver hunting-cup embossed with hunting-scenes, presented to him in 1831 by the local farmers as an "expression of their gratitude".

Mr Postlethwaite had married in 1823 Agnes, the daughter of William Lewthwaite, Esq. of Broadgate in Cumberland, himself a Justice of the Peace and Deputy Lieutenant of his county.

Branwell, as has been seen, described his employer as "a large landowner, and of a right hearty and generous disposition", and his lady as "a quiet, silent, and amiable woman". Of the two boys he said that they were "fine, spirited lads". Unlike his sisters, he does not seem to have disliked his employers on sight.

Their demands, moreover, do not seem to have been excessive, and to judge by the evidence that has come to light he was left a very free hand in planning his pupils' lessons. That the outdoor life suited him his letter to John Brown attests. To have beautiful scenery to sketch, and the use of a horse to ride to Ulverston was exactly the kind of activity he liked, and the very fact that, as he declared to John Brown, he meant "to continue in their good opinion", is proof that he was satisfied.

He did not live at Broughton House but lodged with a Dr Gibson, the local surgeon referred to in his letter. Whether the attractions of the daughter were all that Branwell retailed or somewhat heightened to arouse the envy of his Haworth cronies, the mere fact of having a feminine audience before whom to perform raised his spirits, and completed the work of restoration begun by his abstinence.

Broughton, in fact, suited him physically and mentally, and he might have done well had the too-easy regime not induced him to believe there were no rules at all worth observing. There were other contacts available, outside his duties, and he found himself in no sense shut off from companionship. At Ulverston there was a Masonic Lodge, the "Oddfellows", to whose members he may have had introductions. The four main hostelries of the town—*The Sun Hotel, The Queen's, The King's Arms* and *The Rose* were not without their attractions, both for their cheer and for their influx of travellers, towards whom the gregarious Branwell naturally gravitated. The bow-fronted shops, displaying in heavy gold lettering on black grounds the enticing choice and variety of the goods obtainable inside, were among the best supplied in his experience.

As the gentlemen rode into town once a week to bank Mr Postlethwaite's rents and fetch the select blend of tea affected by his wife, the tutor, temporarily in funds for the first time in years, could contemplate the purchase of Macassar oil or of a Havana cigar, listed among the specialities to be obtained at the "Perfumers and Chymist's". It was not a disagreeable life.

The doorway of the bank to which Branwell rode every week

with his employer, the Lancaster Banking Co. in King Street, stands yet today. It had the distinction of being the oldest joint stock bank in England. Though the bank moved premises long ago, the pillared portico and high pedimented windows of the original building can still be seen forming part of an ironmongers' store.

That Branwell had plenty of leisure and used some of it, at least, to a good purpose, may be judged by the work he put into his translation of Horace's Odes, a specimen of which he sent to Hartley Coleridge on 20th April.

As spring advanced he had increasing opportunities, also, of visiting the beautiful country spread on every side. Black Combe lay only five miles to the west of Broughton and that it was not merely a landmark on his horizon but a closely observed and intimate presence, the sonnet to which he gave its name attests.

BLACK COMB

Far off, and half revealed, 'mid shade and light,
Black Comb half smiles, half frowns; his mighty form
Scarce bending into peace, more formed to fight
A thousand years of struggles with a storm
Than bask one hour subdued by sunshine warm
To bright and breezeless rest; yet even his height
Towers not o'er this world's sympathies; he smiles—
While many a human heart to pleasure's wiles
Can bear to bend, and still forget to rise—
As though he, huge and heath-clad on our sight,
Again rejoices in his stormy skies.
Man loses vigour in unstable joys.
Thus tempests find Black Comb invincible,
While we are lost, who should know life so well.

The excellence of his Horace translations, attested by classical scholars and poets alike, and upon which he busied himself at Broughton, prompted him yet once again to try his luck at a literary career.

Translations from the classical—and, for that matter, from the Continental—poets were a paying proposition at the time, and far more likely to bring an unknown young writer before the public than original composition—unless it were of an outstanding character. Branwell was aware perhaps of the benefit to his own formless and diffuse style of writing of the terse phrase and rigid frame of the Latin poet, and hoped more might be achieved by his Horace Odes than from all his other verse put together. To make security doubly sure, on 15th April he wrote to De Quincey—since 1809 the tenant of Wordsworth's "Dove Cottage"—enclosing the completed version of "The Wanderer" now re-named "Sir Henry Tunstall", and on 20th April to Hartley Coleridge, enclosing two of his "Horace Odes" and his poem "At dead of midnight, drearily" (Harriet II).

His letter to De Quincey has not been preserved; the text of his letter to Hartley Coleridge reads:

Broughton-in-Furness,
Lancashire, April 20th, 1840.

Sir

It is with much reluctance that I venture to request, for the perusal of the following lines, a portion of the time of one upon whom I can have no claim, and should not dare to intrude; but I do not, personally, know a man on whom to rely for an answer to the question I shall put, and I could not resist my longing to ask a man from whose judgement there would be little hope of appeal.

Since my childhood I have been wont to devote the hours I could spare from other and very different employments to efforts at literary composition, always keeping the results to myself, nor have they in more than two or three instances been seen by any other. But I am about to enter active life, and prudence tells me not to waste the time which must make my independence; yet, sir, I love writing too well to fling aside the practice of it without an effort to ascertain whether I could turn it to account, not in *wholly* maintaining myself, but in *aiding* my maintenance, for I do not sigh after fame and am not ignorant of the folly or the fate of those who, without ability, would depend for their lives upon their pens; but I do seek to know, and venture, though with shame, to ask from one whose word I must respect: whether, by periodical or other writing, I could please myself with writing, and make it subservient to living.

I would not, with this view, have troubled you with a composition in verse, but any piece I have in prose would too greatly trespass upon your patience, which, I fear, if you look over the verse, will be more than sufficiently tried.

I feel the egotism of my language, but I have none, sir, in my heart, for I feel beyond all encouragement from myself, and I hope for none from you.

Should you give any opinion upon what I send, it will, however condemnatory, be most gratefully received by—Sir, your most humble servant,

P. B. Brontë.

The result was an invitation to go over to Ambleside to visit Coleridge, which Branwell did on 1st May 1840.

It was a day that would remain for ever memorable to Branwell —one of the rare days in his unlucky life when he was accepted on terms of equality by a man of letters, one of the illustrious fortunate, so poor Branwell thought, who had climbed the hard slopes of Parnassus and was securely placed upon its snowy peak.

As it happened, there was a strange similarity of temperament and of fortune discernible between these two, which may explain the instant bond of sympathy that sprang up between them.

Hartley Coleridge was considerably the older man, at that time already forty-five and losing fast that uncanny childish look which had puzzled and fascinated friends and critics alike.

His precocity as a child had far out-distanced Branwell's. With such a father and such an uncle as he had, with Coleridge, Southey, and Wordsworth too bent over his cradle and watching his every stirring of consciousness, it was little surprising that at four he was an argumentative metaphysician, prodigiously concerned with the nature and appearance of Reality, discoursing upon the difference between "Me" and "I", and illustrating his deductions by seizing his own left arm with his right hand and saying: ". . . there's a deal of Hartleys. There's Picture-Hartley [pointing to the portrait Hazlitt had painted of him] and there's Shadow-Hartley [looking behind him in the sunlit room], there's Echo-Hartley and there's Catch-me-fast-Hartley."

This adored child, whose sweetness of disposition was equal only to his precocious wisdom, had created at the age of six a world in all things comparable to Branwell's "Glass Town", and which he called "Ejuxria", imagining that it was sprung from a cataract in a field adjoining his happy home at Greta Hall. To this cataract he gave the name of "Jug-force"—from which his kingdom was called "Jug-forcia" and, later, Ejuxria.

It was a dream world that wholly occupied him and gave him much concern. His father asking him one day as they were walking out together what made him so thoughtful, Hartley answered: "My people are too fond of war, and I have just made an eloquent speech in the Senate, which has not made any impression on them, and to war they will go." This was language that would have been wholly understandable to "Little Bany".

Alas for Hartley Coleridge! He, too, throughout his childhood was subject to violent rages, which his younger and very perceptive brother, Derwent, remembered later and diagnosed with great sagacity as "the disguise of pity, self-accusation or other painful emotion", and, in the final analysis, as "an organic defect, a congenital imperfection", that recalls forcibly Charlotte's words about young Victor Crimsworth. Hartley's excessive sensibility made him tremble all his life at receipt of a letter, and caused him to shy away from all responsibility and pain.

Unlike Branwell, he had had some regular schooling—though his profound scholarship must chiefly be attributed to the companionship of his father, the Wordsworths, his Uncle Southey, and the latter's notable library at Greta Hall containing more than 30,000 titles. Thanks to his Uncle Southey, also, Hartley went up to Merton College, Oxford, and was later even elected a Fellow of Oriel. The cloistered life, however, had nothing to charm his restless spirit and he chafed under the restraint. Literature was all his passion and a failure to secure the Newdigate Prize almost unhinged his mind. In still closer affinity to Branwell Brontë, under the bitterness of disappointment he took to drink, a course which inevitably lost him his Fellowship. He took his dismissal gladly, seeing in the academic world nothing but injustice and chicanery, and joyfully made his way back to the Lakes. It was the only place where his spirit felt at home and where his genius found an outlet. He earned a desultory living, going as far as Leeds, as has been seen, to write his "Northern Worthies", teaching for a term here and there in boys' schools, treading very much the same path as his friend Branwell, but all the while writing copiously poetry, drama, and criticism. He wrote fairly regularly also for *The London Magazine* and *Blackwood's*. His connections with the great triumvirate, Coleridge, Southey and Wordsworth, brought him the friendship of such men as John Wilson, editor of *Blackwood's*—whose lovely home, Elleray, on the banks of Lake Windermere, was a constant refuge for Hartley Coleridge. His "table talk" was almost as delectable as his father's and as eagerly sought.

John Wilson's daughter, remembering those frequent visits, wrote later: "Everyone loved Hartley Coleridge; there was something in his appearance that evoked kindliness. Extremely boyish in aspect, his juvenile air was aided not a little by his general mode of dress—a dark blue cloth round jacket, white trousers, black silk handkerchief tied loosely round his throat; sometimes a straw hat covered his head, but more frequently it was bare, showing his black, thick, short, curling hair. His eyes were large, dark and expressive, and a countenance almost sad in expression was relieved by the beautiful smile which lighted it from time to time. The contrast between him and the Professor [her father] as they walked up and down the drawing-room at Elleray was very striking. My father's rapid sweeping steps would soon have distanced poor Coleridge if he had not kept up with him by a sort of short trot . . . the Professor's athletic form, stately and free in action, and his clear blue eyes and flowing hair contrasting with Hartley's diminutive stature and dark complexion. . . ."

By the terms of his father's will, a trust fund was set up to secure to poor Hartley some comfort in his declining years. In touching terms, wherein the confession both of his son's and his own sadly unpractical nature was made, Samuel Taylor Coleridge wrote in July 1830:

"Most desirous to secure, as far as in me lies, for my dear son, Hartley Coleridge, the tranquillity indispensable to any continued and successful exertion of his literary talents, and which, from the like characters of our minds in this respect, I know to be especially requisite for his happiness . . . I affix this codicil to my last will and testament. . . ."

Since 1837 Hartley had been living in a dream cottage on the shores of Rydal Water, mid-way between Ambleside and Grasmere and within a few minutes' walk of Rydal Mount, where lived his life-long friends the Wordsworths. There he pursued the only existence for which he was fit, the life of a poet and philosopher in closest communion with Nature.

Here, to Nab Cottage, came Branwell Brontë on that 1st May 1840 appointed by Hartley Coleridge for their meeting. The cottage still stands today, almost flush with the winding high road, and sheltered and over-shadowed through all the months of summer by the giant beech trees that border the lake. It is a long low structure darkened by the mass of ivy that clusters round its porch and up its chimney-stack. Little patches of cottage garden flank it on either side, and behind it fields rise sharply towards the precipitous flank of Nab Scar. A description of its interior as it was when Branwell visited it, fortunately exists:

Most days the window blind was down, so that when you were in the room you had "a light much like a shade". Hartley was seldom in in summer or fine weather; one side was occupied by something which resembled a pigeon-box rather than a book-case; then there was a door covered with red-baize, that looked like the entrance to a closet, but which you found to be a receptacle for a little white-curtained bed. The fire-place had large hobs and what school-boys would call "caves" where pipes rested. Over the mantel-piece hung a cocked hat and feather, and a sword—I believe his father's—and a print of one of his father's earliest friends. Within arm's length of an old-fashioned chair, with claws and grotesque arms, was the book he most used, Anderson's *British Poets*. Floor and table and window-seat were piled up with dusty papers. . . .

How Hartley appeared to strangers, another pen has described in recounting a visit made only four years after Branwell's. Of Hartley issuing from his cottage, Aubrey De Vere wrote in 1844: "He could scarcely be said to have walked, for he seemed with difficulty to keep his feet on the ground, as he wavered about near us with arms extended like wings. Everything that he said was strange and quaint . . . always representing a mind whose thoughts dwell in regions as remote as the antipodes. After 50 years of ill-fortune the man before us was still the child described by Wordsworth. . . . It was a strange thing to see Hartley Coleridge fluctuating about the room, now with one hand on his head, now with both arms extended like a swimmer's. There was some element wanting in his being. He could do everything but keep his footing, and, doubtless, in his inner world of thought, it was easier for him to fly than to walk, and to walk than to stand. There seemed to be no gravitating principle in him."

Such was the host who came forward to greet Branwell. If one aspect, more than another, of Hartley Coleridge, was calculated to set Branwell at ease, it was his diminutive figure, allowing Branwell for once in his life that coveted sense of superiority which in his special relationships he had all too frequently been denied.

Hartley was small and sympathetic. He might truthfully see in the ardent young man before him the image of what he himself might have been, but for the security of an income, and if family connections had not everywhere opened the doors of literary coteries to him.

Hartley had unquestionably the finer mind, the deeper erudition, the more genuine talent, and, in most respects, a better character than Branwell Brontë. For him, sponsored by his father and his father's illustrious friends, the dedication to literature had been a natural choice and demanded no disguise or secrecy, as for the parsonage children. For them Blackwood's lay at the ends of the earth, inaccessible except to infinitely daring assault, but to Hartley Coleridge it lay just round the corner in Mr Wilson's luxurious drawing-room at Elleray. When the two are fairly compared it is impossible not to reflect what Branwell Brontë might have achieved with Hartley's connections and with Hartley's luck.

Judging Branwell by the quality of the "Odes" submitted to him and unaware of all the starts and set-backs of his chequered youth, seeing only his inexperience and his ardour, Hartley generously advised him to stick to it and make of literature the object of his life.

The advice was intoxicating and never forgotten by Branwell, even in his darkest hour. Hartley urged him to finish translating the First Book of the Odes and promised to read it, when finished, and to use his influence in finding a publisher for it. He also read to Branwell—and gave him—his own translation of the thirty-eighth ode, the only one, strangely enough, he had attempted. Of this ode, the last of Book I, Branwell wrote at the conclusion of his manuscript on 27th June:

"This Ode I have no heart to attempt, after having heard Mr H. Coleridge's translation, on May day, at Ambleside."

It needed no more encouragement than this to raise Branwell to the zenith of hope and enthusiasm and to make him believe that he had one foot already on the stirrup of Pegasus. Patrick Benjamin Wiggins lay not all that distance behind him, and either to stand on his head or to cast himself prostrate before the feet of Great Men was still his first reflex.

Hartley Coleridge entertained him, more than probably at the *Low-Wood Inn*, where he was a regular customer and where the landlord, Jackson, was a generous friend, often asking no more in payment for a glass than a song from his eccentric little customer.

That Branwell's return from Ambleside was both late and inebriated was hardly surprising; nor that a report of the occurrence should reach the ears of his employer. Mentally Mr Postlethwaite made a note to keep a closer watch on his sons' tutor, with a rider that "the sort of poet chap" with whom he had spent the day must be "no go".

Coleridge's advice worked in Branwell like a ferment. From then on there was no more attempt to "continue in the good opinion of his employers". He threw discretion to the winds, and, in the lovely early summer weather, ranged far abroad irrespective of his duties and regardless of time.

Leyland reports how "on one of his pedestrian excursions, he had stepped into a wayside inn, and was seated musing before the parlour fire, when a young gentleman entered the room. Branwell turned round, and recognised at once a friend of the name of Ayrton, whose acquaintance he had formed at Leeds. The surprise and delight at this unexpected meeting was mutual; and Branwell's friend, who was driving about the country, requested his company for some distance on the journey, for the purpose of prolonging the interview, and of continuing the conversation that had been begun. The young tutor drove some ten miles with his friend, utterly regardless of the long return to Ulverston."

Whether the Ayrton of this story were a poet or no, tradition in the Postlethwaite family has it that the end of Branwell's engagement came suddenly in consequence of his going off without leave with "a poet friend" on a prolonged carouse. When night came and he had not returned, the alarm was given and Mr William Postlethwaite, the brother of Branwell's employer, Mr Robert, rode off in search of him. To the ignominious and drunken return that followed there could be but one consequence: dismissal. Mr Brontë's dereliction as a tutor had been gone into by Mr Postlethwaite and on questioning the boys it had been found that latterly he had taught them very little, spending most of their lesson-times in sketching and making up stories in connection with his pictures.

So ended his engagement at Broughton. That he gave a different reason from the true one to his family, appears from the fact that he succeeded in getting his father to write to Mr Postlethwaite and request that he be sent home.

Overjoyed at his regained liberty and burning to get at his translation of Horace, Branwell reappeared in Haworth in June with all the semblance of an injured party. His sisters' experience of teaching in private houses would wholly predispose them to take his part in whatever unpleasantness had occurred between him and his employer.

On 27th June, having finished his translation of Horace, Branwell wrote the following letter to Hartley Coleridge:

Haworth, near Bradford, Yorkshire
27th June, 1840

Sir

You will, perhaps, have forgotten me, but it will be long before I forget my first conversation with a man of real intellect, in my first visit to the classic lakes of Westmorland.

During the delightful day which I had the honour of spending with you at Ambleside, I received permission to transmit to you, as soon as finished, the first book of a translation of Horace, in order that, after a glance over it, you might tell me whether it was worth further notice or better fit for the fire.

I have—I fear most negligently, and amid other very different employments—striven to translate two books, the first of which I have presumed to send you, and will you, sir, stretch your past kindness by telling me whether I should amend and pursue the work or let it rest in peace?

Great corrections I feel it wants, but till I feel that the work might benefit me,

I have no heart to make them; yet if your judgment prove in any way favourable, I will re-write the whole, without sparing labour to reach perfection.

I dared not have attempted Horace but that I saw the utter worthlessness of all former translations, and thought that a better one, by whomsoever executed, might meet with some little encouragement. I long to clear up my doubts by the judgment of one whose opinion I should revere, and—but I suppose I am dreaming —one to whom I should be proud indeed to inscribe anything of mine which any publisher would look at, unless, as is likely enough, the work would disgrace the name as much as the name would honour the work.

Amount of remuneration I should not look to—as anything would be every-thing—and whatever it might be, let me say that my bones would have no rest unless by written agreement a division should be made of the profits (little or much) between myself and him through whom alone I could hope to obtain a hearing with that formidable personage, a London bookseller.

Excuse my unintelligibility, haste, and appearance of presumption, and— Believe me to be, Sir, your most humble and grateful servant,

P. B. Brontë.

If anything in this note should displease you, lay it, sir, to the account of inex-perience and *not* impudence.

So far as is known, the attempt to get his translation published never went any further. Either Hartley, in a period of more than ordinarily muddled thinking and living, took no further steps in the case, or he was unsuccessful in placing Branwell's manuscript. The latter seems the more likely because there is evidence, contained in one of Charlotte's letters to M. Heger four years later, that she too had written to Hartley Coleridge and received encouragement from him. This she would hardly have done if Hartley had treated Bran-well with any want of heart.

The attempt, if ever made, remained unsuccessful, and the need for Branwell to fix upon some more secure source of income than translations from the Latin, again made itself pressingly felt.

His next venture, into a quite different world from any of which he had yet had experience, did not take him from home till the end of September. During the whole of that summer he was at Haworth where he found all his sisters reunited, in an exceptional interval of freedom.

At Haworth, too, were William Weightman, his father's new curate, and Mary Taylor, Charlotte's old school friend, by that time twenty-three years of age and so pretty that Miss Wooler had declared her "too pretty to live".

If over the years Mary stayed less often at the parsonage than Ellen Nussey, it was not that she was less often invited or less loved, for undoubtedly she was the more valued friend of the two. She had her reasons for shunning such visits as, later, she had her reasons for destroying the great bulk of Charlotte's letters. That these were highly confidential is evident from Mary's comment upon them years later to Mrs Gaskell: "I wish I had kept Charlotte's letters now," she wrote, when Mrs Gaskell was engaged in writing Charlotte's *Life*; "I never felt safe to do so until latterly that I have a home of my own. . . ."

Mary migrated to New Zealand in 1845 and at that distance could be—and was—Charlotte's confidante in a way which Ellen Nussey, closely involved in the family's affairs, could less freely be.

There can be no doubt that to Mary Charlotte very fully opened her heart upon the subject which eventually became the skeleton in the Brontë family cupboard: the moral and physical ruin of the only son of the house. That this subject was one of special import to Mary Taylor the evidence remains to show, for she was in love with Branwell Brontë and her love once given, as her friend Charlotte perceived, was incapable of change. Of all the unlikely attachments she could have formed, this was the unlikeliest. High-minded, strong-willed, upright to the core of her being, neither poetical nor romantic, but energetically practical and realistic in all her outlook, born and bred of Dissenting and Radical stock, a rebel burning to break the chains by which Victorian women—and particularly Victorian ladies—were bound, Mary Taylor was of the stuff to mother the Gracchi. Instead, she fell in love with Branwell Brontë and for all her fine intelligence, had the simplicity to let him see it.

The same attraction by opposites had operated in Branwell's case; he, too, had fallen in love with Mary. They were of an age and Mary's dazzling prettiness and strength of character appealed to his congenital weakness and offered a prop without which he could not stand.

The opportunities were not many, and it must have been on a visit of hers during the summer of 1838 when Branwell was just home from Bradford, that the impression was created. A glimpse of them together, afforded in a letter of Charlotte's of the time, conveys the very flutter of first unconscious feeling.

Charlotte, writing to Ellen of the visit of their mutual friends Mary and Martha Taylor on 9th June 1838, mentions "Mary's lively spirits and bright colour" and concludes her note: "They are making such a noise about me I cannot write any more. Mary is playing on the piano; Martha's chattering as fast as her little tongue can run; and Branwell is standing before her, laughing at her vivacity. . . ."

He might be laughing at Martha's vivacity but it was to Mary's playing he was listening, Mary being a passionate lover of music like himself.

On his return from Broughton in June 1840 he found Mary at the parsonage once more. It was during the second half of June and Charlotte, as her correspondence shows, had gone to some pains to time Mary's visit for that particular period.

Writing to Ellen during the visit itself, which "—has been a very pleasant one to us, and I believe to herself also . . ." Charlotte mentions Mary in relationship only to Mr Weightman the curate, with whom she "had several games at chess which generally terminated in a species of mock hostility . . .".

The omission of all mention of Branwell at this stage was not duplicity on Charlotte's part; that Ellen already knew something of the matter appears from a further letter of Charlotte's written late that autumn, when the poor little flower of Mary's romance had already been crushed; it had barely survived the year.

Only as a reflection upon yet another surprising facet of Branwell's character is it a matter of interest now, but to Ellen Nussey, all too susceptible to attentions from the flirtatious Mr Weightman and other gentlemen, the disembalming of Mary's secret was, in Charlotte's view, to serve as a lesson. No young woman should have the folly to give her heart before her hand, and woe to the simpleton who allowed her heart's feelings to show in her face, was the gist of Charlotte's warning. Preaching on this text to the susceptible Ellen (who was, even then, debating upon the suitability of yet another suitor besides Mr Weightman) Charlotte came out with the point of her sermon:

Did I not once tell you of an instance of a Relative of mine who cared for a young lady till he began to suspect that she cared more for him and then instantly conceived a sort of contempt for her? You know to what I allude—never as you value your ears mention the circumstance—but I have two studies—*you* are my study for the success . . . of a quiet, tranquil character. Mary is my study—for the contempt, the remorse,—the misconstruction which follow the development of feelings in themselves noble, warm—generous—devoted and profound—but which being too freely revealed—too frankly bestowed—are not estimated at their real value—God bless her—I never hope to see in this world a character more truly noble—she would *die* willingly for one she loved—her intellect and her attainments are of the very highest standard yet I doubt whether Mary will ever marry.

Nab Cottage, Rydal Water, the home of Hartley Coleridge
from 1837 to 1849

Hartley Coleridge in 1848, after the painting by William Bowness

"It was a white-haired apparition—wearing in all other
respects the semblance of youth."—*Aubrey de Vere*

What Branwell Brontë's destiny might have been could he have measured up to the standards of such a love will remain a teasing question to the end. That he cared for her "till he began to suspect that she cared more for him and then instantly conceived a sort of contempt for her", is but another instance of his incapacity to come to terms with life. So long as it was an unattainable ideal, the love of Mary burned strongly in his heart. Directly it became an accessible reality, he shrank away from it both in scorn and fear.

Mary Taylor, who never married, had ample time in her long and useful life to grieve over the tragedy of her only lover, for whose life, as Charlotte knew, she would once so willingly have given her own.

Whether to flee Mary Taylor the more easily, or from a genuine ripening of sympathy, Branwell spent much time with his father's curate that summer at Haworth. Since both had "classical attainments of no mean order", it is likely that Branwell would show Willy Weightman his Horace translations and get his views on them. They went out with the guns when the shooting season opened, and when Weightman went away to pass his final ordination examinations at Ripon, he wrote to Branwell as to an old friend, "describing certain balls at which he had figured, and announcing that he had been twice over head and ears, desperately in love. . . .".

The friendship thus formed, which Branwell was later to say was one of the dearest in his life, held nothing but benefits in it for him, for, though Weightman talked flightily, he was a strong character, full of life and kindness, and brought Branwell the understanding tolerance his sisters were unable to give.

The "friendly intercourse" related by Francis Leyland, which had occurred between Branwell and Mr Woolven (his fellow traveller at the *Castle Tavern*) during his Bradford days and rambles in the Todmorden district, came to a head this summer with the extension beyond Littleborough and Hebden Bridge of the Manchester-Leeds railway on which Mr Woolven was officially employed.

There can be little doubt, though Leyland does not specifically say so, that it was on inside information received from Mr Woolven that Branwell was prompted to apply for a post with the Manchester-Leeds Railway Company—a post so out of keeping with all his previous experience and training as to have astonished his sisters' biographers ever since. The fact was that Branwell's status as artist and author could not support him any longer, and that so far as a career was concerned, the classics had had their day with him.

According to the minutes of the Company, applications for appointments were being received by the Superintendent of the Line, Captain Laws, R.N., as from 6th July 1840. Only after investigations into character, etc., had been made and the decision to engage the applicant had been taken by Captain Laws, was the appointment laid before the Board.

Branwell's appointment was confirmed at the Board meeting held at Hunt's Bank, Manchester, on 31st August 1840. He was engaged as "Assistant Clerk in Charge" at Sowerby Bridge Station (just about to be opened) at a salary of £75 a year—to increase by £10 every year up to a maximum of £105.

Branwell's superior, the "Clerk in Charge" at Sowerby Bridge —a man called George Duncan—was engaged on the same day at a starting salary of £130 a year, rising to a maximum of £150. The extent—or rather the limitations—of his prospects were thus fully known to Branwell before launching on his new career. Salaries were paid quarterly, an inconvenience which was remedied only towards the end of Branwell's connection with the railways two years later. Branwell thus entered on his new post at a salary of £18.15.0 the quarter.

The appointment carried with it the obligation on the part of the applicant to find "satisfactory security for the Amount of two years salary at their highest rates". On 12th October 1840 (after Branwell had begun working for the Company) his father was accepted as a surety for the sum of £210, but Branwell's other surety, his friend Thomas Sugden the landlord of the *Black Bull*, was *not* found to be a "sufficient surety". It says much for Branwell's friendless state that when it came to finding a guarantor to take Sugden's place, it had to be Miss Elizabeth Branwell, whose security was accepted by the railway company at their board-meeting of 2nd November 1840. Even so, Miss Branwell's respectability had to be vouched for by her bankers at Skipton.

Branwell's appointment to the new station at Sowerby Bridge, two miles south-west of Halifax, was thus announced by Charlotte to Ellen Nussey on 29th September. Anticipating her friend's incredulity before the *fait accompli*, Charlotte adopted a tone of forced liveliness little in keeping with her true feelings which, in comparison with the family's once inordinate ambitions for Branwell, must have been of unequivocal disappointment.

". . . A distant relation of mine," she wrote (using the same paraphrase for Branwell as in her letter regarding Mary Taylor) "one Patrick Boanerges, has set off to seek his fortune in the wild, wandering, adventurous, romantic, knight-errant-like capacity of clerk on the Leeds and Manchester Railroad. Leeds and Manchester, where are they? Cities in a wilderness—like Tadmor, alias Palmyra —are they not? . . ."

One of Branwell's great incentives in applying for the post at Sowerby Bridge had been, according to Francis Leyland, the proximity of Halifax, where Joseph Bentley Leyland, his sculptor friend of Bradford days, had now permanently returned to live, and where he was assured of as congenial society as anywhere in England.

Branwell's appointment to the railways, regarded by most Brontë biographers as a definite *déclassement* and the result of a life of failure up to then, was hardly so envisaged by Branwell himself at the time.

The very newness and adventure associated with the pioneer days of the railway were full of attraction and hope for him. Listening to Mr Woolven's optimistic pronouncements, reading the Company's prospectuses in the papers, watching the feats of engineering required to tunnel the line through the mountainous barrier of rock dividing Lancashire from Yorkshire, he might indeed feel that he was living at the centre of a new and exciting age in which a place existed for him and where, for the first time, he could compete on a footing of equality with his young contemporaries.

Chapter Fourteen

CLERK TO THE RAILWAY

His arrival at Sowerby Bridge had been timed to precede by a few days the opening, on 5th October, of the new stretch of line, thus proudly announced by its promoters in the *Halifax Guardian* of 3rd October, under the heading "Manchester and Leeds Railway":

The public are respectfully informed, that on and after October 5th 1840, this line will be Further Opened, for the Conveyance of Passengers and General Merchandise between Leeds and Hebden Bridge; and the Trains will start from each of these places, and depart from the intermediate Stations as follows:

Start from Heb. Brd Morning	dep. from Sow. Brd	Arrive Leeds
8 o'clock	15 past 8	50 past 9

Passengers may be booked through to Manchester by the above Leeds train and will be conveyed from Hebden Bridge to Littleborough by Coaches provided by the Company.

dated September 29th 1840.   By Order of the Directors.

The actual opening was reported in the *Leeds Mercury* thus:
". . . At Sowerby Bridge an immense number of persons congregated, and upon the rocks, and all along the valley every eminence was occupied. The shrill bandit-like whistle of the engine was at length heard, and in a few moments the valley resounded with the hoarse puffing of the engine. The train proceeded at a relatively slow speed, a wise and prudent precaution on the part of the engineers. . . ."

Sowerby Bridge in Branwell's day was far removed from the "world's end" successive Brontë biographers have made it appear. It was, on the contrary, at the noisy and stirring van of a prosperous enterprise soon to become nation-wide. In 1831, when the Manchester-Leeds line was first projected, it had, even, been mooted as the first possible terminus. It had remained a key-position throughout the three successive stages in which the line was built, particularly during the two last and most difficult ones—with which Branwell was connected—before the linking of Littleborough to Todmorden and Hebden Bridge by the Summit Tunnel through Blackstone Edge, where, as the Company's prospectus advertised, passengers had to be "conveyed by coach" to make the connection. The tunnel, completed two months after Branwell's arrival, was 1,171 yards long and made engineering history in its day. Something of the excitement of those concerned in the operation, and in those witnessing its first effects, reaches us in contemporary press reports. Describing the opening of the stretch of line from Littleborough to Todmorden on 4th December 1840, the *Leeds Mercury* says: "To mark the auspicious occasion cannon were fired from the hillside and workmen were regaled within the tunnel."

The locality, whose rocky and mountainous nature had been indicated by the *Mercury's* reporter, was elsewhere thus described in its pages:

"The high chain of hills which separates the counties of York and Lancaster is only intersected by one valley, the Valley of the Calder—so narrow, winding, full of natural irregularities . . . so preoccupied by the turnpike road, the river and the canal . . . as to make it exceedingly difficult to carry a railway through it."

To Sowerby Bridge, straddling across both flanks of the Calder, with its sheer hillsides and rural heights dotted by mills, sudden life and prominence had come. The nearest point to Halifax on the line—Halifax to its intense chagrin getting no railway station until 1844—Sowerby Bridge was an important trade centre. Goods brought by train as far as Sowerby Bridge, were there shipped on barges to pursue their route by the Calder-Hebble-Rochdale canal.

To this strange new world of active, confident men, Branwell arrived in that autumn of 1840 and found himself at once in the centre of a shifting scene.

Nothing was as yet fixed or permanent, except the track of the railway which ran almost within view of his bedroom windows. Neither the station offices nor the station-master's house were as yet completed. The tender for their construction (for the sum of £551) had only been accepted by the Company at their board-meeting of 8th June, and work was still in progress. The offices in temporary use by Branwell, wooden and corrugated-iron structures, were part of the subsequent goods yard and can yet be seen today. Well-founded local tradition has it that Branwell lodged in Sowerby Street—the road nearest the station—with the family of Ely Bates whose house, later No. 22 and licensed as the *Pear Tree Inn*, was then no more than a "beer-house", one of a row of Stuart houses with wooden shutters and arched doorways, demolished in 1927. Steeply climbing to the village of Sowerby, by Haugh End House and Quarry Lane, Sowerby Street is very reminiscent of Branwell's own Main Street in Haworth, with a narrow cobbled side-walk and, at a bend half-way up, a noble ale-house—*The Royal Oak.*

The proximity of *The Royal Oak*—only three doors up from his lodgings—assured for Branwell one welcome centre at least in his new surroundings. Sowerby Bridge, indeed, was not deficient in houses of entertainment, and in Branwell's day—whereas the whole community numbered 5,000 inhabitants (and 700 houses)—there were seven inns. Of these, *The Bull's Head*, both by its central position and its old-established fame, *The Royal Oak* for its proximity to the railway yards, and *The Wharfe* for the "professional" character of its clientele, became Branwell's favoured haunts.

But the chief attraction for him in his new situation was its proximity to Halifax and his Halifax friends, and the artistic and literary stimulus they could bring.

The road to Halifax from Sowerby Bridge is an unending climb, and the reverse a prodigious drop, which, viewed from the standpoint of his cultural ambitions, might be taken to symbolise his whole situation.

By March 1841 there were five morning and four afternoon trains running daily from Manchester to Leeds and the same number in the contrary direction. On Sundays there were two morning and one afternoon train in either direction. Such a time-table left Branwell with considerable leisure which, in his first autumn in the Calder valley, he spent constantly with his friends in Halifax.

By great good luck for him, his friend Joseph Leyland had returned there the previous year. A member of an old professional and highly respected family, he had many connections in the town. His grandfather, William Leyland, was principal for over fifty years of an academy in Wade Street, where both Joseph himself and his far more conventional brother, Francis, received their education. Their own father, Roberts Leyland, set up as bookseller and printer, with his house and business premises at No. 15 Corn Market, where he lived and died. Among his other activities, Roberts Leyland was for some time editor of the *Halifax Guardian*, a weekly newspaper in those days, but his main interest was with books, publishing many by local authors whom he thus encouraged and publicised. Among these were William Dearden, who became one of Branwell's friends, George Hogarth, Dickens' father-in-law,

and John Nicholson, the Airedale poet. Among books of antiquarian interest published by him was *Buildings in the Town and
Parish of Halifax*, with illustrations drawn by the local artist John
Horner, which had considerable success. Roberts Leyland was also
a keen naturalist, and an early council member of the Halifax
Literary and Philosophical Society. By the time Branwell came to
live in the district, he had added a circulating library to his printing
and publishing works, and was, as can be seen, on his own account
a source of information and interest for a young man with Branwell's
tastes and talents.

Leyland's two sons, Joseph Bentley and Francis Alexander, born
respectively in 1811 and 1813, were both endowed with many of
their father's gifts, as well as some others of their own, and in their
individual and very differing ways, had both a strong attraction for
Branwell Brontë.

With Branwell Joseph Leyland had much in common, being,
in the words of a descendant, "self-opinionated, sarcastic and un-
reliable, scornful of religion and of anyone who disagreed with him,
only working when the spirit moved him" and preferring to spend
long convivial hours with chosen companions to the drudgery of
completing a commissioned work. He was, however, a true artist,
with genuine genius, capable of achieving works of noble integrity,
which no considerations of money or patronage would deflect him
from executing as he conceived them. He was, also, to his misfortune, a generous and kind-hearted man who could not bear to see
his friends in trouble, and added incalculably to his own already
considerable burden in extricating his friends from theirs. Brilliant
as had been his beginnings and assured as his London successes had
seemed to make his future, he no sooner returned to Halifax than
the period of his misfortunes began. Strangely parallel and tragic
were his and Branwell Brontë's destinies.

Francis Leyland, Joseph's younger brother, was of a very different
temperament. He was learned, pious and dependable, succeeding
his father as head of the publishing house and carrying on the
business with his widowed mother. He was a noted antiquarian,
with a great knowledge of medieval art. It was he who was called
on to design the seal of Halifax Corporation, and later the Arms
of the town.

But in 1840 when Branwell came to live in the district, the
Leyland family was as yet prosperous, united and happy. They all

lived together over the printing works in Corn Market, Joseph having his own studio at No. 10 Square Road, just off the famous Piece Hall at the very centre of Halifax life. Here Branwell constantly came to see him and watch him at work. Leyland was occupied at that time with the relievo in white marble of the head of an African bloodhound which he had owned and which had served as model for his famous group, "African Bloodhounds".

From the studio the friends would sally forth to one or other of Halifax's main hostelries, *The Old Cock* or *The Talbot* by preference, to meet their friends and discuss art and letters until such time as Branwell Brontë had to stumble back the two miles to Sowerby Bridge.

Very early in Branwell's stay at Sowerby Bridge Joseph Leyland brought over his brother Francis to see him. Recollecting that first meeting almost forty years later when writing his *Brontë Family*, Francis wrote:

It was on a bright Sunday afternoon in the autumn of 1840, at the desire of my brother, the sculptor, that I accompanied him to the station at Sowerby Bridge to see Branwell. The young railway clerk was of gentleman-like appearance, and seemed to be qualified for a much better position than the one he had chosen. In stature he was a little below the middle height; not "almost insignificantly small", as Mr Grundy states, nor had he "a downcast look": neither was he "a plain specimen of humanity". He was slim and agile in figure, yet of well-formed outline. His complexion was clear and ruddy, and the expression of his face, at the time, lightsome and cheerful. His voice had a ringing sweetness, and the utterance and use of his English was perfect: Branwell appeared to be in excellent spirits, and showed none of those traces of intemperance with which some writers have unjustly credited him about this period of his life. My brother had often spoken to me of Branwell's poetical abilities, his conversational powers, and the polish of his education; and, on a personal acquaintance I found nothing to question in this estimate of his mental gifts, and of his literary attainments.

The friendship of Francis Leyland brought Branwell, besides recognition and encouragement, an outlet for his long-suppressed yearning to appear in print. Through the family's connection with the *Halifax Guardian*, Branwell was able to get several of his poems inserted in its columns. Between August 1841 and July 1842, six of his poems were thus first published in the paper—a circumstance which, either not known or overlooked by his sisters' biographers, proves Branwell to have been the first of his family (except, of course, their father) to appear in print.

Other friends from his Bradford days had gravitated to Halifax in the interval and with them Branwell also renewed acquaintance. There was, notably, the landscape painter, John Wilson Anderson, born at Halifax in 1792, who after an unprofitable career at Bradford returned to his native town as "Keeper of the Baths", described in Walker's Directory for 1845 as "the most extensive suite of baths in Yorkshire, consisting of cold, tepid, hot, swimming, shower, vapour and sulphur baths, with suitable and convenient dressing-rooms. A spacious bowling green is attached and the grounds have recently been tastefully laid out by the present occupant—Mr J. W. Anderson. . . ."

Part of the "tasteful lay-out" of the grounds due to their artistic owner was the exhibition permanently held there of various works of art, among them statuary of Leyland's which, as time went on and the effects of exposure made themselves felt, suffered grievous damage and eventual decay. The very size of poor Leyland's works, when not placed in churches and private collections, made their preservation a constant problem and eventually an impossibility. Poverty obliging him, later, to use perishable materials, the majority have, regrettably, been lost.

Wilson Anderson who was, in the words of his obituary, "a very genial and social man, fond of company—easy going—never doing to-day what could be put off to to-morrow . . ." added yet another Bohemian figure to the background of Branwell's new life with the railways.

In William Dearden, schoolmaster, author and critic, he renewed an old family acquaintance (Dearden had been a schoolmaster at Keighley and had known Mr Brontë since 1829), and made a friend for life—and a somewhat unwise champion after death. Dearden was a local man with many connections in the Halifax area. To these he was only too eager to introduce Branwell, ranking his gifts so far above their desert as eventually to believe him capable of having written *Wuthering Heights*.

With such companionship offering him the stimulus—if not the practice—of all the arts he had most ardently loved and pursued since childhood, it is hardly surprising that Branwell's mind was not so much on his employers' work, as on his friends'. Yet, to begin with, there were no complaints lodged against him, and promotion came his way.

On 1st April 1841 Branwell was transferred to the station at Luddenden Foot, one mile farther up the line towards Hebden

Bridge, where his post was that of "Clerk in Charge", at a starting salary of £130 a year.

Charlotte, governess at the time with the Whites of Rawdon, outside Bradford, thus commented on the change to Emily at home in a letter dated 2nd April: ". . . I have not heard from Branwell yet. It is to be hoped that his removal to another station will turn out for the best. As you say, it *looks* like getting on at any rate."

The station at Luddenden Foot lay one mile to the north-west of Sowerby Bridge (to which it was linked by means of a tunnel 657 yards long) and was literally blasted out of the overhanging rock—a circumstance which creates still today an impression of perpetual shade and moisture, since the rock's beaded surface seems to glisten perpetually in a minelike darkness.

In contrast to Sowerby Bridge, where the line ran alongside the Calder and the waters of the canal in a verdant hollow, there is something sinister about the cavernous chill of Luddenden Foot; the place is at once grander and more inimical than Sowerby Bridge. Quite naturally the eye of the beholder is impelled upwards and away towards the towering heights where pastures and farmsteads dot the hillside, and where the roofs of Luddenden village to the north seem by contrast to shine in a paradisian light. That Branwell should by preference have sought that refuge to his actual place of employment need not surprise us.

The village of Luddenden straggles up the hillside in terraces, presenting an almost alpine appearance with its roofs at varying levels. Its main street, so narrow and steep that at the turnings the houses almost touch, finally abuts on to a small square at the top which, like Haworth, is crowned by a church and an inn.

For Branwell the church had life-long and peculiar associations as the last resting-place to which was borne, all the way from Haworth across the moors, the body of William Grimshaw, his father's almost legendary predecessor in the curacy of Haworth. On the story of that funeral and of the undying love of which it was a symbol—of Grimshaw's will expressed formally and legally to be buried in the Luddenden grave of his long-dead wife—the little Brontës had been brought up. It was a story after their own passionate hearts; they understood it, tiny as they were, when they first heard it from the lips of Tabby. In every Brontë was born or early implanted the acceptance of love as the very principle of life, as the eloquent negation of death. The story, sown early in that fertile soil, would bear its bitter fruit in all of them—in Branwell especially —and come to its triumphal flowering in *Wuthering Heights*.

There was, and still is, something supernatural about the setting of Grimshaw's grave—that low, sunken, stone-flagged churchyard by the rushing Calder, embowered in high trees where poplars predominate. Though Grimshaw's grave itself had been taken in by the enlargement of the church, even in Branwell's time, the poetry he was soon to write would show how potent was still the spell exercised by the old name, the old associations, the old faith of which Branwell, unlike his sisters, could only preserve the horror without the hope.

With the inn, the *Lord Nelson*, he would have many and close connections as time went on and the misery of his situation drove him towards the nearest—and strongest—anodyne within reach.

Luddenden Foot was ranked as a "second-class station" by the Railway Company, and, as at Sowerby Bridge, Branwell had the misfortune to be appointed before the station offices were actually built. The Company's minutes show that it was not until 9th May 1842 (just after Branwell's dismissal) that the decision was taken to build "a small station at Luddenden Foot similar to that at Elland, with lodging-rooms above for the Clerk". The buildings completed then can still be seen today, a decent little four-roomed house, the sizeable fire-place of Adam design and the skylight in the clerk's office, creating an impression of space and warmth and light that argues a certain attention on the Company's part to the well-being of its personnel. But Branwell was not to know these relative comforts.

The line here was double and the traffic considerably greater than at Sowerby Bridge. Branwell had the post of responsibility— corresponding to that of stationmaster today—with one porter under him, a man of the name of Walton.

From his office window overlooking the line, when the last coach had passed, there was nothing but the distant hills above to catch his eye. Within a few months of settling in, he would thus graphically describe his outlook and his day.

> I . . . sat amid
> The bustle of a Town-like room
> 'Neath skies, with smoke-stain'd vapours hid—
> By windows, made to show their gloom.
> The desk that held my ledger book

> Beneath the thundering rattle shook
> Of engines passing by;
> The bustle of the approaching train
> Was all I hoped to rouse the brain
> Of stealthy apathy. . . .

The traffic during those early months of the line was predominantly goods, of which many indications are scribbled in the notebook Branwell used at the time. Of a handy size for the pocket, measuring 5 inches by $3\frac{1}{2}$ inches and consisting of twenty pages of cartridge paper obviously intended for sketching, the little book came to contain in a strange medley—very descriptive of its owner's mind—unfinished sketches of his colleagues, some of his finest poetic outpourings and the memoranda of his daily functions. Thus we read:

> 10.6 per ton to Liverpool
> 6s. to Manch^r
> Perhaps 200 tons or 300 go weekly towards Manch^r and Liverpool but chiefly Manch^r at 6s p^r ton would be 2500 p^r year
>
> Note: 3 waggons & 3 covers for Sowerby—

8^T 8^c of coal carriage	0.	17. 6
price paid to Walton		
To Utley 4^T 4^c	0.	8. 6
,, 4^T 4^c 7. 6	1.	11. 6

Beside coal, the chief commodity carried on the line was wool, for which he makes a hasty jotting on December 10th 1841, "Wool 1^T (ton) 4^c (cwt)" without destination or price.

That he took interest in his work to begin with and brought some practical sense to bear, is shown in the minutes of the Company which record a meeting of the Directors held at Manchester on 4th October 1841 when a "letter from Mr Brontë in reference to certain alterations required at the Luddenden Foot Station" was brought before them, "approved and confirmed" and "ordered to be done".

But this is to anticipate.

Branwell's first impressions of Luddenden Foot were received in spring and the recollections of his Halifax friends, the Leylands and Grundy in particular, are of Sunday outings in the enlivening weather, when the friends ranged far afield through Luddenden Dene up the wooded slopes of Heptonstall, over the moorland heights of Wadsworth, and up the Hebden Valley to Cragg Vale.

The region is precipitous, richly wooded and rocky, the cliff faces overgrown with sycamore, birch and oak, and broken by swift currents of water—the becks in their stony beds—racing through narrow channels at what appear great depths below. Branwell, approaching it in boyhood from the opposite direction of Haworth Moor, had often walked to Hardcastle Craggs above Hebden Bridge and, when the children could secure the Haworth gig, had escorted his sisters there on summer picnics, and in autumn when the undergrowth of bracken is purple with wild orchids.

With Joseph Leyland and Francis Grundy he ranged the district now, ending the long day's exploration either at the *Cragg Vale Inn*, *The White Horse* at Hebden Bridge or *The White Lion* at Heptonstall—or at all three in succession, becoming soon a very regular customer at every one.

Francis Henry Grundy was a new acquaintance whose recollections of Branwell, preserved in his *Pictures of the Past* published in 1879, give him a stake in the Brontë family story. He was the Manchester-born son of a Unitarian minister and at the time Branwell met him an engineer on the new railway line between Leeds and Bradford. He was living in lodgings at Halifax where, to use his own expression, he "chummed in" with George Robert Stephenson (nephew of the railway king), sharing with him "a large double-bedded room", and enjoying to the top of his bent his first release from his widowed mother's apron strings.

Grundy was twenty-one and Branwell twenty-four, a difference in age which made Grundy (who called him "much my senior") look up to Branwell as an experienced man of the world. Branwell, though narrowly educated, was far better read than Grundy and could give him much, and genuinely Grundy admired him.

". . . What a splendid specimen of brain power running wild he was! What glorious talent he had still to waste!" Grundy exclaimed in retrospect. Yet he had something in abundance which poor Branwell totally lacked, and that was animal spirits. Grundy enjoyed to the full the good things of this world—among them "twenty-year-old Port at 2/6 the bottle"—and knew not what it was to feel a qualm of conscience, far less to be shadowed and haunted with conscience as Branwell was, for all his bravado, upon the least excess.

Grundy was a new type to him, a product of the scientific age from which, until recently, Branwell had lived so remote a life.

Grundy was material-minded, practical, astute, pushing, hearty, and innately vulgar—qualities conspicuously absent from Branwell's austerely intellectual home.

Grundy possessing a pass on the railways, as, indeed, Branwell did also, the two frequently met and ranged abroad together.

"I always liked scamps with brains," confessed Grundy. "Here was one, as great a scamp as could be desired and with an unexpected stock of brains indeed. He took to me amazingly, for I was very young and had the ideas and habits of a gentleman. Nay, I could meet him sometimes with quotation for quotation even in the languages other than English, which he most affected. On his side, he had a fund of information, experience and anecdote, which he poured forth freely for my benefit, not at first showing me anything of the rough side of his nature."

Grundy's recollections of Branwell, written thirty-eight years after the event, must be examined with caution, both for the natural effects of time upon any human memory, and for the boastful streak in the writer who wished to pose as an intimate not only of Branwell but of the whole Brontë family. This he could never be, for the good reason that during Branwell's year at Luddenden Foot, when Grundy claimed that "at times we would drive over in a gig to Haworth (twelve miles) and visit his people", describing *all* Branwell's sisters as "red-haired, long-toothed and wearing glasses", only Emily was at home. From references in letters of Charlotte made at the end of the year we learn that Branwell never went near his home after the month of July (pretexting work), so that the probability is that Grundy accompanied him once or twice during the summer holidays which brought Charlotte and Anne home, on which occasions Grundy had a glimpse of them and no more. Their absolute reticence in the presence of strangers, and particularly of bumptious strangers, would sufficiently account for Grundy's pique in describing them years later.

Yet his insight into Branwell's dual nature was remarkable. "He was ever in extremes," noted Grundy, "gloriously great or ingloriously small." Where his evidence can be trusted is in the actual circumstances of Branwell's life that he witnessed at Ludden-den Foot and of them he had this to say:

. . . When I first met him he was station-master at a small roadside place on the Manchester-Leeds Railway, Luddendenfoot by name. The line was only just opened. . . . Had a position been chosen for this strange creature for the express purpose of driving him several steps to the bad, this must have been it. Alone, in the wilds of Yorkshire, with few books, little to do, no prospects, and wretched pay, with no society congenial to his better tastes, but plenty of wild, rollicking, hard-headed half-educated manufacturers, who would welcome him to their houses, and drink with him as often as he chose to come, what was this morbid man who couldn't bear to be alone to do?

Grundy who himself got on and reached the head of his profession, obviously expected no effort to be made by Branwell. He understood him, perhaps, all the better for the complete contrast in their natures. Branwell, in his eyes, was an oddity, out of place in his world:

One of Brontë's peculiarities was a habit of making use of the word "Sir" when addressing even his most intimate friends and acquaintances; and if he made a quotation in Greek or Latin or French, he always translated it: "Fiat justitia, ruat coelum", that means "Justice must be done though the Heavens fall". I beg your pardon, Sir, but I have been so much amongst the barbarians of the hills that I forgot.

Had Grundy really known the Brontë family as he claimed, he would have known that this habit of calling his interlocutor "Sir" was wholly derived from Branwell's father, as well as his fad for Latin tags—an artless imitation harking back to Branwell's boyhood.

Grundy's evidence, supplied many years after the story of Branwell Brontë's ruin was public property, tends to confirm an already established picture, but Francis Leyland, who knew Branwell over a longer period and in a far closer degree of friendship and sympathy, did not see his position at Luddenden Foot in the same shameful light. His circle and influence were, admittedly, superior to Grundy's. He counted among his friends such men as Sutcliffe Sowden—in after years well known to Charlotte, and the officiating clergyman at her marriage with Arthur Bell Nicholls. Sowden was incumbent of nearby Mytholm when Branwell was at Luddenden Foot and, through Francis Leyland, the two struck up a friendship—Sowden, like Branwell, having a passion for nature—and often explored the district together on foot.

Leyland, who probably ignored Branwell's worst excesses, considered that he "magnified the common pleasures and enjoyments of his leisure hours into crimes and omissions of duty", and, far from being a drinker or cynic himself, thought that the company Branwell found at *The Red Lion* or *Shuttle and Anchor* was congenial and enough to "banish all solitude". It says much for the chameleon-like nature of Branwell's mind that two friends observing the same circumstances could see them so differently. To Grundy alone, it would seem, Branwell took off the mask, and met cynicism with cynicism.

Certain it was that the dread of solitude, noted by Grundy, was fast becoming a phobia with Branwell. The need for society, even totally uncongenial society, drove him among men with whom he had nothing in common, either in conversation or background, and by the blaze of great inn fires to absorb oblivion by the glass.

When the last train of the day was gone—and, as time wore on, before the last train was gone, leaving the issue of tickets to Walton —Branwell would flit up the hill to the refuge awaiting him inside the hospitable walls of the *Lord Nelson*. The place had everything to attract him—antiquity, style, and a long tradition of hospitality behind it. It was a Stuart building, L-shaped, straggling, low, with a veritable jungle of chimney-stacks and roof-tops tilted at oblique angles, with part of its eaves resting on the slopes of the higher road which wound farther up the hill beyond the summit of Luddenden.

It had long been a gentleman's private residence (it still bears the initials and the date of the original owner, Gregory Patchett— "G.P. 1634"—carved in stone over the door) and was first licensed in the mid-eighteenth century. Long known as the *White Swan* it was only after the fame of Trafalgar that its name was altered to the *Lord Nelson*.

The *Lord Nelson* combined the sort of contrasting clientele the most likely to appeal to Branwell—the rough types and the culti- vated gentlemen. Predominantly commercial, in that wool-growing district, it had also, strange to say, some particular clerical connec- tions, having indeed at one time been the actual property of a clergyman—the Rev. Thomas Greenwood of Mirfield—and owing its major attraction, a remarkable circulating library, to the gift of a clergyman. The incumbents of Luddenden, living in such close proximity to the inn, had at all times entertained their guests to dinner at the *White Swan* and during the work of restoration on old Grimshaw's church from 1810 to 1814, had regularly performed their baptismal services there.

The Luddenden circulating library (whose remaining volumes are today preserved in Sowerby Bridge Reference Library) was created in 1781 and counted over nine hundred volumes in Bran- well's day. It was famous in all the region and ruled by a set of

Sowerby Bridge and the Calder Valley in 1845,
at the coming of the railways

Portrait of Francis Alexander Leyland,
Branwell's biographer

Portrait of Joseph Bentley Leyland,
Branwell's sculptor friend

strict rules to which members had scrupulously to adhere or else suffer fines and eventual exclusion. A few of its Memorandum books exist yet today, recording the members' names, the amount of their subscriptions, the cost of "repairs and candles" disbursed each month in the upkeep of the books, and the peculiarly secretive system by which the books were catalogued. These were not listed by title or author but by a number given to each. Thus the records of each member's reading showed only a number, which, in default of the key catalogue, would reveal nothing.

The surviving volumes—some ninety in all—are bound in vellum, showing every sign of the care taken of them as recorded in the Memorandum books where the condition of each, after each monthly meeting of the library, was minutely set down, thus: "stained in the corner", "moth eaten", "torn at the edge", "loos leaf", "holes in the binding".

Members paid a monthly contribution of 4d each which, according to the number at the time, seems to have brought in anything from 4s 10d to 10s 8d a month. This sum was disbursed in further purchases of books (which, incidentally, were bought from Leyland's father, the Halifax bookseller and publisher), in repairs and bindings for old volumes, and on candles—the outlays on the latter commodity figuring in every month's accounts at 7d a pound.

The membership seems never to have been large and during Branwell's period did not alter from twenty-two, but counted the main mill-owners and shopkeepers in the district among its number. On no list does Branwell's name appear, although local and well-substantiated tradition confirms the fact of his using the library.

Books were kept in the great panelled room on the first floor at the *Lord Nelson* and if any might doubt the suitability of the place to the pursuit, reference to the library's Rules will show that its committee were well prepared for all contingencies. One Rule reads:

> . . . If any member come to the said meeting drunk so that he be offensive to the company and not fit to do his business he shall forfeit 2d.

"Swearing an oath" during the evening's proceedings was also considered offensive and incurred a 2d fine. The popularity or novelty of some works making them obvious favourites, the committee took its precautions how to prevent a free-for-all during the changing of books. ". . . For the sake of good order," it was ruled,

o

"it is agreed that all the books shall be conveniently placed, and that one member elected by the majority shall reach any book chosen by the member whose call it is, the rest keeping their seats."

By the volumes that have survived and by rare occasional naming of some particular work to be re-bound or otherwise repaired in the Memorandum books (*Tom Jones* and *Roderick Random* are so mentioned) some idea of the kind of books kept at the Luddenden library can be formed.

They included a large quantity of theological and political works, some of which, dating from the period of the French Revolution, were the object of a special purge in 1830. We read that a meeting of members was convened for Tuesday, 1st February 1830 "to remove all seditions and deistical works" from the library.

In a Memorandum book of "Reviews and Periodicals", appear some titles possibly coming under that category—a 1796 edition of Paine's *Age of Reason*, some numbers of a periodical called *The Patriot* and Cooper's *Reply to Burke*.

Among existing volumes of interest are: *The Newgate Calendar*, *The Pictorial History of England* in six volumes, the *Gospel Magazine*, the *Young Gentleman's and Lady's Philosophy*, Debrett's *Peerage and Baronetage*, Percy's *Anecdotes* in fifteen volumes—a collection of true and fictional tales of enormous range and erudition by the author of the *Reliques* and peculiarly attractive reading, one feels, for Branwell.

That the volumes of the library, stored in the upper room of the *Lord Nelson*, were a boon to Branwell and eagerly devoured by him at hours unsuspected by the prudent library committee, is local knowledge. How he spent other hours at the inn, in very different pursuits, reference to his notebook reveals. As easy of access as his sisters were distant, Branwell made himself agreeable to all and sundry and in his urgent need of companionship exchanged confidences with any who chose to drink with him. That his affability and talents were soon exploited can be seen from various memoranda scribbled in his notebook, side by side with the hours of trains and the poems on eternal damnation.

He was obviously soon regarded by the youths of the village in the light of a public scribe, for they brought him their business letters of a delicate nature to write, like the following for which Branwell made memoranda:

To Jim Darwin from H. Craven. Jim should have received from R. of Stubbing £3 for H's use in losing him in his scrape about the child which H. was compelled by court to pay. Now H. has never received the cash and he wishes to know whether J. has received it and if so why he has not acquainted him or sent him the money. H. says he will not be responsible and if Jim does not pay or say why not—Law must be entered into when he can make Jim suffer for forgery of his name.

Money left from Luke's father for L's benefit, for £200 out of it this man is paying four per cent interest to Luke's benefit (interest received about old Christmas) Luke wants man to pay into his hands the full sum within 14 days from receipt of the letter.

The gentleman's steward is the man to be addressed. An answer requested as soon as possible because necessity presses.

In what spirit of repentance—or reformation—the following entry was made, with its concluding resolution, it would be difficult to say. On the very first page of his notebook he entered: "At R. Col last night with G. Thompson, & Titterington, R. Col, H. Killiner and another. Quarrelled with J. T. about going but after a wrestle met him on the road and became friends. Quarrelled almost on the subject with G. Thompson. Will have no more of it. P.B.B.

The entry is followed by a note for "Curled Greens for Mr W—" (possibly his porter Walton) and the cry three times repeated: "JESU—JESU—JESU—".

Neither his work nor his leisure could secure him from the fierce urgency of these returns to God which, in this place more than in any other, were the inevitable corollary to debauch. Above the rattle of the railways, the crack of mirth, the heat and pressure in the inn bar, the voices of his ghosts wailed in his ears: "Remember me!"

The first in constance and intensity—the ghost of Maria—had been with him ever since his London failure, but here at Luddenden Foot she was almost crowded out by the ghost of his old ambitions and, more horrific still, the ghost of his old beliefs, summoned from a lethargy of years by the imperious presence in Luddenden Church of Grimshaw—beliefs whose heart-rending probings into his fall from grace only heightened the torture begun by drink and drugs. In bursts of occasional noble verse he eased his mind, fast cracking under the triple strain.

> Amid the world's wide din around,
> I hear from far a solemn sound
> That says, "Remember me!—"

he wrote on 11th September in a strangely percipient statement of the contrast between his present lot and the extravagant anticipations

of his boyhood. Jotted down in italic script in his notebook, with
very few alterations, the poem describes how the voice of Maria
came to him in his station office so vividly that, though he well
knew it came from no "Ruby lips and sapphire eyes", he knew its
origin—as certainly as Jane Eyre recognised the voice of Rochester.
To the Brontës such things occurred and were not queried. Charlotte Brontë, indeed, when questioned by Mrs Gaskell on the point
years later, simply replied: "It is a true thing; it really happened."

The voice of Maria, stirring all Branwell's memories of those
beginnings of life in which she had shared, brings the realisation of
his failure home to him as nothing else in his situation can do.

> Why did it bring such scenes to mind
> As Time has left so long behind?—
> Those summer afternoons, when I
> Lay basking 'neath a glorious sky,
> Some noble page beneath me spread,
> Some bright cloud floating overhead,
> And sweet winds whispering in the tree
> A wondrous future meant for me!
>   Why did it bring, my eyes before,
> The hours spent wandering on the moor,
> Beneath a grey and iron sky,
> With nothing but the waters still
> To break the stern monotony
> Of darksome heath and windless hill?—
> While fancy, to the heedless child,
> Revealed a world of wonders wild—
> Adventures bold and scenes divine
> Beyond the horizon's gloomy line—
> Until he thought his footsteps trod
> The pathless plains round Volga's flood,
> Or paced the shores of Grecia's sea,
> Or climbed the steep of Calvary.
>   Why did I think I stood once more
> At night beside my father's door?—
> And, while far up in heaven the moon
> Through clear and cloud was driving on,
> A moment dark but bursting soon
>   Upon the heaven she made her own,
> I often times would think that she
> Was some bold vessel o'er a sea
>   'Mid unknown regions gliding—
> Perhaps with Parry in the north
> On strange discovery venturing forth,
>   On stormy waters riding;

Perhaps with Sinbad 'mid those Isles
Where Genii haunt and sunshine smiles;
Perhaps—and nobler still than these—
With Vincent guarding England's seas
From might of foreign war;
Or bearing Nelson o'er the wave
To find a glorious Hero's grave
On deathless Trafalgar!

The mention of Nelson in the concluding lines of this poem is indicative of a strange preoccupation with the fame and destiny of that hero that he suffered at the time, his notebook containing several early drafts of a poem which he only subsequently completed under the title: "The Triumph of Mind over Body".

It was doubtless by the extremes of contrast with his own fate that he fixed on Nelson—so blessed in all his enterprises—his bewildered gaze. Feeling for him something like kinship (for the first draft of the poem, we learn from Grundy, was called "Brontë"), there was in this exploration of a destiny so dissimilar to his own, an inversion of the sentiment, "There, but for the grace of God, go I!"

Branwell's Luddenden Foot notebook contains several jottings of the names of great men, sometimes listed, as in the case of "Tasso, Galileo, Milton, Otway, Johnson, Cowper, Burns", to serve as examples of the triumph of the soul over adversity. While he saw the hopeless issue to which his own youthful ambitions had come, he was capable yet at times of the energy of thought to wish himself otherwise. That in moments of inspiration and fervour the wish to become resolved itself into a positive faith in becoming and reliance upon the compassion of God to aid, is revealed in the fine flight, jotted down at Luddenden, with which he ultimately finished the poem on Nelson.

Give me Great God, give all beneath thy sway
Soul to command and body to obey
When dangers threat a heart to beat more high
When doubts confuse a more observant eye;
When fate would crush us down a steadier arm
A firmer front as stronger beats the storm.
We are thy likeness—give us on to go
Through life's long march of chance and change below.
Resolved thine image shall be sanctified
By humble confidence not foolish pride.
We love our task so let us do it well;

Nor barter ease on earth with pain in hell.
We have our Talents from Thy Treasury given
Let us return Thee good account in Heaven.
    I see thy world—this age is marching on,
Each year more Wondrous than its parent gone;
And shall my own drag heavily and slow,
With wish to rise yet grovelling far below?
Forbid it God who madest what I am,
Nor made to honour let me sink in shame;
But as yon moon that *seems* through clouds to glide
Whose dark breasts ever seek her beams to hide
Shines *really* heedless of that earthly sway,
In her own heaven of glory far away!
So may my soul that seems involved below
In life's conflicting mists of care and woe
For far remote from its own heaven look down
In clouds of fleecy shine or stormy frown,
And while—so often eclipsed—men pity me
Gaze steadfast at their life's inconstancy
But feel myself like her at home in heaven with Thee.

That Luddenden had the power to turn his thoughts inward
upon himself as no place had done for years, is instanced yet again
in the poem dated "Dec. 19, 1841, at Luddenden Church", where in
language—and courage—worthy of his sisters, he implores God to
give him "the stern sustaining power" to face his end.

O God! while I in pleasure's wiles
    Count hours and years as one,
And dream that, wrapt in pleasure's smiles,
    My joys can ne'er be done,

Give me the stern sustaining power
    To look into the past,
And see the darkly shadowed hour
    Which I must meet at last;

The hour when I must stretch this hand
    To give a last adieu
To those sad friends that round me stand,
    Whom I no more must view.

For false though bright the hours that lead
    My present passage on,
And when I join the silent dead
    Their light will all be gone.

> Then I must cease to seek the light
>   Which fires the evening heaven,
> Since to direct through death's dark night
>   Some other must be given.

He was obsessed with the thought of death and judgment, a condition not only provoked by his sense of sin, but by the more real and urgent decline in his physical health to which his poems of the time bear several allusions. His natural debility had been placed under perpetual strain for years now by drink and opium. Grundy, meeting him at Luddenden Foot for the first time, claimed that Branwell had previously "undergone the torture of the damned" through opium, but that he "recovered himself of his habits there after my advent". Whether this is true or not, Branwell himself was aware how ill he was. An entry in his notebook shows at what straws he was ready to clutch—be they only supplied by quack advertisements.

> "Manhood—the causes of its premature decline"
>   by J. I. Austin
>   3-6d.   No. 4, St. Ann's Street
>   Manchester.

Both the physical and mental wreck are feelingly described in a poem written while it was yet summer: "Brearly Hill Aug 8 1841", a poem singularly hushed and humble, as though the vitality to resist his fate further were already gone.

> Oh Thou, whose beams were most withdrawn
>   When should have risen my morning sun,
> Who, frowning most at earliest dawn,
>   Foretold the storms through which 'twould run;
>
> Great God! when hour on hour has passed
>   In an unsmiling storm away,
> No sound but bleak December's blast,
>   No sights but tempests, through my day,
>
> At length, in twilight's dark decline,
>   Roll back the clouds that mark Thy frown,
> Give but a single silver line—
>   One sunblink, as that day goes down.
>
> My prayer is earnest, for my breast
>   No more can buffet with these storms;
> I must have one short space of rest
>   Ere I go home to dust and worms;

I must a single gleam of light
　　Amid increasing darkness see,
Ere I, resigned to churchyard night,
　　Bid day farewell eternally!

My body is oppressed with pain,
　　My mind is prostrate 'neath despair—
Nor mind nor body may again
　　Do more than call Thy wrath to spare,

Both void of power to fight or flee,
　　To bear or to avert Thy eye,
With sunken heart, with suppliant knee,
　　Implore a peaceful hour to die.

When I look back on former life,
　　I scarcely know what I have been,
So swift the change from strife to strife
　　That passes o'er the 'wildering scene.

I only feel that every power—
　　And Thou hadst given much to me—
Was spent upon the present hour,
　　Was never turned, my God, to Thee;

That what I did to make me blest
　　Sooner or later changed to pain;
That still I laughed at peace and rest,
　　So neither must behold again.

The appeal to God though characteristically devoid of hope, is an instance of those frequent "struggles after the good" reported by Grundy even in the midst of the life Branwell then led, and on which he was himself to cast, later, so searing a condemnation. "Poor, brilliant, gay, moody, moping, wildly excitable, miserable Brontë!" wrote Grundy. "No history records your many struggles after the good—Your wit, brilliance, attractiveness, eagerness for excitement—all the qualities which made you such 'good company' and dragged you down to an untimely grave—".

Viewing it in perspective after it was over, Branwell thus summed up his life at Luddenden Foot: ". . . I would rather give my hand than undergo again the grovelling carelessness, the malignant yet cold debauchery, the determination to find how far mind could carry body without both being chucked into hell, which too often marked my conduct when there, lost as I was to all I really liked. . . ."

The end came suddenly and not surprisingly. At the end of Branwell's year of office, when the accounts came to be audited, they were found deficient. He was summoned to appear before the audit of the Company, his porter with him; the sum of £11 1s 7d was in question. He could give no satisfactory account of it and indeed, when his ledgers were looked into, the margins were found to be scribbled all over with drawings and caricatures—showing how little attention he had paid to his employers' business.

He was, inevitably, dismissed. The minutes of the Company, reporting the circumstance, could not be more laconic, less expressive of what must have been Branwell's feelings in the event. The extract of the meeting of the Directors of the Manchester and Leeds Railway, held at Hunts Bank, Manchester, on 4th April 1842 says, under the heading "Mr Bronte": "Report from Messrs Robinson and Greenish on certain irregularities of the Clerk in Charge at the Luddenden Foot Station, Mr Bronte, who had been found deficient £11. 1. 7. He had been discharged in consequence and the amount deducted from his quarter's salary."

Grundy, who was himself an employee of the railways, has vouched for the fact that Branwell "was not suspected of the theft himself", only convicted "of constant carelessness". His absences from his post, Grundy admitted, "carousing with congenial drinkers", had been "of days' continuance". The porter, left increasingly in charge of the ticket office, had helped himself from the till.

The fact that Branwell was not guilty of the worst offence could not save him in the Company's opinion. That an appeal was made by local and influential patrons of the line, has come to light in examining the Company's minutes. On 11th April 1842 it is recorded that the Directors read a "Memorial from certain Merchants, Millowners, etc. residing at Luddenden Foot interceding for the re-employment of Mr Bronte, discharged from the situation of Clerk in Charge at the Station there (Particulars reported last week). Upon a consideration of the case the Board determined to adhere to their former decision".

Branwell's salary, amounting to £32 10s 0d the quarter, when the missing sum was deducted, left him little to pay his liabilities at Luddenden—the many debts his whole way of life had contracted there. His plight was real, indeed, and, though brought on himself in great measure, was not so exceptional among railway employees as might at first sight appear. In an article published in *Herapath's*

Railway Magazine for 22nd May 1841, the whole question of the underpayment of railway clerks is vented; Branwell's own case might be under discussion, so similar are those instanced:

> No Railway situation can indeed be compared to a mercantile one, either in its present pay or future prospects. . . . The salaries of the clerks are too low. . . . Can it be expected that young men of good families and steady habits will eke out their lives on the miserable pittances allowed them of £50, £60 or £80 a year which are worse . . . than the pay of day labourers? . . . If the Directors want good servants, they must make the places worth having. . . . Let us suppose . . . for we have been informed of such cases . . . that one of these under-paid clerks shows a defalcation in his accounts, is it not naturally to be expected that the equally underpaid clerk who is employed to check him, should be ready to protect his poor brother rather than the hard-dealing Co? Can we be astonished if such things take place? *They do take place.* . . .

Branwell's own particular disaster, whatever the alleviating circumstances attending the defalcations of others, was aggravated, as he himself was the first to feel, by those very standards of rectitude in which he had been brought up. Coming from such a family, what valid excuses had he? His dismissal from the Railway Company sent him home, in good earnest this time, a ruined man.

PART FIVE

NORTHANGERLAND

*

Chapter Fifteen

AGAINST THE ROPES

Branwell came home to find all his sisters away. Charlotte and Emily had gone to school in Brussels on the previous 8th February and Anne continued at her post with the Robinson family near York. The utter lack of confidants on whom to relieve his bursting heart precipitated the breakdown towards which he had long been heading. Alone with his father and aunt there was nothing—and no one—to avert the despair that now overwhelmed him, a despair far more rationally provoked than any he had yet endured, for his situation was, indeed, appalling.

He had not a penny to call his own, and, at the age of twenty-five, had to depend wholly upon his father—a father who, for all his life-long partiality and patience, had now proof of his son's dissolute, if not dishonourable, conduct. Brought up as Branwell had been to precepts of absolute integrity, what could be worse to live down than such disgrace? It was little attenuation to the circumstances that he was not actually accused of stealing the money; his whole way of life was exposed for what it had been, drunken, idle, debauched.

In that silent family those words, had they been uttered, would have hurt less than the incredulous stupefaction of the elders confronted with this prodigal's return. How explain to them what had happened? The attempt was impossible. Under the strain, mind and body collapsed and he was seriously ill for many weeks.

Dismissed on 31st March (1842), he was five weeks at home before life and spirits revived to any degree. The extremity of his depression inevitably provoked a sudden revulsion of hope and brought him to his feet again. He might, in the language of his

205

favourite sport, have been knocked into the ropes, but the very violence of the blow sent him staggering back again into the centre of the ring.

His first action on feeling better was to write to his Halifax friends, Leyland and Grundy, on whom he had come to rely so entirely during his late experiences. To them, in the absence of his sisters, he could open his heart. "I cannot avoid the temptation to cheer my spirits by scribbling a few lines to you," he wrote to Grundy on Sunday, 22nd May, already so sick to death of home and inaction as to contemplate a return to work. To the practical Grundy, intimate as he was with the Stephensons, uncle and nephew, Branwell naïvely looked for help to get work again on the railway. The letter, which had a practical purpose, is also Branwell's most revealing statement of his attitude to home—to the spiritual atmosphere in which he had been brought up and with which he would never again be in harmony.

I cannot avoid . . . scribbling a few lines to you while I sit here alone—all the household being at Church—the sole occupant of an ancient parsonage among lonely hills, which probably will never hear the whistle of an engine till I am in my grave.

. . . After experiencing, since my return home, extreme pain and illness, with mental depression worse than either, I have at length acquired health and strength and soundness of mind, far superior I trust, to anything shown by that miserable wreck you used to know under my name. I can now speak cheerfully and enjoy the company of another without stimulus of six glasses of whiskey; I can write, think, and act with some apparent approach to resolution, and I only want a motive for exertion to be happier than I have been for years. But I feel my recovery from almost insanity to be retarded by having nothing to listen to except the wind moaning among old chimneys and older ash trees, nothing to look at except heathery hills walked over when life had all to hope for and nothing to regret with me—no one to speak to except crabbed old Greeks and Romans who have been dust the last five thousand years. And yet this quiet life, from its contrast, makes the year passed at Luddenden Foot appear like a nightmare, for I would rather give my hand than undergo again the grovelling carelessness, the malignant yet cold debauchery, the determination to find how far mind could carry body without both being chucked into hell, which too often marked my conduct when there, lost as I was to all I really liked, and seeking relief in the indulgence of feelings which form the black spot on my character.

Yet I have something still left in me which may do me service. But I ought not to remain too long in solitude, for the world soon forgets those who have bidden it "Good-bye". Quiet is an excellent cure, but no medicine should be continued after a patient's recovery, so I am about, though ashamed of the business, to dun you for answers to . . . [followed by enquiries after jobs].

Excuse the trouble I am giving to one on whose kindness I have no claim, and for whose services I am offering no return except gratitude and thankfulness, which are already due to you. Give my sincere regards to Mr Stephenson. A word or two to show that you have not altogether forgotten me will greatly please yours, etc.

P. B. Bronte.

With Leyland, Branwell's revived interests were of a different order. Unhappily for Leyland he was in no position to succour Branwell—on the contrary the uncertainties of the artistic career had brought the fine and successful sculptor to a position of such financial straits as to oblige him to take hack work, while his great pieces of sculpture waited for a buyer. He was advertising for work in the *Halifax Guardian*—work of a commercial order, more suitable to a stonemason than to a romantic sculptor. "Halifax Marble Works, Square Road," his advertisement read: "J. B. Leyland, Sculptor—Monuments, busts, tombs, tablets, chiffonier slabs and all kinds of marble work used in the upholstery business, made to order. A variety of marble chimney pieces on view, cleaned, repaired or set up."

The opportunity to serve Leyland occurred to Branwell at this very time, and was seized upon with all the eagerness of a naturally generous nature all too seldom placed in the position to confer benefits.

On 3rd May there died at Haworth Mr Thomas Andrew, the local surgeon. His loss was generally deplored in Haworth and a committee was set up to raise a monument to him in the church. This was no sooner mooted than Branwell sent John Brown (a practising stonemason himself) over to Halifax to offer the commission to Leyland. His letter of 15th May relating further to the subject is self-explanatory:

Dear Sir,

I have received great pleasure from the examination of the three Drawings which you put into the hands of Mr. J. Brown and it appears to me that the Design at £40, No. 2 has received the greatest approbation from the Committee appointed to carry into effect the erection of a monument to the late Mr. Andrews [*sic*].

If you could come over to Haworth on the Afternoon of Friday May 20th, during the evening of which day the Committee will sit, they will be able to speak more distinctly to you than I have the power to do—and I am sure my father would be pleased to see you if you can make it convenient to visit us before the meeting.

Mr. Brown will be thankful for any instructions you may be pleased to give him, and as he expects an order for two more monuments, of course through your hands, he will be thankful for some information respecting the best method of colouring letters *sunk* in marble tablets.

Excuse the extreme illegibility of this scrawl as I am scarcely recovering from
severe indispositions, and, with a hope, to see you on Friday, Believe me, Dear
Sir, Yours most respectfully

P. B. Bronte

Leyland's brother Francis, commenting on the event, reports
that Joseph went over to Haworth on the 20th, as requested, and
"partook of Mr Brontë's hospitality; and in the evening, accompanied by the incumbent and his son, appeared before the monument committee".

In the mere fact that Mr Brontë extended hospitality to Leyland
can be seen something of his attitude to Branwell's derelictions from
duty. Quite obviously, Mr Brontë did not blame them on his son's
bohemian friends—as many another country clergyman of his day
would have done. His deep-rooted reverence for all "men of
genius" would make him regard Leyland's visit as an honour, to be
marked with all possible respect. In such gestures he showed himself the true father of his children.

That the Committee's notion of what was due to genius did not
square up with its Chairman's is obvious from the corollary. Bent
no doubt on getting its pennyworth out of the "off-comed'un"
artist, it was such as to put Branwell to shame. Sending Leyland
the text of the inscription for the monument, he wrote on 29th June:

Dear Sir,

I think it my duty to send you a copy of the inscription intended for Mr.
Andrew's monument.

It is not such a one as would have best pleased myself, but I was compelled to
frame it so as to please others, as to whose taste and judgement you will some time
since have formed a tolerably correct opinion.

I have not often felt more heartily ashamed than when you left the committee
at Haworth; but I did not like to speak on the subject then, and I trusted that you
would make that allowance which you have perhaps often ere now had to do,
for gothic ignorance and ill-breeding, and one or two of the persons present,
afterwards felt they had left by no means an enviable impression on your mind.

Though it is but a poor compliment—I long much to see you again at Haworth
and forget for half a day the amiable society in which I am placed, where I never
hear a word more musical than an ass's bray. . . .

I remain, dear Sir, Yours respectfully and sincerely,

P. B. Bronte.

The matter of Mr Andrew's memorial tablet dragged on through
the summer and was the object of several letters from Branwell to
Leyland—showing his genuine wish to serve his friend, and his
revived energy and health. On 12th July he wrote:

Mr John Brown understands from Mr Newsholme of Haworth, who lately called upon you, that you will be prepared to bring the Tablet hither on Friday, and he wishes to know whether it will be your pleasure to do so, and thus have the letters blackened and all completed under your own eye; or whether you intend that he shall bring it over to Halifax on Saturday and complete it there?

He would also be much obliged by being informed whether or not it will injure the work to clear the slab from the yolk laid on it, *before* it is blackened. . . .

By 10th August Branwell was able to report to his friend that "Your work at Haworth has given to all who have seen it the most unqualified satisfaction even where they understood nothing of its real merit. . . ."

A contributing factor to his recovery was undoubtedly the publication in the *Halifax Guardian* and *Leeds Intelligencer* of several of his poems that early summer. (Hitherto it has been believed that only one poem of Branwell's was published in his lifetime, his lines on the "Afghan War" printed in the *Leeds Intelligencer* on 7th May 1842.) Recalling the long years of frustration behind him, it cannot be doubted that their publication brought Branwell that indefinable elation known only to the creative artist in communicating his ideal experience and in seeing it recognised.

The poems, which include two excerpts from the "Caroline" sequence, represent some of his most mature thought, and most shapely and condensed writing, as the following sonnets bear witness. Under the title "On the callousness produced by Cares", the first appeared in the *Halifax Guardian* of 7th May 1842.

> Why hold young eyes the fullest fount of tears;
> And why do youthful breasts the oftenest sigh,
> When fancied friends forsake, or lovers fly
> Or fancied woes and dangers wake their fears?
> Ah! he who asks has seen but springtide years;
> Or Time's rough voice had long since told him why!
> Increase of days increases misery,
> And misery brings selfishness, which sears
> The heart's first feelings: 'mid the battle's roar
> In death's dread grasp, the soldier's eyes are blind
> To comrades dying, and he whose hopes are o'er
> Turns coldest from the sufferings of mankind;
> A bleeding spirit oft delights in gore;
> A tortured heart oft makes a tyrant mind.

The second, given the title "Peaceful Death and Painful Life", appeared in the *Halifax Guardian* on 14th May:

Why dost thou sorrow for the happy dead?
For if their life be lost, their toils are o'er
And woe and want shall trouble them no more,
Nor ever slept they in an earthly bed
So sound as now they sleep while, dreamless, laid
In the dark chambers of that unknown shore
Where Night and Silence seal each guarded door:
So, turn from such as these thy drooping head
And mourn the "Dead alive" whose spirit flies—
Whose life departs before his death has come—
Who finds no Heaven beyond Life's gloomy skies
Who sees no Hope to brighten up that gloom,
'Tis HE who feels the worm that never dies—
The REAL death and darkness of the tomb.

They show sufficiently the disillusioned path Branwell was treading. Significantly enough, they were signed by his new pseudonym, "Northangerland", new not in nomenclature, but in the identification of himself with his Angrian rebel whose characteristics—fraud, hypocrisy, boldness and treachery, so alien to one side of Branwell's nature—he was now increasingly to assume.

Grundy, answering his appeal for work, had no comfort to bring. "... I should have been a fool, under present circumstances," Branwell answered him on 9th June, "to entertain any sanguine hopes respecting situations. ..."

Better placed than Branwell to gauge the hopelessness of all attempts at re-employment by the railway, Grundy had suggested other careers. The gulf between his commercial outlook and Branwell's classical and unpractical education was only too clear to the latter. "You ask me why I do not turn my attention elsewhere," Branwell wrote, "and so I should have done, but that most of my relatives and more immediate connections are clergymen, or by a private life somewhat removed from this busy world. As for the Church—I have not one mental qualification, save, perhaps, hypocrisy, which would make me cut a figure in its pulpits. Mr James Montgomery, and another literary gentleman who have lately seen something of my 'head work' wish me to turn my attention to literature, and along with that advice, they give me plenty of puff and praise. All very well, but I have little conceit of myself, and great desire for activity. ..."

Self-delusive words, if ever any were spoken, for a great ill from which Branwell suffered then and for the rest of his life, was wounded

Hardcastle Craggs, the scene of many of Branwell's walks

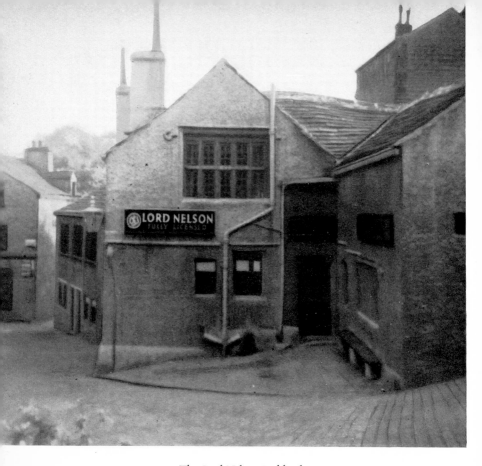

The *Lord Nelson*, Luddenden

"I would rather give my hand than undergo
again . . . the cold debauchery . . . which
marked my conduct there. . . ."—*Branwell Brontë*

vanity. The praise, which he received in abundance, was never enough to appease his hunger for fame.

Through Grundy, surprisingly enough, he made yet another literary contact that summer. A close friend and colleague of Grundy's father, the Unitarian minister, was the Rev. James Martineau, brother of Harriet, to whom Grundy now offered to forward some of Branwell's work. He sent his poem on Nelson, with its original title "Bronté", which Grundy later claimed to have submitted to Leigh Hunt as well as to Harriet Martineau.

James Martineau made himself their spokesman in writing to Branwell a letter of "most kindly and truthful criticism—at least in advice, though too generous far in praise . . ." to which Branwell referred in a letter to Grundy of 25th October.

The praise, only further irritating his sense of frustration, did little to ease the bitter mood.

Recalling his animadversions against clergymen and the hypocrisy of their lives, one might be surprised to find that he made fast friends with his father's curate, Mr Weightman, with whom he was thrown into close contact that summer. Mr Weightman he liked, inordinately—all the more because there was no cant there. With him he could range the moors, follow the guns, even share a bottle, without reprobation. William Weightman was a well-read, romantic young man with whom Branwell could discourse on his favourite topics and authors, and feel himself not totally lost to literary stimuli.

In mid-June Anne came home for part of her holidays; the other part was spent every summer in accompanying her employers to Scarborough. Her return gave Branwell his first opportunity in years of getting to know what sort of girl his youngest sister was.

As "absolutely nothing" he had dismissed her, in his bumptious days of Patrick Benjamin Wiggins—"next to an idiot". Anne at twenty-two, with three years' experience of governess work behind her, had very definite notions of her own and was far from being the nonentity her silence and shrinking sensitivity led superficial observers to suppose. She had passed through, and barely survived, a searing religious crisis during which every inculcated tenet of her aunt's had been tried in the fire of her own compassionate and truth-loving nature, and found wanting both in love and vision. Having cast off the doctrines of Predestination and Election in which she had been reared, and filled with an unbounded faith in the salvation of

P

sinners, Anne had but to see her brother's distress to resolve to save him.

She was drawn irresistibly to all creatures smaller and weaker than herself—including animals and sinners—and adopted Branwell from that time on as her special charge. Either then, or very shortly after, she obtained for him a post with her employers as tutor to the only son of the family.

For Branwell, come to an ignominious halt in his devious path towards celebrity, there were not many openings left (short of becoming a soldier, and even that prospect was debarred him by his height) and a ready-found post where no reference, other than his sister's, was required, was too good a chance to refuse. He jumped at it, probably unaware of the sacrifice Anne had made. For she hated her position with the Robinsons, hated their worldly ways, their lack of high principle, their want of harmony. She had wished to leave them already the previous year, though they, more than satisfied with her, wished as eagerly to retain her. Now a double incentive prompted her to stay: Charlotte wrote in July from Brussels saying that she and Emily were unlikely to return home in September, the school's principals, Monsieur and Madame Heger, having offered them advantageous pupil-teacher terms to stay for another year.

What other hopes Anne had for a happier future, connected neither with drudgery nor home, she certainly did not confide to Branwell those holidays—only to the poetry written to ease her heart; but she had loved Willy Weightman ever since he came to Haworth three years before, and had perceived recently a change in him towards herself, a greater frequency in

> That Angel smile that late so much
> Could my fond heart rejoice—

that transported her with joy. She allowed herself to hope. In the words of her *Agnes Grey* even then springing to life out of her own experiences, she asked herself: "Who can tell what this one month may bring forth? I have lived nearly three and twenty years, and I have suffered much, and tasted little pleasure yet; is it likely my life all through will be so clouded? is it possible that God may hear my prayers, disperse those gloomy shadows, and grant me some beams of heaven's sunshine yet?"

It was not to be. The friend whose merry heart had so captivated her sad one, the good companion who had been like a brother to Branwell, was stricken down in the last days of August with cholera —a visitant all too frequent at Haworth in those days—and after a fortnight's illness, died on 6th September, to the dismay of all. Branwell wrote on 25th October to Grundy, who was complaining of his neglect:

My dear Sir,
     There is no misunderstanding. I have had a long attendance at the death-bed of the Rev. Mr Weightman, one of my dearest friends. . . .

Even as Branwell wrote those words, another domestic loss was imminent. At the funeral of Willy Weightman conducted by Mr Brontë—and the occasion of a fine tribute to the departed whom he had loved "as a son"—Branwell appeared alone in the family pew, where his presence, after years of absence, and his audible sobs, were alike remarked upon by the congregation. Miss Branwell was absent. She was already ill and within the space of a fortnight lay dying.

     In the same letter to Grundy in which he described his "attendance at the death-bed of the Rev. Mr Weightman", Branwell went on ". . . and now I am attending at the death-bed of my aunt, who has been for twenty years as my mother. I expect her to die in a few hours. . . ."

     Writing four days later, on 29th October, Branwell had indeed to report that his aunt had died:

My dear Sir,
     As I don't want to lose a *real* friend, I write in deprecation of the tone of your letter. Death alone has made me neglectful of your kindness, and I have lately had so much experience with him, that your sister would not now blame me for indulging in gloomy visions either of this world or another. I am incoherent, I fear, but I have been waking two nights witnessing such agonising suffering as I would not wish my worst enemy to endure; and I have now lost the guide and director of all the happy days connected with my childhood. I have suffered such sorrow since I last saw you at Haworth that I do not now care if I were fighting in India or—since, when the mind is depressed, danger is the most effectual cure. But you don't like croaking, I know well, only I request you to understand from my two notes that I have not forgotten *you* but *myself.* Yours etc. . . .

As Branwell mentioned in his letter to Grundy, all his sisters being away, the whole burden of the illness and death of his aunt had fallen on him. Nothing shows more effectively the superficial and unnatural quality of his usual cynicism—a cynicism assumed as armour against the world—than the genuine feeling he showed over his aunt's death; at heart he remained a child.

The immediate and practical effect of Miss Branwell's death was to bring Charlotte and Emily straight back from Brussels. They arrived home on 8th November and found Anne there. Anne, sent for urgently, should have reached home in time to see her aunt alive, but Mrs Robinson had not granted her leave in time.

Thus suddenly and unexpectedly reunited, the four young people took stock of their new situation. The girls, being scrupulously honest with themselves, recognised that the death of their aunt was not a heart-searching sorrow. They had respected her greatly, but love had never entered into their sentiments towards a relative so little resembling them in temperament.

Inviting Ellen Nussey to come and visit them, Charlotte could say on 20th November: ". . . Do not fear to find us melancholy or depressed. We are all much as usual. You will see no difference from our former demeanour. . . ."

On Branwell, as has been seen, had wholly fallen the shock and ordeal of his aunt's illness and death, and of the genuineness of his pang in losing her there can be no doubt.

She had indeed been a good friend to him; coming forward with help whenever help was needed; paying for extra painting lessons, standing surety for him with the Railway Company, and doubtless performing numerous other acts of generosity and kindness; best of all perhaps, never letting him feel that she had lost faith in him. To her at least he remained the favoured nephew. There is absolutely no truth in Mrs Gaskell's assertion, so often repeated, that his aunt cut Branwell out of her will. Reference to the terms of it effectively explodes that contention.

The will, drawn up in April 1833, when Branwell was not quite sixteen, made financial provision for her nieces only (the three Brontë nieces and the daughter of her sister, Jane Kingston) supposing, as was normal at the time, that her nephew would sufficiently make his own way in the world.

To each of the young Brontës Miss Branwell left a personal memento specifically named in her will: to Charlotte her "Indian workbox", to Emily her "workbox with a china top", together with her ivory fan, to Anne, her watch "with all that belongs to it, as also my eye-glass and its chain . . ." and to Branwell, the more distinctly masculine bequest, of her "Japan dressing-box". The will was proved in the prerogative court of York on 28th December 1842 by two of its four executors, Mr Brontë and Mr George Taylor of Stanbury, the testatrix's total effects being "sworn under £1500".

In Charlotte's notes to Ellen during the holidays that followed, the allusions to Branwell suggest no dramatic change in attitude to him, nor, indeed, any prolonged return of depression on his part. He would appear to be borne up on the crest of the wave once again, and to have regained much of his old brio in public. ". . . Branwell wants to know why you carefully exclude all mention of him when you particularly send your regards to every other member of the family?" Charlotte teases her friend after Ellen's visit to Haworth in early January 1843. "He desires to know whether and in what he has offended you, or whether it is considered improper for a young lady to mention the gentlemen of the house. We have been one walk on the moors since you left. . . ."

To the obvious reply Ellen returned, Charlotte answered on 15th January: "I will deliver Branwell your message."

In the same letter she confirmed, what her friend already knew by her recent visit, that Charlotte herself was returning to Brussels very shortly. It was not necessary to explain further the rest of the family's plans, since they were known to Ellen.

On Miss Branwell's death, the need for one of the girls to remain at home as her father's housekeeper had become self-evident, and Emily chose to be that one. She was both the best suited by her housewifely capacity and the most eager to remain at home. She had "worked like a horse" in Brussels, as Charlotte said, to learn all she could, but had had enough of foreign exile to last her a lifetime.

There was thus an element of fate in the solution of the family's problems, by which Charlotte returned to Brussels (as she longed to do) and Anne returned to Thorp Green, with the consequent intro-duction of Branwell into the family of her employers.

Charlotte left home for Brussels on Friday, 27th January 1843, by which date Anne and Branwell had already gone to Thorp Green.

Chapter Sixteen

LYDIA

Until Anne had negotiated his engagement as tutor in the family of her own employers, Branwell had probably taken very little interest in them or their concerns. But now that he was speeding towards York in the new railroad from Leeds with Anne by his side, anything that she could tell him about the Robinsons would be of help in his first contacts with the family. Although his particular functions would relate to his pupil mainly, the temper of the parents was of vital import to his happiness, as his previous experience at Broughton had shown. What were Mr and Mrs Robinson like?

It was not from Anne that he would receive a glowing account, for she liked and approved neither of them. But her reasons, founded upon an innate distaste for worldliness, would not necessarily sway Branwell. In the event, they did exactly the contrary.

How much Anne herself knew of their history and connections, after two years' service in the family, cannot be guessed. Research into their family papers, however, shows that the Manor of Thorp Green came into their possession only three generations back, in 1795. The Robinson family were collaterals of the Marquis of Ripon, and had connections in the peerage, parliament and the Church.

Mr Robinson himself was a clerk in Holy Orders, but never at any time officiated in that capacity, save only on the occasions of his children's christenings. He was, at that time, in his forty-third year, having been born on 2nd February 1800. He had inherited the Thorp Green estate in infancy, his father having died at the premature age of thirty-three, leaving his estate and his heir in the capable and businesslike hands of his widow, Mrs Elizabeth Robinson who, together with an unmarried daughter, Jane, still spent a great part of each year on the family estate. A second daughter, Mary, had married the Venerable Charles Thorpe, D.D., Archdeacon of Durham, and lived at Ryton in the County of Durham.

In 1824 Mr Robinson had married Lydia, daughter of the Rev. Thomas Gisborne, Canon of Durham, of Yoxall Lodge, Yoxall, Staffordshire, and by her had had five children, of whom four sur-

vived, Anne's pupils over the last two years. They were: Lydia
Mary, born 25th October 1825, Elizabeth Lydia, born 10th January
1827, Mary, born 6th May 1828, and Edmund, the only boy and
Branwell's prospective pupil, born on 19th February 1832—by
which count he was at the beginning of the year 1843 on the eve of
his eleventh birthday.

Mrs Robinson, on her side, was co-heiress to her father's considerable estate. Her only sister had married William Evans, Esq.,
of Allestree Hall in the county of Derby, and Park House, Kensing-
ton, member of parliament for North Derbyshire. Upon her
marriage Mrs Robinson had received a marriage portion of £6,000,
over which she had absolute control and which was not without its
effect on the subsequent story—and the destiny of Branwell Brontë
in particular.

When Anne had first been engaged to teach the Robinson
children in March 1841, she had been required to coach Edmund in
Latin, on the understanding that he was shortly to be sent to a
public school. That eventuality had been constantly deferred, both
by his inability to learn and his mother's indulgence, until the
decision was taken, in this January of 1843, to engage a tutor for him
instead.

It has, fortunately, been possible to establish at what salaries
Anne and Branwell were engaged. Mr Robinson's last personal
cash account book, luckily yet preserved among the family papers,
shows that Branwell was paid £20 a quarter and Anne £10.
According to *Agnes Grey* she had been engaged at £50 per annum
(a good salary for those days and exactly double that offered her by
her first employers, the Ingham family of Blake Hall) but the
deduction of £10, though not redounding to her employers'
generosity after two years' service, would seem to correspond with
her being relieved of Edmund's education in 1843.

That Branwell's engagement should positively have reduced her
own earnings would but be characteristic of Anne. By that time,
also, she may have been relieved of teaching Lydia, her eldest pupil,
who had turned seventeen in the previous October and was already
attending balls and parties with her mother.

If there was one thing that appealed to Branwell in all this tale,
it was the social position of his prospective employers. The fact that
Mr Robinson was related to the Marquis of Ripon and Mrs Robinson had a sister married to the member of parliament for North

Derbyshire were matters so flattering to his vanity that he would still boast of them three years later when confiding in his friends Leyland and Grundy the whole unpredicted outcome of his adventure. Always "gloriously great or ingloriously small", as the astute Grundy had noticed, Branwell liked extremes, and if he was to be employed by *anyone*, it might as well be people of rank and fashion.

The Robinsons' estate must, similarly, have left him nothing to desire, combining genuine antiquity with up-to-date elegance. Its history stretched back to 1292 when the Convent of Fountains had obtained a licence of free warren there. The resultant "Grange" was regarded by the Abbot of Fountains and his monks as a choice retreat for "their solace, profit and pleasure" and served for centuries as a resting-place on their frequent journeys from Fountains to York. In the actual fourteenth-century building in which Branwell would be lodged, the "Monks' House"—in size and function serving in those latter days rather as a dower house within the estate—an Abbot of Fountains, John de Ripon, had died in 1435, and within sight of its gabled windows was still preserved the monks' circular "stew pond" where plenteous supplies of fish were stored in anticipation of the passing wayfarer.

Such romantic antecedents could but heighten for Branwell the attractions of the place. The drawing he sent home of his lodgings at the Monks' House—recognisably exact even today when the timbered and wattled building is a century older—can still be seen at the Brontë Parsonage Museum, Haworth.

The Thorp Green Hall Anne and Branwell knew, almost completely destroyed by fire at the beginning of this century, was a Georgian mansion set in "11 acres of Gardens, Pleasure Grounds and Paddock" and owned the "exclusive right of shooting over nearly 2,000 acres of land". It was situated a mile and a half from Little Ouseburn, midway between Green Hammerton and Boroughbridge and some twelve miles from York.

Fortunately, a description has been preserved in a "To Let" notice dating from shortly after the departure of Anne and Branwell. This gives a very clear idea of the house. Anne, writing of it as "Horton Lodge" in *Agnes Grey* outlined it as a large house with "a stately portico and long windows descending to the ground".

In the words of the advertisement appearing in the *York Gazette* and the *Leeds Mercury* in February 1848, the house comprised: "Entrance Hall, Dining Room (32 ft. 4 in. by 18 ft.) Drawing

Room (30 ft. by 19 ft.) Library (19 ft. 7 in. by 18 ft. 4 in.) Spacious Breakfast, Ante and other Rooms, large and convenient Kitchens, Servants' Hall, Cellars, and other offices; Eight Lodging Rooms on the first floor and Nine Lodging Rooms on the second floor.

"The outbuildings comprise Brewhouse, Wash-house, Laundry, Dairy, Stabling for 14 horses, Loose-Box, Coach-house, Hay Chambers, Saddle Rooms etc. . . ."

Of its position, the advertisement could boast that "Thorp Green is beautifully situated in a rich and finely wooded district, about 12 miles from York, 5 from Borough-bridge, 9 from Knaresbrough, and 11 from Ripon; . . . and within reach of the York & Ainsty, Bramham Moor & Bedale Packs of Hounds. . . ."

The latter detail calls to mind that Anne recorded of her employer that he was more often gone with the hounds than at home, and that at least *one* of her young lady pupils had no interests outside the stables, or conversation but for stable-boys.

For the same reason that the house became vacant shortly after Anne and Branwell left in 1845, an inventory of the contents and its furniture was taken, which permits of a more distinct idea of their surroundings than any fictional description could afford.

It was the period when mahogany was much in vogue and we find it predominating in all the reception and main bedrooms throughout the house. The great drawing-room contained: "a Piano Forte, Brussels Carpet, Large Chimney Glass, Pair fire screens, Arm chairs, Music chair, Pair of Globes, Painted Table, Mahogany Chiffoneer, Mahogany Card-tables, 2 Conversational chairs, 2 Rosewood Chiffoneers with marble tops, Sofa Table, Work Table, 2 Stained Rosewood sofas, Devotional chairs, 6 Mahogany easy chairs, Large Ottoman, Pembroke Table, 12 Stained Chairs, Chess Table, India Cabinet, . . . 3 sets of Moreen Window Curtains, Blinds, Rollers", together with "soft hassocks" and "footstools", "soft cushions" and "Moreen cushions", etc.

The dining and breakfast rooms were furnished with equal comfort and style. Only the "school-room" furnishings afford an eloquent commentary on the consideration shown to dependants in that household. It recalls a trait in the character of "Mrs Hargrave" in *The Tenant of Wildfell Hall* (noticeably modelled upon Mrs Robinson in her ultimate relations with her daughters), of whom Anne recorded that though very comfortably off, " . . . she grinds her dependants, pinches her servants . . ."

The school-room in which Anne had spent the major part of her two years at Thorp Green, was inventoried as furnished with a "Drugget & hearth rug (old) Fender, fire-irons, etc., Dining table, Set painted book-shelves, Couch & cover, 6 chairs & covers, 1 Book Case and books, 20 pictures".

The school-room books (like all the books, indeed, catalogued in the house) are no reflection on the mainly worldly and sporting characters of its owners. Collected very likely by Mr Robinson's parents, they attest to wide and cultured interests. They included, in their original texts, the works of Herodotus, Xenophon, Thucydides, Sophocles, Euripides, Pindar, Cicero, Virgil—books on mathematics and chemistry, Rapin's *History of England* in five volumes, a very small but choice collection of English authors— Bell's *Shakespeare, Paradise Lost,* Pope's *Odyssey* and *Iliad,* Boswell's *Corsica,* Scott's *Works,* Cook's *Voyages,* and among a wide assortment of dictionaries only one foreign text: the *Lettres Choisies de Sévigné.*

Let it be said at once that the degree of advancement in her pupils' studies described by Anne in *Agnes Grey* at no period reached the standard of the authors quoted here, which represented no doubt little more than the conventional basis for a school-room library.

In the rest of the house, in the library itself, in the drawing and breakfast rooms, were some hundreds of other volumes, mainly theology and classics in the former, history, travel, fiction and poetry in the two latter. Among standard English authors like Addison and Steele, Gibbon, Goldsmith, Thompson, Southey, Scott, More, were volumes of travel, books on gardening, on "Natural History" (twenty-six volumes), volumes of sermons, Italian poets in their original texts, etc.

Mrs Robinson could be accounted a regular reader, even if mainly of light literature, for there is proof to show that she had a subscription to the circulating library run by Bellerby and Sampson at 13 Stonegate, York, for which she paid two guineas annually (and postage of 4s 1d on the "Library Box" in which her books were sent out and returned).

Her tastes would not appear to have descended to her children. Of the girls' disinclination for any intellectual effort, for any studies other than "showy accomplishments—music, singing, dancing, drawing", Anne has eloquently written in *Agnes Grey.* That Mrs Robinson supported them against their governess in doing everything they liked and nothing that irked them, she has also written.

What was true for the girls, was true in a far higher degree of the boy. Edmund, with whose Latin studies Anne struggled for two years, never got beyond the Valpy's *Delectus* stage, of which her own annotated copy can still be seen at the Brontë Parsonage Museum at Haworth. She was, as she recorded in *Agnes Grey*, expected to get "the greatest quantity of Latin Grammar and Valpy's *Delectus*" into her pupil's head without any effort on his part.

Echoes of her lessons with Edmund abound in *Agnes Grey*:

Master Charles was his mother's peculiar darling. . . . At ten years old he could not read correctly the easiest line in the simplest book; and as, according to his mother's principle, he was to be told every word before he had time to hesitate or examine its orthography, it is not surprising that he made little progress during the two years I had charge of his education. His minute portions of Latin grammar, etc. were to be repeated over to him till he chose to say he knew them. If he made mistakes in his little easy sums in arithmetic, they were to be shown to him at once, and the sum done for him, instead of his being left to exercise his faculties in finding out for himself. . . .

She describes Edmund, further, as

a pettish, cowardly, capricious, selfish little fellow, only active in doing mischief, and only clever in inventing falsehoods, not merely to hide his faults, but, in mere malicious wantonness to bring odium upon others. . . . It was a trial of patience to live with him peaceably; to watch over him was worse; and to teach him, or pretend to teach him, was inconceivable.

Such was the pupil committed to Branwell's care in that January of 1843. Lest Anne be accused of invention or flagrant exaggeration of the portrait, confirmation from a quite different source exists. The tutor to whom young Edmund was eventually sent in default of a public school, while writing flattering eulogiums to his mother on the score of his "innocence and purity", was obliged to conclude: "that his mental acquirements are so very inferior is his infelicity rather than his fault . . .".

That Branwell very early in his role of preceptor gauged his pupil's capacity and the mother's inordinate fondness for her son appears by the sequel. To the delight—and incredulity of all at home, and of Charlotte in far-away Brussels—Branwell was very soon reported to be "doing well" and being "in good odour" with his new employers. The eulogies did not rest there. They only rose to a crescendo over the years and "Anne and Branwell are *both*

wondrously valued in their situations . . ." Charlotte could report a
full year after Branwell had arrived at Thorp Green.

That he was resolved not to fail again was evident; the post was
too good to lose for the price of folly. (Looking back on the years
at Thorp Green later, Branwell was able to boast: ". . . in my last
situation I was so much master, and gave myself so much up to
enjoyment . . .".) The comfort, the security, the air of luxury,
strongly appealing to the snob in him, all roused his latent capacities
for showmanship. He realised that his position hung on his handling
of Edmund, and adroitly he must have steered his course to achieve
so early the wholehearted commendation of his employers. Obviously, to Edmund was not applied the scalp-lifting discipline
reserved for Branwell's Sunday-school scholars. To gain his pupil's
good graces was to ensure those of the pupil's doting mother, and
though, doubtless, Branwell's chief aim in settling down at Thorp
Green was to do precisely this, the result exceeded every expectation.
Intentional as his flattery and subservience would be to gain his
pupil's mother to his cause, he hardly expected the rapidity or the
completeness with which he did so.

That something in his situation was causing him a strange dis-
quiet, a perturbation of the spirit as unwelcome as it was obsessing,
the verses he wrote barely two months after arriving at his post
reveal. Dated 30th March they run:

> I sit this evening, far away
> From all I used to know,
> And nought reminds my soul to-day
> Of happy long ago.
>
> Unwelcome cares, unthought-of fears
> Around my room arise;
> I seek for suns of former years,
> But clouds o'ercast my skies. . . .

Of Mrs Robinson, soon to fill his entire universe, several
glimpses are afforded in *Agnes Grey*. Writing of Mrs Murray, the
mother of her pupils, Anne described her as "a handsome dashing
lady of forty, who certainly required neither rouge nor padding to
add to her charms, and whose chief enjoyments were, or seemed to
be, in giving or frequenting parties . . .".

The first error that must be corrected in writing of Mrs Robinson
and Branwell Brontë is that originally made by Mrs Gaskell and

repeated ever since by Brontë biographers in describing Mr Robinson as an elderly invalid and his wife as many years his junior. She
was, in fact, of the same age as her husband, having been born like
him in 1800. At the time of Branwell's arrival at Thorp Green, she
was, therefore in her forty-third year—seventeen years his senior.

To understand something of the complexity of Mrs Robinson's
very superficiality, her letters and personal papers, of which great
numbers are still preserved among the family documents, must be
read. She reveals herself as an intelligent woman with an excellent
head for business, writing a beautiful hand and expressing herself
fluently. Obviously accustomed to unquestioning service and
flattery, difficulties made her peevish; when hard pressed she fell
back on an assumption of weakness, patently foreign to her character. At all times she liked to pose as a victim. She was a lady who
took her social obligations seriously. As Mrs Gaskell reported of her
years later, she was given to many charitable and religious causes,
and expressed herself with becoming zeal upon many matters
touching the welfare of the dispossessed. She gave regularly to
"the Poor of Little Ouseburn", paid for "Poor Scholars" to be
taught "Reading, Writing & Arithmetic" at Great Ouseburn
School; subscribed annually to the "Society for the Propagation of
the Gospel" and to the "Society for the Promotion of Christian
Knowledge" (one guinea each) while as regularly running up bills
with her Hanover Square dressmaker for sums that put her charities
in the shade.

She was, as every complaint of Anne Brontë attests, an over-
indulgent mother, pampering her children in all their propensities—
until they ran counter to her own and their worldly interests when,
as the long contentions over her daughters' marriages reveal, Mrs
Robinson could be as ruthless as a far more authoritarian parent.

While fulfilling the obligations incumbent on a lady of her
station with punctilious exactitude, as her accounts reveal, she had
little feeling for the predicament of a shy stranger like Anne cast
alone in her household. Writing of her again in *Agnes Grey*, Anne
says: "Mrs Murray was so extremely solicitous for the comfort
and happiness of her children and continually talking about it, she
never once mentioned mine, though they were at home surrounded by friends, and I an alien among strangers; and I did not
yet know enough of the world not to be considerably surprised at this
anomaly. . . ."

The "anomaly", when it came to Mrs Robinson's treatment of her son's new tutor, would be a matter for still greater surprise, for none of the arrogance and neglect that had marked her treatment of Anne for two years were shown to Branwell at all.

The truth of what in fact were Branwell's relations with his employer's wife at Thorp Green was, for obvious reasons, so obscured by the Robinson and Brontë families that it can be discovered only by indirect means.

Branwell wrote some twenty letters on the subject to his friends Grundy and Leyland but all after the event. The only contemporary document to remain is his verses written at Thorp Green two months after his arrival there. From these unsatisfactory sources, from a handful of remarks in subsequent letters of Charlotte's, from Anne's evidence which comes down to us only as reflected in the attitudes of Branwell's sisters, and above all of Branwell's father, must the truth be derived.

Fully cognisant as the world is today of the nature and consequences of Branwell's infatuation for Mrs Robinson, the proof no longer exists of what her feelings were for him. They remain an enigma. Yet when the issue is faced which of the two must be held responsible for what happened, the evidence points to Mrs Robinson. This is not to say that she lost her head over her son's under-sized tutor; she had too much worldly wisdom and wide social experience for that. But that her conduct was such as to convince Branwell of her love, and Branwell's sister Anne, appears all too clearly.

". . . for four years (including one year of absence)", Branwell subsequently wrote to Leyland, "a lady intensely loved me as I did her, and each sacrificed to that love all we had to sacrifice, and held out to each other HOPE for our guide to the future. She was all I would wish for in a woman, and vastly above me in rank, and she loved me even better than I did her. . . ."

And again, in a letter to Grundy: ". . . This lady showed me a degree of kindness which . . . ripened into declaration of more than ordinary feeling . . . all combined to an attachment on my part and led to reciprocation which I had little looked for. . . ." And again, in a letter to Leyland, he spoke of "her horror at having been the first to delude me into wretchedness" and of his own misery in having "fixed his soul on a being worthy of all love and who for years had given him all love . . .".

Branwell's evidence not only claims that the love between Mrs

Robinson and himself was mutual, but that it existed almost from the very beginning of their acquaintance. To this the verses written only two months after his arrival would seem to attest.

Mrs Robinson showed him the kindest attentions from the first, so much is evident: that Branwell also mistook their nature, is very likely. That she was immensely relieved to find her son's tutor to be a gentle young man with discreet manners and amusing artistic gifts is understandable; that she showed her satisfaction by a gracious manner and even a benevolent encouragement for his many talents, is a likely consequence. But that Branwell, in his utter ignorance of such a society woman's very language and demeanour, might easily mistake their intention, is a likely consequence also. Encouragement to Branwell acted always like an intoxicant—especially at that period when he had received all too little of it for years, and it would not need much consideration and sympathy on her part to enslave him. The opposite is more difficult to believe. Yet flattery and a dog-like devotion are sometimes acceptable whatever their source, and Branwell could, as all his friends attest, when speaking of subjects near his heart, electrify an audience with his eloquence. That he did so, not once, but constantly, in the presence of Mrs Robinson, cannot have been without its effect on her. For, if she was an unknown quantity to Branwell, it must also be remembered that he was a new type for her.

He would succeed in entertaining her. And, experienced as she was in worldly pleasures, the very novelty of what he had to offer would make it doubly effective. Bent on charitable purposes, no doubt, Mrs Robinson would seek to know where and how her patronage could advance the prospects of the little poet who read aloud with such extraordinary pathos while she sat like the heroine in the novel he would come to write, bent over "the beads that were gradually forming the roses and tulips . . ." of her work.

By what process she imperceptibly drifted into a less superficial and more positive feeling, can only be surmised. Even allowing for exaggerations on Branwell's part, before a year was out, it must have warranted the absolute assurance with which he regarded her as won by the early summer of 1844.

To a man with his life-long frustrations, what circumstance could have more completely pandered to his vanity? They each represented a new star on the other's horizon, attractive by its very remoteness and novelty. Only Branwell, being a Brontë and attuned to supernatural agencies, would follow that star to the world's end, though it killed him. Mrs Robinson, when she did come to recognise the portents, would retreat with all the strategy of a practised general, calculating as unavoidable the devastation wrought.

There was in their relationship another element. Untrue as the allegations have been proved by which Mrs Robinson was made to appear as the neglected wife of an elderly invalid, there was perhaps enough of disharmony between the pair to warrant Branwell in considering her unappreciated. Writing to Grundy after the event, he said she had received "but unrequited return where most should have been given . . .". Whether this was so or not, he saw himself in the role of her knight-errant, a role not so new to him as might be supposed. He came to it already prepared by years of identification of himself with "Northangerland", one of whose outstanding characteristics was to step in between husbands and their neglected wives. On that shadier side of his nature, evolved from the old Angrian influences of his boyhood, Branwell took a satanic delight in the evil of his creations for the sake of evil. As far back as 1837, in the poem called "Harriet I" he had described his heroine receiving her guests in a scene of splendid festivity, her husband standing at her side, and covertly watched by her former lover, Northangerland, even then returned from exile and disguised as a minstrel. To his eye she was patently

> wedded to an Iron Breast
> Whose feelings ne'er replied to thine . . .

to a husband

> Who stood
> Apart in black and brooding mood,
> The gloomy partner of that lot
> Which he embittered with a life
> Of wild debauchery and strife
> And serpent-like revenge . . .

Seeing her thus mated, Northangerland vows to shame the husband and revenge himself by reconquering the wife. The very thought

> gave his fiery heart the rein
> Heedless of punishment or pain.

His scowling look attracts Harriet's attention.

Thorp Green Hall, front view

Thorp Green Hall, rear view

Branwell's lodgings at Thorp Green, 1844

> . . . She saw the shade severe . . .
> Collected on his forehead high,
> And o'er his deep unquiet eye,
> But in its glance of dissolute joy
> That truly sparkled to destroy
> Her fond heart traced with answering thrill
> The old impassioned feeling still. . . .

In the poem, Northangerland easily attains his end, Branwell glorying in his hero-villain's utter amorality.

> . . . there is something in his face
> Beyond its outward form of grace—
> A forehead dark with frowning ire,
> An eye of fierce, unholy fire,
> A lip of scorn . . .
> And noble though the features be
> They are marked with hidden treachery,
> And sickness left from hours gone by
> Of riot and debauchery. . . .

Though the attributes little fitted him, in fact Branwell might well imagine himself into the role of seducer so familiar to his hero, and Mrs Robinson, fancying herself, or in fact, neglected by her husband, might welcome his championship at a critical moment in her marital relations. The scene thus set, the protagonists had but to play their parts. The actual facts, recorded at the time in family correspondence respecting Branwell's and Anne's sojourn at Thorp Green, are meagre and certainly afford no glimmering of the drama being enacted there.

In late April 1843, barely four months after Branwell had taken up his post, Mr Brontë visited his children, doubtless at Mr Robinson's invitation, and had nothing but good to report to Charlotte in Brussels.

Commenting on the news in a letter of 1st May, Charlotte wrote to Branwell:

Dear Branwell
   I hear you have written a letter to me; this letter, however, as usual, I have never received, which I am exceedingly sorry for, as I have wished very much to hear from you. Are you sure that you put the right address and that you paid the English postage, 1s. 6d? Without that, letters are never forwarded. I heard from papa a day or two since—all appears to be going on reasonably well at home—I grieve only that papa is so solitary but however you and Anne will soon be returning for the holidays which will cheer the house for a time.
   Are you in better health and spirits, and does Anne continue to be pretty well?

I understand papa has been to see you. Did he seem cheerful and well? Mind when you write to me you answer these questions, as I wish to know. Also give me a detailed account as to how you get on with your pupil and the rest of the family. I have received a general assurance that you do well and are in good odour, but I want to know particulars. . . . Be sure you write to me soon, and beg Anne to inclose a small billet in the same letter, it will be a real charity to do me this kindness. Tell me everything you can think of.

As by a strange premonition of the spiritual as well as the geographical void that would soon part them for ever, Charlotte returned for a brief moment to the bond of their closest union, their imaginary world of Angria, only to leave it and him in sorrowing valediction, never to return again. She continued:

It is a curious metaphysical fact that always in the evenings when I am in the great dormitory alone, having no other company than a number of beds with white curtains, I always recur as fanatically as ever to the old ideas, the old faces, and the old scenes in the world below. *?*

Give my love to Anne, and believe me yourn—
Dear Anne, write to me, Your affectionate

Schwester
C. B.

She had closed her letter, only to open it again to add a post-script—of very little interest to Branwell no doubt, but which in the sheer rapture of the moment she could not have omitted writing, if she had had to strike off her right hand.

Mr Heger has just been in and given me a little German Testament as a present. I was surprised, for since a good many days he has hardly spoken to me.

By the sequel it would appear that Branwell had already passed beyond her ken. Writing to Emily on 29th May Charlotte said: "I have written to Branwell though I never got a letter from him."

Charlotte's letter of 1st May 1843 remains, in the absence of all others, the last gesture of love ever exchanged between them. Already sinking beneath her own heart-searching sorrow, she was as yet unaware of his, or of how completely and inevitably it would split them.

The summer holidays brought Anne and Branwell home. In a note to Ellen Nussey, dated 22nd May, Emily announced that "all here are in good health, so was Anne according to her last letter. The holydays will be here in a week or two and then if she be willing I will get her to write you a proper letter—a feat that I have never performed. . . ."

Their return would be at most for three weeks or a month before they joined their employers as usual for a month at Scarborough.

To Anne these visits to the sea had already brought their train of compensating joys and lasting memories, which would colour both her writings and her mind with indelible hues. Branwell, too, was to have his experiences of Scarborough, and that they would be inextricably bound with his love for Mrs Robinson was only natural.

There is a passage in his unfinished novel, "And the Weary are at Rest", written two years later, that attests to this, as, also, to his very exact knowledge of the Scarborough front.

. . . I once sat not far from Scarboro' under a black, wet semicircle of rock, with no objects in sight except sand and starfish for a few yards in front and the tidal waves framed in the dark rocks of my cove, which ended in a grey background of sea stretching parallel to a milky sky. Now, one might ask where lay the charm that could keep me half an hour biting my cane . . . when, if the prospect did embrace the three great objects of Nature—Heaven, Earth and Ocean —they would all have been seen to better advantage on the walls of the National Gallery. . . . Would not a *railway cutting* show rockwork in a more scientific as well as more shapely form than the shapeless and useless piles that girdled me? Would not even the little Circular Museum hold forth . . . more interesting specimens of geological and zoological history than those afforded by the cornelian pebbles or limpit shells or starfish that sprawled among . . . the sand and seaweed? Very true— . . . but neither science and the picturesque combined . . . can produce . . . the incommunicable emotion of an inward reflected joy.

The journey to Scarborough, not yet performed by rail (Branwell would just catch the opening of the York-Scarborough line in July 1845 on his last visit to Scarborough) was made by coach from York from the yard of the famous *George Hotel* in Coney Street, York was the Robinsons' shopping centre and both Branwell and Anne had frequent occasions for accompanying their pupils there, Echoes of the school-room party's shopping excursions are frequently found in Mr Robinson's cash accounts, and in such an invoice as the following from the family's bookseller and stationer at York, Robert Sunter of 23 Stonegate, for:

Eton Latin Grammar	2	0
2 copy books 1/6	3	0
Box of best pens		
Valpy's Latin Delectus	8	6
Le Petit Courrier for		
January to June	1 4	0
3 quires notepaper	2	4
13 Packets broad-bordered		
envelopes, etc.		

There were other visits, too, for Branwell and Anne on the rare occasions of their half-holidays, when they might at their own leisure visit the city's countless beauties and antiquities. What York Minster had meant to Anne over the years of her residence at Thorp Green was only finally revealed to Charlotte and Ellen Nussey when they accompanied her there on her last journey. That it brought Branwell the very highest aesthetic delight when he first saw it, is shown by contrast with his utter indifference to it—and to all great artistic stimuli—before his end. Reviewing his fallen state in a letter to Leyland written in January 1847, he wrote: ". . . my total want of happiness, were I to step into York Minster now, would be far, far worse . . ." than the loss of material possessions to the poor.

The Robinsons always stayed in furnished rooms at Scarborough and annually patronised the same establishment. This was "Wood's Lodgings", situated on St Nicholas Cliff overlooking the South Bay, and commanding the finest views in the town.

The house which, together with its two adjoining cottages, figures in many old prints of Scarborough, was large, three storeyed and contained no less than thirteen separate suites of rooms. In returning every summer as they did to Scarborough, the Robinsons sometimes booked one suite and sometimes another, according to the number in their party at the time. The *Scarborough Gazette*, appearing on Thursdays throughout the season, published a weekly visitors' list by which the arrivals and departures of the Robinson family—among others—can be traced. Often accompanied by Mrs Robinson, senior, and Miss Jane Robinson, the family when at full complement—with "3 Misses Robinson" and "Master Robinson"—required lodgings at "No 3" comprising: "Drawing Room, Dining Room and 8 or 9 beds" as well as lodgings at "No 7a" which consisted of: "Drawing Room, Dining Room, Breakfast Room, Parlour and 12 beds". Advertising his apartments at the beginning of each season, Mr Wood inserted the following advertisement in the *Scarborough Record*:

W. Wood informs the Nobility & Gentry visiting Scarborough, that his Houses, situated on the Cliff, are of different sizes, containing from Five to Fifteen Beds. W. Wood engages to give every attention to the comfort of those who may patronise his Lodgings.
Address—Hope Cottage, Cliff.

The Scarborough season did not get into full swing until the end

of June, and regularly the Robinsons had taken up their residence by the first week in July. By then, all the pleasures of the season were available. John Walshaw, "Sea-Bather", could proudly advertise "this opportunity of returning his best thanks to his numerous friends, the Visitors and Inhabitants of Scarborough for the decided preference given to him during the last 3 seasons . . . and respectfully informs them that his Machines are now on the sands. . . . Invalids especially attended to.
N.B. J. W's Machines are the nearest to the Spa and their tops are painted red and white stripes".

By 5th July, when the Robinsons usually had reached Scarborough, "Mr Kohler, leader of the Talented Band", could announce to his patrons "that the Spa Saloon Concerts have recommenced and will be continued every Tuesday & Friday evening during the season. Tickets of admission, 1/- each." In other and more detailed advertisements Mr Kohler announced that "selections from the works of Auber, Donizetti, Labitsky, Jullien, Koenig and other eminent composers, will be performed *daily* on and after the 3rd day of July next. N.B. To Subscribers to the Cliff Bridge Gardens to see that they are furnished with tickets."

Mr Kohler further added to his seasonal activities and his income by advertising "lessons on the Flageolet, Cornet, Flute, Guitar". At least during his first summer at Scarborough, when nothing clouded Branwell's sky, Mr Kohler would have been a man after his own heart.

The ubiquitous Mr Kohler it was, also, who every season "commencing on 4th July", announced his intention of giving "a series of 6 full dress balls in the Town Hall, having again secured the services of Mr Corri, the favourite M.C." Mr Corri, lest new visitors to Scarborough might be under the disadvantage of not knowing his fame, inserted his own advertisement in the local *Gazette*:

Mr Sidney Corri, M.C. at the Queen's Concert Rooms, Hanover Square, Will's, St James's, and other places of fashionable resort in London respectfully informs the Nobility, Gentry, etc that during the season he intends to give private lessons in all fashionable dancing now extant—
Three private lessons—One guinea. . . .

That Mr and Mrs Robinson, staying within a stone's throw of the Cliff Bridge and its Gardens and the Spa Saloon, availed themselves of the elegant pleasures spread at their door, Mr Robinson's cash accounts show. There are entries of 5s at a time for the "Scarbro' Band", for "Sea Bathing", for "Sea Baths", for divers excursions and the hire of a piano for four weeks, etc. They also patronised the local theatre, which they would doubtless have prohibited their daughters from attending could they have foreseen subsequent events.

The "Theatre Royal" was situated in St Thomas's Street, almost in a direct line with the Cliff lodgings, and was owned and managed by Samuel Roxby, a remarkably gifted member of a theatrical family. Consisting of several generations and collaterals, the family counted among its existing members Samuel (the owner of the Scarborough Theatre Royal), Robert, and William Beverley Roxby, accounted the most famous scene-painter of his time, with numerous successes to his score at Drury Lane, and in the field of pure art contributing regularly to the Royal Academy. Among the younger generation of this family was Henry Roxby, the company's leading man—acting under his stage name of "Harry Beverley"— and "Mrs Beverley", who played all the leading female parts from Shakespearean tragedy to contemporary farce.

The plays of Sheridan Knowles were constantly being billed, *The Love Chase* and *Virginius* in particular, alternating with such historical dramas as Bulwer's *Richelieu* and *Eugene Aram*, Shakespeare's comedies, and popular farces like *The Happiest Day of My Life*, *The Waterman*, *The Bee Hive*, *Secrets Worth Knowing* and *The Dancing Barber*.

Pleasures of another kind were assured to Scarborough's seasonal visitors by Theakston's Circulating Library in St Nicholas Street, which, together with its News-Room, was open to the public daily.

There the gentlemen could await the arrival of the London papers, or study the movement of the tides, while the ladies of the family changed their novels, of which Mr Theakston proudly advertised each year that "All the New Popular Novels have recently been added to the Circulating Library. . . ."

Multiple as the allurements were to every form of pleasure and entertainment for Scarborough's visitors, reminders of their higher obligations were also not lacking in the press. With the opening of the season, Christ Church, Vernon Road, would advertise in the *Scarborough Gazette*, under the heading "Additional Services" that: "The Vicar proposes holding a second Morning Service in Christ

Church after the commencement of July and to continue such for 3 or 4 months, so as to accommodate the visitors to Scarborough" and set out his times of services at 10 a.m., 12 noon, 3 p.m. and 7 p.m. Christ Church, the nearest to Wood's Lodgings, and the one in which Anne Brontë's funeral service was held in 1849, would be the Robinsons' place of worship, though readers of *Agnes Grey* know also that to Anne the Parish Church of St Mary's on the Castle Cliff was intimately known and loved, and its graveyard chosen eventually for her resting place.

This is the Scarborough Branwell knew. To the "little Circular Museum", with its flat Doric columns, remembered by him in his novel, he would have accompanied his pupil on rainy days, and tried to draw some spark of instruction for him from the geological exhibits displayed within its walls.

But to rejoin Mrs Robinson, to carry her plaid, to fetch her book, to post her letters, to read aloud to her on indolent afternoons when the sun beat too fiercely on the promenade and it was fresher to remain indoors by the great windows open to the sea—was all his longing. Unlike Anne, the vision of the sea, the shining rocks, the ruined castle on the Cliff, held no message for him other than the reminder that "Lydia" was more beautiful than they.

No greater proof of his mental preoccupation at Thorp Green can be found than in the almost total cessation of creative writing which marked those years. After March 1843 when he wrote the verses already referred to above, he wrote no more poetry till the early summer of 1845, when the great shock of the severance from the woman he loved drove him back on the consolation of literature.

As with his writing, so with his painting. Scarborough, that great stimulus to Anne, seems not to have tempted him back to his palette. Nor can the prolonged silence of his Thorp Green years be attributed to over-work; all too much leisure was on his hands, but he spent it like a somnambulist, moving about in the middle of his dream.

How long Mr Robinson's unqualified satisfaction with his son's tutor lasted cannot be gauged. No indication of the dates of certain scenes later described by Branwell to his friends can be surmised. "This lady," Branwell wrote to Grundy in October 1845, "(though her husband detested me) showed me a degree of kindness which, when I was deeply grieved one day at her husband's conduct, ripened into declarations of more than ordinary feeling. . . ." And again, writing to Leyland on 25th November 1845 he gave the following glimpse of Mr Robinson: ". . . my late employer shrank from the bare idea of my being able to write anything, and had a day's sickness after hearing that Macaulay had sent me a complimentary letter. . . ."

Whatever Mr Robinson's aversion and however early formed (and the first of these two statements would suggest that it dated from almost the beginning of their relations), Mrs Robinson's satisfaction alone seems to have been sufficient to ensure the continued engagement of the tutor—an engagement which, it must not be overlooked, lasted fully two and a half years.

On 1st January 1844 Charlotte returned home from Brussels and found Anne and Branwell there for their Christmas holidays. By the 23rd they were gone again and Charlotte wrote to Ellen Nussey: ". . . Anne and Branwell have just left us to return to York. They are both wondrously valued in their situations. . . ."

Before the next return home at mid-summer, the Rubicon had been passed in Branwell's relations with Mrs Robinson. Charlotte, Emily and their father noticed a complete change in his manner. He was in extravagant spirits one moment and in the depths of despair the next, irritable and impatient only for his return to Thorp Green. Alluding to this later, Charlotte wrote to Ellen on 13th January 1845: ". . . Branwell and Anne leave us on Saturday. Branwell has been quieter and less irritable on the whole this time than he was in the summer. . . ."

Branwell, in fact, by that January 1845, was more certain of himself than at any time in his life. By then, all the ambiguities in his position had been clarified—to his own satisfaction at least. He entertained no doubt whatever that Mrs Robinson loved him and further intended to marry him when she should be widowed—a circumstance which the rapid deterioration in her husband's health rendered highly probable.

By that time the final pattern of Branwell's and Anne's sojourn at Thorp Green had taken shape. Mr Robinson, become a chronic sufferer from dyspepsia, had often to stay whole days in bed. The children, less and less subject to any form of discipline, became increasingly rebellious. By then, the two eldest, Lydia and Elizabeth—aged respectively nineteen and a half and eighteen—had passed out of Anne's control and were openly flouting that of their mother. Their emancipation from the school-room and Anne's continued confinement there with the youngest girl, Mary, may the more readily explain both their increasing insubordination and Anne's comparative ignorance of what was going on in the rest of the house. That this was so for some time at least can alone explain the apparent countenance she gave her brother's conduct. Struggling to the last to inculcate some principle and sense into her young pupil, for whom she had a greater regard than for either the showy Lydia or the horsey Bessie, Anne was perhaps the one adult in the establishment who was for a long time ignorant of what was going on. That she disliked and disapproved the slack moral code of the family, its connections and circle, appeared in her ultimate study of it in *Wildfell Hall*: but that more than a suspicion of her brother's and Mrs Robinson's relations reached her before the end, cannot be supposed. When it did so, finally, she decided to leave, with whatever consequences. How deeply her spirit was marked by what she had lived through, she confided to the diary paper written after her return home, on Emily's birthday in 1845, in which she wrote that during her stay she had "some very unpleasant and undreamt of experience of human nature. . .".

Whatever the governess, shut away in the school-room with Mary, may not have known, Lydia, Elizabeth and, above all, young Edmund were fully cognisant of it, as appears from the evidence of their subsequent behaviour towards their parents. By mid-summer when the crash came, upon the least remonstrance on their mother's part, they were openly threatening her "to tell Papa about Mr Brontë".

The most dangerous to his mother's peace—and to his tutor's security—was undoubtedly young Edmund, and very closely they both had to supervise his chatter. That it did great damage the subsequent attitude of his uncles, the Venerable Charles Thorpe and Mr Evans, shows. They were the trustees appointed under Mr Robinson's will, upon whom Mrs Robinson became wholly dependent during her widowhood, and were frequently referred to by Branwell in the event. There is a revealing letter of Mrs Robinson's extant, which, in the general destruction of the evidence, speaks volumes. Writing to her lawyer some year and a half after her husband's death, she says: "I return Dr Thorpe's letter, and I hope he will pursue his present pacific plan of acting, and give us no further trouble and expense. . . . I hope Dr T. may be less unguarded in questioning Edmund than he used to be . . . for I am well aware of things he has said to me concerning Thorp Green and *all* which had better *not* have been said.

"And I am *very* glad you talked to my son upon it by naming 'him' in Dr Thorpe's presence . . ." Who was referred to by this ambiguous pronoun, can leave little doubt in our mind. Branwell, writing continually and incoherently after the event to his friends, was all too certain of the implacable enmity to his cause of Edmund's uncles.

Two allies Branwell believed he had secured to himself while at Thorp Green, whose names would recur in all his subsequent letters: the family doctor, Dr Crosby of Great Ouseburn, and Mrs Robinson's confidential maid, Ann Marshall.

Francis Leyland, in his *Brontë Family*, mentioned that, while at Thorp Green, Branwell had "soon formed acquaintances in the neighbourhood, and among them was Dr — physician to the family in which he was a tutor. Besides being possessed of a fund of anecdote, combined with an entertaining manner of relating stories, that alone made him excellent company, Branwell was found to be a thorough musician, for he had further cultivated the taste and acquired considerable skill in performance. . . ."

Dr Crosby had come to Great Ouseburn in 1829, and lived in a double-fronted Georgian house in the centre of the village. Here Branwell found a ready welcome. Dr Crosby was a fellow Mason, a member of the Oddfellows branch, of Loyal Providence Lodge, Great Ouseburn. Whether he had a keen appreciation for music, as Leyland reported, or relished a good tale wittily told, his intimacy with Branwell was chiefly founded on a very different knowledge of his friend's affairs. No circumstances of Branwell's relations with Mrs Robinson can have been hidden from him for, upon Branwell's dismissal, he acted as their go-between, and the agent through whom Branwell applied for financial help, and Mrs Robinson sent it. Incredible as this circumstance appears, and more discreditable to either party than all the rest of their conduct, it is a fact attested by a number of Branwell's letters and confirmed by Charlotte Brontë. Dr Crosby, moreover, figures frequently in Mrs Robinson's cash accounts for sums not *always* entered under "medical attendance".

A greater ambiguity surrounds the conduct and exact role of Branwell's other confidante, Ann Marshall, Mrs Robinson's confidential maid. By all his accounts, Ann Marshall was not only in her mistress's confidence, but in his. After Branwell's dismissal she wrote to him over a length of time, keeping him informed of her mistress's condition. And Branwell, as fully, confided his hopes and fears to her.

Yet, examination of the Robinson family papers brings a different light to bear on Ann Marshall's role in the household, revealing her not so much as her mistress's confidential maid, as her master's. In a number of promissory notes signed with his hand, Mr Robinson made cash presents to Ann Marshall, amounting in the end to £520, a sum all the more considerable and surprising by contrast to Ann's wages, which we learn were £12 per annum.

The first of these promissory notes is dated "July 4th 1843" and reads:

I promise to pay Anne [*sic*] Marshall or Order on demand the sum of Three hundred and fifty pounds with interest after the rate of three per cent per annum for value received.

£350   Edmund Robinson
                                        Thorp Green.

On 4th January 1844 (exactly six months later) Mr Robinson signed a second promissory note drawn up in precisely the same terms and for a sum of £200. This was followed on 19th August 1844 (a little more than six months later) with yet another, for the sum of £50. And finally, on 19th March 1845, Mr Robinson signed a promissory note for the sum of £100. In every case the wording was alike, the money being given "for value received".

The sums involved, their regular recurrence, the secrecy with which they were conferred (contrasting as they do with the annual entry of Ann's wages in Mr Robinson's cash accounts) and above all, their incidence only during the period of Branwell's residence at Thorp Green, invests them with a peculiar interest for the biographer and makes it impossible not to ask: did they represent Ann Marshall's price for spying into her mistress's affairs? That Mr Robinson had conduct to repent of towards his wife, Branwell ultimately declared in his letters.

On the other hand, the promissory notes could relate to matters quite unconnected with Branwell and concerning Mr Robinson alone.

The role of Ann Marshall, no matter on whose behalf she acted, was of sufficient importance to make her the object later of close questioning and investigation. On the evidence of her nephew, a Mr Atkinson, in whom she confided, she "was much worried and

troubled by being examined and cross-examined at Thorp Hall".
Certain it is that the promissory notes became known to Mrs
Robinson after her husband's death, and figure repeatedly in her
correspondence with her solicitors. Ann herself never enjoyed her
prize, dying of consumption at the age of thirty-eight on 16th April
1847, but the sum was paid by Mrs Robinson, with accrued interest,
to Ann's mother. The family solicitor took it upon himself to "put
up a gravestone to poor Ann's memory", describing her as "for
many years a most respected servant of the Rev. Edmund Robinson
of Thorp Green".

A last glimpse into Branwell's state of mind before his dream
shattered about his head is afforded by the two sonnets he wrote in
May 1845, and with which he broke the strange silence of his two
years at Thorp Green. To both he gave the one name, "The Emi-
grant", as though in preparation and acceptance of a future which
broke completely with his past.

I

When sink from sight the landmarks of our home,
And—all the bitterness of farewells o'er—
We yield our spirit upon ocean's foam,
And in the new-born life which lies before,
On far Columbian or Australian shore,
Strive to exchange time past for time to come:
How melancholy, then, if morn restore—
(Less welcome than the night's forgetful gloom)
Old England's blue hills to our sight again,
When we, our thoughts seemed weaning from her sky—
That *pang* which wakes the almost silenced pain!
Thus, when the sick man lies, resigned to die,
A well-loved voice, a well-remembered strain,
Lets Time break harshly in upon Eternity.

II

When, after his long day, consumed in toil,
'Neath the scarce welcome shade of unknown trees,
Upturning thanklessly a foreign soil,
The lonely exile seeks his evening ease—
'Tis not those tropic woods his spirit sees;
Nor calms, to him, that heaven, this world's turmoil;
Nor cools his burning brow that spicy breeze.
Ah no! the gusty clouds of Englands isle
Brings music wafted on their stormy wind,
And on its verdant meads, night's shadows lower,
While "Auld Lang Syne" the darkness calls to mind.

Thus, when the demon Thirst, beneath his power
The Wanderer bows—to feverish sleep consigned,
He hears the rushing rill, and feels the cooling shower.

After that, events moved swiftly to their climax. Examination
of Mr Robinson's cash accounts shows that he was constantly seeing
his doctors, Dr Crosby, and a Dr Simpson called in for consultations
from the beginning of the year 1845 as the deterioration in his health
gained momentum.

On 10th February he made an entry as paying " 'Miss Brontè's'
salary, £10" and on 21st April he paid " 'Mr Brontè's' salary £20".
Branwell, who had, of course, arrived two years after Anne, was
paid at different quarters from her. His next quarter's salary was
therefore due on 21st July, but on 11th June the following entry
shows that he received it considerably in advance.

| Miss Brontè | 3. | 10. | 0 |
| Mr Brontè (due July 21) | 20. | 0. | 0 |

(The £3 10s od paid to Anne was, obviously, on a pro rata basis, the
money due to her for one month's salary—in this case, something in
the nature of a gratuity, maybe, on the occasion of her leaving.)

On that day—11th June—or at latest the next, Anne and Branwell
went home for the holidays, as Charlotte mentioned in a letter to
Ellen dated 18th June. Discussing the possibility of accepting an
invitation to the Nusseys', Charlotte wrote: "You thought I refused
you coldly, did you? It was a queer sort of coldness, when I would
have given my ears to be able to say yes, and felt obliged to say no.

"Matters are now however a little changed, Branwell and Anne
are both come home, and Anne I am rejoiced to say has decided not
to return to Mr Robinson's—*her* presence at home certainly makes
me feel more at liberty. . . ."

That no inkling of a crisis in Branwell's affairs had reached the
family is apparent from Charlotte's next letter to Ellen. Writing
on 24th June she said: ". . . Branwell only stayed a week with us
but he is to come home again when the family go to Scarbro'. . . ."

By 19th or 20th June, as Charlotte's letter therefore shows,
Branwell had returned to Thorp Green.

On Friday, 4th July, the Robinsons went to Scarborough. Mr
Robinson entered the fact in his cash accounts, and the *Scarborough
Herald* for 10th July corroborated the fact. All the family—"the

Rev. E. & Mrs Robinson & 3 Misses Robinson"—had arrived, with the exception of Edmund, who, the same paper shows, joined them only on 17th July.

Whether Edmund had been left behind at Thorp Green in charge of Branwell for some special coaching is not clear, but the fact remains that on the very day he joined his parents at Scarborough Mr Robinson wrote a letter dismissing Branwell, who had by then reached home. He was struck almost senseless with the terms of the letter, which Charlotte reported as ". . . sternly dismissing him and intimating that he had discovered his proceedings, which he characterised as bad beyond expression, and charging him on pain of exposure to break off instantly and for ever all communication with every member of his family . . .".

Whether Mr Robinson had acted after long deliberation, or in the very moment of discovery, whether it was upon a statement of Edmund's, or on some complaint of his wife's, will never now be known.

The strong likelihood that the blow was struck by Mrs Robinson herself, seems to be borne out by subsequent events. That Branwell was making himself impossible and threatening not only her present but her future security would be in character, and was exactly what she had to combat later. If Mr Robinson's discovery implicated his wife, in his opinion, just as much as the tutor, the consequences must in some way have been visited on her; whereas quite the contrary seems to have been the case. The fact emerges that during the days immediately following Branwell's dismissal—days that one would imagine were fraught with extreme delicacy, if not danger, to Mrs Robinson's domestic peace—days during which Branwell, as Charlotte reported, was thinking "of nothing but stunning or drowning his distress of mind . . .", and during which "no one in the house could have rest . . ." Lydia Robinson was receiving almost daily presents from her husband. In his cash accounts for those days at Scarborough can be seen his repeated entries for such costly items as "Lydia's chain £4. 0. 0—Lydia's Shawl £1. 17. 6—Lydia's brooch £1. 8. 0—Lydia's Scarf—" and the conclusion has most unequivocally to be made, that Mrs Robinson had secured her peace at the price of treachery.

If Branwell was not wholly deluding himself, if what he later repeatedly averred was true, that for more than three years he had "loved and been loved", and had every reason to hope that "ere very long I should be the husband of a lady whom I loved best in the world . . ." then undoubtedly Mrs Robinson's situation had become critical, and the more Mr Robinson's health declined and the tutor's pretensions grew, the more imperative for her peace became the need to be rid of him. Unwittingly, Anne may have paved the way to this when she gave her employers notice. It made the break with the brother easier still.

If this seems an unduly harsh judgment on Mrs Robinson's conduct, it alone would merit the stigma cast on her by Mr Brontë years later when writing to Mrs Gaskell. Congratulating her on her just published *Life* of his daughter, he wrote on 2nd April 1857: ". . . The pictures of my brilliant and unhappy son, and of his diabolical seducer, are master-pieces. . . ." Sharing a bedroom with Branwell for the last three years of his life as he did, during nights of candid revelation (as well as of drunken ravings), not much of the truth of what happened at Thorp Green can have remained hidden from Mr Brontë. His stern judgment on that evidence was corroborated, it must not be forgotten, by the witness of his daughter Anne as well. Subsequent events would only strengthen and confirm the unshakable opinion of the Brontë family on Mrs Robinson, summed up in the words of Charlotte: ". . . that woman is a hopeless being; calculated to bring a curse wherever she goes, by the mixture of weakness, perversion, and deceit in her nature . . .", and ". . . a worse woman, I believe, hardly exists . . .".

Evidence of a quite unbiased nature has come to light which only endorses the opinion of Branwell's family. During his illness, which was ultimately declared as "dyspepsia" of many years standing, culminating in "phthisis", Mr Robinson was attended by his usual doctors, Dr Crosby and Dr Simpson. But on occasions he also called in, as a consultant, a Dr William Hall Ryott from Thirsk, who was considered a very go-ahead man for the time. Dr Ryott went over to Thorp Green on several occasions to examine Mr Robinson, when he would spend the night at the Hall, and his impressions of the situation there included some of a non-medical character. What he saw and heard was enough to impress him forcibly with the fact that Mrs Robinson, and not Branwell, was wholly to blame for what happened. Recalling those visits many years later when the truth had become partially known to the world, he would say that he wholeheartedly pitied Branwell and condemned the lady. He often saw Anne and spoke of her as "sweet" and "very pretty". Dr Ryott's evidence (given to the present author by his grand-daughter), standing outside the Brontë-Gaskell-Robinson controversy as it does, is invaluable in apportioning the blame, if any doubt yet subsists on that score.

Mrs Gaskell heard reports of a clandestine meeting at Harrogate after the rupture, and of a wild proposal on Mrs Robinson's part to leave her husband and her fortune and run away with Branwell. (That the Robinsons spent a day at Harrogate on 3rd September 1845 is confirmed by an item in Mr Robinson's cash accounts where he entered £2 for the day's expenses.) On reflection it would appear that Mrs Robinson saw the wisdom of preserving her fortune and of bestowing such part of it only on Branwell Brontë from time to time as charity might suggest. Charity occupied much of Mrs Robinson's thoughts, as has already been seen. In a letter written shortly after her husband's death to her daughters' trustee she specifies: "With regard to Charities *I am pained* that *any one* should miss any help I could ever give them. . . ."

The account given to Branwell by Dr Crosby and Ann Marshall of what actually happened between husband and wife, was the least likely, as may be supposed, to damage Mrs Robinson in Branwell's eyes. Writing to Grundy in October 1845 he told him: ". . . Three months since, I received a furious letter from my employer, threatening to shoot me if I returned from my vacation, which I was passing at home, and letters from her lady's-maid and physician informed me of the outbreak, only checked by her firm courage and resolution that whatever harm came to her, none should come to me. . . ."

Mrs Robinson's version of the "dénouement" as presented to Branwell, was such as effectively to preserve his good opinion to the end. He never wavered in his trust of the woman he loved.

Nevertheless, the shock was greater than his physique could bear. His grief was frenzied and he gave way to it without any attempt at self-control as we have seen from Charlotte's letter. Branwell, telling Grundy about it later, said: "I dreaded . . . the wreck of my mind and body, which, God knows, during a short life have been severely tried. Eleven continuous nights of sleepless horror reduced me to almost blindness. . . ." Drink and drugs aiding, his madness and violence made him so unmanageable at home that Mr Brontë had to send him away to the sea in charge of John Brown. They went to Liverpool on 29th July and from there into Wales for a week, where "the sweet scenery, the sea, the sound of music",

Ann Marshall, the Robinsons' confidential maid

"Our Lady of Greif", drawing by Branwell Brontë,
April 1846

"We need not entertain a doubt as to
whom it is intended to represent."
—F. A. Leyland

Branwell later told Grundy, "caused me fits of unspeakable distress".

Yet, almost as soon as he got to Liverpool, Branwell so far pulled himself together as to write to Charlotte to express "some sense of contrition for his frantic folly . . ." and to "promise amendment on his return . . .".

The resolution to do better is symptomatic of the period that was to follow during which, in spite of the death blow he had received, Branwell was still buoyed up with the secret hope of before long possessing the woman he loved. He was alone so to be beguiled. Charlotte, commenting on his promises of improvement to Ellen had no illusions: ". . . so long as he remains at home, I scarce dare hope for peace in the house . . .".

Her loss of all patience and confidence in her former confederate was now to prove the last disaster of Branwell's unfortunate life, the causes of the radical change in her being probably not even surmised by him.

R

Chapter Seventeen

MARIA THURSTON

A year and a half had elapsed since Charlotte returned from Brussels and during that period neither Branwell nor Anne had seen her for more than three weeks at a time. Only Emily could have any knowledge of the state of near mental collapse in which Charlotte had come home and the intense depression of spirits that had weighed on her almost ever since.

The resolution to quit Brussels, taken when she had come to realise the impossible nature of her feelings for M. Heger, had taken a toll of all her reserves of strength. She came home exhausted with the moral and physical struggle of her last six months under M. Heger's roof, only to find that the heroism of which she had been capable, in his presence, had cruelly deserted her now that she was materially removed from him. When all the embargoes to her love were out of sight and she could see him as she pleased in the mind's eye alone—in the role of teacher, adviser, friend—intolerable longing could take full possession of her heart and imagination, and wear her down with unrelenting insistence.

The absolute purity of her desires, her sense of triumphant virtue in having denied herself even such innocent happiness as his friendship gave, were contributing factors in exacerbating Charlotte's nerves and temper and keeping her in a perpetual state of irritation. The restlessness of her mind is apparent in the many visits she paid her friends Ellen Nussey and Mary Taylor, and in the plans, successively discarded, for occupying her time. At the period of Branwell's dismissal from Thorp Green, she was playing with the idea of going abroad again—to Paris—as Anne noted in her diary paper of 31st July 1845. Anything to flee the realisation of her loss. By 1845 its irreparable nature was fully borne in on her by the failure of M. Heger to respond to her one poor little remnant of consolation, the correspondence to which, in parting, he had given his consent.

Then began for Charlotte the worst torment of any yet endured, the added suffering of feeling that she was misjudged and despised.

"Monsieur," she wrote to him on 8th January 1845, "the poor have not need of much to sustain them—they ask only for the crumbs that fall from the rich man's table. But if they are refused the crumbs they die of hunger."

Perceptive, even from the centre of the furnace in which her heart burned alive, of the real enemy working behind her master, Charlotte had this terrible message to send to Mme Heger. ". . . I have a hidden consciousness that some people, cold and common-sense, in reading it [her letter] would say—'She is talking nonsense'—I would avenge myself on such persons in no other way than by wishing them one single day of the torments which I have suffered for eight months. We should then see if they would not talk non-sense too. . . ."

She wrote again in May. She wrote again in November and humbled herself to ask: "May I write to you again next May? I would rather wait a year, but it is impossible—it is too long. . . ."

The letter of May 1846 was never written. Something, not only the chords of a heart stretched to its ultimate capacity of suffering, had snapped, but an indifference born of very excess had succeeded the crisis, like a sleep after fever. The great illness that was her love for M. Heger, burned itself out, leaving her temporarily numbed.

It was Branwell's crowning misfortune that his own calamity should coincide with Charlotte's.

Because of what she had just endured, when in July 1845 the astounded family first heard of Branwell's love for Lydia Robinson, none was more wholly unsympathetic towards it than Charlotte herself. From the first, she gave Branwell no credit for attempting to fight his sorrow; she immediately gave up his case as hopeless. It is notable that her sisters did not share this view.

On the very day, 31st July, that Charlotte was writing with unenviable clairvoyance as we have seen to Ellen of Branwell, then away with John Brown, Emily and Anne were recording in their diary papers that Branwell had recently ". . . had much tribulation and ill-health" and were severally but jointly hoping that "he would be better and do better hereafter".

All too perceptive of her brother's weakness as she was, Charlotte's incredulity from that time on of any possibility of reform either in his conduct or intentions will be seen to help create, rather than prevent, the very condition she deplored.

Like a leitmotiv, her condemnation of Branwell punctuated all her letters of the time. "My hopes ebb low indeed about Branwell," she wrote on 18th August to Ellen. "I sometimes fear he will never be fit for much—his bad habits seem more deeply rooted than I thought. . . ." "Things here at home are much as usual . . ." she wrote a few days later, "not very bright as regards Branwell, though his health, and consequently his temper have been somewhat better this last day or two, because he is now forced to abstain. . . ."

The impossibility of entertaining visitors, even intimates like Ellen, had of course to be laid to Branwell's account. "Branwell makes no effort to seek a situation," she wrote on 8th September, "and while he is at home I will invite no one to come and share our discomfort. . . ." And again on 7th October she writes: "I have told you without apology that I cannot ask you to Haworth at present. I told Miss Wooler the same. . . ." By 4th November, the accumulated irritability and frustration of the past weeks bursts out into the open declaration: "I wish I could say one word to you in his favour, but I cannot, therefore I will hold my tongue. . . ."

On 31st December it is: "You say well in speaking of Branwell that no sufferings are so awful as those brought on by dissipation . . ." and by the beginning of the New Year, her condemnation is final: "Branwell offers no prospect of hope—he professes to be too ill to think of seeking for employment—he makes comfort scant at home. . . ."

Branwell may never have seen the manuscript of his sister's story relating to Elizabeth and Henry Hastings, but the relationship there described had been a very real thing of which he, more than anyone, had been aware.

What had now changed was not the brother's role—that remained constant—it was the sister whose outlook had been totally modified. The effect now of so startling an alteration in her was only to drive Branwell back upon himself. Secret as every circumstance of his love obliged him to be, he hid from his family even the few attempts he made at resuming a normal life. Indicative of this were the contacts he strove to establish at that very time with the outside world, and which prove that while Charlotte was inveighing against him for, among other things, making no attempt to find work, he was in fact trying to get back upon the Railway. On 23rd October 1845 he wrote to the Secretary of the Manchester and Hebden Bridge Railway Company:

Dear Sir

  I respectfully beg leave to offer myself as candidate for the situation of Secretary to the Manchester & Hebden Bridge & Keighley & Carlisle Junction Railway.

··· I trust to be able to produce full testimonials as to my qualifications and Securities, if required, to any probable amount.

I am,

Dear Sir,

Your most respectful and

obdt Servt

P. B. Brontë.

At the same time, he wrote to Grundy, who had returned to the district and from whom, before anyone else, Branwell might hope to get a testimonial for the Company. The letter to him written during the same month of October, is his first full personal statement of what happened at Thorp Green. It reads:

October 1845

I fear you will burn my present letter on recognising the hand-writing; but if you will read it through, you will perhaps rather pity than spurn the distress of mind which could prompt my communication, after a silence of nearly three (to me) eventful years. While very ill and confined to my room, I wrote to you two months ago, hearing that you were resident engineer of the Skipton Railway, to the inn at Skipton. I never received any reply, and as my letter asked only for one day of your society to ease a very weary mind in the company of a friend who *always* had what I always wanted, but most want now, *cheerfulness*, I am sure you never received my letter, or your heart would have prompted an answer.

Since I last shook hands with you in Halifax, two summers ago, my life till lately has been one of apparent happiness and indulgence. You will ask "Why does he complain then?" I can only reply by showing the under-current of distress which bore my bark to a whirlpool, despite the surface waves of life that seemed floating me to peace. In a letter begun in the spring and never finished, owing to incessant attacks of illness, I tried to tell you that I was tutor to the son of [Mr Edmund Robinson, Thorp Green Hall] a wealthy gentleman whose wife is sister to the wife of — M.P. for the county of — and the cousin of Lord —. This lady, (though her husband detested me) showed me a degree of kindness which, when I was deeply grieved one day at her husband's conduct, ripened into declarations of more than ordinary feeling. My admiration of her mental and personal attractions, my knowledge of her unselfish sincerity, her sweet temper, and unwearied care for others, with but unrequited return where most should have been given . . . although she is seventeen years my senior, all combined to an attachment on my part, and led to reciprocations which I had little looked for. During nearly three years I had daily "troubled pleasure soon chastised by fear". Three months since, I received a furious letter from my employer, threatening to shoot me if I returned from my vacation, which I was passing at home; and letters from her lady's-maid and physician informed me of the outbreak, only checked by her firm courage and resolution that whatever harm came to her, none should come to me. . . . I have lain during nine long weeks utterly shattered in body and broken down in mind. The probability of her becoming free to give herself and estate never rose to drive away the prospect of her decline under her present grief. I dreaded, too, the wreck of my mind and body, which, God knows, during a short life have been severely tried. Eleven continuous nights of sleepless horror reduced me to almost blindness, and being taken into Wales to recover, the sweet scenery, the sea, the sound of music caused me fits of unspeakable distress. You will say, "What a fool!" but if you knew the many causes I have for sorrow which I cannot even hint at here, you would perhaps pity as well as blame. At the kind request of Mr. Macaulay and Mr. Baines, I have striven to arouse my mind by writing something worthy of being read, but I really cannot do so. Of course, you will despise the writer of all this. I can only answer that the writer does the same, and would not wish to live if he did not hope that work and change may yet restore him.

Apologising sincerely for what seems like whining egotism, and hardly daring to hint about days when in your company I could sometimes sink the thoughts which "remind me of departed days", I fear departed never to return, I remain, etc.

P. B. Bronte.

The mention of striving to arouse his mind "by writing something worthy of being read . . ." relates to another plan he had under review at the time and which he had confided to his friend Leyland in a letter written the previous month:

Haworth,
Sept. 10th, 1845.

My Dear Sir,

I was certainly sadly disappointed at not having seen you on the Friday you named for your visit, but the cause you alledge for not arriving was justifiable with a vengeance—I should have been as cracked as my cast had I entered a room and seen the labours of weeks or months destroyed (apparently not, I trust, really) in a moment.

That vexation is I hope over and I build upon your renewed promise of a visit, for nothing cheers me so much as the company of one whom I believe to be a MAN, and who has known care well enough to be able to appreciate the discomfort of another, who knows it too well.

Never mind the lines I put into your hands, but come hither with them, and if they shall have been lost out of your pocket on the way, I wont grumble, provided you are present to apologise for the accident.

I have, since I saw you at Halifax, devoted my hours of time snatched from downright illness, to the composition of a three volume *Novel*—one volume of which is completed—and along with the two forthcoming ones, has been really the result of half a dozen by-past years of thoughts about, and experience in, this crooked path of Life.

I felt that I must rouse myself to attempt something while roasting daily and nightly over a slow fire—to wile away my torment and I knew that in the present state of the publishing and reading world a Novel is the most saleable article, so that where ten pounds would be offered for a work the production of which would require the utmost stretch of a man's intellect—two hundred pounds would be a refused offer for three volumes whose composition would require the smoking of a cigar and the humming of a tune.

My novel is the result of years of thought and if it gives a vivid picture of human feelings for good and evil—veiled by the cloak of deceit which must en-wrap man and woman—If it records as faithfully as the pages that unveil man's heart in Hamlet or Lear, the conflicting feelings and clashing pursuits in our uncertain path through life, I shall be as much gratified (and as much astonished) as I should be if in betting that I could jump over the Mersey I jumped over the Irish Sea. It would not be more pleasant to light on Dublin instead of Birkenhead than to leap from the present bathos of fictitious literature on to the firmly fixed rock honoured by the foot of a Smollet or Fielding.

That jump I expect to take when I can model a rival to your noble Theseus who haunted my dreams when I slept after seeing him—but meanwhile I can try my utmost to rouse myself from almost killing cares, and that alone will be its own reward.

Tell me when I may hope to see you and believe me, dear Sir,

Yours,

P. B. BRONTË

Both prospects—that of getting work again on the Railway, and that of writing a novel—are of importance, mainly as showing that Branwell had still, in those first months following his dismissal from Thorp Green, enough hope and energy left to turn his mind to some regular occupation, buoyed up as he still was by the secret conviction that Mrs Robinson, as soon as her husband was dead, would give herself to him.

To Leyland, more completely than to Grundy, he could un-burden his heart. Almost immediately on being dismissed from Thorp Green, even before the trip to Liverpool, he had gone over to Halifax and on the very day after his return, 4th August, had written to Leyland:

Dear Sir

John Brown wishes to know whether or not, you can make your intended visit to Haworth this week.

Of course he awaits, and will be ready for your own convenience, in naming your week or your day.

I need hardly add that I shall myself be most delighted to see you, as God knows I have a tolerably heavy load on my mind just now, and would look to an hour spent with one like yourself as a means of at least temporarily, lightening it.

I returned yesterday from a week's journey to Liverpool and North Wales, but I found during my absence that wherever I went a certain woman robed in black, and calling herself "MISERY" walked by my side, and leant on my arm as affectionately as if she were my legal wife.

Like some other husbands I could have spared her presence.

Yours most sincerely,

P. B. BRONTË.

The sequel, dated 19th August, reads:

My dear Sir,

John Brown wishes to know whether the payment due for the monument will be most acceptable this week, as, if so he can get it from the parties before Saturday and give it into your hands.

They had not the required sum in the house or he would have recieved it to-day.

The Tablet has fully satisfied all who have seen it. As to my own affairs I only wish I could see one gleam of light amid their gloom. You, I hope, are well and cheerful.

Yours sincerely,
P. B. Brontë.

That he was capable at that time of giving his mind to extraneous subjects, the references to John Brown's goings and comings between Haworth and Halifax and to the execution of a mural tablet go to show. The tablet, subscribed for by the people of Haworth, was the memorial to poor Willie Weightman, dead three years before. Even at that crisis in his affairs, Branwell was not so lost to all his old connections as not to secure for Leyland the commission of designing and executing the tablet—worth from £40 to £60.

To Leyland also on 25th November, he sent the text of a poem, "Penmaenmawr", written during his trip to Wales with John Brown, which he asked his friend to insert, as usual, in the *Halifax Guardian*. He gave as his reason for doing so, the specific purpose of reaching Mrs Robinson, without arousing the suspicions of Mr Robinson. The accompanying letter fully explained his motives.

My dear Sir,

I send through yourself the enclosed scrap for the Halifax Guardian—and I ought to tell you why I wish anything of so personal a nature to appear in print.

I have no other way, not pregnant with danger, of communicating with one whom I cannot help loving. Printed lines with my usual signature "Northangerland" would excite no suspicion—as my late employer shrank from the bare idea of my being able to write anything, and had a day's sickness after hearing that Macaulay had sent me a complimentary letter so *He* won't know the name.

I sent through a private channel one letter of comfort in her great and agonizing present afflictions, but I recalled it through dread of the consequences of a discovery.

These lines only have one merit—that of really expressing my feelings while sailing under the Welsh mountain, when the band on board the steamer struck up "Ye banks and Braes"—and God knows that, for many different reasons, these feelings were far enough from pleasure.

I suffer very much from that mental exhaustion, which arises from brooding on matters useless at present to think of, and active employment would be my greatest cure and blessing—for really after hours of thoughts which business would have hushed I have felt as if I could not live, and, if long continued, such a state will bring on permanent affection of the heart, which is already bothered with most uneasy palpitations.

I should like extremely to have an hour's sitting with you, and if I had the chance, I would promise to try not to be gloomy. You said you would be at Haworth e're long, but that '*e're*' has doubtlessly changed to '*ne'er*', so I must wish to get to Halifax sometime to see you.

I saw Murray's monument praised in the papers, and I trust you are getting on well with Beckwith's, as well as with your own personal statue of living flesh and blood. Mine, like your Theseus, has lost its hands and feet, and, I fear, its head also, for it can neither move, write or think as it once could.

I hope I shall hear of you on John Brown's return from Halifax whither he has gone, and apologising honestly for putting you to the trouble of placing the enclosed in the hands of the newspaper editor—if you choose to do so.

I remain,

Dear Sir,

Yours most sincerely,

P. B. Brontë.

The poem, evoking the unshakable firmness of the mountain in the face of Nature's rages and History's depredations, and calling on it to help the writer stand "as moveless through sun and shine", contained a direct allusion to his love in the lines:

> I knew a flower, whose leaves were meant to bloom
> Till Death should snatch it to adorn a tomb,
> Now, blanching 'neath the blight of hopeless grief,
> With never blooming, and yet living leaf;
> A flower on which my mind would wish to shine,
> If but one beam could break from mind like mine.
> I had an ear which could on accents dwell
> That might as well say "perish" as "farewell!"
> An eye which saw, far off, a tender form,
> Beaten, unsheltered, by affliction's storm;
> An arm—a lip—that trembled to embrace
> My angel's gentle breast and sorrowing face;
> A mind that clung to Ouse's fertile side
> While tossing—objectless—on Menai's tide!

The river Ouse here invoked flows through Little Ouseburn.

The conviction was unshakable that it was Mrs Robinson who needed his pity and his support. Even in his own mental collapse, it gave him the illusion of being the stronger of the two, an illusion by which, nevertheless, he managed to live.

Not even indirect news was reaching him of Mrs Robinson during the autumn and winter following their separation, and his imagination was free to picture her despair in tones as unrelieved as was his own.

Not until the next summer would Branwell learn of one very cogent cause of upheaval affecting the family at Thorp Green. On 20th October 1845, Lydia, the worldly, dashing, pleasure-seeking eldest daughter of the house, eloped to Gretna Green with Henry Roxby, the leading actor of Scarborough's Theatre Royal. The event, creating the stir that can be imagined, was thus recorded by a Great Ouseburn villager at the time: "Miss Lydia Robinson made her exit with Henry Roxby, a play-actor, Monday Morning, Oct. 20th. They went to Gretna Green and got married that night. She was just a fortnight turned 20 years that day. A bad job." The misalliance, so wounding to the family pride, cost Lydia her dowry. "Cut off without a shilling" by her father, as Branwell was later to report, she was even deprived of her third share of her mother's dowry, the £6,000 settled on her at marriage, which in due course, on the judicious marriages of Elizabeth and Mary, was equally divided between them. Lydia's distress in the immediate years following her marriage was occasionally met by insignificant gifts from her mother—such as £6 on learning that Mr Roxby had been ill—and after much tribulation a weekly allowance of 30s was finally settled on her. She and her husband were once received at Thorp Green shortly after their marriage, but that was all.

For a time, as the fifty-eight pages of the novel mentioned to Leyland attest, Branwell bent his mind upon his writing. The need for some such stimulus was all the more desperately felt as time dragged on and his isolation at home became more pronounced each day. His family's incomprehension was gradually assuming as big a part in his mental dejection as his separation from the woman he loved. As he wrote to Leyland:

> When I fall back on myself, I suffer so much wretchedness that I cannot
> d my temptation to get out of myself. . . . The quietude of home, and
> lity to make my family aware of the nature of most of my sufferings
> ine write:
>
> > Home thoughts are not, with me,
> > Bright as of yore . . .
> > My home has taken rest
> > In an afflicted breast
> > Which I have often pressed
> > But—may no more!

His misfortune was not only heightened by his inability to make the family aware of *his* sufferings, but by his inability to imagine, and relieve *theirs*. That his sisters had made sacrifices over years to help him upon his devious course had never even been remarked by him. It paled into insignificance now, beside the permanent sacrifice he exacted of them—the peace of their own fireside. Tragic, indeed, was the pass to which they now were come, in which, boxed up together in the old home, bent on the self-same task of literary fulfilment, they lived in complete seclusion from each other, the brother from the sisters, each side unknowing what the other did.

In the autumn of 1845, while the "Poems" of Currer, Ellis and Acton Bell were being collated for publication, the wretched brother of the Bells—who could have added some verses at least worthy of inclusion with theirs—was offered no share in the venture and, if Charlotte is literally to be believed, remained unaware to the end that his sisters "had ever published a line".

He, for his part, wrote in secret from them, and occupied much of that autumn and winter in writing the novel of whose existence they probably never heard.

It has been suggested that the writing of "And the Weary are at Rest" dates from 1842, but this is not only to disregard the whole nature of the experience described in the novel, but to overlook such internal evidence of its later composition as the very exact description of "the little Circular Museum" at Scarborough and the reference to the conservatory at Chatsworth built only after Branwell had gone to Thorp Green in 1843.

The manuscript with the title "And the Weary are at Rest" has been preserved and represents Branwell's last contribution to literature. The culmination of his Angrian cycle, it is above all important for its reflection of his experiences at Thorp Green, thinly disguised as they are in the characters of his prototype, Alexander Percy, Earl of Northangerland, and his heroine, Maria Thurston.

Left incomplete, the story shows no signs of having a beginning. It starts *in mediis rebus*, with a reflection of Percy's strangely obsessive fears for his health, an obsession which, as Branwell's own letters show, was personal to him at the time. "I dread a single hint at physical decay as the criminal does each tick of the clock which must toll his knell. When this firm foot can no longer tread the heather, this warm blood no longer thrill to a woman's touch, this working brain no longer teem with thick-coming fancies, this omnivorous stomach no longer bear its three bottles or 20 tumblers—then what the devil is Alexander Percy to do! . . . I am not a woman to bear pains with patience so the life of an invalid would kill me or drive me mad. . . ."

It is noteworthy that the obsession with physical decay coincides with the change in the conception of Alexander Percy himself. In this his final appearance before the public, he is presented despoiled of the last vestiges of his Angrian exterior, the coal-black hair and whiskers included, and is presented in his true likeness, that of Patrick Branwell Brontë—the *alter ego* hidden in his breast—with his "curly auburn hair, a sad pale face and quivering lips, laid low on a restless pillow and showing every feature in sickly guise save the wicked blue eyes . . .".

Percy is staying with Mr and Mrs Thurston at their country house on the moors, to attend the opening of the grouse season on 12th August. The moorland district in which the house is set is recognisably Haworth—with its highest viewpoint named, without disguise, as Boulsworth Hill. Obviously recognisable, too, as the Sladen Valley waterfall is the place where ". . . at noontide, the diverging groups of Sportsmen and attendants met at a lonely spring, whose diamond water gushed up through deep green mosses in a dell of knee-deep heather under a semi-circle of Whinstone rock . . .". Percy, disgusted with the company (a re-assortment of the old Angrian crew—Montmorency, Gordon, O'Connor, Quashia Quamina) and intent only on seeking out Maria Thurston, hurries back to the house by a typical moorland track ". . . across the gulley and down the long cartruck which served as path from the peat pits to the farmsteads of a more civilised land . . .".

Successful in eluding his companions, Percy regains the house and finds Maria Thurston, as he counted on doing, "already seated at her little work-table" and pretends to examine her embroidery frame. He loses little time in coming to the point and in telling her: "You know you are a lady, and that a man, if worthy of the name, can neither dislike or even feel indifferent to you. You know you are *a neglected* lady, and that I know you are so."

So Branwell had conceived of Mrs Robinson, whether in effect she were a neglected wife or no. The supposition made the man's role easier, in giving him an excuse to push his suit. Branwell's analysis of Percy's calculations is very revealing. To declare himself, he ponders, might provoke three disagreeable consequences: "The ruin of a lady whom his very soul did love just then; the risk of a bullet through his bosom from the pistol of the dark, bilious-faced person under whose roof he abode, and, worst of all, denial of love. . . . He dreaded every movement of Mrs Thurston lest it should announce her departure from the room. . . ." (The epithet "bilious-faced" reminds us that Mr Robinson suffered from a chronic liver complaint.)

Mrs Thurston is represented as much attracted to Percy, but terrified of a jealous husband. Her checks upon Percy's ardour have, to begin with, a quiet dignity. When he tries to wring a confession of wretchedness from her and discontent with her lot, she answers: "We have guides, Sir, in even the most intricate journey. . . . Duty is one very safe. . . . Rectitude of conduct points out the straightest road from this to the other world. . . . Resignation I would recommend as a faster friend than either, for it neither craves for hope nor fears despair. . . ."

Though in ambiguous terms, Percy begs her to replace his dead wife in his lonely existence, but makes himself sufficiently clear for her to cry: "Sir, Sir, you must restrain this speech. I cannot bear it, and beg you as a gentleman to spare me. . . ."

To win Maria Thurston Percy resorts to a farcical and expensive piece of buffoonery, which throws a very revealing light on Branwell's inside knowledge of dissenting circles.

Abandoning his hostess for the day, Percy takes up his residence at the local hotel—The Thurston Arms—where, conspicuously dressed in black, he sets about organising a "Special Extraordinary Meeting of the Wesleyan Methodist Society" for 6 p.m. that evening at the local "Sanctification Chapel". He gives the chambermaid a sovereign to buy mob-caps for herself, and also a quantity of tracts to distribute on every tray and on every bed in the hotel—tracts printed at the "Wesleyan Repository in London"—and sets about coaching his disreputable friends, Hector Montmorency, O'Connor, Gordon, Quamina, in their new parts.

Percy is attended by a fanatical manservant called Bob who belongs to the "Primitive Methodists called Ranters" and, believing in the signs of grace in his master, enjoins on him and his abandoned friends: ". . . donnat pray like frightened folk. Pray with a thundering roar—pray till your legs kick out like stallians—If Heaven's grace will na' come, yaw mun mak' it come!" Of his peculiar brand of piety, Branwell has this to say: "I shall not give the report of Bob's prayer as—though too true to nature and what

I have often heard in Yorkshire and Lancashire, it would very justly be pronounced impious by all not instinctively acquainted . . . with all the deliria of revivals and experiences. . . ."

Branwell's own profound experience of the degrees of dissent—its tenets and phraseology—as debated by the Calvinists and Arminians in his aunt's Methodist magazines, as well as of the clergy of the Established Church, is shown in passage after passage that follows, illuminating, if need existed, his deep-rooted aversion to them all.

"I am sure from your chambermaid's pretty mouth," says Montmorency, breaking into Percy's bedroom, where he is practising a hymn under Bob's tuition, "that she has a sweet treble. We'll make up 4 parts. . . . I am a Calvinist and believe Jerry and Quamina and O'Connor and Gordon were predestined to the fire-grate, so I won't call them in to join us."

"Oh, but Hector," expostulated Percy, "I am not a Calvinist. I am as good a Wesleyan as was ever hatched and I insist that *all* shall be saved."

At breakfast, where he pronounces a long Grace, Percy asks the waiter whether there are any resident "teachers of the Gospel" in the district, and is told that "Mr Scarlet, the Curate, is a capital judge of horseflesh" and that the Rev. Matthew Rasper who "weighs 18 stone, and can scarce go to cover" has "as good a drop of wine in his cellars" as the hotel has, which the Dean says is "not to be beaten at the Bishop's . . . and I am sure the Dean is a judge, Sir."

"Are there any here of the Lord's Labourers in the Wesleyan or Primitive Methodist Vineyards?" Percy pursues his inquiries, and orders the waiter to send for "the local Wesleyan Preacher and to bring a brace of Class-Leaders along with him".

At the same time he orders his friends of the shooting party "to be off the moors and down at the Hotel by 5 in the afternoon, for the Lord has work for them". Montmorency, who knows Percy's depths, and sees through his play-acting, remarks that he always had an idea "that the black coat carries it with the lassies over the red and green"—a philosophy of life pursued by Branwell himself, it will be remembered, when employed at the Postlethwaites.

At the summons from the "rich gentleman" at *The Thurston Arms*, the local preacher, "the Rev. Simon Slugg", knocked over his breakfast table with its ham and eggs and barked his shins, in his eagerness to obey. En route, he was in a "whirl of calculations . . . about the chapel debt, quarterly subscriptions, donations to a dozen

Percy, Earl of Northangerland, drawn by J. B. Leyland
and said to resemble Branwell Brontë

"and the weary are at rest"
the lap against which my temples
used to beat was not that of a Mother
or daughter but of a WIFE and if I
appear outwardly forgetful of her now
do I not inwardly think of her till sleep
snatches away remembrance? I have
no longer the half bashful half delighted cheek to blush to my morning salut-
ations no longer the evening solace for
the past days cares but of those cares
themselves I have plenty who as each
fresh one enters my bosom brings tidings
of others on the road and if this strong
frame and iron constitution of mine fail
me - good God! What should I do! I
dread a single hint at physical decay
as the criminal does each tick of the clock
which must toll his knell - When this
firm foot can no longer tread the heather
this warm blood no longer thrill to a wom
-ans touch this working brain no lon
-ger teems with thick coming fancies this

Facsimile of first page of "And the weary are at rest"

"I have, since I saw you at Halifax, devoted my time
to the composition of a 3-volume Novel—one of
which is completed."—*Branwell Brontë*, 1845

It was a point constantly stressed by Branwell in his letters to his friends, that Mrs Robinson was neglected by her husband.

Pleading their past unhappy lives, Percy uses this as an argument to grasp at happiness now. "The balm of our mutual love may be before us for I know that thou lovest me. . . ." After "one look of almost vindictive fierceness, one close embrace . . ." Mrs Thurston abandons herself to Percy's arms, "in the whirl of her own feelings", not knowing "whether she were alive or dead . . .". Sensing her abandon, Percy "threw open the window which admitted of immediate access to the lawn . . ." (we are reminded of Anne's "long windows reaching to the ground") and "taking her arm first and next her waist, compelled her . . . to resign herself to his direction . . .". Together they go out to the shrubberies—the trysting-place of other illicit amours, as described by Anne in *The Tenant of Wildfell Hall*.

In the abandoned breakfast room, "the grim portrait of Mr Thurston frowned over the mantelpiece. The fair, but wan-looking lady of the mansion smiled sorrowfully from her gilded frame beside it. . . ."

Fair apparently in beauty, but not in colour, for when the couple return from the shrubberies, "Mrs Thurston's raven tresses were disordered . . .".

In the scene that follows, the signs of their guilty understanding are given a prominence that the foregoing incidents in no way warranted; they relate, all too obviously, to real, and not fictional, experience.

They are joined by Montmorency, and, Mrs Thurston moving to lift a "very large folio of local antiquities, Percy so far forgot himself as to say, imperiously and warmly: 'Halt, darling, I'll carry it!' and, as she coloured violently and could not speak, he muttered: 'Damn these slips of the tongue. . . .' "

Montmorency also noticed that she "could not tear herself from the sofa, and allowed Percy's hand to fall on her own without noticing the 'accident' . . .".

Unlike Jane Eyre and Helen Huntingdon, Maria Thurston has no clear idea of sin, of duty or dereliction from duty. Left to herself, she tries to probe into her feelings. "Have I sinned?" she asks herself. She knows only so much that she is being impelled by a power she cannot resist. "I only know that I cannot help myself," she says, "that I am going whither my every feeling leads me. . . . A long

s

dark future may be preparing for me . . . but how can I shake off what my heart clings to?"

She finds a ready excuse in her husband's neglect. "I gave myself to one who promised what he did not perform. . . ." Not without a conscience, or a knowledge of what religion teaches, Maria Thurston argues with her God. "I long to be his own," she muses upon Percy, "but I have, through my life, longed to be Thine own. I cannot be both. . . ." The final responsibility, she claims with Machiavellian casuistry, is surely not hers but God's, who made her as she is. "I am as Thou hast formed me," she concludes, "I feel as Thou hast caused me to feel. I am Thine with whom to do what Thou pleasest —but I am another's also!"

There the fragment ends. Lively, occasionally witty, but marred with all Branwell's old literary faults, confusion, diffuseness, vulgarity, it is yet the best thing he ever wrote and is an earnest both as observation and experience of what, given health and time, he might have come to write. Because of claims made later by certain of his friends that Branwell wrote *Wuthering Heights*, the importance of the fragment cannot be exaggerated, for it supplies of itself both the refutation and the explanation of so exorbitant a claim.

The impetus to write, "to wile away my torment", as he had told Leyland, neither lasted nor succeeded; the manuscript remained incomplete and his grief as entire. Poetry occupied him sporadically, and one poem in particular carries echoes of his Thorp Green experience. In Mr Robinson's library, as the inventory shows, were the two volumes of Anson's *Voyages*. Obviously read by Branwell during his residence there, the tale of Anson's tribulations during the 1740 campaign against Spain worked on his memory and inspired the poem, written at this time, which he called "Juan Fernandez".

Robinson Crusoe's Isle, Juan Fernandez was also the haven towards which Anson and his ships—two only out of his original flotilla of six—hurried, but all too late to save his men from dying of scurvy. The lesson of hope deferred—and too late realised—sank deep into Branwell's heart. Waiting and wishing for the one issue that could bring him his desire—the death of Mr Robinson—he despaired as often as he hoped, sensing that, even when it came, it would come too late for him.

Against the last stanza of the original manuscript he had written "Lydia" in Greek letters. The passage reads:

Anson—upon the sea of life
The worn and wasted soul like thee,
Mid winds and waves of care and strife
A rest like Juan's Isle may see—
May to its woodlands wish to roam,
Forgetting in that happy home
The rough Cape Horn of agony.

I'd long been tossed like withered leaf
That eddying blasts whirl round and round,
And born through many a gust of grief
While to the port of pleasure bound.
I saw at last Fernandez' Isle—
I saw a heart that beat for me,
A look that gave not friendship's smile
Or kindness of affinity—
The intercourse 'twixt man and man,
The kindnesses by kindred shown,
Though not extinguished, were outshone
When Nature's deeper power began
To point the mental sight afar
To love's own sun from friendship's star.
Sunlike, my own Fernandez shines,
While early eve o'er me declines,
Laid like a log with—deep beneath—
The scarce unwelcome gulph of Death.
Tossed overboard, my perished crew
Of Hopes and Joys sink, one by one,
To where their fellow-thoughts have gone
When past gales breathed or tempests blew
Each last fond look ere sight declines
To where my own Fernandez shines.
Without one hope that they may e'er
Storm-worn, decline in sunshine there.

The slow winter crept with frozen paces towards the spring.
The situation with his family further deteriorated: even the tolerant
Emily came to declare him to be "a hopeless being". Charlotte,
returning from a visit to Ellen on 2nd March 1846, reported on her
home-coming: ". . . I found Papa very well—his sight much the
same—Emily and Anne were gone to Keighley to meet me—unfortunately I had returned by the old road while they were gone by
the new—and we missed each other. . . . I went into the room
where Branwell was to speak to him about an hour after I got home
—it was very forced work to address him—I might have spared
myself the trouble as he took no notice and made no reply—he was

stupefied. My fears were not vain. Emily tells me that he got a sovereign from Papa while I have been away under the pretence of paying a pressing debt—he went immediately and changed it at a public-house—and has employed it as was to be expected—she concluded her account with saying he was a hopeless being—it is too true—in his present state it is scarcely possible to stay in the room where he is—what the future has in store I do not know. . . ."

While Branwell sat alone in his room, stupefied by opium, staring back at the old print on the wall of "The Death of Wolfe", his sisters foregathered in the dining-room, correcting the proof-sheets of their volume of verse, even then going through the presses of Messrs Aylott and Jones of Paternoster Row.

They, too, were approaching their "Juan Fernandez" after shipwreck and much tribulation, buoyed up with the one hope of that slender volume appearing at last in print, only to find that it was too late to bring them the dreamed-of joy.

By one of those cruel coincidences that marked so many of their final relationships, the *Poems of Currer, Ellis and Acton Bell* appeared early in May, barely two weeks before the news reached Branwell for which he had been waiting so long.

The Yorkshireman for 30th May 1846 bore this announcement in its obituary column:

On Tuesday last [May 26th] at Thorp Green near Boroughbridge, aged 46, the Rev. Edmund Robinson. He died as he had lived, in firm and humble trust in his Saviour.

Copied by the *Leeds Mercury* the news was read by Branwell with the effect that can be imagined. Years later the barmaid at the *Bull* (another "Anne") remembered how "he fair danced down the churchyard as if he were out of his mind" at the news. He prepared for the journey to Thorp Green, which ever since his separation from Lydia he had been rehearsing over and over in his mind. Either on that same day, or the next, before he could complete his arrangements, he received a message at the parsonage that he was wanted at the *Bull*. A messenger had come over for him from Thorp Green. What the interval of delirious joy wrought in him of anticipation as he dressed himself to meet his visitor, can only be measured by its consequences.

On reaching the *Bull* he found the Robinsons' coachman, George Gooch, awaiting him and hurried him into the little back parlour that they might be private and discuss their business over a bottle of wine.

Time passed, and, busy as the barmaid was, she did not notice that, when the visitor called for his horse and paid his count, Branwell had not gone with him. Only much later, on hearing a strange noise—which she remembered to the end of her days, "like the bleating of a calf", she hurried to the little parlour and found Branwell in a fit on the floor.

George Gooch had been the bearer of no letter, as Branwell had fondly supposed, convening him to Thorp Green. Guessing exactly what Branwell's reactions would be when he saw the death of Mr Robinson announced in the papers, Mrs Robinson and her advisers —the trustees appointed under her husband's will, the Venerable Charles Thorpe and Mr Evans—had despatched Gooch with a verbal statement purporting to come from the lady alone. The effect to be created on Branwell by the messenger—and very successfully the coachman carried out his part—was to deter him for the lady's sake from ever again seeking to communicate with her. Knowing how unreasonable Branwell could be, a sufficient reason had to be found to warn him off for ever, and in so doing, both Mrs Robinson and the trustees did not scruple to make use of an argument which was totally untrue.

Gooch was employed to tell Branwell that Mr Robinson had made a codicil to his will by which his wife would forfeit every penny of the inheritance, and the care of her children be removed from her and confided to the trustees, if she ever again saw Branwell.

Branwell had certainly counted on Mrs Robinson's fortune— some of his statements to his friends on the subject read uncommonly as though the money were a *great* attraction: "I had reason to hope that ere long I should be the husband of a Lady . . . with whom in more than competence, I might live at leisure . . ." he had written to Leyland, and Mrs Robinson's advisers had given him credit for *no other* motive in pursuing her. But, in the event, their calculations were wrong. Branwell was a Brontë for whom, in the final analysis, the only values that mattered were spiritual values—among which the Brontës emphatically counted romantic love.

Mrs Robinson's fortune, as an adjunct to her *person*, was an acceptable aid to the kind of life it was still Branwell's ambition to live—the life of a creative writer—but it never at any time ranked before her person, or in lieu of it, in Branwell's dreams.

To lose her fortune would not, by itself, have deterred him
from pursuing her still and this, it would seem, even Mrs Robinson
perceived. Knowing Branwell better than her brothers-in-law
could do, she was aware that an appeal to his sentiments would be
far more potent than any stern prohibition on her part. What
George Gooch had to say respecting his mistress's mental and moral
sufferings and her physical collapse had exactly the desired effect on
Branwell. Stricken to the soul himself, he readily visualised her in a
like condition, and, bereft himself of all will to live, eagerly embraced
the image of his Lydia as like to die.

Always "gloriously great or ingloriously small", Branwell
accepted the decree of Fate without a struggle, and certain it is that
when George Gooch arrived back at Thorp Green he was able to
report that "Mr Brontë" had taken matters very well.

Chapter Eighteen

"OUR LADY OF GREIF"

The fit in which he was found did not prove fatal. He was able indeed to write next day about the event to Leyland, but very certain it is that he was sincere in saying that he wished his head were as cold as the bas-relief medallion his friend had modelled of him. His suffering was heightened by a strange clairvoyance into his own case. "... I am too hard to die, and too wretched to live. ..."

The letter, written in a large uncontrolled hand, sloping violently to right and left and blotted throughout, is painfully indicative of the tempest in his mind. The insistence on Mrs Robinson's sufferings shows how successfully the coachman had accomplished his mission. Neither dated nor addressed, it reads:

My dear Sir,

I should have sent you "Morley Hall" ere now, but I am unable to finish it at present from agony to which the grave would be far preferable.

Mr. Robinson of Thorp Green is dead, and he has left his widow in a dreadful state of health. She sent the coachman over to me yesterday, and the account which he gave of her sufferings was enough to burst my heart.

Through the will she is left quite powerless, and her eldest daughter who married imprudently, is cut off without a shilling.

The Executing Trustees detest me, and one declares that if he sees me he will shoot me.

These things I do not care about, but I do care for the life of the one who suffers even more than I do. Her Coachman said that it was a pity to see her, for she was only able to kneel in her bedroom in bitter tears and prayers. She has worn herself out in attendance on him, and his conduct during the few days before his death was exceedingly mild and repentant, but that only distressed her doubly. Her conscience has helped to agonize her, and that misery I am saved from.

You, though not much older than myself, have known life. I now know it with a vengeance—for four nights I have not slept—for three days I have not tasted food—and when I think of the state of her I love best on earth, I could wish that my head was as cold and stupid as the medallion which lies in your studio.

I write very egotistically but it is because my mind is crowded with one set of thoughts, and I long for one sentence from a friend.

What I shall do I know not—I am too hard to die, and too wretched to live. My wretchedness is not about castles in the air, but about stern realities; my hardihood lies in bodily vigour; but, dear Sir, my mind sees only a dreary future which I as little wish to enter on as could a martyr to be bound to the stake.

I sincerely trust that you are well, and hope that this wretched scrawl will not make me appear to you a worthless fool, or a thorough bore.

Believe me,

Yours most sincerely,

P. B. Brontë.

To Grundy he also wrote, prefacing his account of what had happened with a renewed request for work. "The gentleman with whom I have been is dead," he proceeds. "His property is left in trust for the family, provided I do not see the widow; and if I do, it reverts to the executing trustees, with ruin to her. She is now distracted with sorrows and agonies; and the state of her case, as given by her coachman who has come to see me at Haworth, fills me with inexpressible grief. Her mind is distracted to the verge of insanity, and mine is so wearied that I wish I were in my grave. . . ."

In a further letter to Grundy, written doubtless on receipt of a reply from him, Branwell reiterated only the main cause of his despair: the accounts of Mrs Robinson's distracted state. ". . . Since I saw Mr George Gooch," he writes, "I have suffered much from the accounts of the declining health of her whom I must love most in this world, and who, for my fault, suffers sorrows which surely were never her due. . . ."

Already, in April, Branwell had sketched Lydia in a letter to Leyland, in the role of "Our Lady of Greif" [sic], with bowed head, streaming hair and clasped hands, and thus his imagination was perpetually kindled to see her now, as the suffering victim of her love for him. It was the one consolation remaining to his ego, that a woman could be distracted for love of him.

How his shattered dream affected the family is told in a letter of Charlotte's written to Ellen Nussey on 17th June.

. . . We, I am sorry to say, have been somewhat more harassed than usual lately. The death of Mr Robinson, which took place about three weeks or a month ago, served Branwell for a pretext to throw all about him into hubbub and confusion with his emotions, etc, etc. Shortly after, came news from all hands that Mr Robinson had altered his will before he died and effectually prevented all chance of a marriage between his widow and Branwell, by stipulating that she should not have a shilling if she ever ventured to reopen any communication with him. Of course, he then became intolerable. To papa he allows rest neither day nor night, and he is continually screwing money out of him, sometimes threatening that he will kill himself if it is withheld from him. He says

Mrs Robinson is now insane; that her mind is a complete wreck owing to remorse for her conduct towards Mr Robinson (whose end it appears was hastened by distress of mind) and grief for having lost him. I do not know how much to believe of what he says, but I fear she is very ill. Branwell declares that he neither can nor will do anything for himself; good situations have been offered him more than once, for which, by a fortnight's work, he might have qualified himself, but he will do nothing, except drink and make us all wretched. . . .

At Thorp Green there were evidently some fears of Branwell's yet attempting a return, and Dr Crosby was deputed to send him an even more alarming account of Mrs Robinson's state than that received before. Coming from a doctor, its terms had a professional value in Branwell's eyes exceeding George Gooch's tale, and coming, moreover, from an ally as Branwell regarded him, it carried more weight than any prohibition from Messrs Thorpe and Evans could have done. Reporting on Dr Crosby's letter to Leyland, Branwell wrote:

Well, my dear Sir, I have got my finishing stroke at last—and I feel stunned into marble by the blow.

I have this morning received a long, kind and faithful letter from the medical gentleman who attended Mr. R. in his last illness and who has since had an interview with one whom I can never forget.

He knows me *well*, and he pities my case most sincerely for he declares that though used to the rough ups and downs of this weary world, he shed tears from his heart when he saw the state of that lady and knew what I should feel.

When he mentioned my name—she stared at him and fainted. When she recovered she in turns dwelt on her inextinguishable love for me—her horror at having been the first to delude me into wretchedness, and her agony at having been the cause of the death of her husband, who, in his last hours, bitterly repented of his treatment of her.

Her sensitive mind was totally wrecked. She wandered into talking of entering a nunnery; and the Doctor fairly debars me from hope in the future.

It's hard work for me dear Sir; I would bear it—but my health is so bad that the body seems as if it could not bear the mental shock.

I never cared one bit about the property. I cared about herself—and always shall do.

May God bless her but I wish I had never known her!

My appetite is lost; my nights are dreadful, and having nothing to do makes me dwell on past scenes—on her own self, her voice, her person, her thoughts, till I could be glad if God would take me. In the next world I could not be worse than I am in this.

I am not a whiner dear Sir, but when a young man like myself has fixed his soul on a being *worthy* of all love—and who for years, has *given* him all love, pardon him for boring a friend with a misery that has only one black end.

I fully expected a change of the will, and difficulties placed in my way by powerful and wealthy men, but I *hardly* expected the hopeless ruin of the mind that I loved even more than its body.

Excuse my egotism, and believe me,

Dear Sir,

Yours,

P. B. Brontë.

Dr Crosby's letter, reporting on "the hopeless ruin" of Mrs Robinson's mind, and on her thoughts of entering a nunnery, was written a month after the death of Mr Robinson, during which period, as an examination of Mrs Robinson's personal papers reveals, she was being very active indeed and exhibiting every sign of being in full possession of a peculiarly lucid mind.

Some ten days before her husband's death she took over his role of accountant of the family expenditure, and entered the daily out-lay as he had done in his cash account book. On 5th June, the very day of his funeral, the expenses attendant on it were entered in her hand (under the heading "Edm's sad funeral"). Mr Lascelles (the clergyman's) fee of £5, the six Bearers, Clerks and Sextons, at a cost of £6; the £1 12s 6d paid to the Singers, in addition to which Mr Lascelles sent in his account for £8 for "funeral fees—per the vaults and Monument".

The estate being in process of probate, Mrs Robinson had per-sonally to attend to all incoming bills and forward them to the trustees for payment. Among the earliest of these were several accounts for attendance and medicines sent in by Dr Crosby.

Mrs Robinson ordered her mourning, the bulk of which, apart from "Caps and bonnets" bought from Midgleys of York, was made by her usual dressmaker, Catherine Harvey of Hanover Square, and which, despite its accretions of "black and white crêpe trimmings" and its "tarlatan caps"—was hardly consonant with the costume of a nun.

Mrs Robinson's father, Canon Gisborne, had died in April shortly before Mr Robinson, and the family discussions arising out of *his* will kept Mrs Robinson fairly busy with her pen in the weeks immediately following her husband's death.

She had, moreover, had to draw up a will herself at this time. Her husband's capital estate, of some £60,000 having been left in trust for Edmund, the only son, Mrs Robinson had the disposal only of her personal dowry, amounting to £7,058 10s 6d, which she now divided in two equal shares between her unmarried daughters,

Elizabeth Lydia and Mary, "for their own absolute use and benefit", thus excluding the unfortunate Lydia Roxby from any share in it.

Mrs Robinson also maintained an arduous and almost daily correspondence with her agent, Daniel Seaton of The Mount, York, whose expense account of £30 for journeys to and from Thorp Green (including the hire of a gig and tolls) for the six months following her husband's death is evidence how constantly he had to consult Mrs Robinson on business, and how closely she was following the details of winding up her husband's estate.

Mrs Robinson's correspondence with Daniel Seaton throughout this period was, of itself, a sufficiently exacting employment for a lady even in the full possession of her mind.

On 14th July 1846, at the very time Dr Crosby wrote to Branwell, Mrs Robinson and her children set out for their summer holidays at the sea. Breaking with a long family tradition, they did not go to Scarborough that year, but a little farther up the coast to Whitby. Painful associations with recent holidays, possibly Lydia's presence at Scarborough, and even the fear of Branwell's following them there, may have dictated the change. Staying only three days at Whitby, the party moved farther up the coast by boat to Hartlepool, where they also stayed three days, moving on finally to Redcar, where they remained three weeks.

It was at this period that the shattered Brontë family experienced yet another severe trial. Mr Brontë's growing blindness from cataract was at length pronounced operable, and with Charlotte to attend him, he went to Manchester on Wednesday, 19th August, and was operated upon on 25th August. They were away from home a full month, during which time Emily and Anne were left alone with Branwell—an ordeal which was thus stoically referred to by Charlotte in a letter to Ellen: ". . . I wonder how poor Emily and Anne will get on at home with Branwell—they too will have their troubles. . . ."

The kind of trouble to which Emily and Anne, and shortly the whole family would be exposed, was Branwell's setting the curtains of his bed alight when in a drunken sleep, and almost destroying himself and the whole house in consequence. The circumstance, noted by John Greenwood, the Haworth stationer, in his diary, is typical of the trials now becoming a familiar pattern of the daily round.

Increasingly, as sleep deserted him at night, Branwell would stay in bed by day—a circumstance to which must certainly be attributed his ignorance of his sisters' growing absorption in their writing, the arrival of proofs from the press, and the daily debates upon the books in hand and the answers to be sent to their publishers. Sometimes, to drown his misery, he would still try to read and take a copy of *Blackwood's* or some old battered favourite to read in bed. Lighting a candle, he would fall asleep, without remembering to blow out the light. On the day in question Anne, going in to see how he was, found the curtains ablaze and Branwell lying in the midst of the fire, insensible either from drink or opium to what was going on. Cry as she would, he did not hear her. Grief and opium were fast making a skeleton of him, but even so he was too heavy for Anne. Greenwood relates how she ran for Emily, who, with absolute self-possession, first sped to the kitchen for a bucket of water, then into Branwell's room, and seizing him bodily, threw him in a heap on the floor, while she tore down the bed-curtains and emptied the water over them. When the fire was out, all Emily said to Anne was: "Don't tell Papa."

This incident, and others like it, together with Branwell's increasing talk of suicide, led to Mr Brontë's insistence on his son's sharing his room. From then on, as Charlotte wrote to Ellen: ". . . he gives Papa no rest either by night or day . . .".

Yet there is evidence that at the very height of that summer's crisis, with Branwell causing the family untold alarms and annoyances, his sisters were yet capable of a gesture that obviously kindled —not only the old vanity in him—but the afflicted heart. It was a kind gesture, conveying better perhaps than words could do at the time, that he was still precious to them. That it was psychologically well timed is revealed by the note Branwell wrote to Leyland about it. Dated 2nd July 1846 it reads:

My Dear Sir,
    John Brown told me that you had a basso relievo of my very wretched self, framed in your studio.
    If it is a *duplicate*, I should like the carrier to bring it to Haworth, not that I care a fig for it, save from regard for its maker, but my sisters ask me to try to obtain it, and I write the note in obedience to them.
    I earnestly trust that you are heartier than I am—and I promise to send you "Morley Hall" as soon as dreary days and nights will give me leave to do so. . . .

There were, however, other subsidiary causes of despair besides the main one pressing on Branwell's mind to complete his mental ruin. He was quite aware that he was fast becoming unemployable and the growing menace of his father's blindness—and also, of his father's death—was a constant terror before which he quailed. It would, as he was quite aware, leave him totally unprovided for.

". . . My father cannot have long to live," he wrote to Leyland at the beginning of 1847, "and . . . when he dies, my evening, which is already twilight, will become night. . . ."

The need of ready money was the most urgent and alarming of all his needs, since, without it, he could not even find oblivion in drink or opium. Cadge as he did from his Halifax friends, they were scarcely in a better position than himself. Whenever fit to dress himself and go out, he would ride over to see them and make a day—and a night—of it at one or other of his favourite inns, which only further plunged him into debt. "I cannot, without a smile at myself, think of my stay of three days in Halifax," he had written Leyland shortly before the death of Mr Robinson, "on a business that need not have occupied 3 hours; but in truth when I fall back on myself I suffer so much wretchedness that I cannot withstand my temptations to get out of myself. . . ."

For months on end he managed to get credit from the landlord of the *Old Cock* at Halifax, his former favourite haunt, but by the first week in December 1846, even the good-natured Thomas Nicholson had had enough of his pie-crust promises to pay, and sent a Sheriff's Officer over to Haworth with a summons. The shock to the family was perhaps greater than any they had yet suffered on Branwell's account, since it involved a primary principle of honour.

Writing to Ellen Nussey on 13th December, Charlotte reported: "You say I am 'to tell you plenty'—What would you have me to say. Nothing happens at Haworth—nothing at least of a pleasant kind—one little incident indeed occurred about a week ago to sting us to life. . . . It was merely the arrival of a Sheriff's Officer on a visit to Branwell—inviting him either to pay his debts or to take a trip to York [to prison]. Of course his debts had to be paid—it is not agreeable to lose money time after time in this way but it is ten times worse to witness the shabbiness of his behaviour on such occasions.—But where is the use of dwelling on this subject, it will make him no better."

Quite obviously, from the context, Branwell's debts were being paid by his sisters, in an endeavour to keep the worst of his conduct from his father. The immediate sum in question was now paid off, but the main debt to Nicholson remained outstanding, as a letter of Branwell's to Leyland early in the new year (1847) shows. In it, for the first time, direct reference is made to a source of supply which was already being made available to him and on which he drew, without remorse or shame, to the end of his life. Mrs Gaskell, who got the story direct from Charlotte, had not hesitated to say that Mrs Robinson "sent Branwell money—£20 at a time"—and although she was obliged to delete the passage in the third edition of her *Life of Charlotte Brontë*, she knew the fact to be true, though she had not all the evidence corroborating it, now available.

"I wish," wrote Branwell to Leyland, shortly after the visit of the Sheriff's Officer, "Mr Thos Nicholson of the 'Old Cock' would send me my bill of what I owe to him, and, the moment that I receive my outlaid cash, or any sum which may fall into my hands through the hands of one whom I may never see again, I shall settle it."

The appeal, made directly to Dr Crosby as the sequel showed, resulted in "a considerable sum" being sent him, which Charlotte reported in the following May. Writing to Ellen on the 12th, she says: "Branwell is quieter now and for a good reason; he has got to the end of a considerable sum of money of which he became possessed in the Spring. . . ." Although not specifically mentioning him yet, Branwell would not hesitate later to name Dr Crosby to Leyland as his source of supply. By July 1848 he was openly writing: ". . . I will write to Dr Crosby, and request an advance through his hands which I am sure to obtain. . . ."

Echoes of Branwell's correspondence with Dr Crosby are contained in his long letter to Leyland of 24th January 1847, in which the latest news from Thorp Green further endorses the previous accounts of Mrs Robinson's mental and physical ruin. The letter reads:

My dear Sir,

I am going to write a scrawl; for the querulous egotism of which I must intreat your mercy, but, when I look *upon* my past, present and future, and then *into* my own self, I find much, however unpleasant, that yearns for utterance.

This last week an honest and kindly friend has warned me that concealed hopes about one lady should be given up, let the efforts to do so cost what it may. He is the Family Medical attendant, and was commanded by Mr. Evans, M.P. for North Derbyshire to return me, unopened, a letter which I addressed to

Thorp Green and which the Lady was not permitted to see. She too, surrounded by powerful persons who hate me like Hell, has sunk into religious melancholy, believes that her weight of sorrow is God's punishment, and hopelessly resigns herself to her doom. God only knows what it does cost, and will, hereafter, cost me to tear from my heart and remembrance the thousand recollections that rush upon me at the thought of four years gone by. Like ideas of sunlight to a man who has lost his sight they must be bright phantoms not to be realized again.

I had reason to hope that ere very long I should be the husband of a Lady whom I loved best in the world, and with whom, in more than competence, I might live at leisure to try to make myself a name in the world of posterity, without being pestered by the small but countless botherments, which like mosquitoes sting us in the world of work-day toil. That hope, and herself are *gone—She* to wither into patiently pining decline—*It* to make room for drudgery falling on one now ill fitted to bear it.

That ill-fittedness rises from causes which I should find myself able partially to overcome had I bodily strength, but with the want of that, and with the presence of daily lacerated nerves the task is not easy. I have been in truth too much petted through life, and in my last situation I was so much master, and gave myself so much up to enjoyment, that now when the cloud of ill-health and adversity has come upon me it will be a disheartening job to work myself up again through a new life's battle, from the position of five years ago to which I have been compelled to retreat with heavy loss and no gain. My army stands now where it did then, but mourning the slaughter of Youth, Health, Hope, and both mental and physical elasticity.

The last two losses are indeed important to one who once built his hopes of rising in the world on the possession of them. Noble writings, works of art, music or poetry now instead of rousing my imagination, cause a whirlwind of blighting sorrow that sweeps over my mind with unspeakable dreariness, and if I sit down and try to write all ideas that used to come clothed in sunlight now press round me in funeral black; for nearly every pleasurable excitement that I used to know has changed to insipidity or pain.

I shall never be able to realize the too sanguine hopes of my friends, for at 28 I am a thoroughly *old man*—mentally and bodily—Far more so indeed than I am willing to express. God knows I do not scribble like a poetaster when I quote Byron's terrible truthful words:

> "No more, no more, oh! never more on me
> The freshness of the heart shall fall like dew,
> Which, out of all the lovely things we see
> Extracts emotions beautiful and new!"

I used to think that if I could have for a week the free range of the British Museum —the Library included—I could feel as though I were placed for seven days in Paradise, but now, really, dear sir, my eyes would roam over the Elgin marbles, the Egyptian saloon and the most treasured volumes like the eyes of a dead cod fish.

My rude rough acquaintances here ascribe my unhappiness solely to causes produced by my sometimes irregular life, because they have known no other pains than those resulting from excess or want of ready cash. They do not know that I would rather want a shirt than want a springy mind, and that my total want of happiness, were I to step into York Minster now, would be far, far worse than their want of an hundred pounds when they might happen to need it, and that if a dozen glasses or a bottle of wine drives off their cares, such cures only make me outwardly passable in company but *never* drive off mine.

I know only that it is time for me to be something when I am nothing. That my father cannot have long to live, and that when he dies, my evening, which is already twilight, will become night—That I shall then have a constitution still so strong that it will keep me years in torture and despair when I should every hour pray that I might die.

I know that I am avoiding, while I write, one greatest cause of my utter despair—but by God sir it is nearly too bitter for me to allude to it!

For four years (including one year of absence) a lady intensely loved me as I did her, and each sacrificed to that love all we had to sacrifice, and held out to each other HOPE for our guide to the future. She was all I could wish for in a woman, and vastly above me in rank, and she loved me even better than I did her —Now what is the result of these four years? UTTER WRECK. The "Great Britain" is not so thoroughly stranded as I am. I have received to-day, since I begun my scrawl, a note from her maid Miss Ann Marshall, and I *know* from it that she has been terrified by vows which she was forced to swear to, on her husband's death-bed, (with every addition of terror which the ghastly dying eye could inflict upon a keenly sensitive and almost *worried* woman's mind) a complete severance from him in whom lay her whole heart's feelings. When that husband was scarce cold in his grave her relations, who controlled the whole property overwhelmed her with their tongues, and I am *quite conscious* that she has succumbed in terror to what they have said.

To no one living have I said what I now say to you, and I should not bother yourself with my incoherent account did I not believe that you would be able to understand somewhat of what I meant—though *not all*, sir—for he who is without hope, and knows that his clock is at twelve at night, cannot cummunicate his feelings to one who finds *his* at twelve at noon.

I long to be able to see you, and I shall try to do so on Friday next—the 29th inst., or on Saturday, if I am at all able to take the journey.

                    Till then, I am, Dear Sir,
                        Yours sincerely,

                                    P. B. BRONTË.

With Dr Crosby's letter had very certainly come the "consider-able sum of money" referred to by Charlotte, and which Branwell received as a token of undying love from the woman whom he believed only the violence of her relatives was keeping away from him.

That Mrs Robinson had motives other than love, or even re-morse or charity in sending help to the unfortunate young man whose health and prospects had been ruined by love of her, neither Branwell nor his sisters could know. The necessity of placating Branwell, of preventing any scandalous outbreak on his part, of

Penmaenmawr. Early nineteenth-century landscape

The *Old Talbot*, Halifax

"If you can see Mrs Sugden of the *Talbot*, tell her that on
receipt of the money I expect shortly, I will transmit her the
account I owe her. . . ."—*Branwell Brontë*

Scene at the *Talbot*, drawing by Branwell Brontë

"The rescue of the punchbowl", January 1848

keeping him at arm's length at all costs, becomes all too evident when the nature of Mrs Robinson's current activities becomes apparent.

While Dr Crosby and Ann Marshall were employed in describing her as "sunk into religious melancholy" and "resigned to her doom", Mrs Robinson was entering on a period of intense activity in pursuit of matrimonial prospects not only affecting her two daughters, but, as the event would soon show, herself as well.

Her correspondence shows that during the first winter and spring following her husband's death, she stayed at the home of her relatives, Sir Edward and Lady Scott at Great Barr Hall in Staffordshire, a removal which, though in no way surprising in her then uncertain circumstances would, within the space of two years—and promptly on the death of Lady Scott—lead to her marriage with the gentleman. Sir Edward Dolman Scott, member of parliament for Lichfield from 1831 to 1837, a relative of Mrs Robinson's and doubtless an acquaintance from her girlhood's days spent at Yoxall in the diocese of Lichfield, was already seventy-three at this time.

With Edmund now off her hands at his tutor's in Somerset, her daughters staying with their uncles in Derbyshire, or with their grandmother in lodgings at York or Scarborough, Mrs Robinson further freed her hands by letting Thorp Green Hall. Bereft of their home, and made increasingly to feel that their mother was anxious to be rid of them, the Robinson girls began to rebel in the spring of 1847. Forbidden ever since their father's death to communicate with their ex-governess (for fear of news reaching Branwell respecting their mother), Elizabeth and Mary Robinson suddenly resumed a correspondence with Anne. Cautious in their comments to begin with, they gradually confided to her the whole course of their mother's astounding conduct. Writing to Ellen on 1st March 1847, Charlotte commented:

... The Misses Robinson—who had entirely ceased their correspondence with Anne for half a year after their father's death have lately recommenced it—for a fortnight they sent her a letter almost every day—crammed with warm protestations of endless esteem and gratitude. ... We take special care that Branwell does not know of their writing to Anne. ...

As their correspondence with Anne became firmly established, Elizabeth and Mary did not scruple to condemn their mother's conduct, and wrote for help and guidance as pressure from their mother was brought to bear to hurry them into marriages for which neither of them had inclination.

The anomalous situation by which Anne was forced into the role of guide and counsellor to the friendless girls in opposition to their own mother, is reflected in the similar situation described in *The Tenant of Wildfell Hall*, where Helen Huntingdon, victim herself of an unhappy marriage, champions young Esther Hargrave against her worldly mother's unscrupulous match-making.

Mrs Robinson was in a hurry to marry off her daughters for a reason which she seemed not even to scruple to hide: her own matrimonial plans. By January 1848 they were sufficiently known to the Brontë family (with the exception of Branwell), to warrant Charlotte's writing to Ellen on the 28th:

> . . . The Robinsons still amaze me by the continued frequency and constancy of their correspondence. Poor girls! they still complain of their mother's proceedings; that woman is a hopeless being; calculated to bring a curse wherever she goes by the mixture of weakness, perversion, and deceit in her nature. Sir Edward Scott's wife is said to be dying; if she goes I suppose they will marry, that is if Mrs R. *can* marry. She affirmed her husband's will bound her to remain single, but I do not believe anything she says. . . .

Lady Scott was not being as co-operative as could have been wished in promoting the happiness of her rival, and, even, it would appear, the comfort of her rival's children, for on 20th January, eight days before Charlotte's letter quoted above, Mrs Robinson, still staying at Great Barr Hall, the Scotts' home, wrote to her agent: ". . . Lady Scott remains in so dangerous a state that my poor girls have little amusement here just now, so I have agreed to their going for a week or two to York to their grandmamma. . . ."

On 2nd February she wrote again to her agent respecting Edmund's holiday plans, which had been upset for the same reason; instructing Seaton to send him £6 travelling expenses and £5 pocket money, Mrs Robinson wrote: ". . . I am very anxious about my son and I am greatly mortified at the illness of Lady Scott which has deranged all our holiday plans. . . ."

In spite of her many trials in attaining her ends, by July Mrs Robinson had succeeded in getting both her daughters engaged, a circumstance which elicited from Charlotte the comment:

> Not one spark of love does either of them profess for her future husband, one of them openly declares that interest alone guides her, and the other, poor thing! is acting according to her mother's wish, . . . a worse woman, I believe, hardly

exists; the more I hear of her the more deeply she revolts me, but I do not like to talk about her in a letter. . . .

At last, on 4th August, Mrs Robinson was able to write her agent: ". . . Lady Scott is *just* gone after a long and distressing illness. . . ." Charlotte, reporting the fact to Ellen, could amplify with some further particulars on 18th August:

. . . The Robinsons are not married yet, but expect to be in the course of a few months. The unhappy Lady Scott is dead, after long suffering—both mental and physical. I imagine she expired two or three weeks ago. Mrs Robinson is anxious to get her daughters husbands of any kind, that they may be off her hands, and that she may be free to marry Sir Edward Scott, whose infatuated slave, it would appear, she is. . . .

It is impossible not to conjecture whether Mrs Robinson's state of infatuation, as described by her daughters to Anne, bore any resemblance to the feelings she had once entertained for Branwell Brontë.

That *his* remained constant, only intensifying in their hallucinating power as his morbid condition worsened, all who knew him have witnessed. There could be no improvement in his case. "Infatuated" to a very different degree from Mrs Robinson, his emotional collapse could only be followed by the rapid degeneration of what physical reserves he had.

To the onlooker, the greatest pathos must ever lie in the contrast between the devouring flame of his love and its unworthy object.

THE BROKEN DREAM

The make-believe world with its protective wrapping of dreams in which Branwell had swathed himself since boyhood like a chrysalis, had shattered about him and left him defenceless against his fate. His wretchedness, as he had the clairvoyance to tell Leyland, was "not about castles in the air, but stern realities", and these neither his temperament nor his training had at any time equipped him to meet. His destruction from then on was a foregone conclusion. The only matter for surprise is that he survived as long as he did.

Given a man of his mentality, the sources of his suffering could only increase. Of these, the rift with his family was to become as constant and incurable, seemingly, as his love for Lydia. Indeed, since he never realised *her* unworthiness, his family's unkindness was the more apparent to him of the two calamities. That this was so is painfully illustrated by Branwell's and Charlotte's correspondence at the time, he confiding in his two friends, Leyland and Grundy, and she in Ellen Nussey.

Branwell's manner of meeting the challenge of fate was not only below Charlotte's and contemptible to her, and a daily reminder of her own past sufferings, but a heightening of present frustrations which, in their different degree, represented suffering quite as intolerable.

When it is considered that the main bulk of the Brontës' published work was produced in three years by Emily and Anne and in eight by Charlotte (her output more than doubled theirs) the value of time in their tragic course can be better understood. They were working against the clock in an unequal race between the maturing of their genius and the rapid decline in their health. That the consciousness of this struggle made Charlotte, at least, more intolerant of the hindrance Branwell represented, is understandable but none the less tragic for him as well as for them.

In all Charlotte's strictures upon Branwell she never complained of the fact of his love (and love for a married woman at that), but of his self-indulgence, his drunkenness, his idleness and his constant hindrance to herself and her sisters in their plans. True as this was and terrible as the constant presence of a drunken drug-addict brother in the house could not fail to be, Branwell's chief fault in Charlotte's eyes was simply that he could not control his passion as she had controlled hers. It would be vain to seek one reference to him in her letters not prompted by the intensest irritation. From the beginning of the crisis, shortly after his dismissal, when she wrote: ". . . I wish I could say one word in his favour, but I cannot . . .", it is a crescendo of blame. To Ellen on 23rd January 1846: ". . . Branwell offers no prospect of hope—he professes to be too ill to think of seeking for employment . . ."; and to Miss Wooler on 30th January 1846: ". . . You ask about Branwell; he never thinks of seeking employment and I begin to fear he has rendered himself incapable of filling any respectable station in life . . . the faculty of self-government is, I fear, almost destroyed in him. . . ."

Added to her contempt for his exhibitionism, came anger at his rising debts and the invidious position in which the family was placed by the advent of the Sheriff's Officer. By 1st March 1847 it is with Branwell's half-truths that she is outraged, as much as with his debts: ". . . Branwell has been conducting himself very badly lately—I expect from the extravagance of his behaviour and from mysterious hints he drops—(for he never will speak out plainly) that we shall be hearing of fresh debts contracted by him soon. . . ."

The absolute need of a little change and pleasure in the increasing isolation of their lives tempted Charlotte in the fine spring of 1847 to invite Ellen to Haworth. (She had not been on a visit since Branwell had come home from Thorp Green.) ". . . I hope you will be decently comfortable," Charlotte wrote on 12th May, concluding the arrangements for Ellen's visit; ". . . Branwell is quieter now and for a good reason; he has got to the end of a considerable sum of money. . . . You must expect to find him weaker in mind, and the complete rake in appearance. I have no apprehensions of his being at all uncivil to you; on the contrary, he will be as smooth as oil. . . ."

In the expression—and the feeling—stronger than any to have escaped Charlotte elsewhere, can be found the trace of that attitude of cynical incredulity towards any signs of amendment in Branwell of which his friend Searle Phillips later so bitterly complained.

Phillips was editor of the *Leeds Times* in 1845-6 and claimed later to have met Branwell often at the *Black Bull*. On one such occasion, he reported, Branwell told him the following tale.

Branwell had been to visit a sick Sunday-school scholar, a young girl likely to die, and told Phillips: ". . . I went to see the poor little thing, sat with her half an hour and read a psalm to her and a hymn at her request. I felt very much like praying with her too"— Phillips, remembering Branwell's actual words, recalled how his voice trembled with emotion in saying this —"but you see I was not good enough. How dare I pray for another who had almost forgotten how to pray for myself? I came away with a heavy heart, for I felt sure she would die, and went straight home, where I fell into melancholy musings. I often do; but no kind word finds its way to my ears, much less to my heart. Charlotte observed my depression and asked what ailed me. So I told her. She looked at me with a look which I shall never forget, if I live to be a hundred years old—which I never shall. It was not like her at all. It wounded me, as if some one had struck me a blow in the mouth. It involved ever so many things in it. It was a dubious look. It ran over me, questioning and examining, as if I had been a wild beast. It said, 'Did my ears deceive me, or did I hear ought?' And then came the painful, baffled expression which was worse than all. It said, 'I wonder if that's true?' But, as she left the room, she seemed to accuse herself of having wronged me, and smiled kindly upon me and said, 'She is my little scholar and I will go and see her.' I said not a word. I was too much cut up. . . ." The end of the tale was doubtless added to point the moral of Branwell's drunkenness— and its cause in the incomprehension of his family. Phillips reported Branwell as saying: "When Charlotte was gone, I came over here to the *Black Bull* and made a night of it in sheer disgust and desperation. Why could they not give me some credit when I was trying to be good?"

The visit of Ellen did not, in effect, take place that summer of 1847; for Branwell's sisters these months were taken up by their novel-writing. It was 15th October before Charlotte wrote again of Branwell to Ellen, and then her comment was "Branwell has been more than ordinarily troublesome and annoying of late; he leads Papa a wretched life. . . ."

By the new year (1848) the physical rather than the moral aspect of Branwell's deterioration was uppermost in her mind: writing on 11th January she told Ellen: ". . . Branwell has contrived by some means to get more money from the old quarter— and has led us a sad life with his absurd and often intolerable conduct—Papa is harassed day and night—we have little peace—he is always sick, has two or three times fallen down in fits—" By "sick" Charlotte always meant "drunk".

At this rate, it is hardly surprising to read in a letter of Charlotte's at the end of July 1848, that Branwell's "constitution seems shattered . . .". The wonder seems rather that it lasted so long.

Alarmed as he himself had been while at Luddenden Foot at certain signs of physical collapse, and constantly as he had written in his poetry of his premature decay, the fact remains that he found it hard to die. He had perfectly diagnosed his own case on receiving the mortal blow from Thorp Green: "I am too hard to die, and too wretched to live. . . ." With nothing to do, no congenial company except for the friends at Halifax to whom he sent out signals of distress whenever he was sufficiently roused from the torpor that now constantly invaded him, his only occupation was to consider his lot. This he succeeded in doing with eloquence, the artist in him aiding him to depict his pitiable case with maximum effect. With potent visions induced by opium operating on his weakened mind, he literally saw his state "roasting daily and nightly over a slow fire . . ." and as often as not illustrated his letters to his friends.

What greatly added to his torment were the occasional flashes of lucidity, the ability to judge his case objectively, to analyse the progress of decay, to contrast and compare his former faculties and all the high hopes entertained for him and by himself, with the absolute ruin from which it was his worst affliction now *not* to be able to save himself.

". . . I suffer very much from that mental exhaustion, which arises from brooding on matters useless at present to think of," he wrote to Leyland even before the death of Mr Robinson finally destroyed his hopes.

Up to the time of Mr Robinson's death in May 1846, Branwell still believed in the power of literature to save him from insanity and occasionally when least oppressed, took some active steps towards writing something (witness his novel "And the Weary are at Rest") and considered approaching publishers. His old bad luck from early days, in all his attempts to interest the editor of *Blackwood's* and established literary figures, held good and dogged him even now.

"Troubles never come alone," he wrote Leyland on 29th April 1846, "—and I have some little troubles astride the shoulders of the big one.

"Literary exertion would seem a resource, but the depression attendant on it, and the almost hopelessness of bursting through the barriers of literary circles, and getting a hearing among publishers, make me disheartened and indifferent. . . ."

When the blow fell and he was made to realise that Mrs Robinson was never to be his, he gave up all talk of writing and publishing for ever. The dream world, in whose atmosphere he had lived since boyhood dissolved about him, and the anguish of living in the real world with a live sorrow was more than he could face. He recognised instinctively its power to kill him. ". . . My wretchedness," he wrote Leyland on the day of awakening, "is not about castles in the air, but about stern realities. . . ."

The recognition that the creative power had died in him, that the creative response, even, was blunted beyond repair, that every feeling that had once made life exciting and desirable, had deserted him, was a new torment to this once spoilt and sanguine child.

". . . I have been in truth too much petted through life," he wrote Leyland in January 1847, ". . . now when the cloud of ill-health and adversity has come upon me it will be a disheartening job to work myself up again through a new life's battle. . . . Noble writings, works of art, music or poetry now instead of rousing my imagination, cause a whirlwind of blighting sorrow that sweeps over my mind with unspeakable dreariness . . . for nearly every pleasurable excitement that I used to know has changed to insipidity or pain. . . ."

The absolute necessity to escape from his suffering, from the small cage in which, like a frantic animal his mind was enclosed, made him desperate for money with which to buy drink and opium. So his last troubles accumulated about him. Troubles which his "rude rough acquaintances" in Haworth (as he spoke of them), and popular imagination ever since, have assigned to the wrong causes. Branwell's wretchedness was not caused by drink and drugs —*they* were but the palliatives of a sorrow which he had not the resolution of soul to surmount. Yet it was not an ignoble sorrow; it was born of the better side of his nature, in which love and the creative urge reigned to the exclusion of self-interest. Had Branwell had a harder heart and been less of an artist, his sufferings might have been subdued; as it was they were incurable.

His Haworth cronies, as he bitterly complained, could understand only a material sorrow, but the grief of the artist for whom aesthetic joys had been everything in life—that was a sorrow which none on earth could share.

Not even his sisters. Their own and separate sorrow, to which Branwell was as much a stranger now as the villagers were to his, was of another order.

Theirs came not from the loss of powers, but from the consciousness of powers matured and no longer to be denied.

To recognise those powers within themselves and, belated as it was, to have the opportunity to give them expression suddenly within their reach—and as suddenly snatched away—that was a sacrifice to which even Branwell's sisters were unequal. Cost what it would—and in the event it cost each one of them their lives—they must fulfil their destiny as creative artists in the face of illness and the flight of time. Their inconceivable ill-fortune decreed that the moral collapse of Branwell was to coincide with the swiftly fatal course of Anne's and Emily's illness.

The real miracle remains how such works as theirs could have been composed in the time—and under conditions so wholly adverse to creation. That they dedicated what time remained to them to that creation is in accord with their genius—it was also Branwell's final misfortune.

That their once-admired brother was excluded from all knowledge of their attempt—to spare him as Charlotte wrote later, "too deep a pang of remorse for his own time misspent, and talents misapplied . . ." is a fact vouched for by the family and only contested by a few ill-judging friends of Branwell who would claim too much for him. While the name of "Bell" was making itself known throughout England and reaching even Mr Brontë and Tabby through the indiscretions of the postman, Branwell, in his increasing isolation, alone remained unaware of its existence.

The measure of his failure is to be found precisely in that fact. From his sisters' literary achievement which filled their existence during the two last years of his life, he was as much excluded as

though he had never, in their brilliant childhood, been the prime
mover, chief instigator and most prolific exponent of their collective
writing. The great objective had been reached; works of imagination capable of publication and noticed in every critical journal of
the capital were leaving the parsonage—he alone had no hand in
them. To the heart-break of losing the woman he loved was added
now the total failure of his life's ambition: the world's recognition
as a writer. Decidedly the *real* world had no place for Branwell
Brontë.

He had reached the last phase of his luckless journey. His state,
from then on, resembled indeed that of the "Castaway" in Cowper's
poem which, Mary Taylor remembered many years later, had always
powerfully moved Branwell in boyhood. Of him it could in those
final months be said that he was

> . . . Of friends, of hope, of all bereft . . .

while his sisters, like the ship-mates in the poem, were borne
irresistibly onward. Of that sad division, certain lines seemed even
to give a prophetic forecast:

> Nor, cruel as it seemed, could he
> Their haste himself condemn,
> Aware that flight, in such a sea,
> Alone could rescue them.
> Yet bitter felt it still to die
> Deserted, and his friends so nigh. . . .

Chapter Twenty

THE WEARY ARE AT REST

From that real world whose hostile encroachments had so effectively destroyed his dream, some ugly sounds were yet to come before he could shut his eyes to it for ever.

On 22nd July 1848 Mr Brontë received by the morning post a letter from the landlord of the *Old Cock* at Halifax, Mr Thomas Watson Nicholson, threatening him that if his son's debts were not paid, he would proceed to a summons.

That their true extent could not be confessed by Branwell is shown by the fact that Mr Brontë gave him ten shillings to cover them and ordered him immediately to pay Mr Nicholson.

Mr Nicholson meant business this time, as the tone of his letter made plainly apparent to Branwell. In a distracted state of mind he wrote to the only two remaining sources of help he could call upon—his unfailing friend Joseph Leyland, and Dr Crosby.

His letter to Leyland reads:

> Haworth
> Keighley
> Saturday morning
> [the date stamped on the letter by the Post
> Office was "Haworth JUL 22nd 1848"]

My dear Sir,
    Mr Nicholson has sent to my father a demand for the settlement of my bill owed to him, immediately, under penalty of a Court Summons.

I have written to inform him that I shall soon be able to pay him the balance left in full—for that I will write to Dr Crosby and request an advance through his hands which I am sure to obtain, when I will remit my amount owed, at once, to the Old Cock.

I have also given to John Brown this morning Ten shillings which John will certainly place in Mr N's hands on Wednesday next.

If he refuses my offer and presses me with law, I am RUINED. I have had five months of such utter sleeplessness, violent cough and frightful agony of mind that jail would destroy me for ever.

I earnestly beg you to see Nicholson and tell him that my receipt of money on asking, through Dr Crosby, is morally certain.

If you conveniently can see Mrs Sugden of the Talbot, and tell her that on receipt of the money I expect so shortly I will transmit her the whole or part of the account I owe her.

Excuse this scrawl. Long have I resolved to write to you a letter of five or six pages, but intolerable mental wretchedness and corporeal weakness have utterly prevented me.

I shall [not] bother you again if this painful business only gets settled.

At present, believe me,

Dear Sir,

Yours sincerely, but nearly worn out,

P. B. Bronte.

On Leyland's shoulders, then, the "painful business" was shunted, and Mr Nicholson and Mrs Sugden were referred to him as their debtor's surety.

From the context of the letter it can be seen that Branwell had neither written nor seen his friend since the previous January when the incident referred to in his last letter to Leyland (January 1848) occurred in Mrs Sugden's hostelry, the *Talbot*. Branwell had then collapsed on his friends and caused a scandal which he had thus excused:

. . . I was *really* far enough from well when I saw you last week at Halifax, and if you should happen shortly to see Mrs. Sugden of the Talbot you would greatly oblige me by telling her that I consider her conduct towards me as most kind and motherly, and that if I did anything during temporary illness to offend her I deeply regret it, and beg her to take my regret as my apology till I see her again, which, I trust, will be ere long.

I was not intoxicated when I saw you last, dear Sir, but I was so much broken down and embittered in heart that it did not need much stimulus to make me experience the fainting fit I had, after you left, at the Talbot, and another, more severe, at Mr. Crowthers [the *Commercial Inn* near the Northgate]. . . .

The letter had, incidentally, been illustrated by Branwell, with a representation of the scene at the *Talbot* during which evidently one of Mrs Sugden's punch-bowls had very nearly been overturned and smashed by Branwell in his cups. His fellow-revellers were each indicated by pseudonyms—"Phidias" for Leyland, "St Patrick" for himself, "Draco—the Fire Drake" a friend of Leyland's (Joe Drake, a carver and gilder living in Halifax)—etc.

Since that night, Branwell had evidently not seen Leyland, and knew little of his actual circumstances.

These had with a tragic persistence steadily deteriorated leaving Leyland in sore financial straits. The friend who had originally sponsored his going to London—Thomas Illidge the portrait painter, who introduced him to Stothard and helped launch him in the art world—wrote frequently imploring him to return to London where his outstanding talents would find their true outlet and give him the position he could long ago have achieved if he had not returned to the provinces. "By staying in the country you are murdering your fame," Illidge wrote, urging him to make up his mind to the move.

But it was too late. Leyland's debts were closing in upon him and his creditors only kept at bay on the security of his commissions. He accepted work of all sorts, funeral tablets in the main, to ward them off, but ill-luck still dogged his efforts. There is the story of a group of his—representing five "Warriors", which he exhibited at Manchester and which, seen and admired by Lord Ribblesdale, was bought by him and ordered to be sent up to Gisburn. But so poor were the only materials Leyland could afford to use, that the group was pulverised in transit.

He had a deep devotion towards his mother and, much as he knew Illidge's advice was right and the only course to save him from ruin, yet he could not make up his mind to leave her.

Since Branwell had seen him, he had received a commission to execute the life-size effigy of Dr Beckwith for York Minster, and the memorial tablet, for Halifax Parish Church, of the Rev. John Murray, for which he received £68. The Beckwith memorial, which took years to complete and for which he was paid a mere mason's fee of £250 kept him in Halifax against the better judgment of his true friends, and contributed to his final ruin.

From that responsibility Branwell Brontë cannot wholly be exempted. He knew Leyland for a generous-hearted man who could not see a friend in trouble without coming to his aid. Because of his commissions, mostly received from civic and public bodies, Leyland's credit was better than that of any other of Branwell's Halifax friends. Leyland's misfortune it was that they all, sooner or later, looked to him to extricate them from their troubles. At the very time that Branwell now appealed to him to placate the two Halifax publicans, Leyland was standing surety for Wilson Anderson who had been summoned by another of Branwell's publican friends, Mrs Crowther of the *Commercial Inn* in North Gate, for a matter of £3.

None of Leyland's artist friends ever honoured their obligations towards him and he was not the man to press them. By the time Leyland was paid for the Beckwith effigy, it was too late to refloat his credit. The monument was erected in the Minster in May 1849, and the occasion may be said to mark the end of Leyland's connection.

with Branwell Brontë. It was John Brown who was sent over to erect it, travelling in the same wagon as the monument. Three months later Leyland had not yet received his money, and John Brown, who had not received his fee either (£5 7s 9d), had to write and claim it from the Lord Mayor and Clerks of the City Council declaring that "if he could not be paid the whole immediately, he must have £3, as he was fast" [a Haworth expression denoting need].

The death of his mother in the next year, and the deep disappointments of a career that had opened with such promise, preyed on Leyland's mind. Arrested for debt in the autumn of 1850, he preferred to declare himself a bankrupt—though it was for a sum of only £150—and went to Manor Gaol, where he died on 28th January 1851. Not a line about him appeared in the *Halifax Guardian*. He had been loved, and was befriended throughout his imprisonment, by a young woman of a deeply religious turn of mind—a Miss Elizabeth Haley of Northowram. Her letters, recalling the happy walks they used to take together on Sundays, were the last signals he received from an ungrateful world.

Branwell's debts to him—of which his family would know nothing—were, of course, never paid.

To Branwell's other plea for help written on that 22nd July 1848 to Dr Crosby, doubtless a satisfactory response was received. By a strange coincidence it would reach its destination about the time when Mrs Robinson was announcing to her agent the death of Lady Scott (4th August), a circumstance which, advancing her own plans so favourably, would make it expedient if not pleasurable once again to send a dole to Branwell Brontë.

How Dr Crosby wrote to him of Mrs Robinson's situation, by then, there is no means of knowing. Gone from Thorp Green as the family were and moving in circles hardly suspected by Branwell—in Staffordshire and Derbyshire principally—Mrs Robinson might hope that the announcement which, of all others, she needed to keep from Branwell's knowledge, would never come to his notice. Fate, which seemed to be favouring all her projects at the moment, worked for her even in this: by the time *The Yorkshireman*, the paper that might have fallen into Branwell's hands, announced her marriage to Sir Edward Dolman Scott on 8th November 1848 Branwell was in his grave.

Preparations for the marriage of her daughter Mary, due to take place in the autumn, principally occupied Mrs Robinson that August.

Elizabeth, whom her mother also hoped shortly to get off her hands, and whose engagement Charlotte mentioned to Ellen in a letter of 28th July 1848, proved not so amenable as her sister. She broke off her engagement and was not married until 1851 when she married William Jessop Esq. of Butterley Hall, Pentrick, Derbyshire.

Business connected with her daughters' settlements and the winding up of many old accounts, occupied Mrs Robinson throughout the weeks following Lady Scott's death. She was finishing her old life and preparing for the new.

In a different context the same might be said of Branwell Brontë. His state of health since the beginning of 1848 had consistently deteriorated. He told Leyland that July of his "five months of utter sleeplessness, violent cough and frightful agony of mind ...": opium had so destroyed his appetite that his clothes hung on him like a scarecrow's. John Brown's wife and daughters, with whom he probably felt more at home than with any family in Haworth, teased him about his clothes which were so much too big for him that they asked him if he was wearing his father's coat. Tabitha Brown, later Mrs Ratcliffe, told Mrs Chadwick that Branwell was a mere skeleton before he died.

Yet he kept out and about. Restlessness was one of his chief miseries. So long as his money lasted he would creep as far as the *Bull*, where the barmaid had compassion on him and served him fivepenny nips of gin and listened to the incoherent reiterations of his tale. He could not keep Mrs Robinson out of his ramblings. "He loved that woman so, he would speak of her to a dog ...", the barmaid recalled years later.

For sixpence also he could buy a measure of laudanum—and oblivion—at Bessy Hardacre's little drug-store opposite the *Bull*, and when he did not have sixpence, he would wheedle some pills of laudanum out of her, for sheer pity of his plight.

The desperate need of a few pence with which to buy a kingdom vaster than his own Angria had become the horizon beyond which this life-long adventurer could no longer look. In default of the charity of Mrs Robinson he had to beg nearer home. Obviously the time was past when his father could be hoodwinked with tales of pressing debts to pay. If his son had to die, in Mr Brontë's broken

heart the one hope that remained was that he might not, positively,
die of drink. Ringing the changes on the few accomplices that yet
remained to him, Branwell scribbled one desperate Sunday morning
the following note to his old confederate John Brown:

Dear John
    I shall feel very much obliged to you if you can contrive to give me Five
pence worth of Gin in a proper measure.
    Should it be speedily got I could perhaps take it from you or Billy [William
Brown] at the lane top, or, what would be quite as well, sent out for, to you.
    I anxiously ask the favour because I know the good it will do me.
    Punctually at Half-past Nine in the morning you will be paid the 5d out of a
shilling given me then.
                                        Yours,
                                            P. B. B.

    The nights, as he told Leyland, were frightful. Not alone for
him, but for his father who kept watch over him, lest he should in
good earnest at last—as he had so often threatened to do—blow his
brains out with his father's pistols. "The poor old man and I have
had a terrible night of it . . ." he would say, staggering downstairs
in the morning. "He does his best, the poor old man, but it's all over
with me." The words, reported by Charlotte to Mrs Gaskell, have
long ago taken their place in English literature.
    The weather that summer was unremittingly bad and only con-
tributed further to his decline. Charlotte and Anne, hurrying across
the fields to catch the train at Keighley on 7th July to visit their
publishers in London—an escapade very certainly kept from Branwell—got drenched in a sudden snow-storm. Writing to Ellen in
August, Charlotte commented that, for the last six weeks, "one
showery day had succeeded another, which circumstance has
caused some dire forebodings about the crops . . .".
    Even had his strength allowed Branwell to ride over to visit his
Halifax friends, the weather was consistently against him. Francis
Leyland recalled seeing Branwell only once at Halifax after he wrote
to Joseph on 22nd July. It was his last visit and may have been the
occasion for writing the following note later discovered among
Joseph Leyland's papers. Written in the 'Commercial Room', *Old
Cock*, New Market, Halifax, it reads: "For mercie's sake come and
see me, for I have sought for you till I dare not risk my knee and my
eyesight any more this evening.
    "I shall have a bad evening and night if I do not see you, but I

Patrick Branwell Brontë, portrait medallion by
J. B. Leyland

"A life-size medallion of him in very high relief,
and the likeness was perfect. . . ."—*F. A. Leyland*

IN MEMORY

OF

PATRICK BRANWELL BRONTE,

WHO DIED

SEPTEMBER 24TH, 1848,

AGED THIRTY YEARS,

Branwell Brontë's funeral card

hardly know where to send the bearer of this note so as to enable him to catch you."

The note was signed in bold capital letters NORTHANGER-LAND—without a doubt the last document to bear that ill-omened name.

It had brought its bearer through eighteen years of revolution and aggression, of ship-wreck, mutiny, repeated imprisonings, through dreams of conquest, crownings, debates and battlefields; through treachery, fraud and the dark abysm of adultery—to end in the back-parlour of a provincial tavern unable to creep away under the stern eye of the landlord, unless a friend came to bale him out. To this end had Northangerland brought Branwell Brontë—in place of the snowy peak of high Parnassus.

Grundy, who had returned to the district after two years' absence, was working on the new line at Skipton (at seventeen miles from Haworth) and, unaware of Branwell's rapid decline since they had last met, wrote inviting him over for a merry meeting at the *Devonshire Hotel*. Grundy's account of what followed one evening in September 1848, published in his *Pictures of the Past* (1879), was contested by Francis Leyland in his *Brontë Family*. Leyland considered that Grundy had purposely altered the date of this meeting from 1846 to 1848 and that the conduct he ascribed to Branwell was either wholly invented, or staged as a joke by Branwell.

In his pious desire to clear Branwell of all imputations of blasphemous and lunatic conduct, Leyland went very far. So far, indeed, as to suppress evidence of conduct of which he himself must very often have been a witness. Grundy, who had no axe to grind except to prove his intimacy with the Brontë family, never hesitated to show Branwell at his most distraught and speaking, as Branwell's letters to him sufficiently show, very often like a madman. Grundy's account of Mr Brontë's incursion into the evening's proceedings point rather to the meeting's having taken place in 1848, since his blindness in 1846 and long indisposition after his eye-operation, would have made it very unlikely that autumn.

Grundy certainly confused his various meetings with Branwell. On one, which he relates as *immediately preceding* the last, he reports that he heard from Branwell's lips "his painful history . . . his happiness, his misery, and the sad story which was the end . . .". Grundy had, of course, as early as October 1845 heard from Bran-

U

well by letter all the circumstances of his devastating disappointment over Mrs Robinson.

Chronologically exact or inexact, Grundy's evidence is unique and has to be repeated.

... He was miserable, [he wrote of Branwell]. At home the sternness of his father had never relaxed and he was unfitted for outside social companionship. He was lost now, for he had taken again to opium.

Very soon I went to Haworth again to see him for the last time. From the little inn I sent for him to the great square cold-looking Rectory. I had ordered a dinner for two and the room looked cosy and warm, the bright glass and silver pleasantly reflecting the sparkling firelight, deeply toned by the red curtains. Whilst I waited for his appearance, his father was shown in. Much of the Rector's old stiffness of manner was gone. He spoke of Branwell with more affection than I had ever heretofore heard him express, but he also spoke almost hopelessly. He said that when my message came, Branwell was in bed, and had been almost too weak for the last few days to leave it; nevertheless, he had insisted upon coming, and would be there immediately. We parted and I never saw him again.

Presently the door opened cautiously and a head appeared. It was a mass of red unkempt uncut hair, wildly floating round a great gaunt forehead; the cheeks yellow and hollow, the mouth fallen, the thin lips not trembling but shaking, the sunken eyes, once small now glaring with the light of madness—I hastened to my friend, greeted him with my gayest manner, as I knew he liked best, drew him quickly into the room and forced upon him a stiff glass of hot brandy. Under its influence, and that of the bright cheerful surroundings, he looked frightened, frightened of himself. He glanced at me for a moment, and muttered something of leaving a warm bed to come out into the cold night. Another glass of brandy and returning warmth gradually brought him back to something like the Bronte of old. He even ate some dinner, a thing which he said he had not done for long; I never knew his intellect clearer. He described himself as waiting anxiously for death— indeed, longing for it, and happy, in these his sane moments, to think that it was so near. He once again declared that that death would be due to the story I knew, and to nothing else. When at last I was compelled to leave, he quietly drew from his sleeve a carving-knife, placed it on the table and holding me by both hands, said that having given up all thoughts of ever seeing me again, he imagined when my message came that it was a call from Satan. Dressing himself, he took the knife, which he had long secreted, and came to the inn, with a full determination to rush into the room and stab the occupant. In the excited state of his mind he did not recognise me when he opened the door, but my voice and manner conquered him and "brought him home to himself". I left him standing bareheaded in the road, with bowed form and dropping tears. A few days afterwards he was dead ....

The picture of Branwell conjured up by that last sentence corroborates the evidence of William Brown, John's brother, who recalled the last time Branwell went into the village. He met him in the lane winding up to the parsonage, "quite exhausted, panting for breath, and unable to proceed . . .". William helped him to the house, which he never left again.

It might, indeed, be asked what his family were doing while he was visibly dying before their eyes. The doctor was evidently called in—on account of his cough if for nothing else—for Charlotte mentioned in a later letter to Ellen that, though "his constitution had been failing all the summer, neither the doctor nor himself thought him so near his end as he was . . .".

There was little, of course, that any of them could do. For a long time now he had passed beyond their reach. The normal means of communication no longer operated between them. He neither spoke nor understood their speech, mazed in his labyrinth of opium.

On Emily, the tallest in the family except their father, had for long devolved the task of dragging him upstairs to his bed on his late returns from the *Black Bull*. But even that time was over now. As an animal senses the good-will of its master without words, without even a touch sometimes, by a mere look only, Emily's brooding glance may at times have penetrated to Branwell's broken heart. He was a "hopeless being", but she understood him. Emily had no particular admiration for success, as the world judged of successful people. She was far more at home among pariahs.

A Gondal poem, written as long ago as November 1839, and already bearing strange premonitions of the theme developed in *Wuthering Heights*, can perhaps best help the world to understand why she undoubtedly—more than anyone in the family—never cast off Branwell.

Though the poem has no title, it is related in subject to a similar lament of Lord Eldred's for the murdered Queen of Gondal ("How few of all the hearts that loved"). Whatever the theme, it refers clearly enough to the sort of being the world censures, but on whom, as on Branwell, Emily had no judgment to pass.

> Well, some may hate, and some may scorn,
> And some may quite forget thy name,
> But my sad heart must ever mourn
> Thy ruined hopes, thy blighted fame.
>
> . . . "Then bless the friendly dust", I said,
> "That hides thy unlamented head.
> Vain as thou wert, and weak as vain,
> The slave of falsehood, pride and pain,
> My heart has nought akin to thine—
> Thy soul is powerless over mine."

But these were thoughts that vanished too—
Unwise, unholy, and untrue—
Do I despise the timid deer
Because his limbs are fleet with fear?
Or do I mock the wolf's death-howl
Because his form is gaunt and foul?
Or hear with joy the leveret's cry
Because it cannot bravely die?

No! Then above his memory
Let pity's heart as tender be:
Say, "Earth lie lightly on that breast,
And, kind Heaven, grant that spirit rest!"

How Anne felt towards him, readers of *The Tenant of Wildfell Hall* are left in no doubt. Her faith rose to the challenge of his ruin. Soon after the Thorp Green disaster she had written:

I mourn with thee, and yet rejoice
That thou should'st sorrow so;
With angel choirs I join my voice
To bless the sinner's woe.

Though friends and kindred turn away,
And laugh thy grief to scorn;
I hear the great Redeemer say,
"Blessed are ye that mourn" . . .

The irreligion of Branwell, commented on by Charlotte after his death, was, of all his father's trials, the worst to bear. For years he had not only refused to go to his father's church and join in the family prayers, but had openly attacked such practices as pure hypocrisy. He had, however, been a little too noisy in his denunciation; he could not let the matter rest, as is apparent to anyone reading his writings. Enlightened by them as, perhaps, his family at the time could never be, the modern reader can judge of Branwell's irreligion for what it truly was—an inverted faith, proceeding from a too entire acceptance of his aunt's Calvinistic tenets. He was never at any time a convinced atheist—his powers of deduction and speculation were not capable of such a thing. Purely emotional and intuitive, his responses to religion proceeded not from strength of reasoning or indifference, but from the bitterness of disappointment, the panic of fear.

The early and exaggerated sense of sin wakened in him had *severed* rather than united him to the promises of religion—for himself he saw no prospect of their being fulfilled—and the *contrary* he dared not face.

"Nay—all is lost!" he had cried in the poem "Misery II".

> I cannot bear
> In mouldering dust to disappear,
> And Heaven will not the gloom dispel,
> Since were there one, my home were Hell—
> No Hope, no Hope, and Oh, farewell
> The form so long kept treasured here
> Must thou then ever disappear?

Ever since his adolescence he had preferred to *deny* the heaven of Maria, rather than bear to be excluded from it; this was, at the same time, the *cause* of his cynicism and of his heartbreak. Not strong enough, as his sisters were in their several ways, to rebuild a heaven of his own (though *not* to the pattern of his aunt's) in discarding *hers*, he had found nothing better to put in its place.

In nothing, perhaps, so much as in philosophic outlook had his sisters outstripped Branwell. Starting from the same point of departure as he had done, from their aunt's knee, where all had absorbed the same relentless doctrines, they had gone their several ways, soon to depart from the beaten track of conventional theology, but *all* except only Branwell to come in sight of a kinder heaven which Emily could hail as a

> long eternity of joy . . .

Unlike Branwell, fear never entered into their conception of a further life. Emily strained towards death as her "Rewarding Destiny!" Anne longed inexpressibly to be delivered from the burden of life and saw death as the beloved element—the sea across which she was fearless to pass.

There is a passage in *Jane Eyre* which, put into the mouth of Helen Burns, sufficiently voices for us Charlotte's creed.

"We are, and must be, one and all, burdened with faults in this world," said Helen Burns, "but the time will soon come when, I trust, we shall put them off in putting off our corruptible bodies . . . and only the spark of the spirit will remain . . . whence it came it will return, perhaps again to be communicated to some being higher than man—perhaps to pass through gradations of glory, from the pale human soul to brighten to the seraph! Surely it will never, on the contrary, be suffered to degenerate from man to fiend? No, I cannot believe that: I hold another creed, which no one ever taught me, and which I seldom mention, but in which I delight, and to which I cling, for it extends hope to all; it makes eternity a rest—a mighty home—not a terror and an abyss. Besides, with this creed, I can so clearly distinguish between the criminal and his crime, I can so sincerely forgive the first while I abhor the last; with this creed, revenge never worries my heart, degradation never too deeply disgusts me, injustice never crushes me too low; I live in calm, looking to the end."

Doubtless because of their individual and very personal faiths, the Brontës had always been noticeably reticent in speaking of religion and much of Branwell's deep division of mind had remained unknown to them. They had heard him mock all his adult life at religion, but they may not have heard of his many hankerings after it—as so much of his poetry attests—and as Francis Leyland had done, and who declared that though Branwell might have lost much of his early piety, he never lost the effect of it.

The family's surprise, therefore, was all the greater when suddenly, within two days of his end, a change came over him. Then "all at once" as Charlotte wrote afterwards, "he seemed to open his heart to a conviction of the existence and worth" of that religion and those principles in which, she said, "he would never believe at all".

The end came very suddenly. Too weak to get up again after that last outing in the village when William Brown had helped him home, Branwell stayed in bed. It was a Saturday, 23rd September, and there was not only this sudden change of heart towards religion, but towards the family, which must have warned them of a still greater change to come. Charlotte, writing to Ellen Nussey away in the south of England, gave her the main facts briefly.

"He was entirely confined to his bed but for one single day, and was in the village two days before his death.

"The end came after twenty minutes' struggle on Sunday morning, 24th September. He was perfectly conscious till the last agony came on. His mind had undergone the peculiar change which frequently precedes death. Two days previously the calm of better feelings filled it. A return of natural affection marked his last moments. . . ."

To Mr Williams who had not, like Ellen Nussey, known all the heart-ache of the previous years nor any of the wrongs committed on either side, Charlotte wrote strangely enough with far greater feeling and at the same time with far greater ease. Speaking of Branwell's change of heart at the last, she wrote: "The remembrance of this strange change now comforts my poor Father greatly. I myself, with painful, mournful joy, heard him praying softly in his dying moments, and to the last prayer which my father offered up at his bedside, he added 'Amen'. How unusual that word appeared from his lips—of course you, who did not know him, cannot conceive. Akin to this alteration was that in his feelings towards his relatives—all bitterness seemed gone. . . ."

Later, in a letter to Ellen Nussey's sister, Charlotte said, further, that the "propitious change" which marked "the last few days of poor Branwell's life—his demeanour, his language, his sentiment—all singularly altered and softened . . . could not be owing to the fear of death, for till within half an hour of his decease he seemed unconscious of danger . . .".

It was early Sunday morning, and while some of the family, at least, were getting ready to go to church, John Brown went up to sit in Branwell's room.

They had, for all their very different natures, found a bond of sympathy between them which went back as far as Branwell could remember. To John he may not have shown the best side of his nature, but he had felt free with him—which was a relief in a life where so much was not avowable.

To Brown it might be easier than to another to confess, as he did then that, in all his life he had "done nothing—either great or good".

The agony began so suddenly that Brown had to call for the family to come quickly. Seizing his hand, Branwell cried loudly: "Oh, John, I'm dying!"

It was the last word John heard from him. As the family came in he slipped away, out of respect for them maybe, but also not to see the going of the bright boy for whom he had once had almost paternal feelings. He hurried down to the church and stood in the belfry door, waiting as he said later, for the signal to ring the passing bell.

It came shortly after 9 o'clock, and within a few minutes all Haworth and the surrounding hamlets knew that "t'parson's Patrick" had gone his erratic way.

Branwell's death, following on so wild and romantic a life, inevitably gave rise to many exaggerated accounts which, for their Gothic and macabre details, would have appealed to Branwell himself. Mrs Gaskell, hearing them years later (certainly not from Charlotte) gave them credence and inserted them in her biography. Francis Leyland, who had the truth direct from the Brown family, emphatically denied Branwell's reported defiance of death; he did not meet it standing, but in his father's arms, to which, in a last gesture of filial love, he resigned himself.

Martha Brown, who was in the room, could also deny the story that Branwell had died with his pockets full of Mrs Robinson's letters. Branwell had no letters from Mrs Robinson. It would be greatly to underestimate her intelligence to suppose she would ever directly have addressed him. Francis Leyland knew that what letters Branwell kept had come solely from Dr Crosby.

How the death of Branwell affected his family it remained for Charlotte to relate. ". . . My poor father naturally thought more of his *only* son than of his daughters," she wrote Mr Williams, "and much and long as he had suffered on his account, he cried out for his loss like David for that of Absalom—my son!—my son!" Closely as she might describe, and clearly analyse the peculiar nature of the family's bereavement in letters to friends, about her personal sorrow she was dumb.

"The noble face and forehead" of her dead brother wrung her heart with a grief she could not explain to Mr Williams or any other sympathising friend. To them she must deplore Branwell's wasted life, but alone with her memories she knew that it was not the man she was mourning, but the "Little King" of their Desert Islands— the wildly enthusiastic "Patrick Benjamin Wiggins" of their ambitious youth—even the "Henry Hastings" of their adult years, towards whom she had shown so premature a wisdom and whom she had known so generously how to forgive. Judge Branwell as Charlotte might to outsiders, and even in her letters describing his end, the real sorrow that bowed her down was the recollection of the long misunderstanding which had broken the magical link with their childhood.

Had his whispered "Amen" conveyed some special meaning for her? Reading her eloquent descriptions of her brother's death, it is impossible not to hope that towards her in particular Branwell showed those signs of reviving love and gentleness of which she spoke, and that his last vision of her was no longer as the implacable justiciar of his last wretched years, but the beloved "Tallii" of his boyhood.

We have buried our dead out of sight [Charlotte wrote to Mr Williams on 2nd October]. A lull begins to succeed the gloomy tumult of last week. It is not permitted us to grieve for him who is gone as others grieve for those they lose. The removal of our only brother must necessarily be regarded by us rather in the light of a mercy than a chastisement. Branwell was his father's and his sisters' pride and hope in boyhood, but since manhood the case has been otherwise. It has been our lot to see him take a wrong bent; to hope, expect, wait his return to the right path; to know the sickness of hope deferred, the dismay of prayer baffled; to experience despair at last—and now to behold the sudden early obscure close of what might have been a noble career.

I do not weep from a sense of bereavement—there is no prop withdrawn, no consolation torn away, no dear companion lost—but for the wreck of talent, the ruin of promise, the untimely dreary extinction of what might have been a burning and a shining light. My brother was a year my junior. I had aspirations and ambitions for him once, long ago—they have perished mournfully. Nothing remains of him but a memory of errors and sufferings. There is such a bitterness of pity for his life and death, such a yearning for the emptiness of his whole existence as I cannot describe. I trust time will allay these feelings.

My unhappy brother never knew what his sisters had done in literature— he was not aware that they had ever published a line. We could not tell him of our efforts for fear of causing him too deep a pang of remorse for his own time mis-spent, and talents misapplied. Now he will *never* know. I cannot dwell longer on the subject at present—it is too painful. . . .

A few days later, on receiving yet another letter from him, she wrote again:

My dear Sir,

I thank you for your last truly friendly letter, and for the number of *Blackwood* which accompanied it. Both arrived at a time when a relapse of illness had depressed me much. Both did me good, especially the letter. I have only one fault to find with your expressions of friendship: they make me ashamed, because they seem to imply that you think better of me than I merit. I believe you are prone to think too highly of your fellow-creatures in general—to see too exclusively the good points of those for whom you have a regard. Disappointment must be the inevitable result of this habit. Believe all men, and women too, to be dust and ashes—a spark of the divinity now and then kindling in the dull heap—that is all. When I looked on the noble face and forehead of my dead brother (nature had favoured him with a fairer outside, as well as a finer constitution, than his sisters) and asked myself what had made him go ever wrong, tend ever downwards, when he had so many gifts to induce to, and aid in, an upward course, I seemed to receive an oppressive revelation of the feebleness of humanity—of the inadequacy of even genius to lead to true greatness if unaided by religion and principle. In the value, or even the reality, of these two things he would never believe till within a few days of his end; and then all at once he seemed to open his heart to a conviction of their existence and worth. The remembrance of this strange change now comforts my poor father greatly. . . .

When the struggle was over, and a marble calm began to succeed the last dread agony, I felt, as I had never felt before, that there was peace and forgiveness for him in Heaven. All his errors—to speak plainly, all his vices—seemed nothing to me in that moment: every wrong he had done, every pain he had caused, vanished; his sufferings only were remembered; the wrench to the natural affections only was left. If man can thus experience total oblivion of his fellow's imperfections, how much more can the Eternal Being, who made man, forgive His creature?

Had his sins been scarlet in their dye, I believe now they are white as wool. He is at rest, and that comforts us all. Long before he quitted this world, life had no happiness for him. . . .

Branwell was buried on Thursday, 28th September, and his funeral service was conducted by his father's old friend William Morgan. The certified cause of death entered was given as "Chronic bronchitis-Marasmus" (a wasting of the flesh from no pronounced disease). The event was reported without comment in the *Leeds Mercury* of 30th September among other deaths for the previous Sunday.

. . . On the same day, aged 30, Patrick Branwell, son of the Rev. P. Bronte incumbent of Haworth. . . .

Since the funeral of Aunt Branwell, six years before, Branwell had not re-entered the old church. Yet if there was one place in the world where he had truly longed to be it was there, where they brought him now, under the stone flags, deep in the family vault, out of the sight of men, in the covering darkness close beside Maria. It was there, released from the long strain of living—from the dreams of grandeur, the thorny path of fame, the mockeries of love—that all his sad life he had really longed to be.

"O, I do seem to see thee now" he had, in a rare moment of hope, written of that reunion,

> Thy smiling eyes and shining brow,
> Thy sunny cheek and golden hair. . . .
> All through the noontide of my years
> How thou didst enter all my fears
> And hopes and joy, and smiles and tears!
> How often have thy bright blue eyes,
> Driven sorrow shrinking from its shrine
> And banished all my misery
> Before one heavenly look of thine!

How different his life might have been had it not been blighted at its outset by that early sorrow, who can tell? But his faults, such as they were, were not *unnatural* faults. They proceeded from lack of character, not lack of heart. Had Branwell been less susceptible, both to love and sorrow, he might have been a stronger and certainly a more successful man, but it was not his destiny to succeed in anything.

Grundy, considering the many injustices heaped against him, had this final word to say in his friend's defence: "... P.B.B. was no domestic demon; he was just a man moving in a mist who lost his way. More sinned against than sinning, at least he proved the reality of his sorrows. They killed him. ..."

It was not Grundy who doubted Branwell's last statement to him that his "death would be due to the story" he knew ,"and to nothing else".

That, so far as we can come at the truth, must be the judgment of posterity. In that one respect, at least, poor Branwell attains a distinction of his own—for none can contest that he was the only Brontë to die of love.

EPILOGUE

Only six weeks after Branwell's death, on Wednesday 8th November, Mrs Robinson married Sir Edward Dolman Scott. The marriage was by special licence and solemnised in the home of Lady Bateman (a sister of Sir Edward's first wife), 19 Marlborough Buildings, in the parish of Walcot, Bath. Only Mr and Mrs Evans were present. The bridegroom was seventy-five, the bride forty-eight.

Writing to her agent from Southampton immediately after the wedding, the new Lady Scott informed him of the honeymoon plans: "We are . . . seeing to the fitting out of Sir Edward's Yacht which is going to meet us at Marseilles. Next Monday I shall be at 45, Bryanston Square . . . previous to leaving Eng^d as we want to get into warmer quarters for the winter on the coast of the Mediterranean. . . ." She did not expect to be back by Christmas and wrote to her agent making every arrangement for Edmund's comfort during the holidays.

Mary Robinson's marriage to Henry Clapham had conveniently taken place on 19th October from her aunt's house at Allestree. By a strange coincidence, her new home was Aireworth House, Keighley, at only four miles' distance from Haworth. But by the time she settled there the circumstance could no longer affect Branwell Brontë. Her sister Elizabeth, until she conformed to her mother's wishes, divided her time between Keighley and Allestree Hall.

It was from Keighley that the "Robinson girls"—as Charlotte still called them—came to see Anne in the first week of December. Writing of their visit to Ellen Nussey on 10th December, Charlotte who had not met them before, said they were "attractive and stylish-looking girls. They seemed overjoyed to see Anne; when I went into the room, they were clinging to her like two children. . . ." The report they brought of their mother was that she was "in the highest spirits".

So far as the Brontë family was concerned, what further happened to Lady Scott was of no importance. She had played a sufficient part in initiating a domestic tragedy that would sweep a whole family into its grave. Only Mr Brontë would survive to know all the tribulations that in due course befell her.

Sir Edward Scott died on 27th December 1851. Mary Clapham, after only seven years of marriage, lost her young husband and with the only child of the marriage, a little girl, went to live with her sister Elizabeth, then settled in Derbyshire, where, in due course, Mary married again.

On 25th March 1857 appeared Mrs Gaskell's *Life of Charlotte Brontë*. (Charlotte had died 31st March 1855.) Without naming Lady Scott, Mrs Gaskell designated her unmistakably as the cause of Branwell Brontë's ruin. The relevant passages occurred in Chapter XIII of Volume I and in Chapter II of Volume II. The first one read: ". . . The story must be told. If I could, I would have avoided it; but not merely is it so well-known to many living as to be, in a manner, public property, but it is possible that, by revealing the misery, the gnawing, life-long misery, the degrading habits, the early death of her partner in guilt . . . to the wretched woman, who not only survives, but passes about in the gay circles of London society, as a vivacious, well-dressed, flourishing widow, there may be awakened in her some feelings of repentance.

"Branwell, I have mentioned, had obtained a situation as a private tutor . . . he took the fancy of a married woman, nearly twenty years older than himself. It is no excuse for him to say that she began the first advances, and 'made love' to him. She was so bold and hardened, that she did it in the very presence of her children; and they would threaten her that, if she did not grant them such and such indulgences, they would tell their bed-ridden father 'how she went on with Mr Brontë . . .' "

The second passage, relating the circumstances of Branwell's death, read: "I have heard from one who attended Branwell in his last illness that he resolved on standing up to die. . . . I have previously stated, that when his fatal attack came on, his pockets were found filled with old letters from the woman to whom he was attached. He died! she lives still—in May Fair. The Eumenides, I suppose, went out of existence at the time when the wail was heard, 'Great Pan is dead.' I think we could better have spared him than those awful Sisters who sting dead conscience into life.

"I turn from her for ever. . . ."

The effect of these passages was to set gossip "seething and circulating in the London coteries", according to the *Athenaeum*, and to prompt Lady Scott to a law suit. Her advisers, however, prevailed on her to keep the case out of the courts and to bring pressure on Mrs Gaskell instead, to publish a retraction of the offensive passages. In her absence abroad, and against her feelings, Mr Gaskell agreed to this and instructed his solicitors, Messrs Shaen & Roscoe, to publish the following letter in *The Times* and *Athenaeum*. It appeared on 30th May 1857.

8 BEDFORD ROW,
LONDON, May 26th, 1957.

Dear Sirs,

As solicitor for and on behalf of the Rev. W. Gaskell and of Mrs. Gaskell his wife, the latter of whom is authoress of the *Life of Charlotte Brontë*, I am instructed to retract every statement contained in that work which imputes to a widowed lady, referred to, but not named therein, any breach of her conjugal, her maternal, or of her social duties, and more especially of the statement contained in chapter 13 of the first volume, and in chapter 2 of the second volume, which imputes to the lady in question a guilty intercourse with the late Branwell Brontë. All those statements were made upon information which at the time Mrs. Gaskell believed to be well founded, but which, upon investigation, with the additional evidence furnished to me by you, I have ascertained not to be trustworthy. I am therefore authorised not only to retract the statements in question, but to express the deep regret of Mrs. Gaskell that she should have been led to make them.—I am, dear sirs, yours truly,

WILLIAM SHAEN.

Messrs Newton P. Robinson, Solicitors, York.

Deleted from the third edition of the *Life of Charlotte Brontë*, the passages have since been re-incorporated in the work, Mrs Gaskell herself maintaining their truth to the end.

With the destruction of all the evidence in what so nearly became the case of "Robinson v. Gaskell", all pointers in the direction of the truth are precious. There exists today in the Parsonage Museum at Haworth the ten-volume set of Campbell's *Lives of the Lord Chancellors of England*, given by Mr Brontë in 1857 to Mr Henry Newton of York, the Robinson solicitor, "in recognition of legal services rendered to Branwell Bronte". Branwell, of course, was dead, but his father's gift, coming so shortly after the suppression of the case that must have dragged his name, with that of Mrs Robinson, before the public, is eloquent enough of the family's pride in accepting no benefits without acknowledgment.

Whether the Eumenides, invoked by Mrs Gaskell, raised their ugly heads once again, or whether remorse had nothing to do with the case, suffice it to say that Lady Scott died only two years after the scandal broke, on 19th June 1859. She was fifty-nine. At all events, she was thus spared the sorrow of learning of her only son's death from drowning in the river Ure, while riding to hounds, on 4th Februry 1869. He was thirty-seven and died unmarried.

By the terms of his will dividing his estate among his sisters, the eldest, Lydia Roxby, by then settled in Liverpool, received an annuity of £500, and there were legacies of £6,000 each to her two sons. With Edmund's death the family name became extinct. Its connection with Thorp Green had been finally severed four years before when he sold the estate for £129,000.

Dr Crosby, a main actor in the Thorp Green drama, died on 1st December 1859 at Great Ouseburn, aged sixty-two. He was buried in Great Ouseburn churchyard where his grave can yet be seen today, marked by an obelisk. In the church, a memorial tablet was erected to his memory by subscription, which states that:

> His Universal kindness
> Professional ability
> benevolent disposition
> and active usefulness
> during a residence of 30 years
> Warmly endeared him
> To a large circle of friends
> Who deeply lament
> His sudden removal.

It was the custom in Haworth at that time—and still is in a mitigated form—for a "Funeral Sermon" to be preached on the Sunday immediately following a burial. Branwell's was held on 1st October. It was noticed that Emily, who caught cold at the service, never went out again. When she died on 19th December of galloping consumption no one in the village hesitated to say she had died of grief for her brother. Anne, whose decline had almost kept pace with Emily's, died in the following May at Scarborough.

These deaths were followed after a six years' lull in suffering by that of Charlotte in 1855.

The extinction of the family was complete. It was as if each individual genius, having come to fruition at the same moment, had been devoured by a single flame. The causes of their deaths were set out on the death-certificates, but it is open to query whether disease alone would have vanquished courage like theirs, had not grief played yet greater havoc with their passionate hearts. It must remain a moot point whether the Brontës might not have lived into middle age if grief had not stood so early at their door. And it was Branwell's final misfortune that he it was who let the enemy in.

Appendix A

THE AUTHORSHIP OF *WUTHERING HEIGHTS*

Excluded as he was from all share in—even from all knowledge of—the publication of his sisters' books, Branwell was yet made posthumously to appear to have had some part in the inspiration and writing of two of them: *Wuthering Heights* and *The Tenant of Wildfell Hall*. These allegations, made by his friends years after the deaths of all the Brontës, must be briefly examined here.

The date of publication of *Wuthering Heights*, it will be remembered, was December 1847. It was published by Thomas Cautley Newby of Mortimer Street, Cavendish Square, as a three-volume novel together with Anne's *Agnes Grey*. After Emily Brontë's death, her sister Charlotte's publishers, Smith Elder & Co. of Cornhill, obtained the book from Newby (this was before the copyright laws were passed) and brought it out in a posthumous edition in October 1850. The original manuscript, whether destroyed by Newby or by Smith Elder, has never since reappeared.

Accepted for publication by Newby in July 1847 after, as Charlotte gave evidence, it had been "... perseveringly obtruded upon various publishers for the space of a year and a half...." the actual writing of the book had therefore been finished some time in the spring of 1846—April or May as correspondence over the publication of the Bells' volume of *Poems* would tend to show. Its actual date of composition can therefore be placed as late as 1845 and as early as 1844.

On 8th June 1867 there was reproduced in the *Halifax Guardian* an anonymous review of *Wuthering Heights* which had just appeared in *The People's Mirror*, in which the writer said among other things:

"Who would suppose that Heathcliff, a man who never swerved from his arrow-straight course to perdition from his cradle to his grave ... had been conceived by a timid and retiring female? But this was the case." The article, read by William Dearden, Branwell's former friend, and headmaster at that time of Warley Grammar School, was immediately taken up and commented on by him in the next issue of the *Halifax Guardian*, that of 15th June 1867.

Though he had not previously come forward upon the subject, he did so now, alleging that his evidence would make Emily's claim to have written *Wuthering Heights* appear "somewhat apocryphal".

Dearden related how he and Branwell, as was often their wont while Branwell was at Luddenden Foot, had agreed that each should write a drama or a poem "relating to real or imaginary existence before the Deluge" and read it aloud before an impartial auditor as judge of their respective merits. The friends appointed as meeting-place the *Cross Roads Inn*, midway between Haworth and Keighley (and a convenient half-way house for travellers from Halifax) and on the appointed night Joseph Leyland rode over from Halifax to be arbiter.

Branwell had no sooner arrived and announced that his contribution was a poem, "Azrael" (written in 1842), and dived into his hat for his papers, than he discovered to his chagrin that he had brought the wrong manuscript. He was for riding straight home and fetching the right one but his friends dissuaded him and prevailed on him to read aloud the manuscript he had brought. It turned out to be the beginning of a novel, and Dearden alleged in his article that "the scene . . . and the characters introduced in it—so far as they developed—were the same as those in *Wuthering Heights*". Dearden never heard more than that opening section, but he quoted another friend of Branwell's, Edward Sloan—already dead at the time Dearden was writing—as having declared that "he no sooner began to read *Wuthering Heights* than he anticipated all the characters and incidents in the story: because Branwell's manuscript which he had heard read portion by portion as the author produced it, had familiarised them to his mind . . .".

Dearden closed his article with a doggerel rhyme, entitled "A Retrospect" which he averred he had written "shortly after the event had occurred" and in which he states that:

> Bronté read
> For one full hour, long chapters of a tale
> To which that monstrous figment, *Wuthering Heights*
> (The credulous world believes as Ellis Bell's)
> Bears in its characters and incidents
> Too strong resemblance ever to be deemed
> Entirely accidental. . . .

Dearden, it should be recalled, had been a schoolmaster at Keighley in the late eighteen-twenties and early thirties, when he had known Mr Brontë. On the publication of Mrs Gaskell's *Life of Charlotte Bronté*, he had rushed to Mr Bronté's defence and had been so importunate in urging him to make a public attack on Mrs Gaskell that Mr Bronté had silenced him with a firm request to busy himself no further on his behalf.

More than one rumour had reached Mr Bronté's ears that doubt had been cast on Emily's authorship of *Wuthering Heights*. Martha Brown recalled how "very indignant he was at what was said in certain quarters as to *Wuthering Heights* being the joint production of Emily and her brother Branwell. He maintained that the latter had no part or share whatever in the book. . . ." And, indeed, on another occasion, Mr Bronté had declared that his son was "wholly incapable of such a production".

Mr Bronté's declared views on the subject might explain why Dearden waited for several years after his death before advancing his own evidence respecting Branwell's authorship. The other witness to the evening at the *Cross Roads Inn*, Joseph Leyland, was also long since dead.

The matter, however, once taken up by Dearden, did not rest there. Grundy, on his return to England after many years overseas, writing in 1879 of his friendship with Branwell—and claiming far more familiarity with Branwell's family than he really possessed—did not hesitate to go a step further. "Patrick Bronté declared to me," he claimed, "and what his sister said bore out the assertion, that he wrote a great portion of *Wuthering Heights* himself. Indeed, it is impossible for me to read that story without meeting with many passages which I feel certain must have come from his pen. The weird fancies of diseased genius with which he used to entertain me in our long talks at Luddenden Foot reappear in the pages of the novel, and I am inclined to believe that the very plot was his invention rather than his sister's."

The bare assumption that Emily Brontë admitted Francis Grundy into her confidence on the authorship of any composition of hers, reduces the evidence to its rightful place, on the rubbish heap.

George Searle Phillips, writing in 1872, also claimed to have heard from Branwell himself that he had written a novel—which Phillips did not pause to consider might *not* be *Wuthering Heights*.

The fact that Branwell was writing a novel—as stated by him in his letter to Leyland of 10th September 1845—was known to all his friends. That he had not decided on a title, Dearden himself confirms in his *Halifax Guardian* article, in which he wrote that Branwell "had not yet fixed on a title for his production". The story, Dearden further reported, "broke off abruptly in the middle of a sentence. . .". This is precisely the case with "And the Weary are at Rest".

If the meeting at the *Cross Roads Inn* when Branwell was engaged on his novel was as late as 1845, the fragment read aloud by him can have been "And the Weary are at Rest"—but then the rest of Dearden's evidence is invalidated as regards the poem freshly written for the contest—the poem "Azrael", written as both Dearden and Leyland agree, as early as 1842. If the meeting took place after Branwell's dismissal from Luddenden Foot in the spring or early summer of 1842 (when the friends had several meetings in Haworth, Halifax or elsewhere), the prose fragment read aloud to them might have been the manuscript known as "Percy". The characters in that fragment and those in "And the Weary are at Rest" are the same (Percy, Montmorency, Quamina, etc.) with the exception of Mr and Mrs Thurston, who were based on the Robinsons and added to the tale after Branwell's Thorp Green experience. The violence, both of language and action, in the "Percy" fragment would fit Dearden's description of the scenes read aloud by Branwell, better than those of the later story. Both, however, are set in wild moorland country and introduce Yorkshire characters freely blaspheming and drinking, of a type that listeners might confound with the characters of *Wuthering Heights*.

To the later fragment, "And the Weary are at Rest", however, belong two distinctive features more readily to be confounded with similar ones in *Wuthering Heights*: the canting man-servant, Robert, speaking nothing but Biblical texts, in whom one might see a pale replica of Joseph, and the memorable scene in a Methodist chapel, complete with pulpit-thumping ranting preacher, who might again, after a lapse of years, have recalled to listeners the vociferations of Jabes Branderham in *Wuthering Heights*.

In no case can Branwell's friends have heard *Wuthering Heights* at the *Cross Roads Inn*, unless he had snatched up his sister's manuscript by mistake and read it aloud as his own!

On the authorship of *Wuthering Heights* the evidence of the Brontë family is conclusive. That Emily wrote it—and Emily alone—Mr Brontë, Charlotte, and Emily herself, attest. Of these, Emily's own acknowledgment of her authorship should be sufficient. Her only subterfuge was to employ a pseudonym. As "Ellis Bell" she sent her book out into the world and endured the ensuing incredulity and alarm with no more than a little scornful smile. Charlotte, in her Preface to the posthumous edition of her sister's work, has some very important evidence to give relating to the period of its composition. She recalls how, when Emily was engaged in writing it, she would read portions of it aloud to her sisters

—this was the girls' nightly habit always—and meet their protests at its ferocious passages with astonishment. "If the auditor of her work," wrote Charlotte, trying to excuse the violence of *Wuthering Heights* to the refined public, "when read in manuscript, shuddered under the grinding influence of natures so relentless and implacable, of spirits so lost and fallen; if it was complained that the mere hearing of certain vivid and fearful scenes banished sleep by night, and disturbed mental peace by day, Ellis Bell would wonder what was meant, and suspect the complainant of affectation . . .".

Writing to her own publisher, Mr Williams, of Smith, Elder & Co., after her first encounter with the heads of the firm when she and Anne travelled to London in July 1848, Charlotte had this to say on the subject of the author of *Wuthering Heights*: ". . . Permit me to caution you not to speak of my sisters when you write to me. I mean, do not use the word in the plural. Ellis Bell will not endure to be alluded to under any other appellation than the 'nom de plume'. I committed a grand error in betraying his identity to you and Mr Smith. It was inadvertent—the words 'we are three sisters' escaped me before I was aware. I regretted the avowal the moment I had made it; I regret it bitterly now, for I find it is against every feeling and intention of Ellis Bell. . . ."

If one thing emerges more clearly than another from Charlotte's references to *Wuthering Heights*, it is her consternation at the sort of notoriety the book had achieved, and at the quasi-diabolical reputation it had won for its author. If she could have done so with any truth, Charlotte would have been only too glad to ascribe the worst elements in it (as the world and even she herself judged them) to a male author and the direct collaboration of Ellis Bell's brother—anything to exonerate her beloved sister from the charge of having written something unbeseeming a woman. The mere fact that Charlotte did *not* bring forward this mitigating circumstance, shows that it did not exist.

In the absence of the original manuscript of *Wuthering Heights*, the final proof of its authorship must be sought in the book itself. If it be argued that the setting could, conceivably, have been re-created by any other of the Brontës from their moorland surroundings, this cannot be said of the subject. For the subject of *Wuthering Heights* is not "a cuckoo's tale" (as Nelly Dean had it), nor a revenge story, nor a tale of avarice, nor a new version of the eternal triangle—but something over and above all these—something relating to experience known only, in all that family, to Emily Brontë herself.

That experience, common to many mystics in divers lands and known under varying titles, of the pursuit by the individual soul of reunion with the universal soul, had been the subject of Emily's deepest philosophical poetry, written during 1844 and 1845—the period immediately preceding and corresponding with the composition of *Wuthering Heights*.

In those poems the subject of loss, treated by all the Brontës at varying times and by Anne and Branwell in particular, was treated by Emily alone in its relation to reunion, to integration achieved even by the living with the object of desire —with the dead.

Anne had wept for Willy Weightman, and Branwell had wept for Maria. But at no time had either "dared the final bound" as Emily had done, and gone out of the body to reach the soul's desire. *That* experience she had known and described in language as lucid as others use to relate a material occurrence.

> But first a hush of peace, a soundless calm descends;
> The struggle of distress and fierce impatience ends;
> Mute music soothes my breast—unuttered harmony
> That I could never dream till earth was lost to me.
>
> Then dawns the Invisible, the Unseen its truth reveals,
> My outward sense is gone, my inward essence feels—
> Its wings are almost free, its home, its harbour found;
> Measuring the gulf it stoops and dares the final bound! . . .

To Emily Brontë was known the penalty paid for such experience in the return, in the separation from the desired object, in the division again into parts of something that had become whole; that agony which she had also been able to relate with absolute precision.

> Oh, dreadful is the check—intense the agony
> When the ear begins to hear and the eye begins to see;
> When the pulse begins to throb, the brain to think again,
> The soul to feel the flesh and the flesh to feel the chain!
>
> Yet I would lose no sting, would wish no torture less;
> The more that anguish racks the earlier it will bless:
> And robed in fires of Hell, or bright with Heavenly shine,
> If it but herald Death, the vision is divine. . . .

These words were written in October 1845, and already by then Emily had realised the desirability of death as the only means by which to recover permanently the state of rapture of which she had, probably on several occasions, been afforded a foretaste and in which her soul had become *one* with its object.

That, of course, is the subject of *Wuthering Heights*—a study of love taken to its logical conclusion beyond the grave.

What startled the first Victorian readers of *Wuthering Heights* was precisely this: the boldness of the author's vision in placing her novel not only in time but in eternity; in the assurance with which she endowed her characters with a sense of their *projected* life, of their transcendent destiny.

Catherine's conscience, when she abandoned Heathcliff for Edgar, told her perfectly clearly that she was, in fact, cheating her soul of its immortal life in exchange for worldly prosperity. She knew perfectly well that such communion as existed between her and Heathcliff could not be severed without deadly sin— and the risk of death. ". . . I've no more business to marry Edgar Linton," she confesses to Nelly, "than I have to be in heaven. . . ." She knows that she belongs to Heathcliff. "Whatever our souls are made of, his and mine are the same. . . ." In that moment of clairvoyance, Catherine recited her creed—identifying herself with Heathcliff, she recognised how her own existence was prolonged in his. "I cannot express it," she said, "but surely you and everybody have a notion that there is or should be an existence of yours beyond you. What were the use of my creation, if I were entirely contained here? My great miseries in this world have been Heathcliff's miseries . . . my great thought in living is himself. If all else persisted, and he remained, I should still continue to be. . . ."

In language almost identical, only transposed upon an ideal plane, Emily Brontë wrote, on 2nd January 1846, in the great poem for which she is chiefly remembered, "No coward soul is mine", the lines:

O God within my breast
Almighty ever-present Deity
Life, that in me has rest
As I Undying Life, have power in Thee . . .
Though Earth and moon were gone
And suns and universes ceased to be
And thou wert left alone
Every Existence would exist in thee. . . .

The thought, working in her, of the multiple nature of her soul, inspired in the
very next month the poem: "Enough of Thought, Philosopher" in which, considering the gods within her breast, she writes:

Heaven could not hold them all, and yet
They all are held in me:
And must be mine till I forget
My present entity. . . .

Even in the moment of recognising the union binding her soul to Heathcliff's
Catherine Earnshaw leapt to a yet greater truth—the sudden realisation that there
was no division between Heathcliff and herself, that they were one. "Nelly, I *am*
Heathcliff! He's always, always in my mind: not as a pleasure, any more than I
am always a pleasure to myself, but as my own being. . . ."

Not confined to Catherine alone, but explored to its furthest limits in Heathcliff, was Emily's study of the soul's progression from a temporal to an eternal
state of being. The rapture of her own spiritual experiences illuminates the descriptions of Heathcliff's approaching death and reunion with Catherine—after
eighteen years of devastating grief. (A like insistence on the time factor in separation
and loss had been the major theme in her poem "Cold in the earth, and fifteen wild
Decembers . . ." written in March 1845.) ". . . I have a single wish," Heathcliff
said as he neared his goal, "and my whole being and faculties are yearning to
attain it. They have yearned towards it so long, and so unwaveringly, that I'm
convinced it *will* be reached—and *soon*—because it has devoured my existence:
I am swallowed up in the anticipation of its fulfilment. . . ."

In almost identical words, Emily had described a similar yearning in the poem
written on 2nd June 1845, "How beautiful the Earth is still", in which, renouncing
what the world had to offer, she declared her whole being as set upon nothing this
side of eternity.

. . . A thoughtful spirit taught me soon
That we must long till life be done;
That every phase of earthly joy
Will always fade and always cloy—

This I foresaw, and would not chase
The fleeting treacheries,
But with firm foot and tranquil face
Held backward from the tempting race,
Gazed o'er the sands the waves efface
To the enduring seas—

There cast my anchor of Desire
Deep in unknown Eternity;
Nor ever let me Spirit tire
With looking for *What is to be*. . . .

Heathcliff, hurrying towards his heaven with "a strange glitter of joy in his eyes that altered the whole aspect of his face", is but the personification of that joy in the anticipation of death that runs through all her poetry like a light from eternity. She had written of it already in "Castle Wood" (2nd February, 1844):

> . . . And who would dread eternal rest
> When labour's hire was agony?
>
> Dark falls the fear of this despair
> On Spirits born for happiness;
> But I was born the mate of care,
> The foster-child of sore distress.
>
> No sighs for me, no sympathy,
> No wish to keep my soul below;
> The heart is dead since infancy,
> Unwept-for let the body go.

The "little glittering spirits" in "A Day Dream" (March 1844) had seemed to sing to her:

> Let Grief distract the sufferer's breast,
> And Night obscure his way;
> They hasten him to endless rest,
> And everlasting day . . .
> And could we lift the veil and give
> One brief glimpse to thine eye
> Thou would'st rejoice for those that live,
> Because they live to die . . .

If Emily Brontë's poetry is a glorification of death as the passage to eternal life, that is also the subject of *Wuthering Heights*.

No further proof than this should surely be required to show that Branwell had no hand in it. In the whole body of his verse he never envisaged death in any other than its purely morbid form—as a destroying and dividing agent, that takes away the beloved object and reduces it to nothing but decay.

Incapable of conceiving the philosophic content of his sister's novel, Branwell was also—as every prose passage quoted from his work abundantly shows—incapable of writing a single one of its sentences. The clarity, brevity, concentration and intensity of Emily's prose are the direct antithesis of his style.

More arguments could be adduced to prove the emptiness of the claim advanced by Branwell's friends—as, for instance, the many humorous passages, which have only to be compared with some intended to be humorous in any prose narrative of Branwell's, for the difference of class and quality to be perceived at once. Branwell's never rise above horse-play. Similarly, there is the essential role played by natural phenomena in *Wuthering Heights*, the close association of nature in every mood of the protagonists—that oneness penetrating humans and trees and rocks and plants, the heavens and the earth beneath, that "sweet influence" which Emily, gazing at the stars had felt

"Thrilled through and proved us One"—

and which, except as a dramatic accessory, in a decorative sense, is totally absent from Branwell's verse and prose.

To the Victorian—and urban—critic, Heathcliff needed explaining, and try as she would, Charlotte could not provide the key. For obvious reasons she preferred to leave it in the door locking away their childhood for ever. Branwell became the necessary scapegoat in the public's eye to explain away the Bells' heroes, all of whom had had long previous existences in the realms of Angria and Gondal. Could the critics have known of the lover of Gondal's Queen, the black Douglas who, like Heathcliff, had a "basilisk eye", and who, like him again

> had been nursed in strife
> And lived upon this weary Earth
> A wanderer, all his life—

a "baited tiger", to use his own words, "athirst for gore", doomed to find no haven upon earth, kindled with only one human feeling, his love for the proud woman who mocked him—"For thee," Douglas cried, with all the vehemence of a Heathcliff,

> through never-ending years,
> I'd suffer endless pain;
> But—only give me back my tears;
> Return my love again!

Had the critics known of *him* they would not have had to look further for the source of that unique creation, Heathcliff.

In so far as Branwell, as well as Charlotte and Emily, had from childhood written and romanced about a black changeling child, "Quashia Quamina", first introduced to them by *Blackwood's*, and appearing in his own name and person in Branwell's "And the Weary are at Rest" as late as 1845, he may be said to have had a part in the inception of Heathcliff.

In one other small particular the trace of Branwell can be found in *Wuthering Heights*. It is in the description given very early in the book of Lockwood's reason for renting Thrushcross Grange—the "perfect misanthropist's heaven", removed "from the stir of society", to which he is happy to flee after the miscarriage of a flirtation. In its peculiar character can be recognised the strange motives dictating Branwell's own flight from Mary Taylor—a fact which, of itself, should prove that it was not Branwell wielding the pen.

"While enjoying a month of fine weather at the sea-coast," relates Lockwood, "I was thrown into the company of a most fascinating creature: a real goddess in my eyes, as long as she took no notice of me. I 'never told my love' vocally; still, if looks have language, the merest idiot might have guessed I was over head and ears: she understood me at last, and looked a return—the sweetest of all imaginable looks. And what did I do? I confess it with shame—shrank icily into myself, like a snail; at every glance retired colder and farther; till finally the poor innocent was led to doubt her own senses, and, overwhelmed with confusion at her supposed mistake, persuaded her mamma to decamp. . . ."

Appendix B

BRANWELL BRONTË AND ARTHUR HUNTINGDON

The belief still persists today that Anne Brontë portrayed her brother as Arthur Huntingdon in *The Tenant of Wildfell Hall*. Fostered by the blurbs to successive reprints of the book, it is one of those baseless theories that are hard to kill. Yet, how unlike Huntingdon was to Branwell becomes clearly evident when a close comparison of the two characters is made. Since this has already been done elsewhere by the present author[1], it is not the purpose to repeat it here, but to add a few relevant facts that may explain the initial error which gave rise to the subsequent confusion. To allow it to persist is to do grave injustice to the memory of Branwell.

When Charlotte Brontë was asked by her publishers to write a prefatory notice to the posthumous edition of her sister's book, she found herself faced with the dilemma of either explaining away the "shocking" nature of Anne's novel, or of leaving a shadow of blame upon her sister's memory. She naturally chose the former course, though by so doing she created a misunderstanding of her sister's true intentions in undertaking *The Tenant of Wildfell Hall*.

From its very beginnings, Charlotte had deplored the whole conception of the book ("... the choice of subject," she had written, "was an entire mistake. Nothing less congruous with the author's nature could be conceived....") and after Anne's death, did her best to dissuade her publishers from reprinting it. "... *Wildfell Hall* it hardly appears to me desirable to preserve ..." she wrote to Mr Williams on 5th September 1850.

That *Wildfell Hall* bristled with problems, the virulence of the critics and of a great section of the public had made her only too aware. Her sister's controversial masterpiece presented a challenge to accepted standards of morality and to the tenets of the established church alike, and Charlotte found herself perplexed indeed in proving her sister's blameless intentions. She could do so only by portraying Anne in a very feeble light and by insinuating that the real blame rested upon quite other shoulders.

To Mr Williams she wrote: "The choice of subject in that work is a mistake; it was too little consonant with the character, tastes, and ideas of the gentle, retiring, inexperienced writer. She wrote it under a strange conscientious, half-ascetic notion of accomplishing a painful penance and a severe duty...."

In the Biographical Notice to the posthumous edition of the works of Ellis and Acton Bell, written in 1850, Charlotte wrote: "*The Tenant of Wildfell Hall* had likewise an unfavourable reception. At this I can not wonder. The choice of subject was an entire mistake.... The author had, in the course of her life, been called on to contemplate, near at hand, and for a long time, the terrible effects of talents misused and faculties abused...."

The contradictions contained in these two passages, written within a few weeks of each other, show the confusion of Charlotte's mind in dealing with the matter.

[1] See *Anne Brontë* (London and Edinburgh: Nelson, 1959).

How best to excuse Anne, she indeed found difficult to decide. In her letter to Mr Williams she laid it to the count of "inexperience"; in the Biographical Notice, to a too long and close contemplation of the terrible effects of talents misused. The very ambiguity and imprecision of her explanations made them susceptible of misinterpretation, with the result that Charlotte herself, in her condemnatory remarks on *Wildfell Hall*, was understood to relate the book's subject directly to her own and Acton Bell's reprehensible brother.

Yet, how untrue to both of them this simplification of the matter could be, Charlotte herself bore witness. Writing to Mr Williams on 14th August 1848 about his views on *Wildfell Hall*, *Jane Eyre* and *Wuthering Heights*, she wrote, ". . . You say Mr Huntingdon reminds you of Mr Rochester. *Does he?*" and goes on to give a very clear picture of *her* views on Huntingdon. They correspond closely enough to the character created by Anne, but in no one particular to the character of Charlotte and Anne's brother—Branwell. Had Charlotte ever remotely considered Branwell as the prototype of Huntingdon, she could never have written what she did to Mr Williams. ". . . there is no likeness between the two", [Huntingdon and Rochester] she protested. "The foundation of each character is entirely different. Huntingdon is a specimen of the naturally selfish, sensual, superficial man whose one merit of a joyous temperament only avails him while he is young and healthy, whose best days are his earliest, who never profits by experience, who is sure to grow worse the older he grows. Mr. Rochester has a thoughtful nature and a very feeling heart. . . ."

Thus, out of her own mouth, Charlotte exploded the theory of Huntingdon's similarity to Branwell; for who can suppose she could write so of Branwell? And indeed who that knows anything of Anne, can imagine her portraying the brother she had greatly served, and still passionately sought to redeem, in the figure of the wholly detestable Huntingdon?

The evidence of Leyland, is, moreover, quite categorical on this point: he denied any resemblance existing between Huntingdon and Branwell, and judged that if Anne was thinking of Branwell's case at all, she did everything in her power to hide his identity under that of an utterly dissimilar character. In Gilbert Markham, the real lover in *Wildfell Hall*, who actually pines for a married woman (Helen) and anxiously awaits the death of her worthless husband, Leyland saw a resemblance to Branwell's case, particularly in the "monomania" to which Gilbert's love reduced him.

That Anne had Branwell and Mrs Robinson never far out of her mind is certain. This is shown in such a circumstance as Gilbert's expecting Helen's husband to alter his will, so as to prevent the remarriage of his widow.

Leyland, in his concern to exonerate Branwell from any connection with the darker side of *Wildfell Hall*, overlooked the character to whom he bore some very close resemblances indeed—both in mind and misfortunes—the character of Lord Lowborough, who, as Huntingdon's victim, plays a part only secondary to him in importance.

Anne describes Lord Lowborough as a man of education and culture and heart, sincerely enamoured of the good and fine things in life, but incapable of standing up to its trials, and as succumbing under its disappointments. Huntingdon said of him, sneeringly, that he was "born under an unlucky star". Early in the description of Lowborough, the reader learns that his sorrows at being jilted by a woman drove him to opium. He is described as "looking like the ghost in Macbeth" and obviously "suffering from the effects of an overdose of his insidious comforter . . .". How the drug operated, Anne Brontë had had only too much experience. In Lowborough's frenzied heart-searchings, his religious melancholy, his many attempts at reform, his disastrous returns to the vicious circle of the friends he despises, his exaggeration, his immoderate "remorse, terrors and woes", his loneliness, his drunkenness, is vividly evoked the portrait of Branwell left by his friend Grundy. "Poor, brilliant, gay, moody, moping, wildly excitable, miserable Brontë! No history records your many struggles after the good—Your wit, brilliance, attractiveness, eagerness for excitement. . . ."

Above all, in his disastrous love for his wife, the unscrupulous Annabella, in whose beauty and depths of perfidy Anne may have portrayed something of Mrs Robinson, the likeness to Branwell is brought to a tragic head. Even in his unsuccessful attempts at suicide, the likeness holds.

To see Branwell in Huntingdon is to miss Anne's main purpose, which is a far wider one than mere condemnation of a man's vice. It is the condemnation of a world that she attempted in *Wildfell Hall*, a world in which innocence, her brother's innocence as well as her own, is exposed to temptations so beyond their experience as to make havoc of conventional precept and virtue. Her own, quite as much as Branwell's tribulations in the alien world of Thorp Green Hall, were the subject of her novel, the motive power behind the indictment of that world which she believed it her duty to undertake.

To read *Wildfell Hall* in the light of Anne's and Branwell's experiences at Thorp Green is the only way to realise the book's true purpose and inspiration—which was not merely the story of Branwell's downfall, but of the world that made such a downfall possible.

ACKNOWLEDGMENTS

I wish to thank the following for their help and kindness in supplying me with, or giving me access to, material necessary for the writing of this book: the Council of the Brontë Society for facilities to study, over a long period, the juvenilia and adult writings of Branwell and Charlotte Brontë preserved in the Brontë Parsonage Museum, Haworth; the Keeper of the Department of Manuscripts at the British Museum, for similar facilities to study the Branwell manuscripts in the Ashley Library; the Keeper of the Brotherton Collection, Brotherton Library, University of Leeds, for facilities to study the Leyland letters, the juvenilia and adult writings of Branwell Brontë, and for permission to quote from them; Dr John D. Gordon, Curator of the H. W. and A. A. Berg Collection, New York Public Library, for photostat copies of Branwell's and Charlotte Brontë's manuscripts preserved there; Miss Elizabeth C. Ford, Curator of the Harry Elkins Widener Memorial Library, Harvard University, Cambridge, Mass., for supplying me with microfilms of Charlotte Brontë's manuscripts "Caroline Vernon" and "Henry Hastings", and for giving me permission to quote from them; the Archivist of the Historic Records Department, British Transport Commission, for permission to study and quote from the Minutes of the Manchester-Leeds Railway, 1840-1843; Messrs Brown & Elmhirst, Solicitors, of York, for their great kindness and hospitality in giving me complete access to the Robinson Papers in their keeping; Mr S. Robinson, Librarian of Sowerby Bridge Reference Library, for his active help in local research and for giving me access to the Memorandum books of the Ludden-den Library, 1781-1843; Miss Fannie E. Ratchford, for permission to quote from *The Brontës' Web of Childhood*; Messrs Basil Blackwell & Mott Ltd., for per-mission to quote from *The Shakespeare Head Brontë*; the late Mrs E. C. Meysey-Thompson of Spellow Hill, Knaresborough, for great personal kindness and for permission to quote from the "Register of Sundries" relating to Great and Little Ouseburn, preserved in her family; Miss Mary Leyland, for permission to quote from her monograph "The Leyland Family" (Halifax Antiquarian Society, April 1954); Canon Postlethwaite and his sister Mrs Margaret Cheyne, of Broughton-in-Furness, for their hospitality and for valuable information concerning Branwell Brontë's sojourn there as tutor to their father and uncle; the Secretary of the Royal Academy of Arts, for information regarding the Academy Schools in the time of the Brontës; Miss Dorothy Erskine-Muir, for supplying me with evidence relat-ing to Branwell Brontë and Lydia Robinson recorded by her grandfather, Dr Hall Ryott of Thirsk; Miss Anna M. Smith of Sowerby Bridge, and Mrs Eleanor Stanton of Haworth, and Miss Florence Edmondson, for helpful details relating to their districts.

While every effort has been made to trace the owners of copyright in Brontë texts it has not always been possible to do so. If there are any others whose per-mission I should have obtained before publishing this book, I beg to tender them my sincere apologies for the omission.

W.G.

SOURCES OF EVIDENCE

I ORIGINAL DOCUMENTS

1   MSS by Branwell Brontë, his family and friends—juvenilia, prose narratives, verse, letters—preserved in
    (a) the Brontë Parsonage Museum, Haworth
    (b) the Department of Manuscripts, British Museum
    (c) the Brotherton Collection, Brotherton Library, University of Leeds
    (d) various collections in the U.S.A., *viz*:
        the Bonnell Collection, Philadelphia
        the Berg Collection, New York Public Library
        Harvard University Library, Cambridge, Mass.
        private collections
    from which photostat and microfilm reproductions have been obtained

2   The paintings, drawings, books and personal effects of Branwell Brontë preserved, for the most part, in the Brontë Parsonage Museum, Haworth, and in the Brotherton Collection, Leeds

3   The Robinson family papers, preserved in the offices of Messrs. Brown & Elmhirst, Solicitors, of York

II OFFICIAL DOCUMENTS

1   Registers of baptisms, marriages and deaths of the following churches: St James's, Thornton; St Lawrence's, Appleby; St Michael and All Angels, Haworth; Holy Trinity, Little Ouseburn; St Mary's, Great Ouseburn; and in the case of births, deaths and marriages taking place after 1837, copies obtained from the General Register Office, Somerset House

2   The Register of the Royal Academy of Arts, Burlington House, London

3   The Minutes of the Manchester-Leeds Railway Company, preserved in the British Transport Commission Historic Records Department, Paddington, London, W.2.

4   Archives of the Railway Museum, York

III PUBLISHED DOCUMENTS

1   Nineteenth-century newspaper files preserved in
    (a) the British Museum Newspaper Library
    (b) the provincial offices of the
        Halifax Guardian
        Leeds Mercury
        Leeds Intelligencer
        Scarborough Herald
        Scarborough Gazette

(c) *The Bookman*, double number, October 1904
(d) *Yorkshire Life Illustrated*, May 1955

2 The Annals of the Bradford Antiquarian Society
The Annals of the Halifax Antiquarian Society

3 Nineteenth-century street directories, maps, prints, borough surveys, etc., preserved in Reference Libraries at Keighley, Bradford, Halifax, Sowerby Bridge, Luddenden, Luddenden Foot, Holborn, York, Ulverston

IV TOPOGRAPHICAL AND LOCAL INFORMATION

Derived on the spot in all places connected with Branwell Brontë: Thornton, Haworth, Bradford, Leeds, Holborn, Ulverston, Broughton-in-Furness, Ambleside, Halifax, Sowerby Bridge, Luddenden, Luddenden Foot, York, Little and Great Ouseburn, Scarborough.

Much valuable information has been derived through personal contacts with families resident in and closely connected with these places, whose forebears had personal dealings with Branwell Brontë. (See list of acknowledgments)
Memoranda of the Luddenden Library
Catalogue of Ponden House Library
Heaton Records, Cartwright Memorial Hall, Bradford

V PRIVATELY OWNED DOCUMENTS
See list of acknowledgments

VI PUBLISHED TEXTS: WORKS BY THE BRONTËS

The Miscellaneous and Unpublished Writings of Charlotte Brontë and Patrick Branwell Brontë, edited by T. J. Wise and J. A. Symington, 2 vols., Oxford, 1934
The Poems of Charlotte Brontë and Patrick Branwell Brontë, edited by T. J. Wise and J. A. Symington, 1 vol., Oxford, 1934
The Brontës: their Lives, Friendships and Correspondence, edited by T. J Wise and J. A. Symington, 4 vols., Oxford, 1932
Poems of Branwell Brontë, published in the press in his lifetime, quoted from texts printed in the *Halifax Guardian* and *Leeds Mercury*
The *Odes* of Horace, Book I. Translated by Branwell Brontë, edited by John Drinkwater, privately printed 1923
"And the Weary are at Rest", by Branwell Brontë *c.* 1845, privately printed 1924
The Poems of Currer, Ellis and Acton Bell (Aylott and Jones) 1846
Currer Bell: Biographical Notice of Ellis and Acton Bell prefixed to the post-humous edition of their works (Smith, Elder & Co) 1850
Jane Eyre by Charlotte Brontë (Smith, Elder & Co) 1880
The Tenant of Wildfell Hall by Anne Brontë (Smith, Elder & Co.) 1880
Wuthering Heights by Emily Brontë, original text, published in World's Classics, Oxford, 1955
The Complete Poems of Emily Jane Brontë, edited by C. W. Hatfield, Oxford, 1941

WORKS ON THE BRONTËS

Every work written on the Brontës, from Mrs Gaskell to the present day, is known to the author and has been studied in reference to the present biography; but only those works which, in effect, have been used and quoted from, are listed here.

1 The "Transactions" of the Brontë Society, 1895–1960, with special reference to the following numbers, authors and subjects:

1895 Yates, W. W.: *The Brontës and Dewsbury*

1899 Nussey, E.: "Reminiscences of Charlotte Brontë, after *Scribner's Magazine* May 1871

1908 Catalogue of the paintings and drawings of P. B. Brontë in the Brontë Parsonage Museum

1921 The suppressed passages from Mrs Gaskell's *Life of Charlotte Brontë*

1922 Bibliography of Charlotte Brontë's early MSS

1925 The letters of P. B. Brontë to J. B. Leyland, ed. Hatfield

1927 Unpublished poems of P. B. Brontë

1927 Branwell Brontë and *Wuthering Heights*

1932 Edgerley, M.: *A National Portrait Vindicated*

1933 Unpublished poem ("Azrael") by P. B. Brontë

1941 Wall, Francis: *The Art and Life of P. B. Brontë*

1945 Olsen, T.: "The Weary are at Rest: A Reconsideration of Branwell Brontë"

1950 Whone, Clifford: "The Keighley Mechanics' Institute: Where the Brontës Borrowed Books"

1951 Preston, Albert: *John Greenwood and the Brontës*

1956 Hustwick, Wade: *Branwell Brontë and Freemasonry*

1958 Holgate, Ivy: *The Key to "Caroline"*

2 1857 Gaskell, Elizabeth: *Life of Charlotte Brontë* (Everyman Edition)

1867 Dearden, William: "Who Wrote Wuthering Heights?" *Halifax Guardian* 15th June

1871 Nussey, Ellen: "Reminiscences of Charlotte Brontë", *Scribner's Magazine* May

1872 Searle Phillips, G.: "Branwell Brontë", *The Mirror*, 28th December

1877 Reid, T. Wemyss: *Charlotte Brontë: A Monograph* (Macmillan)

1879 Grundy, F. H.: *Pictures of the Past* (Griffin & Farrar)

1883 Duclaux, Mary Robinson: *Emily Brontë: A Memoir* (W. H. Allen)

1885 Leyland, F. A.: *The Brontë Family, with Special Reference to Branwell Brontë*

1885 Noble, J. Ashcroft: Review of Leyland's book in *The Academy*, 14th November

1886 The Saturday Review: "Branwell Brontë", *idem*, 2nd January

1896 Shorter, C. K.: *The Brontës and their Circle* (Hodder & Stoughton)

1914 Chadwick, Ellis: *In the Footsteps of the Brontës* (Pitman)

1935 Harrison, G. Elsie: *Methodist Good Companions* (Epworth Press)

1936 Cooper, Irene Willis: *The Authorship of Wuthering Heights* (Hogarth Press)

1937 Harrison, G. Elsie: *Haworth Parsonage* (Epworth Press)
1941 Ratchford, F. E.: *The Brontës' Web of Childhood* (Columbia University Press)
1947 Christian, Mildred: *A Census of Brontë MSS in the U.S.A.*
1947 Hinkley, Laura: *The Brontës: Charlotte and Emily*
1948 Harrison, G. Elsie: *The Clue to the Brontës* (Methuen)
1954 Leyland, Mary: The Leyland Family, Halifax Antiquarian Society Annals, April
1955 Blondel, Jacques: *Emily Brontë: Expérience Spirituelle et Création Poétique* (Presses Universitaires de France)
1958 Visick, Mary: *The Genesis of Wuthering Heights* (Hong Kong University Press)
1959 Gérin, Winifred: *Anne Brontë* (Nelson)

3 GENERAL WORKS

Art

Bewick, Thomas: *A History of British Birds*, 2 vols., 1847 (Blackwell & Co., Newcastle)
vol. 1, *Land Birds*
vol. 2, *Water Birds*
Barbier, C. P.: *Samuel Rogers and William Gilpin: their Friendship and Correspondence*, Oxford, 1959
Dayot, Armond: *The Vernets: Joseph, Carl, and Horace*, Paris, 1898
Fuseli, Henry: *Album of Drawings* (Paul Ganz, Berne, 1947)
Hyatt Mayor, A.: *Piranesi, Giovanni Battista Etchings*, New York, 1952
Constable, W. G.: *John Flaxman* (University of London Press, 1927)
Haydon, B. R.: *Autobiography* (World's Classics, 1927)

Literature

Blackwood's Edinburgh Magazine, 1822-8 inclusive
Fraser's Magazine, 1831
Annual Register, 1834, 1835, 1839
De Quincey, Thomas: *Confessions of an English Opium Eater*, 1821
Oliphant, Mrs: *Annals of a Publishing House* (Macmillan, 1897)
Coleridge, Hartley: *Complete Poetical Works* (Routledge)
Cowper, William: *Poems* (Macmillan, 1883)
Dearden, William: *The Death of Leyland's African Bloodhound* (Longmans, 1837)
Disraeli, Benjamin: *Coningsby* (Everyman Edition)
Lytton, Bulwer Edward: *Eugene Aram*

History and Social Background

Young, G. M.: *Victorian England* (Oxford, 1957)
Trevelyan, G. M.: *English Social History* (Longmans, 1947)
Greevey, T.: *Memoirs*, 1828-1838 (John Murray, 1948)
Airlie, Countess of: *Lady Palmerston and her Times*, 1922
Guedalla, Philip: *The Duke* (Hodder and Stoughton, 1940)
Egan, Pierce: *Book of Sports* (London, 1832)
Rolt, L. T. C.: *George and Robert Stephenson* (Longmans, 1960)

Topographical Works

Turner, J. Horsfall: *Haworth Past and Present*, Brighouse, 1897
Scruton, William: *Thornton and the Brontës*, Bradford, 1898
Pen and Pencil Pictures of Bradford, Bradford, 1889
James, John: *History and Topography of Bradford* (Longmans, 1841)
Collingwood, W. G.: *The Lake Counties* (Dent, 1934)
The Halifax Directory, 1842, 1845
Official Guides to: Ulverston; Sowerby Bridge; Bolton Abbey and Woods; Holborn; York
Theakston: *Guide to Scarborough*, 8th ed., 1860
Whiteley-Turner: *A Springtime Saunter*, Halifax, 1913
Rawnsley, H. D.: *Literary Associations of the English Lakes*, Glasgow, 1894
Past and Present at the English Lakes, Glasgow, 1916

ABBREVIATIONS

AB	Anne Brontë
BPM	Brontë Parsonage Museum
BST	Brontë Society Transactions
BTC	British Transport Commission Historic Records Department
CB	Charlotte Brontë
DNB	*Dictionary of National Biography*
EJB	Emily Jane Brontë
EN	Ellen Nussey
PBB	Patrick Branwell Brontë
RA	Royal Academy of Arts
SBC	Shorter: *The Brontës and their Circle*
W & S	Wise and Symington: *The Brontës: their Lives, Friendships and Correspondence*, 1932
W & S Prose	Wise and Symington: *The Miscellaneous and Unpublished Writings of Charlotte Brontë and Patrick Branwell Brontë*, 1934
Poems	Wise and Symington: *The Poems of Charlotte and Patrick Branwell Brontë*, 1934
Butler-Wood	"Bradford Artists", *Bradford Antiquary*, 1893
Chadwick	*In the Footsteps of the Brontës*, 1914
Colles	*The Complete Poems of Hartley Coleridge*
Dearden	"Who Wrote Wuthering Heights?" *Halifax Guardian*, 15th June, 1867
Duclaux	*Emily Brontë: A Memoir*, 1885
Egan	*Book of Sports*, 1832
Gaskell	*The Life of Charlotte Brontë*
Greenwood	Diary of John Greenwood, *Brontë Society Transactions*, 1951
Grundy	*Pictures of the Past*, 1879
Harrison	*The Clue to the Brontës*
Hatfield	*The Complete Poems of Emily Jane Brontë*
Haydon	*The Autobiography of B. R. Haydon*
Herapath	*Railway Magazine*, 22nd and 29th May 1841
Horsfall-Turner	*Haworth Past and Present*, 1879
Leyland	*The Brontë Family, with Special Reference to Patrick Branwell Brontë*, 1885
Mary Leyland	"The Leyland Family", Halifax Antiquarian Society, April 1954

Meysey-Thompson	"Register of Sundries", relating to Great and Little Ouseburn families, in the possession of the late Mrs E. C. Meysey-Thompson
Nussey	"Reminiscences of Charlotte Brontë", *Scribner's Magazine*, May 1872
Oliphant	*Annals of a Publishing House*, 1897
Phillips	"Branwell Brontë", *The Mirror*, December 1872
Ratchford	*The Brontës' Web of Childhood*
Rawnsley	*Literary Associations of the English Lakes*, 1894
Scruton	*Pen and Pencil Pictures of Bradford*, 1889
Scruton "Thornton"	*Thornton and the Brontës*, 1898
Theakston	*Guide to Scarborough*
Wemyss-Reid	*Charlotte Brontë: A Monograph*

NOTES

Part One

Chapter One

page

2 CB's recollection of her mother: Gaskell 33; Leyland I, 62

2 "Warner Howard Warner": BPM

3 Miss Branwell and her nieces: Chadwick 68

Chapter Two

6 "Misery II": *Poems*

7 PBB's poem "Caroline": Leyland I, 224

7 Christmas music: AB's poem "Music on Christmas Morn", published 1846

8 Haworth Grammar School: SBC 114

12-16 "Caroline": Leyland I, 217-22

Chapter Three

17 Haworth Grammar School: Horsfall-Turner 133-6

21 Mad dog bite: Chadwick 113

22 "Keighley Feast": Leyland I, 87-9

Chapter Four

28 "History of the Young Men": Ashley Library, British Museum

29 PBB's letter to *Blackwood's*: W & S. Quotation from *Blackwood's Magazine*, January, 1828

30 CB's "Play of the Islanders": Berg Collection, New York

34 PBB's "Battell Book": BPM

Part Two

Chapter Five

Chapter Six

Chapter Seven

Part Three

Chapter Eight

Chapter Thirteen

Chapter Fourteen

Part Five

Chapter Fifteen

Chapter Sixteen

Chapter Seventeen

Chapter Eighteen

Part Six

Chapter Nineteen

Chapter Twenty

Epilogue

Robinson Papers; General Register, Somerset House; Letters of CB, W & S; Gaskell; *The Athenaeum* 6th June 1857; *The Times* 30th May 1857; Annual Register 1859; Registers of Great Ouseburn

Appendix A

BST 1927; Scruton "Thornton", p. 132; *Halifax Guardian* 15th June 1867; Visick; Cooper

Appendix B

This subject has also been extensively investigated by the present author in her *Anne Brontë* (Nelson 1959)

INDEX